Great Christian Thinkers

GREAT CHRISTIAN THINKERS

FROM THE EARLY CHURCH THROUGH THE MIDDLE AGES

POPE BENEDICT XVI

Fortress Press
Minneapolis

GREAT CHRISTIAN THINKERS
From the Early Church through the Middle Ages

First Fortress Press edition 2011

Cover image: A.M. Rosati/Art Resource, NY
Cover design: Alisha Lofgren

Library of Congress Cataloging-in-Publication Data
Benedict XVI, Pope, 1927-
Great Christian thinkers: from the early church through the Middle Ages / Pope Benedict XVI.—1st Fortress Press ed.
    p. cm.
Includes index.
ISBN 978-0-8006-9851-5 (alk. paper)
1. Religious thought—To 600. 2. Church history—Primitive and early church, ca. 30-600. 3. Religious thought—Middle Ages, 600-1500. 4. Church history—Middle Ages, 600-1500. I. Title.
BR162.3.B46 2011
230.092'2—dc22   2011016179

Manufactured in the U.S.A.

15   14   13   12   11   1   2   3   4   5   6   7   8   9   10

CONTENTS

v

Part Four   MYSTICS, MENDICANTS, AND SCHOLASTICS

PUBLISHER'S FOREWORD

IT IS A MATTER OF PARTICULAR PRIDE at Fortress Press that we offer this compilation of brief portraits composed and presented by Pope Benedict XVI on key figures from Christian history. Over the last several years, week after week, Benedict has devoted most of his public audiences to depicting some of the most important figures of the tradition—theologians and philosophers but also spiritual guides, eremites and monks, abbots and abbesses, popes and bishops, founders and reformers, mystics and missionaries.

The result is a set of seventy expert and reliable yet quite accessible introductions to the key framers of the pre-Reformation tradition, East and West, as useful for personal reading or study as for classroom or congregation. As one might expect of someone who brings decades of his own teaching and research to the task, Benedict's pieces are not only illuminating historical sketches but also often surprisingly personal reflective meditations on the perennial challenges of theology, spirituality, devotion, and corporate religious life—in short, of thinking about and wrestling daily with the mysteries that envelop all our lives and struggles.

The editors of Fortress Press are grateful to the Vatican Library Press for their enthusiasm for the project and willingness to facilitate it by providing lucid and accessible translations.

PART ONE

HEIRS OF THE APOSTLES

St. Clement, Bishop of Rome

After the first witnesses of the Christian faith, mentioned in the New Testament writings, we find the Apostolic Fathers, that is, to the first and second generations in the Church subsequent to the Apostles. And thus, we can see where the Church's journey begins in history.

St. Clement, bishop of Rome in the last years of the first century, was the third successor of Peter, after Linus and Anacletus. The most important testimony concerning his life comes from St. Irenaeus, bishop of Lyons until 202. He attests that Clement "had seen the blessed Apostles," "had been conversant with them," and "might be said to have the preaching of the Apostles still echoing [in his ears], and their traditions before his eyes" (*Adversus Haer.* 3, 3, 3). Later testimonies, which date back to between the fourth and sixth centuries, attribute to Clement the title of martyr.

The authority and prestige of this bishop of Rome were such that various writings were attributed to him, but the only one that is certainly Clement's is the *Letter to the Corinthians.* Eusebius of Caesarea, the great "archivist" of Christian beginnings, presents it in these terms: "There is extant an epistle of this Clement which is acknowledged to be genuine and is of considerable length and of remarkable merit. He wrote it in the name of the Church of Rome to the Church of Corinth, when a sedition had arisen in the latter church. We know that this epistle also has been publicly used in a great many churches both in former times and in our own" (*Hist. Eccl.* 3, 16).

An almost canonical character was attributed to Clement's *Letter.* At the beginning of this text, written in Greek, Clement expressed his regret that "the sudden and successive calamitous events which have happened to ourselves" (1, 1) had prevented him from intervening sooner. These "calamitous events" can be identified with Domitian's persecution: therefore, the *Letter* must have been written just after the emperor's death and at the end of the persecution, that is, immediately after the year 96.

Clement's intervention—we are still in the first century—was prompted by the serious problems besetting the Church in Corinth: the elders of the community, in fact, had been deposed by some young contestants. The sorrowful event was recalled once again by St. Irenaeus, who wrote: "In the time of this Clement, no small dissension having occurred among the brethren in Corinth, the Church in Rome dispatched a most powerful letter to the Corinthians exhorting them to peace, renewing their faith and declaring the tradition which it had lately received from the Apostles" (*Adv. Haer.* 3, 3, 3).

Thus, we could say that Clement's *Letter* was a first exercise of the Roman primacy after St. Peter's death. His *Letter* touches on topics that were dear to St. Paul, who had written two important letters to the Corinthians, in particular the theological dialectic, perennially current, between the *indicative* of salvation and the *imperative* of moral commitment. First of all came the joyful proclamation of saving grace. The Lord forewarns us and gives us his forgiveness, gives us his love and the grace to be Christians, his brothers and sisters. It is a proclamation that fills our life with joy and gives certainty to our action: the Lord always forewarns us with his goodness, and the Lord's goodness is always greater than all our sins. However, we must commit ourselves in a way that is consistent with the gift received and respond to the proclamation of salvation with a generous and courageous journey of conversion.

In comparison with the Pauline model, the innovation is that Clement adds to the doctrinal and practical sections, found in all the Pauline Letters, a "great prayer" that virtually concludes the *Letter*.

The *Letter*'s immediate circumstances provided the bishop of Rome with ample room for an intervention on the Church's identity and mission. If there were abuses in Corinth, Clement observed, the reason should be sought in the weakening of charity and of the other indispensable Christian virtues. He therefore calls the faithful to humility and fraternal love, two truly constitutive virtues of being in the Church: "Seeing, therefore, that we are the portion of the Holy One," he warned, "let us do all those things which pertain to holiness" (30, 1).

In particular, Clement recalls that the Lord himself "has established where and by whom he wishes liturgical functions to be carried out, so that all may be devoutly performed in accordance with his wishes and in a manner acceptable to him. . . . For his own peculiar services are assigned to the high priest, and their own proper place is prescribed to the priests, and their own special ministries devolve on the Levites. The layman is bound by the laws that pertain to laymen" (40, 1–5: it can be noted that here, in this early first-century letter, the Greek word *laikós* appears for the first time in Christian literature, meaning "a member of the *laos*," that is, "of the People of God"). In this way, referring to the liturgy of ancient Israel, Clement revealed his ideal Church. She was assembled by "the one Spirit of grace poured out upon us," which breathes on the various members of the Body of Christ, where all, united without any divisions, are "members of one another" (46, 6–7).

The clear distinction between the "layperson" and the hierarchy in no way signifies opposition, but only this organic connection of a body, an organism with its different functions. The Church, in fact, is not a place of confusion and anarchy where one can do what one likes all the time: each one in this organism, with an articulated structure, exercises his ministry in accordance with the vocation he has received.

With regard to community leaders, Clement clearly explains the doctrine of Apostolic Succession. The norms that regulate it derive ultimately from God himself. The Father sent Jesus Christ, who in turn sent the Apostles. They then sent the first heads of communities and established that they would be succeeded by other worthy men. Everything, therefore, was made "in an orderly way, according to the will of God" (42). With these words, these sentences, St. Clement underlined that the Church's structure was sacramental and not political.

The action of God who comes to meet us in the liturgy precedes our decisions and our ideas. The Church is above all a gift of God and not something we ourselves created; consequently, this sacramental structure does not only guarantee the common order but also this precedence of God's gift which we all need.

Finally, the great prayer confers a cosmic breath to the previous reasoning. Clement praises and thanks God for his marvelous providence of love that created the world and continues to save and sanctify it.

The prayer for rulers and governors acquires special importance. Subsequent to the New Testament texts, it is the oldest prayer extant for political institutions. Thus, in the period following their persecution, Christians, well aware that the persecutions would continue, never ceased to pray for the very authorities who had unjustly condemned them. The reason is primarily christological: it is necessary to pray for one's persecutors, as Jesus did on the cross.

But this prayer also contains a teaching that guides the attitude of Christians toward politics and the state down the centuries. In praying for the authorities, Clement recognized the legitimacy of political institutions in the order established by God; at the same time, he expressed his concern that the authorities would be docile to God, "devoutly in peace and meekness exercising the power given them by [God]" (61, 2). Caesar is not everything. Another sovereignty emerges whose origins and essence are not of this world but of "the heavens above": it is that of Truth, which also claims a right to be heard by the state.

Thus, Clement's Letter addresses numerous themes of perennial timeliness. It is all the more meaningful since it represents, from the first century, the concern of the Church of Rome, which presides in charity over all the other churches. In this same Spirit, let us make our own the invocations of the great prayer in which the bishop of Rome makes himself the voice of the entire world: "Yes, O Lord, make your face to shine upon us for good in peace, that we may be shielded by your mighty hand . . . through the High Priest and guardian of our souls, Jesus Christ, through whom be glory and majesty to you both now and from generation to generation, forevermore" (60–61).

—7 *March 2007*

St. Ignatius of Antioch

Saint Ignatius was the third bishop of Antioch, from 70 to 107, the date of his martyrdom. At that time, Rome, Alexandria, and Antioch were the three great metropolises of the Roman Empire. The Council of Nicaea mentioned three "primacies": Rome, but Alexandria and Antioch also participated in a certain sense in a "primacy."

St. Ignatius was bishop of Antioch, which today is located in Turkey. Here in Antioch, as we know from the Acts of the Apostles, a flourishing Christian community developed. Its first bishop was the Apostle Peter—or so tradition claims—and it was there that the disciples were "for the first time called Christians" (Acts 11:26). Eusebius of Caesarea, a fourth-century historian, dedicated an entire chapter of his *Church History* to the life and literary works of Ignatius (cf. 3:36). Eusebius writes:

> The report says that he [Ignatius] was sent from Syria to Rome, and became food for wild beasts on account of his testimony to Christ. And as he made the journey through Asia under the strictest military surveillance" [he calls the guards "ten leopards" in his *Letter to the Romans 5*, 1], he fortified the parishes in the various cities where he stopped by homilies and exhortations, and warned them above all to be especially on their guard against the heresies that were then beginning to prevail, and exhorted them to hold fast to the tradition of the Apostles.

The first place Ignatius stopped on the way to his martyrdom was the city of Smyrna, where St. Polycarp, a disciple of St. John, was bishop. Here, Ignatius wrote four letters, respectively to the churches of Ephesus, Magnesia, Tralli, and Rome. "Having left Smyrna," Eusebius continues, Ignatius reached Troas and "wrote again": two letters to the churches of Philadelphia and Smyrna, and one to Bishop Polycarp.

Thus, Eusebius completes the list of his letters, which have come down to us from the Church of the first century as a precious treasure. In reading these texts one feels the freshness of the faith of the generation which had still known the Apostles. In these letters, the ardent love of a saint can also be felt.

Last, the martyr traveled from Troas to Rome, where he was thrown to fierce wild animals in the Flavian amphitheater.

No Church Father has expressed the longing for *union* with Christ and for *life* in him with the intensity of Ignatius. We therefore read the Gospel passage on the vine, which according to John's Gospel is Jesus. In fact, two spiritual "currents" converge in Ignatius; that of Paul, straining with all his might for *union* with Christ, and that of John, concentrated on *life* in him. In turn, these two currents translate into the *imitation* of Christ, whom Ignatius several times proclaimed as "my" or "our God."

Thus, Ignatius implores the Christians of Rome not to prevent his martyrdom since he is impatient "to attain to Jesus Christ." And he explains, "It is better for me to die on behalf of Jesus Christ than to reign over all the ends of the earth. . . . Him I seek, who died for us: him I desire, who rose again for our sake. . . . Permit me to be an imitator of the passion of my God!" (*Romans* 5–6).

One can perceive in these words on fire with love the pronounced christological "realism" typical of the Church of Antioch, more focused than ever on the Incarnation of the Son of God and on his true and concrete humanity: "Jesus Christ," St. Ignatius wrote to the Smyrnaeans, "was *truly* of the seed of David," "he was *truly* born of a virgin," "and was *truly* nailed [to the cross] for us" (1, 1).

Ignatius's irresistible longing for union with Christ was the foundation of a real "mysticism of unity." He describes himself: "I therefore did what befitted me as a man devoted to unity" (*Philadelphians* 8, 1). For Ignatius, unity was first and foremost a prerogative of God, who, since he exists as three persons, is one in absolute unity. Ignatius often repeated that God is unity and that in God alone is unity found in its pure and original state. Unity to be brought about on this earth by Christians is no more than an imitation as close as possible to the divine archetype.

Thus, Ignatius reached the point of being able to work out a vision of the Church strongly reminiscent of certain expressions in Clement of Rome's *Letter to the Corinthians*. For example, he wrote to the Christians of Ephesus: "It is fitting that you should concur with the will of your bishop, which you also do. For your justly renowned presbytery, worthy of God, is fitted as exactly to the bishop as the strings are to the harp. Therefore, in your concord and harmonious love, Jesus Christ is sung. And one by one, you become a choir, that being harmonious in love and taking up the song of God in unison you may with one voice sing to the Father" (4, 1–2).

And after recommending to the Smyrnaeans, "Let no man do anything connected with Church without the bishop," he confides to Polycarp: "I offer my life for those who are submissive to the bishop, to the presbyters, and to the deacons, and may I along with them obtain my portion in God! Labor together with one another; strive in company together; run together; suffer together; sleep together; and awake together as the stewards and associates and servants of God. Please him under whom you fight, and from whom you receive your wages. Let none of you be found a deserter. Let your baptism endure as your arms; your faith as your helmet; your love as your spear; your patience as a complete panoply" (*Polycarp* 6, 1–2).

Overall, it is possible to grasp in the *Letters* of Ignatius a sort of constant and fruitful dialectic between two characteristic aspects of Christian life: on the one hand, the hierarchical structure of the ecclesial community, and on the other, the fundamental unity that binds all the faithful in Christ. Consequently, their roles cannot be opposed to one another. On the contrary, the insistence on communion among believers and of believers with their pastors was constantly reformulated in eloquent images and analogies: the harp, strings, intonation, the concert, the symphony. The special responsibility of bishops, priests, and deacons in building the community is clear.

This applies first of all to their invitation to love and unity. "Be one," Ignatius wrote to the Magnesians, echoing the prayer of Jesus at the Last Supper: "one supplication, one mind, one hope in love. . . . Therefore, all run together as into one temple of God, as to one altar, as to one Jesus Christ who came forth from one Father, and is with and has gone to one" (7, 1–2).

Ignatius was the first person in Christian literature to attribute to the Church the adjective "catholic" or "universal": "Wherever Jesus Christ is," he said, "there is the Catholic Church" (*Smyrnaeans* 8, 2). And precisely in the service of unity to the Catholic Church, the Christian community of Rome exercised a sort of primacy of love: "The Church which presides in the place of the region of the Romans, and which is worthy of God, worthy of honor, worthy of the highest happiness . . . and which presides over love, is named from Christ, and from the Father" *(Romans,* Prologue).

As can be seen, Ignatius is truly the "Doctor of Unity": unity of God and unity of Christ (despite the various heresies gaining ground that separated the human and the divine in Christ), unity of the Church, unity of the faithful in "faith and love, to which nothing is to be preferred" (*Smyrnaeans* 6, 1).

Ultimately, Ignatius's realism invites the faithful of yesterday and today, invites us all, to make a gradual synthesis between *configuration to Christ* (union with him, life in him) and *dedication to his Church* (unity with the bishop, generous service to the community and to the world).

To summarize, it is necessary to achieve a synthesis between *communion* of the Church within herself and *mission*, the proclamation of the gospel to others, until the other speaks through one dimension and believers increasingly "have obtained the inseparable Spirit, who is Jesus Christ" (*Magnesians* 15).

Imploring from the Lord this "grace of unity" and in the conviction that the whole Church presides in charity (cf. *Romans,* Prologue), I address to you yourselves the same hope with which Ignatius ended his *Letter to the Trallians*: "Love one another with an undivided heart. Let my spirit be sanctified by yours, not only now but also when I shall attain to God. . . . In [Jesus Christ] may you be found unblemished" (13). And let us pray that the Lord will help us to attain this unity and to be found at last unstained, because it is love that purifies souls.

—*14 March 2007*

ST. JUSTIN, PHILOSOPHER AND MARTYR

SAINT JUSTIN, PHILOSOPHER AND MARTYR, was the most important of the second-century apologist Fathers.

The word *apologist* designates those ancient Christian writers who set out to defend the new religion from the weighty accusations of both pagans and Jews, and to spread the Christian doctrine in terms suited to the culture of their time. Thus, the apologists had a twofold concern: that most properly called "apologetic," to defend the newborn Christianity (*apología* in Greek means, precisely, "defense"), and the pro-positive, "missionary" concern, to explain the content of the faith in a language and on a wavelength comprehensible to their contemporaries.

Justin was born in about the year 100, near ancient Shechem, Samaria, in the Holy Land. He spent a long time seeking the truth, moving through the various schools of the Greek philosophical tradition. Finally, as he himself recounts in the first chapters of his *Dialogue with Trypho*, a mysterious figure, an old man he met on the seashore, leads him into a crisis by showing him that it is impossible for the human being to satisfy his aspiration to the divine solely with his own forces. He then pointed out to him the ancient prophets as the people to turn to in order to find the way to God and "true philosophy." In taking his leave, the old man urged him to pray that the gates of light would be opened to him.

The story foretells the crucial episode in Justin's life: at the end of a long philosophical journey, a quest for the truth, he arrived at the Christian faith. He founded a school in Rome where, free of charge, he initiated students into the new religion, considered as the true philosophy. Indeed, in it he had found the truth, hence, the art of living virtuously.

For this reason, he was reported and beheaded in about 165, during the reign of Marcus Aurelius, the philosopher-emperor to whom Justin had actually addressed one of his *Apologia*.

These—the two *Apologies* and the *Dialogue with the Hebrew, Trypho*—are his only surviving works. In them, Justin intends above all to illustrate the divine project of creation and salvation, which is fulfilled in Jesus Christ, the *Logos,* that is, the eternal Word, eternal Reason, creative Reason. Every person as a rational being shares in the *Logos,* carrying within himself a "seed," and can perceive glimmers of the truth. Thus, the same *Logos* who revealed himself as a prophetic figure to the Hebrews of the ancient law also manifested himself partially, in "seeds of truth," in Greek philosophy. Now, Justin concludes, since Christianity is the historical and personal manifestation of the *Logos* in his totality, it follows that "whatever things were rightly said among all men are the property of us Christians" (*Second Apology of St. Justin Martyr* 13, 4).

In this way, although Justin disputed Greek philosophy and its contradictions, he decisively oriented any philosophical truth to the *Logos*, giving reasons for the unusual "claim" to truth and universality of the Christian religion. If the Old Testament leaned toward Christ, just as the symbol is a guide to the reality represented, then Greek philosophy also aspired to Christ and the gospel, just as the part strives to be united with the whole. And he said that these two realities, the Old Testament and Greek philosophy, are like two paths that lead to Christ, to the *Logos*. This is why Greek philosophy cannot be opposed to gospel truth, and Christians can draw from it confidently as from a good of their own.

Therefore, my venerable predecessor Pope John Paul II described St. Justin as a "pioneer of positive engagement with philosophical thinking—albeit with cautious discernment. . . . Although he continued to hold Greek philosophy in high esteem after his conversion, Justin claimed with power and clarity that he had found in Christianity 'the only sure and profitable philosophy' (*Dial.* 8, 1)" (*Fides et Ratio*, n. 38).

Overall, the figure and work of Justin mark the ancient Church's forceful option for philosophy, for reason, rather than for the religion of the pagans. With the pagan religion, in fact, the early Christians strenuously rejected every compromise. They held it to be idolatry, at the cost of being accused for this reason of "impiety" and "atheism." Justin in particular, especially in his first *Apology*, mercilessly criticized the pagan religion and its myths, which he considered to be diabolically misleading on the path of truth.

Philosophy, however, represented the privileged area of the encounter between paganism, Judaism, and Christianity, precisely at the level of the criticism of pagan religion and its false myths. "Our philosophy . . .": this is how another apologist, bishop Melito of Sardis, a contemporary of Justin, came to define the new religion in a more explicit way (*Ap. Hist. Eccl.* 4, 26, 7).

In fact, the pagan religion did not follow the ways of the *Logos* but clung to myth, even if Greek philosophy recognized that mythology was devoid of consistency with the truth. Therefore, the decline of the pagan religion was inevitable: it was a logical consequence of the detachment of religion—reduced to an artificial collection of ceremonies, conventions, and customs—from the truth of being.

Justin, and with him other apologists, adopted the clear stance taken by the Christian faith for the God of the philosophers against the false gods of the pagan religion. It was the choice of the *truth* of being against the myth of *custom*. Several decades after Justin, Tertullian defined the same option of Christians with a lapidary sentence that still applies: "*Dominus noster Christus veritatem se, non consuetudinem, cognominavit*—Christ has said that he is truth not fashion" (*De Virgin. Vel.* 1, 1).

It should be noted in this regard that the term *consuetudo*, used here by Tertullian in reference to the pagan religion, can be translated into modern languages with the expressions: "cultural fashion," "current fads." In a time like ours, marked by relativism in the discussion on values and on religion—as well as in interreligious dialogue—this is a lesson that should not be forgotten. To this end, I suggest to you once again—and thus I conclude—the last words of the mysterious old man whom Justin the Philosopher met on the seashore: "Pray that, above all things, the gates of light may be opened to you; for these things cannot be perceived or understood by all, but only by the man to whom God and his Christ have imparted wisdom" (*Dial.* 7, 3).

—*21 March 2007*

St. Irenaeus of Lyons

IN REFLECTING ON THE PROMINENT FIGURES of the early Church, we come to the eminent personality of St. Irenaeus of Lyons. The biographical information on him comes from his own testimony, handed down to us by Eusebius in his fifth book on Church history.

Irenaeus was in all probability born in Smyrna (today, Izmir in Turkey) in about 135–140, where in his youth, he attended the school of Bishop Polycarp, a disciple in his turn of the Apostle John. We do not know when he moved from Asia Minor to Gaul, but his move must have coincided with the first development of the Christian community in Lyons: here, in 177, we find Irenaeus listed in the college of presbyters. In that very year, he was sent to Rome bearing a letter from the community in Lyons to Pope Eleutherius. His mission to Rome saved Irenaeus from the persecution of Marcus Aurelius, which took a toll of at least forty-eight martyrs, including the ninety-year-old Bishop Pontinus of Lyons, who died from ill-treatment in prison. Thus, on his return Irenaeus was appointed bishop of the city. The new pastor devoted himself without reserve to his episcopal ministry, which ended in about 202–203, perhaps with martyrdom.

Irenaeus was first and foremost a man of faith and a pastor. Like a good pastor, he had a good sense of proportion, a wealth of doctrine, and missionary enthusiasm. As a writer, he pursued a twofold aim: to defend true doctrine from the attacks of heretics and to explain the truth of the faith clearly. His two extant works—the five books of *The Detection and Overthrow of the False Gnosis* and *Demonstration of the Apostolic Teaching* (which can also be called the oldest "catechism of Christian doctrine")—exactly corresponded with these aims. In short, Irenaeus can be defined as the champion in the fight against heresies. The second-century Church was threatened by the so-called *Gnosis,* a doctrine which affirmed that the faith taught in the Church was merely a symbolism for the simple, who were unable to grasp difficult concepts; instead, the initiates, the intellectuals—*Gnostics,* they were called—claimed to understand what was behind these symbols and thus formed an elitist and intellectualist Christianity. Obviously, this intellectual Christianity became increasingly fragmented, splitting into different currents with ideas that were often bizarre and extravagant, yet attractive to many. One element these different currents had in common was "dualism": they denied faith in the one God and Father of all, Creator and Savior of man and of the world. To explain evil in the world, they affirmed the existence, besides the Good God, of a negative principle. This negative principle was supposed to have produced material things, matter.

Firmly rooted in the biblical doctrine of creation, Irenaeus refuted the Gnostic dualism and pessimism, which debased corporeal realities. He decisively claimed the original holiness of matter, of the body, of the flesh no less than of the spirit. But his work went far beyond the confutation of heresy: in fact, one can say that he emerges as the first great Church theologian who created systematic theology; he himself speaks of the system of theology, that is, of the internal coherence of all faith. At the heart of his doctrine is the question of the "rule of faith" and its transmission. For Irenaeus, the "rule of faith" coincided in practice with the Apostles' Creed, which gives us the key for interpreting the gospel, for interpreting the creed in light of the gospel. The creed, which is a sort of gospel synthesis, helps us understand what it means and how we should read the gospel itself.

In fact, the gospel preached by Irenaeus is the one he was taught by Polycarp, bishop of Smyrna, and Polycarp's gospel dates back to the Apostle John, whose disciple Polycarp was. The true teaching, therefore, is not that invented by intellectuals, which goes beyond the Church's simple faith. The true gospel is the one imparted by the bishops who received it in an uninterrupted line from the Apostles. They taught nothing except this simple faith, which is also the true depth of God's revelation. Thus, Irenaeus tells us, there is no secret doctrine concealed in the Church's common creed. There is no superior Christianity for intellectuals. The faith publicly confessed by the Church is the common faith of all. This faith alone is apostolic; it is handed down from the Apostles, that is, from Jesus and from God. In adhering to this faith, publicly transmitted by the Apostles to their successors, Christians must observe what their bishops say and must give special consideration to the teaching of the Church of Rome, preeminent and very ancient. It is because of her antiquity that this Church has the greatest apostolicity; in fact, she originated in Peter and Paul, pillars of the Apostolic College. All churches must agree with the Church of Rome, recognizing in her the measure of the true Apostolic Tradition, the Church's one common faith. With these arguments, summed up very briefly here, Irenaeus refuted the claims of these Gnostics, these intellectuals, from the start. First of all, they possessed no truth superior to that of the ordinary faith, because what they said was not of apostolic origin; it was invented by them. Second, truth and salvation are not the privilege or monopoly of the few, but are available to all through the preaching of the successors of the Apostles, especially of the bishop of Rome. In particular—once again disputing the "secret" character of the Gnostic tradition and noting its multiple and contradictory results—Irenaeus was concerned to describe the genuine concept of the Apostolic Tradition, which we can sum up here in three points.

1. Apostolic Tradition is "public," not private or secret. Irenaeus did not doubt that the content of the faith transmitted by the Church is that received from the Apostles and from Jesus, the Son of God. There is no other teaching than this. Therefore, for anyone who wishes to know true doctrine, it suffices to know "the Tradition passed down by the Apostles and the faith proclaimed to men": a tradition and faith that "have come down to us through the succession of bishops" (*Adversus Haereses* 3, 3, 3–4). Hence, the succession of bishops, the personal principle, and Apostolic Tradition, the doctrinal principle, coincide.

2. Apostolic Tradition is "one." Indeed, whereas Gnosticism was divided into multiple sects, Church Tradition is one in its fundamental content, which—as we have seen—Irenaeus calls precisely *regula fidei* or *veritatis*: and thus, because it is one, it creates unity through the peoples, through the different cultures, through the different peoples; it is a common content like the truth, despite the diversity of languages and cultures. A very precious saying of St. Irenaeus is found in his book *Adversus Haereses*: "The Church, though dispersed throughout the world . . . having received [this faith from the Apostles] . . . as if occupying but one house, carefully preserves it. She also believes these points [of doctrine] just as if she had but one soul and one and the same heart, and she proclaims them, and teaches them and hands them down with perfect harmony as if she possessed only one mouth. For, although the languages of the world are dissimilar, yet the import of the tradition is one and the same. For the churches which have been planted in Germany do not believe or hand down anything different, nor do those in Spain, nor those in Gaul, nor those in the East, nor those in Egypt, nor those in Libya, nor those which have been established in the central regions of the world" (1, 10, 1–2). Already at that time—we are in the year 200—it was possible to perceive the Church's universality, her catholicity, and the unifying power of the truth that unites these very different realities, from Germany, to Spain, to Italy, to Egypt, to Libya, in the common truth revealed to us by Christ.

3. Last, the Apostolic Tradition, as he says in the Greek language in which he wrote his book, is "pneumatic," in other words, spiritual, guided by the Holy Spirit: in Greek, the word for "spirit" is *pneuma*. Indeed, it is not a question of a transmission entrusted to the ability of more or less learned people, but to God's Spirit, who guarantees fidelity to the transmission of the faith. This is the "life" of the Church, what makes the Church ever young and fresh, fruitful with multiple charisms.

For Irenaeus, Church and Spirit were inseparable: "This faith," we read again in the third book of *Adversus Haereses,* "which, having been received from the Church, we do preserve, and which always, by the Spirit of God, renewing its youth as if it were some precious deposit in an excellent vessel, causes the vessel itself containing it to renew its youth also. . . . For where the Church is, there is the Spirit of God; and where the Spirit of God is, there is the Church and every kind of grace" (3, 24, 1). As can be seen, Irenaeus did not stop at defining the concept of Tradition. His tradition, uninterrupted Tradition, is not traditionalism, because this Tradition is always enlivened from within by the Holy Spirit, who makes it live anew, causes it to be interpreted and understood in the vitality of the Church. Adhering to her teaching, the Church should transmit the faith in such a way that it must be what it appears, that is, "public," "one," "pneumatic," "spiritual." Starting with each one of these characteristics, a fruitful discernment can be made of the authentic transmission of the faith in the *today* of the Church. More generally, in Irenaeus's teaching, the dignity of man, body and soul, is firmly anchored in divine creation, in the image of Christ and in the Spirit's permanent work of sanctification. This doctrine is like a "high road" in order to discern together with all people of goodwill the object and boundaries of the dialogue of values, and to give an ever new impetus to the Church's missionary action, to the force of the truth which is the source of all true values in the world.

—*28 March 2007*

CLEMENT OF ALEXANDRIA

CLEMENT OF ALEXANDRIA, a great theologian, was probably born in Athens at around the middle of the second century. From Athens he inherited that marked interest in philosophy which was to make him one of the pioneers of the dialogue between faith and reason in the Christian tradition. While he was still young, he arrived in Alexandria, the "city-symbol" of that fertile junction between the different cultures that was a feature of the Hellenistic age. He was a disciple of Pantaenus until he succeeded him as head of the catechetical school. Many sources testify that he was ordained a priest. During the persecution of 202–203, he fled from Alexandria, seeking refuge in Caesarea, Cappadocia, where he died in about 215.

Of his most important works three are extant: the *Protrepticus,* the *Paedagogus*, and the *Stromata*. Although it does not seem that this was the author's original intention, it is a fact that these writings constitute a true trilogy, destined to effectively accompany the Christian's spiritual growth. The *Protrepticus,* as the word itself suggests, is an "exhortation" addressed to those who are starting out and seek the path of faith. Better still, the *Protrepticus* coincides with a person: the Son of God, Jesus Christ, who makes himself the exhorter of men and women so that they will set out toward the Truth with determination.

Jesus Christ himself becomes the *Paedagogus,* that is, the "tutor" of those who, by virtue of baptism, have henceforth become children of God. Last, Jesus Christ himself is also the *Didascalos,* the "Master" who presents the most profound teachings. These are gathered in Clement's third work, the *Stromata*, a Greek term which means "tapestries": indeed, they are a random composition of different topics, direct fruits of Clement's customary teaching.

Overall, Clement's catecheses accompanied the catechumens and the baptized step by step on their way, so that with the two "wings" of faith and reason they might reach intimate knowledge of the Truth, which is Jesus Christ, the Word of God. Only this knowledge of the person who is Truth is the "true *gnosis,*" a Greek term which means "knowledge" or "understanding." It is the edifice built by reason under the impetus of a supernatural principle.

Faith itself builds true philosophy, that is, true conversion on the journey to take through life. Hence, authentic "gnosis" is a development of faith inspired by Jesus Christ in the soul united with him. Clement then distinguishes two steps in Christian life. The first step: believing Christians who live the faith in an ordinary way, yet are always open to the horizons of holiness. Then the second step: "gnostics," that is, those who lead a life of spiritual perfection.

In any case, Christians must start from the common basis of faith through a process of seeking; they must allow themselves to be guided by Christ and thus attain knowledge of the Truth and of truth that forms the content of faith. This knowledge, Clement says, becomes a living reality in the soul: it is not only a theory, but it is also a life force, a transforming union of love. Knowledge of Christ is not only thought, but is also love which opens the eyes, transforms the person and creates communion with the *Logos*, with the divine Word, who is Truth and life. In this communion, which is perfect knowledge and love, the perfect Christian attains contemplation, unification with God.

Finally, Clement espouses the doctrine which claims that one's ultimate end is to liken oneself to God. We were created in the image and likeness of God, but this is also a challenge, a journey: indeed, life's purpose, its ultimate destination, is truly to become similar to God. This is possible through the co-naturality with God that humans received at the moment of creation, which is why, already in himself—already in himself—he is an image of God. This co-naturality makes it possible to know the divine realities to which humanity adheres, first of all out of faith, and second, through a lived faith the practice of virtue can grow until one contemplates God.

On the path to perfection, Clement thus attaches as much importance to the moral requisite as he gives to the intellectual. The two go hand in hand, for it is impossible to know without living and impossible to live without knowing. Becoming likened to God and contemplating him cannot be attained with purely rational knowledge: to this end, a life in accordance with the *Logos* is necessary, a life in accordance with truth. Consequently, good works must accompany intellectual knowledge just as the shadow follows the body.

Two virtues above all embellish the soul of the "true gnostic." The first is freedom from the passions (*apátheia*); the other is love, the true passion that assures intimate union with God. Love gives perfect peace and enables the "true gnostic" to face the greatest sacrifices, even the supreme sacrifice in following Christ, and makes him climb from step to step to the peak of virtue. Thus, the ethical ideal of ancient philosophy, that is, liberation from the passions, is defined by Clement and conjugated with love in the ceaseless process of making oneself similar to God.

In this way, the Alexandrian creates the second important occasion for dialogue between the Christian proclamation and Greek philosophy. We know that St. Paul, at the Aeropagus in Athens where Clement was born, had made the first attempt at dialogue with Greek philosophy—and by and large had failed—but they said to him: "We will hear you again."

Clement now takes up this dialogue and ennobles it to the maximum in the Greek philosophical tradition.

As my venerable predecessor, John Paul II, wrote in his encyclical *Fides et Ratio,* Clement of Alexandria understood philosophy "as instruction which prepared for Christian faith" (n. 38). And in fact, Clement reached the point of maintaining that God gave philosophy to the Greeks "as their own Testament" (*Strom.* 6, 8, 67, 1). For him, the Greek philosophical tradition, almost like the law for the Jews, was a sphere of "revelation"; they were two streams which flowed ultimately to the *Logos* himself.

Thus, Clement continued to mark out with determination the path of those who desire "to account" for their own faith in Jesus Christ. He can serve as an example to Christians, catechists, and theologians of our time, whom, in the same encyclical, John Paul II urged "to recover and express to the full the metaphysical dimension of faith in order to enter into a demanding critical dialogue with both contemporary philosophical thought and with the philosophical tradition in all its aspects."

Let us conclude by making our own a few words from the famous "prayer to Christ the *Logos*" with which Clement concludes his *Paedagogus.* He implores: "Be gracious . . . to us your children. . . . Grant us that we may live in your peace, be transferred to your city, sail over the billows of sin without capsizing, be gently wafted by your Holy Spirit, by ineffable Wisdom, by night and day to the perfect day . . . giving thanks and praise to the one Father . . . to the Son, Instructor and Teacher, with the Holy Spirit. Amen!" (*Paed.* 3, 12, 101).

—*18 April 2007*

ORIGEN OF ALEXANDRIA

His Life and Work

In our meditations on the great figures of the early Church, we now become acquainted with one of the most remarkable. Origen of Alexandria truly was a figure crucial to the whole development of Christian thought. He gathered up the legacy of Clement of Alexandria, on whom we meditated in the last chapter, and launched it for the future in a way so innovative that he impressed an irreversible turning point on the development of Christian thought.

He was a true "maestro," and so it was that his pupils remembered him with nostalgia and emotion: he was not only a brilliant theologian but also an exemplary witness of the doctrine he passed on. Eusebius of Caesarea, his enthusiastic biographer, said, "His manner of life was as his doctrine, and his doctrine as his life. Therefore, by the divine power working with him he aroused a great many to his own zeal" (cf. *Church History* 6, 3, 7).

His whole life was pervaded by a ceaseless longing for martyrdom. He was seventeen years old when, in the tenth year of the reign of Emperor Septimius Severus, the persecution against Christians was unleashed in Alexandria. Clement, his teacher, fled the city, and Origen's father, Leonides, was thrown into prison. His son longed ardently for martyrdom but was unable to realize his desire. So he wrote to his father, urging him not to shrink from the supreme witness of faith. And when Leonides was beheaded, the young Origen felt bound to welcome the example of his father's life.

Forty years later, while preaching in Caesarea, he confessed: "It is of no use to me to have a martyr father if I do not behave well and honor the nobility of my ancestors, that is, the martyrdom of my father and the witness that made him illustrious in Christ" (*Hom. Ez.* 4, 8). In a later homily—when, thanks to the extreme tolerance of the emperor Philip the Arab, the possibility of bearing witness by shedding one's blood seemed no longer to exist—Origen exclaims: "If God were to grant me to be washed in my blood so as to receive the second baptism after accepting death for Christ, I would depart this world with assurance. . . . But those who deserve such things are blessed" (*Hom. Iud.* 7, 12). These words reveal the full force of Origen's longing for baptism with blood.

And finally, this irresistible yearning was granted to him, at least in part. In the year 250, during Decius's persecution, Origen was arrested and cruelly tortured. Weakened by the suffering to which he had been subjected, he died a few years later. He was not yet seventy.

We have mentioned the "irreversible turning point" that Origen impressed upon the history of theology and Christian thought. But of what did this turning point, this innovation so pregnant with consequences, consist? It corresponds in substance to theology's foundation in the explanation of the Scriptures.

Theology to him was essentially explaining, understanding Scripture; or we might also say that his theology was a perfect symbiosis between theology and exegesis. In fact, the proper hallmark of Origen's doctrine seems to lie precisely in the constant invitation to move from the letter to the spirit of the Scriptures, to progress in knowledge of God. Furthermore, this so-called allegorism, as von Balthasar wrote, coincides exactly "with the development of Christian dogma, effected by the teaching of the Church Doctors," who in one way or another accepted Origen's "lessons."

Thus, Tradition and the magisterium, the foundation and guarantee of theological research, come to take the form of "Scripture in action" (cf. *Origene: Il mondo, Cristo e la Chiesa* [Milan, 1972], 43). We can therefore say that the central nucleus of Origen's immense literary opus consists in his "threefold interpretation" of the Bible.

But before describing this "interpretation," it would be right to take an overall look at the Alexandrian's literary production. Saint Jerome, in his *Epistle* 33, lists the titles of 320 books and 310 homilies by Origen. Unfortunately, most of these works have been lost, but even the few that remain make him the most prolific author of Christianity's first three centuries. His field of interest extended from exegesis to dogma, to philosophy, apologetics, ascetical theology, and mystical theology. It was a fundamental and global vision of Christian life.

The inspiring nucleus of this work, as we have said, was the "threefold interpretation" of the Scriptures that Origen developed in his lifetime. By this phrase, we wish to allude to the three most important ways in which Origen devoted himself to studying the Scriptures: they are not in sequence; on the contrary, more often than not they overlap.

First of all, he read the Bible, determined to do his utmost to ascertain the biblical text and offer the most reliable version of it. This, for example, was the first step: to know truly what is written and what a specific scriptural passage intentionally and principally meant.

He studied extensively for this purpose and drafted an edition of the Bible with six parallel columns, from left to right, with the Hebrew text in Hebrew characters—he was even in touch with rabbis to make sure he properly understood the Bible's original Hebrew text—then the Hebrew text transliterated into Greek characters, and then four different translations in Greek that enabled him to compare the different possibilities for its translation. Hence comes the title of *Hexapla* ("six columns"), attributed to this enormous synopsis. This is the first point: to know exactly what was written, the text as such.

Second, Origen read the Bible systematically with his famous *Commentaries*. They reproduced faithfully the explanations that the teacher offered during his lessons at Alexandria and Caesarea. Origen proceeded verse by verse with a detailed, broad, and analytical approach, with philological and doctrinal notes. He worked with great precision in order to know completely what the sacred authors meant.

Last, even before his ordination to the priesthood, Origen was deeply dedicated to preaching the Bible and adapted himself to a varied public. In any case, the teacher can also be perceived in his *Homilies*, wholly dedicated as he was to the systematic interpretation of the passage under examination, which he analyzed step by step in the sequence of the verses.

Also in his *Homilies,* Origen took every opportunity to recall the different dimensions of the sense of Sacred Scripture that encourage or express a process of growth in the faith: there is the "literal" sense, but this conceals depths that are not immediately apparent. The second dimension is the "moral" sense: what we must do in living the Word; and finally, the "spiritual" sense, the unity of Scripture which throughout its development speaks of Christ.

It is the Holy Spirit who enables us to understand the christological content, hence, the unity in diversity of Scripture. It would be interesting to demonstrate this. I have made a humble attempt in my book *Jesus of Nazareth* to show in today's context these multiple dimensions of the Word, of Sacred Scripture, whose historical meaning must in the first place be respected.

But this sense transcends us, moving us toward God in the light of the Holy Spirit, and shows us the way, shows us how to live. Mention of it is found, for example, in the ninth *Homily on Numbers*, where Origen likens Scripture to [fresh] walnuts: "The doctrine of the Law and the Prophets at the school of Christ is like this," the homilist says; "the letter is bitter, like the [green-covered] skin; second, you will come to the shell, which is the moral doctrine; third, you will discover the meaning of the mysteries, with which the souls of the saints are nourished in the present life and the future" (*Hom. Num.* 9, 7).

It was especially on this route that Origen succeeded in effectively promoting the "Christian interpretation" of the Old Testament, brilliantly countering the challenge of the heretics, especially the Gnostics and Marcionites, who made the two Testaments disagree to the extent that they rejected the Old Testament.

In this regard, in the same *Homily on Numbers*, the Alexandrian says, "I do not call the law an 'Old Testament' if I understand it in the Spirit. The law becomes an 'Old Testament' only for those who wish to understand it carnally," that is, for those who stop at the literal meaning of the text. But "for us, who understand it and apply it in the Spirit and in the gospel sense, the law is ever new, and the two Testaments are a new Testament for us, not because of their date in time but because of the newness of the meaning. . . . Instead, for the sinner and those who do not respect the covenant of love, even the gospels age" (cf. ibid., 9, 4).

I invite you—and so I conclude—to welcome into your hearts the teaching of this great master of faith. He reminds us with deep delight that in the prayerful reading of Scripture and in consistent commitment to life, the Church is ever renewed and rejuvenated. The Word of God, which never ages and is never exhausted, is a privileged means to this end. Indeed, it is the Word of God, through the action of the Holy Spirit, which always guides us to the whole truth (cf. Benedict XVI, *Address at the International Congress for the 50th Anniversary of* Dei Verbum, *L'Osservatore Romano*, English edition, 21 September 2005, 7). And let us pray to the Lord that he will give us thinkers, theologians, and exegetes who discover this multifaceted dimension, this ongoing timeliness of Sacred Scripture, its newness for today. Let us pray that the Lord will help us to read Sacred Scripture in a prayerful way, to be truly nourished with the true Bread of Life, with his Word.

His Thought

We have examined the life and literary opus of the great Alexandrian teacher, identifying his threefold interpretation of the Bible as the life-giving nucleus of all his work. Now we take up two aspects of Origenian doctrine that I consider among the most important and timely: his teachings on prayer and the Church.

In fact, Origen—author of the important and ever timely treatise *On Prayer*—constantly interweaves his exegetical and theological writings with experiences and suggestions connected with prayer. Notwithstanding all the theological richness of his thought, his is never a purely academic approach; it is always founded on the experience of prayer, of contact with God. Indeed, to his mind, knowledge of the Scriptures requires prayer and intimacy with Christ even more than study. He was convinced that the best way to become acquainted with God is through love and that there is no authentic *scientia Christi* without falling in love with him.

In his *Letter to Gregory*, Origen recommends:

> Study first of all the *lectio* of the divine Scriptures. Study them, I say. For we need to study the divine writings deeply . . . and while you study these divine works with a believing and God-pleasing intention, knock

at that which is closed in them and it shall be opened to you by the porter, of whom Jesus says, "To him the gatekeeper opens."
    While you attend to this *lectio divina*, seek aright and with unwavering faith in God the hidden sense which is present in most passages of the divine Scriptures. And do not be content with knocking and seeking, for what is absolutely necessary for understanding divine things is *oratio*, and in urging us to this the Savior says not only "knock and it will be opened to you," and "seek and you will find," but also "ask and it will be given you." (*Ep. Gr.* 4)

The "primordial role" played by Origen in the history of *lectio divina* instantly flashes before one's eyes. Bishop Ambrose of Milan, who learned from Origen's works to interpret the Scriptures, later introduced them into the West to hand them on to Augustine and to the monastic tradition that followed.

As we have already said, according to Origen the highest degree of knowledge of God stems from love. Therefore, this also applies for human beings: only if there is love, if hearts are opened, can one person truly know the other. Origen based his demonstration of this on a meaning that is sometimes attributed to the Hebrew verb *to know*, that is, when it is used to express the human act of love: "Adam knew Eve his wife, and she conceived" (Gen 4:1). This suggests that union in love secures the most authentic knowledge. Just as the man and the woman are "two in one flesh," so God and the believer become "two in one spirit."

The prayer of the Alexandrian thus attained the loftiest levels of mysticism, as is attested to by his *Homilies on the Song of Songs*. A passage is presented in which Origen confessed: "I have often felt—God is my witness—that the Bridegroom came to me in the most exalted way. Then he suddenly left, and I was unable to find what I was seeking. Once again, I am taken by the desire for his coming and sometimes he returns, and when he has appeared to me, when I hold him with my hands, once again he flees from me, and when he has vanished I start again to seek him" (*Hom. in Cant.* 1, 7).

I remember what my venerable predecessor wrote as an authentic witness in *Novo Millennio Ineunte,* where he showed the faithful "how prayer can progress, as a genuine dialogue of love, to the point of rendering the person wholly possessed by the divine Beloved, vibrating at the Spirit's touch, resting filially within the Father's heart."

"It is," John Paul II continues, "a journey totally sustained by grace, which nonetheless demands an intense spiritual commitment and is no stranger to painful purifications. . . . But it leads, in various possible ways, to the ineffable joy experienced by mystics as "nuptial union'" (n. 33).

Finally, we come to one of Origen's teachings on the Church, and precisely—within it—on the common priesthood of the faithful. In fact, as the Alexandrian affirms in his ninth *Homily on Leviticus*, "This discourse concerns us all" (*Hom. in Lev.* 9, 1). In the same *Homily*, Origen, referring to Aaron's prohibition, after the death of his two sons, from entering the *Sancta sanctorum* "at all times" (Lev 16:2), thus warned the faithful:

> This shows that if anyone were to enter the sanctuary at any time without being properly prepared and wearing priestly attire, without bringing the prescribed offerings and making himself favorable to God, he would die. . . .
>   This discourse concerns us all. It requires us, in fact, to know how to accede to God's altar. Oh, do you not know that the priesthood has been conferred upon you too, that is, upon the entire Church of God and believing people? Listen to how Peter speaks to the faithful: "Chosen race," he says, "royal, priestly, holy nation, people whom God has ransomed."
>   You therefore possess the priesthood because you are "a priestly race" and must thus offer the sacrifice to God. . . . But to offer it with dignity, you need garments that are pure and different from the common clothes of other men, and you need the divine fire. (ibid.)

Thus, on the one hand, "girded" and in "priestly attire" mean purity and honesty of life, and on the other, with the "lamp ever alight," that is, faith and knowledge of the Scriptures, we have the indispensable conditions for the exercise of the universal priesthood, which demands purity and an honest life, faith, and knowledge of the Scriptures.

For the exercise of the ministerial priesthood, there is of course all the more reason why such conditions should be indispensable.

These conditions—a pure and virtuous life, but above all the acceptance and study of the Word—establish a true and proper "hierarchy of holiness" in the common priesthood of Christians. At the peak of this ascent of perfection, Origen places martyrdom. Again, in his ninth *Homily on Leviticus*, he alludes to the "fire for the holocaust," that is, to faith and knowledge of the Scriptures which must never be extinguished on the altar of the person who exercises the priesthood. He then adds: "But each one of us has within him" not only the fire; but he "also has the holocaust and from his holocaust lights the altar so that it may burn forever. If I renounce all my possessions, take up my cross, and follow Christ, I offer my holocaust on the altar of God; and if I give up my body to be burned with love and achieve the glory of martyrdom, I offer my holocaust on the altar of God" (*Hom. in Lev.* 9, 9).

This tireless journey to perfection "concerns us all," in order that "the gaze of our hearts" may turn to contemplate Wisdom and Truth, which are Jesus Christ. Preaching on Jesus' discourse in Nazareth—when "the eyes of all in the synagogue were fixed on him" (cf. Lk 4:16-30)—Origen seems to be addressing us:

> Today, too, if you so wished, in this assembly your eyes can be fixed on the Savior.
>
> In fact, it is when you turn the deepest gaze of your heart to the contemplation of Wisdom, Truth, and the only Son of God that your eyes will see God. Happy the assembly of which Scripture attests that the eyes of all were fixed upon him!
>
> How I would like this assembly here to receive a similar testimony, and the eyes of all—the non-baptized and the faithful, women, men, and children—to look at Jesus, not the eyes of the body but those of the soul! . . .
>
> Impress upon us the light of your face, O Lord, to whom be the power and the glory for ever and ever. Amen! (*Hom. in Lk* 32: 6)

—25 April and 2 May 2007

TERTULLIAN

WE CONTINUE TO SPEAK OF the ancient Church's great personalities. They are teachers of the faith also for us today and witnesses of the perennial timeliness of the Christian faith.

I wish to discuss now an African, Tertullian, who from the end of the second and beginning of the third century inaugurated Christian literature in the Latin language. He started the use of theology in Latin. His work brought decisive benefits that it would be unforgivable to underestimate. His influence covered different areas: linguistically, from the use of language and the recovery of classical culture, to singling out a common "Christian soul" in the world and in the formulation of new proposals of human coexistence.

We do not know the exact dates of Tertullian's birth and death. Instead, we know that at Carthage, toward the end of the second century, he received a solid education in rhetoric, philosophy, history, and law from his pagan parents and tutors. He then converted to Christianity, attracted, so it seems, by the example of the Christian martyrs.

He began to publish his most famous writings in 197. But a too-individualistic search for the truth, together with his intransigent character—he was a rigorous man—gradually led him away from communion with the Church to belong to the Montanist sect. The originality of his thought, however, together with an incisive efficacy of language, assured him a high position in ancient Christian literature.

Tertullian's apologetic writings are above all the most famous. They manifest two key intentions: to refute the grave accusations that pagans directed against the new religion; and, more proactive and missionary, to proclaim the gospel message in dialogue with the culture of the time.

His most famous work, *Apologeticus*, denounces the unjust behavior of political authorities toward the Church; explains and defends the teachings and customs of Christians; spells out differences between the new religion and the main philosophical currents of the time; and manifests the triumph of the Spirit that counters its persecutors with the blood, suffering, and patience of the martyrs: "Refined as it is," the African writes, "your cruelty serves no purpose. On the contrary, for our community, it is an invitation. We multiply every time one of us is mowed down. The blood of Christians is effective seed" (*semen est sanguis christianorum! Apologeticus 50, 13*).

Martyrdom, suffering for the truth, is in the end victorious and more efficient than the cruelty and violence of totalitarian regimes.

But Tertullian, as every good apologist, at the same time sensed the need to communicate the essence of Christianity positively. This is why he adopted the speculative method to illustrate the rational foundations of Christian dogma. He developed it in a systematic way, beginning with the description of "the God of the Christians": "He whom we adore," the Apologist wrote, "is the one, only God." And he continued, using antitheses and paradoxes characteristic of his language: "He is invisible even if you see him; difficult to grasp even if he is present through grace; inconceivable even if the human senses can perceive him; therefore, he is true and great!" (cf. ibid., 17, 1–2).

Furthermore, Tertullian takes an enormous step in the development of Trinitarian dogma. He has given us an appropriate way to express this great mystery in Latin by introducing the terms "one substance" and "three persons." In a similar way, he also greatly developed the correct language to express the mystery of Christ, Son of God and true Man.

The Holy Spirit is also considered in the African's writings, demonstrating his personal and divine character: "We believe that, according to his promise, Jesus Christ sent, by means of his Father, the Holy Spirit, the Paraclete, the sanctifier of the faith of all those who believe in the Father, Son, and Holy Spirit" (ibid., 2, 1).

Again, there are in Tertullian's writings numerous texts on the Church, whom he always recognizes as "mother." Even after his acceptance of Montanism, he did not forget that the Church is the mother of our faith and Christian life.

He even considers the moral conduct of Christians and the future life. His writings are important, as they also show the practical trends in the Christian community regarding Mary most holy, the sacraments of the eucharist, matrimony, and reconciliation, Petrine primacy, prayer. . . . In a special way, in those times of persecution when Christians seemed to be a lost minority, the Apologist exhorted them to hope, which in his treatises is not simply a virtue in itself but something that involves every aspect of Christian existence.

We have the hope that the future is ours because the future is God's. Therefore, the Lord's Resurrection is presented as the foundation of our future resurrection and represents the main object of the Christian's *confidence*: "And so the flesh shall rise again," the African categorically affirms, "wholly in every man, in its own identity, in its absolute integrity. Wherever it may be, it is in safe keeping in God's presence, through that most faithful Mediator between God and man, Jesus Christ, who shall reconcile both God to man and man to God" (*Concerning the Resurrection of the Flesh*, 63, 1).

From the human viewpoint, one can undoubtedly speak of Tertullian's own drama. With the passing of years he became increasingly exigent in regard to the Christians. He demanded heroic behavior from them in every circumstance, above all under persecution. Rigid in his positions, he did not withhold blunt criticism, and he inevitably ended by finding himself isolated.

Many questions still remain open today, not only on Tertullian's theological and philosophical thought, but also on his attitude in regard to political institutions and pagan society. This great moral and intellectual personality, this man who made such a great contribution to Christian thought, makes me think deeply. One sees that in the end he lacked the simplicity, the humility to integrate himself with the Church, to accept his weaknesses, to be forbearing with others and himself.

When one only sees his thought in all its greatness, in the end, it is precisely this greatness that is lost. The essential characteristic of a great theologian is the humility to remain with the Church, to accept his own and others' weaknesses, because actually only God is all holy. We, instead, always need forgiveness.

Finally, the African remains an interesting witness of the early times of the Church, when Christians found they were the authentic protagonists of a "new culture" in the critical confrontation between the classical heritage and the gospel message.

In his famous affirmation according to which our soul "is *naturally* Christian" (*Apologeticus* 17, 6), Tertullian evokes the perennial continuity between authentic human values and Christian ones. Also in his other reflection borrowed directly from the gospel, according to which "the Christian cannot hate, not even his enemies" (cf. *Apologeticus* 37), is found the unavoidable moral resolve, the choice of faith which proposes "nonviolence" as the rule of life. Indeed, no one can escape the dramatic aptness of this teaching, also in light of the heated debate on religions.

In summary, the treatises of this African trace many themes that we are still called to face today. They involve us in a fruitful interior examination to which I exhort all the faithful, so that they may know how to express in an always more convincing manner the *rule of faith,* which—again, referring to Tertullian—"prescribes the belief that there is only one God and that he is none other than the Creator of the world, who produced all things out of nothing through his own Word, generated before all things" (cf. *Concerning the Prescription of Heretics* 13, 1).

—*30 May 2007*

St. Cyprian

WE COME NOW TO AN EXCELLENT AFRICAN BISHOP of the third century, St. Cyprian, "the first bishop in Africa to obtain the crown of martyrdom." His fame, Pontius the Deacon, his first biographer, attests, is also linked to his literary corpus and pastoral activity during the thirteen years between his conversion and his martyrdom (cf. *Life and Passion of St. Cyprian* 19, 1; 1, 1).

Cyprian was born in Carthage into a rich pagan family. After a dissipated youth, he converted to Christianity at the age of thirty-five. He himself often told of his spiritual journey, "When I was still lying in darkness and gloomy night," he wrote a few months after his baptism,

> I used to regard it as extremely difficult and demanding to do what God's mercy was suggesting to me. I myself was held in bonds by the innumerable errors of my previous life, from which I did not believe I could possibly be delivered, so I was disposed to acquiesce in my clinging vices and to indulge my sins. . . .
>
> But after that, by the help of the water of new birth, the stain of my former life was washed away, and a light from above, serene and pure, was infused into my reconciled heart. . . . A second birth restored me to a new man. Then, in a wondrous manner every doubt began to fade. . . . I clearly understood that what had first lived within me, enslaved by the vices of the flesh, was earthly and that what, instead, the Holy Spirit had wrought within me was divine and heavenly. (*Ad Donatum*, 3–4)

Immediately after his conversion, despite envy and resistance, Cyprian was chosen for the priestly office and raised to the dignity of bishop. In the brief period of his episcopacy, he had to face the first two persecutions sanctioned by imperial decree: that of Decius (250) and that of Valerian (257–258).

After the particularly harsh persecution of Decius, the bishop had to work strenuously to restore order to the Christian community. Indeed, many of the faithful had abjured or at any rate had not behaved correctly when put to the test. They were the so-called *lapsi*—that is, the "fallen"—who ardently desired to be readmitted to the community.

The debate on their readmission actually divided the Christians of Carthage into laxists and rigorists. These difficulties were compounded by a serious epidemic of the plague, which swept through Africa and gave rise to anguished theological questions both within the community and in the confrontation with pagans. Last, the controversy between St.

Cyprian and Stephen, bishop of Rome, concerning the validity of baptism administered to pagans by heretical Christians, must not be forgotten.

In these truly difficult circumstances, Cyprian revealed his choice gifts of government: he was severe but not inflexible with the *lapsi*, granting them the possibility of forgiveness after exemplary repentance. Before Rome, he staunchly defended the healthy traditions of the African Church; he was deeply human and steeped with the most authentic gospel spirit when he urged Christians to offer brotherly assistance to pagans during the plague; he knew how to maintain the proper balance when reminding the faithful—excessively afraid of losing their lives and their earthly possessions—that true life and true goods are not those of this world; he was implacable in combating corrupt morality and the sins that devastated moral life, especially avarice.

"Thus he spent his days," Pontius the Deacon tells at this point, "when at the bidding of the proconsul, the officer with his soldiers all of a sudden came unexpectedly upon him in his grounds" (*Life and Passion of St. Cyprian* 15, 1). On that day, the holy bishop was arrested and, after being questioned briefly, courageously faced martyrdom in the midst of his people.

The numerous treatises and letters that Cyprian wrote were always connected with his pastoral ministry. Little inclined to theological speculation, he wrote above all for the edification of the community and to encourage the good conduct of the faithful.

Indeed, the Church was easily his favorite subject. Cyprian distinguished between the *visible*, hierarchical Church and the *invisible*, mystical Church but forcefully affirmed that the Church is one, founded on Peter. He never wearied of repeating that "if a man deserts the Chair of Peter upon whom the Church was built, does he think that he is in the Church?" (cf. *De unit*. [*On the Unity of the Catholic Church*] 4).

Cyprian knew well that "outside the Church there is no salvation" and said so in strong words (*Epistles* 4, 4 and 73, 21); and he knew that "no one can have God as Father who does not have the Church as mother" (*De unit*. 6). An indispensable characteristic of the Church is unity, symbolized by Christ's seamless garment (ibid., 7). Cyprian said this unity is founded on Peter (ibid., 4) and finds its perfect fulfillment in the eucharist (*Epistle* 63, 13).

"God is one and Christ is one," Cyprian cautioned, "and his Church is one, and the faith is one, and the Christian people is joined into a substantial unity of body by the cement of concord. Unity cannot be severed. And what is one by its nature cannot be separated" (*De unit*. 23).

We have spoken of his thought on the Church but, last, let us not forget Cyprian's teaching on prayer. I am particularly fond of his treatise on the Our Father, which has been a great help to me in understanding and reciting the Lord's Prayer better.

Cyprian teaches that it is precisely in the Lord's Prayer that the proper way to pray is presented to Christians. And he stresses that this prayer is in the plural in order that "the person who prays it might not pray for himself alone. Our prayer," he wrote, "is public and common; and when we pray, we pray not for one, but for the whole people, because we the whole people, are one (*De Dom. orat.* [*Treatise on the Lord's Prayer*] 8). Thus, personal and liturgical prayer seem to be strongly bound. Their unity stems from the fact that they respond to the same Word of God. The Christian does not say "*my* Father" but "*our* Father," even in the secrecy of a closed room, because he knows that in every place, on every occasion, he is a member of one and the same Body.

"Therefore let us pray, beloved Brethren," Cyprian wrote,

> as God our Teacher has taught us. It is a trusting and intimate prayer to beseech God with his own word, to raise to his ears the prayer of Christ. Let the Father acknowledge the words of his Son when we pray, and let him also who dwells within our breast himself dwell in our voice. . . .
>
> But let our speech and petition when we pray be under discipline, observing quietness and modesty. Let us consider that we are standing in God's sight. We must please the divine eyes both with the position of the body and with the measure of voice. . . .
>
> Moreover, when we meet together with the brethren in one place, and celebrate divine sacrifices with God's priest, we ought to be mindful of modesty and discipline—not to throw abroad our prayers indiscriminately, with unsubdued voices, nor to cast to God with tumultuous wordiness a petition that ought to be commended to God by modesty; for God is the hearer, not of the voice, but of the heart *(non vocis sed cordis auditor est)*. (3–4)

Today too, these words still apply and help us to celebrate the holy liturgy well. Ultimately, Cyprian placed himself at the root of that fruitful theological and spiritual tradition which sees the "heart" as the privileged place for prayer.

Indeed, in accordance with the Bible and the Fathers, the heart refers to the intimate depths of the person, the place in which God dwells. In it occurs the encounter in which God speaks to man, and man listens to God; man speaks to God and God listens to man. All this happens through one divine Word. In this very sense—re-echoing Cyprian—Smaragdus, Abbot of St. Michael on the Meuse in the early years of the ninth century, attests that prayer "is the work of the heart, not of the lips, because God does not look at the words but at the heart of the person praying" (*Diadema monachorum* [*Diadem of the monks*] 1).

Let us make our own this receptive heart and "understanding mind" of which the Bible (cf. 1 Kgs 3:9) and the Fathers speak. How great is our need for it! Only then will we be able to experience fully that God is our Father and that the Church, the holy Bride of Christ, is truly our Mother.

—6 *June 2007*

Eusebius of Caesarea

In the history of early Christianity, there is a fundamental distinction between the first three centuries and those that followed the Council of Nicaea in 325, the First Ecumenical Council. Like a "hinge" between the two periods are the so-called conversion of Constantine and the peace of the Church, as well as the figure of Eusebius, bishop of Caesarea in Palestine. He was the most highly qualified exponent of the Christian culture of his time in very varied contexts, from theology to exegesis, from history to erudition. Eusebius is known above all as the first historian of Christianity, but he was also the greatest philologist of the ancient Church.

It was to Caesarea, where Eusebius was born probably in about the year 260, that Origen had fled from Alexandria. And in Caesarea, Origen founded a school and a huge library. A few decades later, the young Eusebius educated himself with these books. In 325, as bishop of Caesarea, he played a lead role at the Council of Nicaea. He signed the creed and the affirmation of the full divinity of the Son of God, who is consequently defined as "one in being with the Father" (*homooúsios tõ Patrí*). The creed we recite every Sunday in the holy liturgy is practically the same.

A sincere admirer of Constantine, who had given peace to the Church, Eusebius in turn was esteemed and respected by Constantine. As well as with his works, Eusebius also celebrated the emperor with panegyrics, which he delivered on the twentieth and thirtieth anniversary of Constantine's ascendance to the throne and upon his death in the year 337. Two or three years later, Eusebius died too.

Eusebius was an indefatigable scholar. In his numerous writings, he resolved to reflect and to give an up-to-date report on the three centuries of Christianity, three centuries lived under persecution, drawing abundantly on the Christian and pagan sources preserved in particular in the great library of Caesarea. Thus, despite the objective importance of his apologetic, exegetical, and doctrinal works, the imperishable fame of Eusebius is still mainly associated with the ten books of his *Ecclesiastical History*. He was the first person to write a history of the Church that continues to be of fundamental importance, thanks to the sources which Eusebius made available to us forever. With this chronicle, he succeeded in saving from the doom of oblivion numerous events, important figures, and literary works of the ancient Church. Thus, his work is a primary source of knowledge of the early centuries of Christianity.

We might wonder how he structured this new work and what his intentions were in compiling it. At the beginning of his first book, the historian lists in detail the topics he intends to treat in his work:

It is my purpose to write an account of the succession of the holy Apostles, as well as of the times which have elapsed from the days of our
Savior to our own; and to relate the many important events which are
said to have occurred in the history of the Church; and to mention those
who have governed and presided over the Church in the most prominent dioceses and those who in each generation have proclaimed the
divine Word either orally or in writing.

It is my purpose also to give the names and number and times of
those who through love of innovation have run into the greatest errors,
and, proclaiming themselves interpreters and promoters of a false
doctrine have, like fierce wolves, unmercifully devastated the flock of
Christ . . . and to record the ways and the times in which the divine
word has been attacked by the Gentiles, and to describe the character
of the great men who in various periods have defended it in the face of
blood and of tortures . . . and finally, the mercy and benevolence which
our Savior has afforded them all. (cf. 1, 1, 1–3)

Thus, Eusebius embraced different spheres: the succession of the
Apostles as the backbone of the Church, the dissemination of the message, the errors and then persecutions on the part of the pagans, and the
important testimonies which are the light in this chronicle.

In all this Eusebius saw the Savior's mercy and benevolence. So it
was that he inaugurated, as it were, ecclesiastical historiography, extend-
ing his account to 324, the year in which Constantine, after defeating
Licinius, was acclaimed as the one emperor of Rome. This was the year
before the important Council of Nicaea, which subsequently offered the
"summa" of all that the Church—doctrinally, morally, and also juridi-
cally—had learned in the previous three hundred years.

The citation we have just quoted, from the first book of the *Ecclesiastical History*, contains a repetition that is certainly intentional. The
christological title *Savior* recurs three times in the space of a few lines
with an explicit reference to "his mercy" and "his benevolence."

Thus, we can grasp the fundamental perspective of Eusebian historiography: his is a "Christocentric" history, in which the mystery of God's
love for humankind is gradually revealed.

Eusebius recognized with genuine amazement that

Jesus alone of all those who have ever existed is even to the present
day called Christ [that is Messiah and Savior of the world] by all men
throughout the world, and is confessed and witnessed to under this
name, and is commemorated both by Greeks and Barbarians and even
to this day is honored as a king by his followers throughout the world,
and is admired as more than a prophet, and is glorified as the true and
only High Priest of God. And besides all this, as the preexistent *Logos*

of God, called into being before all ages, he has received august honor from the Father, and is worshiped and adored as God. But most wonderful of all is the fact that we who have consecrated ourselves to him honor him not only with our voices and with the sound of words, but also with complete elevation of soul, so that we choose to give testimony unto him rather than to preserve our own lives. (cf. 1, 3, 19–20)

Another feature thus springs to the fore that was to remain a constant in ancient ecclesiastical historiography: it is the "moral intention" that presides in the account. Historical analysis is never an end in itself; it is not made solely with a view to knowing the past; rather, it focuses decisively on conversion and on an authentic witness of Christian life on the part of the faithful. It is a guide for us too.

Thus, Eusebius strongly challenges believers of all times on their approach to the events of history and of the Church in particular. He also challenges us: what is our attitude with regard to the Church's experiences? Is it the attitude of those who are interested in it merely out of curiosity, or even in search of something sensational or shocking at all costs? Or is it an attitude full of love and open to the mystery of those who know—through faith—that they can trace in the history of the Church those signs of God's love and the great works of salvation wrought by him? If this is our attitude, we can only feel stimulated to a more coherent and generous response, to a more Christian witness of life, in order to bequeath the signs of God's love also to the generations to come.

"There is a mystery," Cardinal Jean Daniélou, an eminent Patristics scholar, never tired of saying: "History has a hidden content. . . . The mystery is that of God's works which constitute in time the authentic reality concealed behind the appearances. . . . However, this history which he brings about for man, God does not bring about without him. Pausing to contemplate the 'great things' worked by God would mean seeing only one aspect of things. The human response lies before them" (*Saggio sul mistero della storia*, Italian edition [Brescia, 1963], 182).

Today, too, so many centuries later, Eusebius of Caesarea invites believers, invites us, to wonder, to contemplate in history the great works of God for the salvation of humankind. And just as energetically, he invites us to conversion of life. Indeed, we cannot remain inert before a God who has so deeply loved us. The specific demand of love is that our entire life should be oriented to the imitation of the Beloved. Let us therefore spare no effort to leave a transparent trace of God's love in our life.

—*13 June 2007*

Part Two

Great Teachers of the Ancient Church

St. Athanasius of Alexandria

CONTINUING OUR REVISITATION of the great teachers of the ancient Church, let us focus our attention on St. Athanasius of Alexandria.

Only a few years after his death, this authentic protagonist of the Christian tradition was already hailed as "the pillar of the Church" by Gregory of Nazianzus, the great theologian and bishop of Constantinople (*Orationes* 21, 26), and he has always been considered a model of orthodoxy in both East and West. As a result, it was not by chance that Gian Lorenzo Bernini placed his statue among those of the four holy Doctors of the Eastern and Western Churches—together with the images of Ambrose, John Chrysostom, and Augustine—that surround the Chair of St. Peter in the marvelous apse of the Vatican Basilica.

Athanasius was undoubtedly one of the most important and revered early Church Fathers. But this great saint was above all the impassioned theologian of the Incarnation of the *Logos,* the Word of God, who—as the Prologue of the Fourth Gospel says—"became flesh and dwelt among us" (Jn 1:14).

For this very reason, Athanasius was also the most important and tenacious adversary of the Arian heresy, which at that time threatened faith in Christ, reduced to a creature "halfway" between God and man, according to a recurring tendency in history which we also see manifested today in various forms.

In all likelihood, Athanasius was born in Alexandria, Egypt, in about the year 300. He received a good education before becoming a deacon and secretary to the bishop of Alexandria, the great Egyptian metropolis. As a close collaborator with his bishop, the young cleric took part with him in the Council of Nicaea, the First Ecumenical Council, convoked by the Emperor Constantine in May 325 to ensure Church unity. The Nicene Fathers were thus able to address various issues and primarily the serious problem that had arisen a few years earlier from the preaching of the Alexandrian priest Arius.

With his theory, Arius threatened authentic faith in Christ, declaring that the *Logos* was not a true God but a created God, a creature "halfway" between God and man who hence remained for ever inaccessible to us. The bishops gathered in Nicaea responded by developing and establishing the "symbol of faith" [creed] which, completed later at the First Council of Constantinople, has endured in the traditions of various Christian denominations and in the liturgy as the Nicene-Constantinopolitan Creed.

In this fundamental text—which expresses the faith of the undivided Church and which we also recite today, every Sunday, in the eucharistic celebration—the Greek term *homooúsios* is featured, in Latin *consubstantialis*: it means that the Son, the *Logos,* is "of the same substance" as the Father, he is God of God, he is his substance. Thus, the full divinity of the Son, which was denied by the Arians, was brought into the limelight.

In 328, when Bishop Alexander died, Athanasius succeeded him as bishop of Alexandria. He showed straightaway that he was determined to reject any compromise with regard to the Arian theories condemned by the Council of Nicaea. His intransigence—tenacious and, if necessary, at times harsh—against those who opposed his episcopal appointment and especially against adversaries of the Nicene Creed, provoked the implacable hostility of the Arians and philo-Arians.

Despite the unequivocal outcome of the council, which clearly affirmed that the Son is of the same substance as the Father, these erroneous ideas shortly thereafter once again began to prevail—in this situation even Arius was rehabilitated—and they were upheld for political reasons by the Emperor Constantine himself and then by his son Constantius II.

Moreover, Constantine was not so much concerned with theological truth but rather with the unity of the empire and its political problems; he wished to politicize the faith, making it more accessible—in his opinion—to all his subjects throughout the empire.

Thus, the Arian crisis, believed to have been resolved at Nicaea, persisted for decades with complicated events and painful divisions in the Church. At least five times during the thirty years between 336 and 366, Athanasius was obliged to abandon his city, spending seventeen years in exile and suffering for the faith. But during his forced absences from Alexandria, the bishop was able to sustain and to spread in the West, first at Trier and then in Rome, the Nicene faith as well as the ideals of monasticism, embraced in Egypt by the great hermit Anthony, with a choice of life to which Athanasius was always close.

St. Anthony, with his spiritual strength, was the most important champion of St. Athanasius's faith. Reinstated in his see once and for all, the bishop of Alexandria was able to devote himself to religious pacification and the reorganization of the Christian communities. He died on 2 May 373, the day when we celebrate his liturgical memorial.

The most famous doctrinal work of the holy Alexandrian bishop is his treatise *De Incarnatione, On the Incarnation of the Word,* the divine *Logos* who was made flesh, becoming like one of us for our salvation. In this work, Athanasius says with an affirmation that has rightly become famous that the Word of God "was made man so that we might be made God; and he manifested himself through a body so that we might receive the idea of the unseen Father; and he endured the insolence of men that we might inherit immortality" (54, 3). With his Resurrection, in fact, the Lord banished death from us like "straw from the fire" (8, 4).

The fundamental idea of Athanasius's entire theological battle was precisely that God is accessible. He is not a secondary God; he is the true God, and it is through our communion with Christ that we can truly be united to God. He has really become "God-with-us."

Among the other works of this great Father of the Church—which remain largely associated with the events of the Arian crisis—let us remember the four epistles he addressed to his friend Serapion, bishop of Thmuis, on the divinity of the Holy Spirit, which he clearly affirmed; and approximately thirty "Festal" letters addressed at the beginning of each year to the churches and monasteries of Egypt to inform them of the date of the Easter celebration, but above all to guarantee the links between the faithful, reinforcing their faith and preparing them for this great solemnity.

Last, Athanasius also wrote meditational texts on the Psalms, subsequently circulated widely, and in particular, a work that constitutes the bestseller of early Christian literature: *The Life of Anthony,* that is, the biography of St. Anthony Abbot. It was written shortly after this saint's death, precisely while the exiled bishop of Alexandria was staying with monks in the Egyptian desert. Athanasius was such a close friend of the great hermit that he received one of the two sheepskins which Anthony left as his legacy, together with the mantle that the bishop of Alexandria himself had given to him.

The exemplary biography of this figure, dear to Christian tradition, soon became very popular, almost immediately translated into Latin, in two editions, and then into various Oriental languages; it made an important contribution to the spread of monasticism in the East and in the West. It was not by chance that the interpretation of this text, in Trier, was at the center of a moving tale of the conversion of two imperial officials whom Augustine incorporated into his *Confessions* (cf. 8, 6, 15) as the preamble to his own conversion.

Moreover, Athanasius himself showed he was clearly aware of the influence that Anthony's fine example could have on Christian people. Indeed, he wrote at the end of this work:

> The fact that his fame has been blazoned everywhere, that all regard him with wonder, and that those who have never seen him long for him, is clear proof of his virtue and God's love of his soul. For not from writings, nor from worldly wisdom, nor through any art, was Anthony renowned, but solely from his piety toward God. That this was the gift of God no one will deny.
>
> For from whence into Spain and into Gaul, how into Rome and Africa, was the man heard of who dwelt hidden in a mountain, unless it was God who makes his own known everywhere, who also promised

this to Anthony at the beginning? For even if they work secretly, even if they wish to remain in obscurity, yet the Lord shows them as lamps to lighten all, that those who hear may thus know that the precepts of God are able to make men prosper and thus be zealous in the path of virtue." (*Life of Anthony*, 93, 5–6)

We have many causes for which to be grateful to St. Athanasius. His life, like that of Anthony and of countless other saints, shows us that "those who draw near to God do not withdraw from men, but rather become truly close to them" (*Deus Caritas Est,* n. 42).

—20 *June 2007*

St. Cyril of Jerusalem

OUR ATTENTION IS FOCUSED now on St. Cyril of Jerusalem. His life is woven of two dimensions: on the one hand, pastoral care, and on the other, his involvement, in spite of himself, in the heated controversies that were then tormenting the Church of the East.

Cyril was born at or near Jerusalem in 315. He received an excellent literary education, which formed the basis of his ecclesiastical culture, centered on study of the Bible. He was ordained a priest by Bishop Maximus.

When this bishop died or was deposed in 348, Cyril was ordained a bishop by Acacius, the influential Metropolitan of Caesarea in Palestine, a philo-Arian who must have been under the impression that in Cyril he had an ally; so as a result Cyril was suspected of having obtained his episcopal appointment by making concessions to Arianism. Actually, Cyril very soon came into conflict with Acacius, not only in the field of doctrine but also in that of jurisdiction, because he claimed his own see to be autonomous from the Metropolitan See of Caesarea.

Cyril was exiled three times within the course of approximately twenty years: the first time was in 357, after being deposed by a synod of Jerusalem; followed by a second exile in 360, instigated by Acacius; and finally, in 367, by a third exile—his longest, which lasted eleven years— by the philo-Arian Emperor Valens. It was only in 378, after the emperor's death, that Cyril could definitively resume possession of his see and restore unity and peace to his faithful.

Some sources of that time cast doubt on his orthodoxy, whereas other equally ancient sources come out strongly in his favor. The most authoritative of them is the Synodal Letter of 382 that followed the Second Ecumenical Council of Constantinople (381), in which Cyril had played an important part. In this letter, addressed to the Roman pontiff, the Eastern bishops officially recognized Cyril's flawless orthodoxy, the legitimacy of his episcopal ordination, and the merits of his pastoral service, which ended with his death in 387.

Of Cyril's writings, twenty-four famous catecheses have been preserved, which he delivered as bishop in about 350. Introduced by a *Procatechesis* of welcome, the first eighteen of these are addressed to catechumens or candidates for illumination (*photizomenoi*, candidates for baptism); they were delivered in the Basilica of the Holy Sepulchre. Each of the first ones (nn. 1–5) respectively treat the prerequisites for baptism, conversion from pagan morals, the sacrament of baptism, the ten dogmatic truths contained in the creed or symbol of the faith.

The next catecheses (nn. 6–18) form an "ongoing catechesis" on the Jerusalem Creed in anti-Arian tones.

Of the last five so-called mystagogical catecheses, the first two develop a commentary on the rites of baptism and the last three focus on the chrism, the body and blood of Christ, and the eucharistic liturgy. They include an explanation of the Our Father (*Oratio dominica*). This forms the basis of a process of initiation to prayer which develops on a par with the initiation to the three sacraments of baptism, confirmation, and the eucharist. The basis of his instruction on the Christian faith also served to play a polemic role against pagans, Judaeo-Christians, and Manichaeans. The argument was based on the fulfillment of the Old Testament promises, in a language rich in imagery.

Catechesis marked an important moment in the broader context of the whole life, particularly liturgical, of the Christian community, in whose maternal womb the gestation of the future faithful took place, accompanied by prayer and the witness of the brethren.

Taken as a whole, Cyril's homilies form a systematic catechesis on the Christian's rebirth through baptism. He tells the catechumen: "You have been caught in the nets of the Church (cf. Mt 13:47). Be taken alive, therefore; do not escape, for it is Jesus who is fishing for you, not in order to kill you but to resurrect you after death. Indeed, you must die and rise again (cf. Rom 6:11, 14). . . . Die to your sins and live to righteousness from this very day" (*Procatechesis* 5).

From the *doctrinal* viewpoint, Cyril commented on the Jerusalem Creed with recourse to the typology of the Scriptures in a "symphonic" relationship between the two Testaments, arriving at Christ, the center of the universe. The typology was to be described decisively by Augustine of Hippo: "In the Old Testament there is a veiling of the New, and in the New Testament there is a revealing of the Old" (*De catechizandis rudibus* 4, 8).

As for the *moral* catechesis, it is anchored in deep unity to the doctrinal catechesis: the dogma progressively descends in souls who are thus urged to transform their pagan behavior on the basis of new life in Christ, a gift of baptism.

The "mystagogical" catechesis, lastly, marked the summit of the instruction that Cyril imparted, no longer to catechumens but to the newly baptized, or neophytes, during Easter week. He led them to discover the mysteries still hidden in the baptismal rites of the Easter Vigil. Enlightened by the light of a deeper faith by virtue of baptism, the neophytes were at last able to understand these mysteries better, having celebrated their rites. Especially with neophytes of Greek origin, Cyril made use of the faculty of sight which they found congenial. It was the passage from the rite to the mystery that made the most of the psychological effect of amazement, as well as the experience of Easter night. Here is a text that explains the mystery of baptism:

> You descended three times into the water, and ascended again, suggesting by a symbol the three days burial of Christ, imitating Our Savior, who spent three days and three nights in the heart of the earth (cf. Mt 12:40). Celebrating the first immersion in water you recall the first day passed by Christ in the sepulcher; with the first immersion you confessed the first night passed in the sepulcher: for as he who is in the night no longer sees, but he who is in the day remains in the light, so in the descent, as in the night, you saw nothing, but in ascending again you were as in the day. And at the self-same moment you were both dying and being born; and that water of salvation was at once your grave and your mother. . . . For you the time to die goes hand in hand with the time to be born: one and the same time effected both of these events. (cf. *Second Mystagogical Catechesis* n. 4)

The mystery to be understood is God's plan, which is brought about through Christ's saving actions in the Church. In turn, the mystagogical dimension is accompanied by the dimension of symbols which express the spiritual experience they "explode." Thus, Cyril's catechesis, on the basis of the three elements described—doctrinal, moral, and, lastly, mystagogical—proves to be a global catechesis in the Spirit.

The mystagogical dimension brings about the synthesis of the two former dimensions, orienting them to the sacramental celebration in which the salvation of the whole human person takes place. In short, this is an integral catechesis which, involving body, soul, and spirit, remains emblematic for the catechetical formation of Christians today.

—*27 June 2007*

St. Basil

His Life and Witness

Let us remember now one of the great Fathers of the Church, St. Basil, described by Byzantine liturgical texts as "a luminary of the Church." He was an important bishop in the fourth century, to whom the entire Church of the East, and likewise the Church of the West, looks with admiration because of the holiness of his life, the excellence of his teaching, and the harmonious synthesis of his speculative and practical gifts.

Basil was born in about 330 into a family of saints, "a true domestic Church," immersed in an atmosphere of deep faith. He studied with the best teachers in Athens and Constantinople. Unsatisfied with his worldly success and realizing that he had frivolously wasted much time on vanities, he himself confessed: "One day, like a man roused from deep sleep, I turned my eyes to the marvelous light of the truth of the Gospel . . . , and I wept many tears over my miserable life" (cf. *Letter* 223: *PG* 32, 824a).

Attracted by Christ, Basil began to look and listen to him alone (cf. *Moralia* 80, 1: *PG* 31, 860bc). He devoted himself with determination to the monastic life through prayer, meditation on the Sacred Scriptures and the writings of the Fathers of the Church, and the practice of charity (cf. *Letters* 2, 22), also following the example of his sister, St. Macrina, who was already living the ascetic life of a nun. He was then ordained a priest and finally, in the year 370, bishop of Caesarea in Cappadocia in present-day Turkey.

Through his preaching and writings, he carried out immensely busy pastoral, theological, and literary activities. With a wise balance, he was able to combine service to souls with dedication to prayer and meditation in solitude. Availing himself of his personal experience, he encouraged the foundation of numerous "fraternities," in other words, communities of Christians consecrated to God, which he visited frequently (cf. Gregory of Nazianzus, *Oratio* 43, 29, *in laudem Basilii: PG* 36, 536b). He urged them with his words and his writings, many of which have come down to us (cf. *Regulae brevius tractatae*, Proemio: *PG* 31, 1080ab), to live and to advance in perfection.

Various legislators of ancient monasticism drew on his works, including St. Benedict, who considered Basil his teacher (cf. *Rule* 73, 5). Indeed, Basil created a very special monasticism: it was not closed to the community of the local Church but instead was open to it. His monks belonged to the particular Church; they were her life-giving nucleus and, going before the other faithful in the following of Christ and not only in faith, showed a strong attachment to him—love for him—especially through charitable acts. These monks, who ran schools and hospitals, were at the service of the poor and thus demonstrated the integrity of Christian life.

In speaking of monasticism, the servant of God John Paul II wrote: "For this reason many people think that the essential structure of the life of the Church, monasticism, was established, for all time, mainly by St. Basil; or that, at least, it was not defined in its more specific nature without his decisive contribution" (Apostolic Letter *Patres Ecclesiae*, n. 2, January 1980; *L'Osservatore Romano*, English edition, 25 February, 6).

As the bishop and pastor of his vast diocese, Basil was constantly concerned with the difficult material conditions in which his faithful lived; he firmly denounced the evils; he did all he could on behalf of the poorest and most marginalized people; he also intervened with rulers to alleviate the sufferings of the population, especially in times of disaster; he watched over the Church's freedom, opposing even the powerful in order to defend the right to profess the true faith (cf. Gregory of Nazianzus, *Oratio* 43, 48–51 *in laudem Basilii: PG* 36, 557c–561c).

Basil bore an effective witness to God, who is love and charity, by building for the needy various institutions (cf. Basil, *Letter* 94: *PG* 32, 488bc), virtually a "city" of mercy, called *Basiliade* after him (cf. Sozomeno, *Historia Eccl.* 6, 34: *PG* 67, 1397a). This was the origin of the modern hospital structures where the sick are admitted for treatment.

Aware that "the liturgy is the summit toward which the activity of the Church is directed," and "also the fount from which all her power flows" (*Sacrosanctum Concilium*, n. 10), and in spite of his constant concern to do charitable acts, which are the hallmark of faith, Basil was also a wise "liturgical reformer" (cf. Gregory of Nazianzus, *Oratio* 43, 34 *in laudem Basilii: PG* 36, 541c). Indeed, he has bequeathed to us a great eucharistic prayer (or *anaphora*) that takes its name from him and has given a fundamental order to prayer and psalmody: at his prompting, the people learned to know and love the Psalms and even went to pray them during the night (cf. Basil, *In Psalmum* 1, 1–2: *PG* 29, 212a–213c). And we thus see how liturgy, worship, prayer with the Church, and charity go hand in hand and condition one another.

With zeal and courage Basil opposed the heretics who denied that Jesus Christ was God as the Father is God (cf. Basil, *Letter* 9, 3: *PG* 32, 272a; *Letter* 52, 1–3: *PG* 32, 392b–396a; *Adv. Eunomium* 1, 20: *PG* 29, 556c). Likewise, against those who would not accept the divinity of the Holy Spirit, he maintained that the Spirit is also God and "must be equated and glorified with the Father and with the Son (cf. *De Spiritu Sancto: SC* 17ff., 348). For this reason, Basil was one of the great Fathers who formulated the doctrine on the Trinity: the one God, precisely because he is love, is a God in three persons who form the most profound unity that exists: divine unity.

In his love for Christ and for his gospel, the great Cappadocian also strove to mend divisions within the Church (cf. *Letters,* 70, 243), doing his utmost to bring all to convert to Christ and to his Word (cf. *De Iudicio* 4: PG 31, 660b–661a), a unifying force which all believers were bound to obey (cf. ibid. 1–3: PG 31, 653a–656c).

Basil spent himself without reserve in faithful service to the Church and in the multiform exercise of the episcopal ministry. In accordance with the program that he himself drafted, he became an "apostle and minister of Christ, steward of God's mysteries, herald of the kingdom, a model and rule of piety, an eye of the body of the Church, a pastor of Christ's sheep, a loving doctor, father and nurse, a cooperator of God, a farmer of God, a builder of God's temple" (cf. *Moralia* 80, 11–20: PG 31, 864b–868b).

This is the program which the holy bishop consigns to preachers of the Word—in the past as in the present—a program that he himself was generously committed to putting into practice. In 379, Basil, who was not yet fifty, returned to God "in the hope of eternal life, through Jesus Christ our Lord" (*De Baptismo* 1, 2, 9). He was a man who truly lived with his gaze fixed on Christ. He was a man of love for his neighbor. Full of the hope and joy of faith, Basil shows us how to be true Christians.

His Teachings and Exhortations

The life and works of St. Basil are full of ideas for reflection and teachings that are also relevant for us today.

First of all is Basil's reference to *God's mystery,* which is still the most meaningful and vital reference for human beings. The Father is "the principal of all things and the cause of being of all that exists, the root of the living" (*Hom.* 15, 2 *de fide: PG* 31, 465c); above all, he is "the Father of our Lord Jesus Christ" (*Anaphora Sancti Basilii*). Ascending to God through his creatures, we "become aware of his goodness and wisdom" (Basil, *Adversus Eunomium* 1, 14: PG 29, 544b).

The Son is the "image of the Father's goodness and seal in the same form" (cf. *Anaphora Sancti Basilii*). With his obedience and his passion, the Incarnate Word carried out his mission as Redeemer of man (cf. Basil, *In Psalmum* 48, 8: PG 29, 452ab; cf. also *De Baptismo* 1, 2: SC 357, 158).

Last, he spoke fully of the Holy Spirit, to whom he dedicated a whole book. He reveals to us that the Spirit enlivens the Church, fills her with his gifts, and sanctifies her.

The resplendent light of the divine mystery is reflected in man, the image of God, and exalts human dignity. Looking at Christ, one fully understands human dignity. Basil exclaims: "[Man], be mindful of your greatness, remembering the price paid for you: look at the price of your redemption and comprehend your dignity!" (*In Psalmum* 48, 8: PG 29, 452b). Christians in particular, conforming their lives to the gospel, recognize that all people are brothers and sisters; that life is a stewardship of the goods received from God, which is why each one is responsible for the other, and whoever is rich must be as it were an "executor of the orders of God the Benefactor" (*Hom. 6 de avaritia*: PG 32, 1181–96). We must all help one another and cooperate as members of one body (*Ep.* 203, 3).

And on this point, he used courageous, strong words in his homilies. Indeed, anyone who desires to love his neighbor as himself, in accordance with God's commandment, "must possess no more than his neighbor" (*Hom. in divites*: PG 31, 281b). In times of famine and disaster, the holy bishop exhorted the faithful with passionate words "not to be more cruel than beasts . . . by taking over what people possess in common or by grabbing what belongs to all (*Hom. tempore famis*: PG 31, 325a). Basil's profound thought stands out in this evocative sentence: "All the destitute look to our hands just as we look to those of God when we are in need."

Therefore, Gregory of Nazianzus's praise after Basil's death was well-deserved. He said: "Basil convinces us that since we are human beings, we must neither despise men nor offend Christ, the common head of all, with our inhuman behavior toward people; rather, we ourselves must benefit by learning from the misfortunes of others and must lend God our compassion, for we are in need of mercy" (Gregory of Nazianzus, *Orationes* 43, 63: PG 36, 580b). These words are very timely. We see that St. Basil is truly one of the Fathers of the Church's social doctrine.

Furthermore, Basil reminds us that to keep alive our love for God and for men, *we need the eucharist,* the appropriate food for the baptized, which can nourish the new energies that derive from baptism (cf. *De Baptismo* 1, 3: SC 357, 192). It is a cause of immense joy to be able to take part in the eucharist (cf. *Moralia* 21, 3: PG 31, 741a), instituted "to preserve unceasingly the memory of the One who died and rose for us" (*Moralia* 80, 22: PG 31, 869b). The eucharist, an immense gift of God, preserves in each one of us the memory of the baptismal seal and makes it possible to live the grace of baptism to the full and in fidelity. For this reason, the holy bishop recommended frequent, even daily, Communion: "Communicating even daily, receiving the holy body and blood of Christ, is good and useful; for he said clearly: 'He who eats my flesh and drinks my blood has eternal life' (Jn 6:54). So who would doubt that communicating continuously with life were not living in fullness?" (*Ep.* 93: PG 32, 484b).

The eucharist, in a word, is necessary for us if we are to welcome within us true life, eternal life (cf. *Moralia* 21, 1: PG 31, 737c).

Finally, Basil was of course also concerned with that chosen portion of the People of God, *the youth,* society's future. He addressed a *Discourse* to them on how to benefit from the pagan culture of that time. He recognized with great balance and openness that examples of virtue can be found in classical Greek and Latin literature. Such examples of upright living can be helpful to young Christians in search of the truth and the correct way of living (cf. *Ad Adolescentes* 3). Therefore, one must take from the texts by classical authors what is suitable and conforms with the truth: thus, with a critical and open approach—it is a question of true and proper "discernment"—young people grow in freedom.

With the famous image of bees that gather from flowers only what they need to make honey, Basil recommends: "Just as bees can take nectar from flowers, unlike other animals which limit themselves to enjoying their scent and color, so also from these writings . . . one can draw some benefit for the spirit. We must use these books, following in all things the example of bees. They do not visit every flower without distinction, nor seek to remove all the nectar from the flowers on which they alight, but only draw from them what they need to make honey, and leave the rest. And if we are wise, we will take from those writings what is appropriate for us, and conforms to the truth, ignoring the rest" (*Ad Adolescentes* 4).

Basil recommended above all that young people grow in virtue, in the right way of living: "While the other goods . . . pass from one to the other as in playing dice, virtue alone is an inalienable good and endures throughout life and after death" (*Ad Adolescentes* 5).

I think one can say that this Father from long ago also speaks to us and tells us important things: In the first place, attentive, critical, and creative participation in today's culture. Then, social responsibility: this is an age in which, in a globalized world, even people who are physically distant are really our neighbors; therefore, friendship with Christ, the God with the human face. And, last, knowledge and recognition of God the Creator, the Father of us all: only if we are open to this God, the common Father, can we build a more just and fraternal world.

—*4 July and 1 August 2007*

St. Gregory of Nazianzus

His Life and Times

After discussing St. Basil, a Father of the Church and a great teacher of the faith, I speak now of his friend Gregory of Nazianzus. Like Basil, he was a native of Cappadocia. As a distinguished theologian, orator, and champion of the Christian faith in the fourth century, he was famous for his eloquence, and as a poet, he also had a refined and sensitive soul.

Gregory was born into a noble family in about 330, and his mother consecrated him to God at birth. After his education at home, he attended the most famous schools of his time: he first went to Caesarea in Cappadocia, where he made friends with Basil, the future bishop of that city, and went on to stay in other capitals of the ancient world, such as Alexandria, Egypt, and in particular Athens, where once again he met Basil (cf. *Orationes* 43, 14–24: SC 384, 146–180).

Remembering this friendship, Gregory was later to write: "Then not only did I feel full of veneration for my great Basil because of the seriousness of his morals and the maturity and wisdom of his speeches, but he induced others who did not yet know him to be like him. . . . The same eagerness for knowledge motivated us. . . . This was our competition: not who was first but who allowed the other to be first. It seemed as if we had one soul in two bodies" (*Orationes* 43, 16, 20: SC 384, 154–156, 164].

These words more or less paint the self-portrait of this noble soul. Yet one can also imagine how this man, who was powerfully cast beyond earthly values, must have suffered deeply for the things of this world.

On his return home, Gregory received baptism and developed an inclination for monastic life: solitude as well as philosophical and spiritual meditation fascinated him. He himself wrote:

Nothing seems to me greater than this: to silence one's senses, to emerge from the flesh of the world, to withdraw into oneself, no longer to be concerned with human things other than what is strictly necessary; to converse with oneself and with God; to lead a life that transcends the visible; to bear in one's soul divine images, ever pure, not mingled with earthly or erroneous forms; truly to be a perfect mirror of God and of divine things, and to become so more and more, taking light from light . . . ; to enjoy, in the present hope, the future good, and to converse with angels; to have already left the earth even while continuing to dwell on it, borne aloft by the spirit." (*Orationes* 2, 7: SC 247, 96)

As he confides in his autobiography (cf. *Carmina [historica]* 2, 1, 11, *De Vita Sua* 340–49: *PG* 37, 1053), Gregory received priestly ordination with a certain reluctance, for he knew that he would later have to be a bishop, to look after others and their affairs, hence, could no longer be absorbed in pure meditation. However, he subsequently accepted this vocation and took on the pastoral ministry in full obedience, accepting, as often happened to him in his life, to be carried by providence where he did not wish to go (cf. Jn 21:18).

In 371, his friend Basil, bishop of Caesarea, against Gregory's own wishes, desired to ordain him bishop of Sasima, a strategically important locality in Cappadocia. Because of various problems, however, he never took possession of it and instead stayed on in the city of Nazianzus.

In about 379, Gregory was called to Constantinople, the capital, to head the small Catholic community faithful to the Council of Nicaea and to belief in the Trinity. The majority adhered instead to Arianism, which was "politically correct" and viewed by emperors as politically useful. Thus, he found himself in a condition of minority, surrounded by hostility. He delivered five *Theological Orations* (*Orationes* 27–31: *SC* 250, 70–343) in the little Church of the Anastasis precisely in order to defend the Trinitarian faith and to make it intelligible. These discourses became famous because of the soundness of his doctrine and his ability to reason, which truly made clear that this was the divine logic. And the splendor of their form also makes them fascinating today.

It was because of these orations that Gregory acquired the nickname: "The Theologian," as he is called in the Orthodox Church. And this is because to his way of thinking theology was not merely human reflection or even less, only a fruit of complicated speculation, but rather sprang from a life of prayer and holiness, from a persevering dialogue with God. And in this very way he causes the reality of God, the mystery of the Trinity, to appear to our reason.

In the silence of contemplation, interspersed with wonder at the marvels of the mystery revealed, his soul was engrossed in beauty and divine glory.

While Gregory was taking part in the Second Ecumenical Council, in 381, he was elected bishop of Constantinople and presided over the Council; but he was challenged straightaway by strong opposition, to the point that the situation became untenable. These hostilities must have been unbearable to such a sensitive soul.

What Gregory had previously lamented with heartfelt words was repeated: "We have divided Christ, we who so loved God and Christ! We have lied to one another because of the Truth, we have harbored sentiments of hatred because of Love, we are separated from one another" (*Orationes* 6, 3: *SC* 405, 128).

Thus, in a tense atmosphere, the time came for him to resign. In the packed cathedral, Gregory delivered a farewell discourse of great effectiveness and dignity (cf. *Orationes* 42: *SC* 384, 48–114). He ended his heartrending speech with these words: "Farewell, great city, beloved by Christ. . . . My children, I beg you, jealously guard the deposit [of faith] that has been entrusted to you [cf. 1 Tm 6:20], remember my suffering [cf. Col 4:18]. May the grace of our Lord Jesus Christ be with you all" (cf. *Orationes* 42, 27: *SC* 384, 112–14).

Gregory returned to Nazianzus and for about two years devoted himself to the pastoral care of this Christian community. He then withdrew definitively to solitude in nearby Arianzo, his birthplace, and dedicated himself to studies and the ascetic life. It was in this period that he wrote the majority of his poetic works and especially his autobiography: the *De Vita Sua,* a reinterpretation in verse of his own human and spiritual journey, an exemplary journey of a suffering Christian, of a man of profound interiority in a world full of conflicts.

He is a man who makes us aware of God's primacy, hence, he also speaks to us, to this world of ours: without God, man loses his grandeur; without God, there is no true humanism. Consequently, let us too listen to this voice and seek to know God's face.

In one of his poems, he wrote, addressing himself to God: "May you be benevolent, you, the hereafter of all things" (*Carmina [dogmatica]* 1, 1, 29: *PG* 37:508). And in 390, God welcomed into his arms this faithful servant who had defended him in his writings with keen intelligence and had praised him in his poetry with such great love.

Instructor of Souls

To fill out this portrait of a great teacher, we shall try to understand some of his teachings.

Reflecting on the mission God had entrusted to him, St. Gregory of Nazianzus concluded: "I was created to ascend even to God with my actions" (*Orationes* 14, 6 *De Pauperum Amore: PG* 35, 865). In fact, he placed his talents as a writer and orator at the service of God and of the Church. He wrote numerous discourses, various homilies and panegyrics, a great many letters and poetic works (almost 18,000 verses!): a truly prodigious output.

He realized that this was the mission that God had entrusted to him: "As a servant of the Word, I adhere to the ministry of the Word; may I never agree to neglect this good. I appreciate this vocation and am thankful for it; I derive more joy from it than from all other things put together" (*Orationes* 6, 5: *SC* 405, 134; cf. also *Orationes* 4, 10).

Nazianzus was a mild man and always sought in his life to bring peace to the Church of his time, torn apart by discord and heresy. He strove with gospel daring to overcome his own timidity in order to proclaim the truth of the faith.

Gregory felt deeply the yearning to draw close to God, to be united with him. He expressed it in one of his poems, in which he writes: "Among the great billows of the sea of life, here and there whipped up by wild winds . . . one thing alone is dear to me, my only treasure, comfort and oblivion in my struggle, the light of the Blessed Trinity" (*Carmina [historica]* 2, 1, 15: PG 37, 1250ff.). Thus, Gregory made the light of the Trinity shine forth, defending the faith proclaimed at the Council of Nicaea: one God in three persons, equal and distinct—Father, Son, and Holy Spirit—"a triple light gathered into one splendor" (*Hymn for Vespers, Carmina [historica]* 2, 1, 32: PG 37, 512).

Therefore, Gregory says further, in line with St. Paul (1 Cor 8:6): "For us there is one God, the Father, from whom is all; and one Lord, Jesus Christ, through whom is all; and one Holy Spirit, in whom is all (*Orationes* 39, 12: SC 358, 172).

Gregory gave great prominence to Christ's full humanity: to redeem man in the totality of his body, soul, and spirit, Christ assumed all the elements of human nature, otherwise man would not have been saved. Disputing the heresy of Apollinaris, who held that Jesus Christ had not assumed a rational mind, Gregory tackled the problem in the light of the mystery of salvation: "What has not been assumed has not been healed" (*Ep.* 101, 32: SC 208, 50), and if Christ had not been "endowed with a rational mind, how could he have been a man?" (*Ep.* 101, 34: SC 208, 50). It was precisely our mind and our reason that needed and needs the relationship, the encounter with God in Christ.

Having become a man, Christ gave us the possibility of becoming, in turn, like him. Nazianzus exhorted people: "Let us seek to be like Christ, because Christ also became like us: to become gods through him since he himself, through us, became a man. He took the worst upon himself to make us a gift of the best" (*Orationes* 1, 5: SC 247, 78).

Mary, who gave Christ his human nature, is the true Mother of God (*Theotokos*: cf. *Ep.* 101, 16: SC 208, 42), and with a view to her most exalted mission was "purified in advance" (*Orationes* 38, 13: SC 358, 132, almost as a distant prelude to the dogma of the Immaculate Conception). Mary is proposed to Christians, and especially to virgins, as a model and their help to call upon in times of need (cf. *Orationes* 24, 11: SC 282, 60–64).

Gregory reminds us that as human persons, we must show solidarity to one another. He writes: "We are all one in the Lord' [cf. Rom 12:5], rich and poor, slaves and free, healthy and sick alike; and one is the head from which all derive: Jesus Christ. And as with the members of one body, each is concerned with the other, and all with all." He then concludes, referring to the sick and to people in difficulty: "This is the one salvation for our flesh and our soul: showing them charity" (*Orationes* 14, 8 *De Pauperum Amore*: PG 35, 868ab). Gregory emphasizes that we must imitate God's goodness and love. He therefore recommends: "If you are healthy and rich, alleviate the need of whoever is sick and poor; if you have not fallen, go to the aid of whoever has fallen and lives in suffering; if you are glad, comfort whoever is sad; if you are fortunate, help whoever is smitten with misfortune. Give God proof of your gratitude, for you are one who can benefit and not one who needs to be benefited. . . . Be rich not only in possessions but also in piety; not only in gold but in virtue, or rather, in virtue alone. Outdo your neighbor's reputation by showing yourself to be kinder than all; make yourself God for the unfortunate, imitating God's mercy" (*Orationes* 14, 26 *De Pauperum Amore*: PG 35, 892bc).

Gregory teaches us first and foremost the importance and necessity of prayer. He says: "It is necessary to remember God more often than one breathes" (*Orationes* 27, 4: PG 250, 78), because prayer is the encounter of God's thirst with our thirst. God is thirsting for us to thirst for him (cf. *Orationes* 40, 27: SC 358, 260). In prayer, we must turn our hearts to God, to consign ourselves to him as an offering to be purified and transformed. In prayer we see all things in the light of Christ, we let our masks fall and immerse ourselves in the truth and in listening to God, feeding the fire of love.

In a poem which is at the same time a meditation on the purpose of life and an implicit invocation to God, Gregory writes:

> You have a task, my soul, a great task if you so desire. Scrutinize yourself seriously, your being, your destiny; where you come from and where you must rest; seek to know whether it is life that you are living or if it is something more. You have a task, my soul, so purify your life: Please consider God and his mysteries, investigate what existed before this universe and what it is for you, where you come from and what your destiny will be. This is your task, my soul; therefore, purify your life. (*Carmina [historica]* 2, 1, 78: PG 37, 1425–26)

The holy bishop continuously asked Christ for help, to be raised and set on his way: "I have been let down, O my Christ, by my excessive presumption: from the heights, I have fallen very low. But lift me now again so that I may see that I have deceived myself; if again I trust too much in myself, I shall fall immediately and the fall will be fatal" (*Carmina [historica]* 2, 1, 67: PG 37, 1408).

So it was that Gregory felt the need to draw close to God in order to overcome his own weariness. He experienced the impetus of the soul, the vivacity of a sensitive spirit, and the instability of transient happiness. For him, in the drama of a life burdened by the knowledge of his own weakness and wretchedness, the experience of God's love always gained the upper hand. You have a task, soul, St. Gregory also says to us, the task of finding the true light, of finding the true nobility of your life. And your life is encountering God, who thirsts for our thirst.

—*8 and 22 August 2007*

St. Gregory of Nyssa

Theologian of Life in the Spirit

In the last chapters, I spoke of two great fourth-century Doctors of the Church, Basil and Gregory of Nazianzus, a bishop in Cappadocia, in present-day Turkey. Today, we are adding a third, St. Gregory of Nyssa, Basil's brother, who showed himself to be a man disposed to meditation with a great capacity for reflection and a lively intelligence open to the culture of his time. He has thus proved to be an original and profound thinker in the history of Christianity.

Gregory was born in about 335. His Christian education was supervised with special care by his brother Basil, whom he called "father and teacher" (*Ep.* 13, 4: *SC* 363, 198), and by his sister Macrina. He completed his studies, appreciating in particular philosophy and rhetoric.

Initially, he devoted himself to teaching and was married. Later, like his brother and sister, he too dedicated himself entirely to the ascetic life. He was subsequently elected bishop of Nyssa and showed himself to be a zealous pastor, thereby earning the community's esteem. When he was accused of embezzlement by heretical adversaries, he was obliged for a brief period to abandon his episcopal see but later returned to it triumphant (cf. *Ep.* 6: *SC* 363, 164–70) and continued to be involved in the fight to defend the true faith.

Especially after Basil's death, by more or less gathering his spiritual legacy, Gregory cooperated in the triumph of orthodoxy. He took part in various synods; he attempted to settle disputes between churches; he had an active part in the reorganization of the Church and, as a "pillar of orthodoxy," played a leading role at the Council of Constantinople in 381, which defined the divinity of the Holy Spirit. Various difficult official tasks were entrusted to him by the Emperor Theodosius, he delivered important homilies and funeral discourses, and he devoted himself to writing various theological works. In addition, in 394, he took part in another synod, held in Constantinople. The date of his death is unknown.

Gregory expressed clearly the purpose of his studies, the supreme goal to which all his work as a theologian was directed: not to engage his life in vain things but to find the light that would enable him to discern what is truly worthwhile (cf. *In Ecclesiasten hom.* 1: *SC* 416, 106–46). He found this supreme good in Christianity, thanks to which "the imitation of the divine nature" is possible (*De Professione Christiana: PG* 46, 244c).

With his acute intelligence and vast philosophical and theological knowledge, Gregory defended the Christian faith against heretics who denied the divinity of the Son and of the Holy Spirit (such as Eunomius and the Macedonians) or compromised the perfect humanity of Christ (such as Apollinaris).

He commented on Sacred Scripture, reflecting on the creation of man. This was one of his central topics: creation. He saw in the creature the reflection of the Creator and found here the way that leads to God. But he also wrote an important book on the life of Moses, whom he presents as a man journeying toward God: this climb to Mount Sinai became for him an image of our ascent in human life toward true life, toward the encounter with God.

He also interpreted the Lord's Prayer, the Our Father, as well as the Beatitudes. In his *Great Catechetical Discourse (Oratio Catechetica Magna)*, he developed theology's fundamental directions, not for an academic theology closed in on itself but in order to offer catechists a reference system to keep before them in their instructions, almost as a framework for a pedagogical interpretation of the faith.

Furthermore, Gregory is distinguished for his spiritual doctrine. None of his theology was academic reflection; rather, it was an expression of the spiritual life, of a life of faith lived. As a great "father of mysticism," he pointed out in various treatises—such as his *De Professione Christiana* and *De Perfectione Christiana*—the path Christians must take if they are to reach true life, perfection. He exalted consecrated virginity (*De Virginitate*) and proposed the life of his sister Macrina, who was always a guide and example for him (cf. *Vita Macrinae*), as an outstanding model of it.

Gregory gave various discourses and homilies and wrote numerous letters. In commenting on human creation, he highlighted the fact that God, "the best artist, forges our nature so as to make it suitable for the exercise of royalty. Through the superiority given by the soul and through the very makeup of the body, he arranges things in such a way that man is truly fit for regal power" (*De Hominis Opificio* 4: PG 44, 136b).

Yet we see that man, caught in the net of sin, often abuses creation and does not exercise true kingship. For this reason, in fact, that is, to act with true responsibility for creatures, he must be penetrated by God and live in his light.

Indeed, man is a reflection of that original beauty which is God: "Everything God created was very good," the holy bishop wrote. And he added: "The story of creation [cf. Gn 1:31] witnesses to it. Man was also listed among those very good things, adorned with a beauty far superior to all of the good things. What else, in fact, could be good, on par with one who was similar to pure and incorruptible beauty? . . . The reflection and image of eternal life, he was truly good; no, he was very good, with the radiant sign of life on his face" (*Homilia in Canticum* 12: *PG* 44, 1020c). Human being was honored by God and placed above every other creature:

> The sky was not made in God's image, not the moon, not the sun, not the beauty of the stars, no other things which appear in creation. Only you (*human soul*) were made to be the image of nature that surpasses every intellect, likeness of incorruptible beauty, mark of true divinity, vessel of blessed life, image of true light, that when you look upon it you become what he is, because through the reflected ray coming from your purity you imitate he who shines within you. Nothing that exists can measure up to your greatness. (*Homilia in Canticum* 2: *PG* 44, 805d)

Let us meditate on this praise of the human being. Let us also see how man was degraded by sin. And let us try to return to that original greatness: only if God is present does man attain his true greatness. Man therefore recognizes in himself the reflection of the divine light: by purifying his heart he is once more, as he was in the beginning, a clear image of God, exemplary Beauty (cf. *Oratio Catechetica* 6: *SC* 453, 174). Thus, by purifying himself, man can see God, as do the pure of heart (cf. Mt 5:8): "If, with a diligent and attentive standard of living, you wash away the bad things that have deposited upon your heart, the divine beauty will shine in you. . . . Contemplating yourself, you will see within you he who is the desire of your heart, and you will be blessed" (*De Beatitudinibus* 6: *PG* 44, 1272ab). We should therefore wash away the ugliness stored within our hearts and rediscover God's light within us. The human goal is therefore the contemplation of God. In God alone can one find one's fulfillment.

To somehow anticipate this goal in this life, one must work ceaselessly toward a spiritual life, a life in dialogue with God. In other words—and this is the most important lesson that St. Gregory of Nyssa has bequeathed to us—total human fulfillment consists in holiness, in a life lived in the encounter with God, which thus becomes luminous also to others and to the world.

Theologian of Human Dignity

I present to you certain further aspects of the teaching of St. Gregory of Nyssa.

First of all, Gregory of Nyssa had a very lofty concept of human dignity. The human goal, the holy bishop said, is to liken oneself to God, and one reaches this goal first of all through the love, knowledge, and practice of the virtues, "bright beams that shine from the divine nature" *(De Beatitudinibus* 6: *PG* 44, 1272c), in a perpetual movement of adherence to the good like a corridor outstretched before oneself. In this regard, Gregory uses an effective image already present in Paul's Letter to the Philippians: *épekteinómenos* (3:13), that is, "I press on" toward what is greater, toward truth and love. This vivid expression portrays a profound reality: the perfection we desire to attain is not acquired once and for all; perfection means journeying on; it is continuous readiness to move ahead because we never attain a perfect likeness to God; we are always on our way (cf. *Homilia in Canticum* 12: *PG* 44, 1025d). The history of every soul is that of a love that fills every time and at the same time is open to new horizons, for God continually stretches the soul's possibilities to make it capable of ever greater goods. God himself, who has sown the seeds of good in us and from whom every initiative of holiness stems, "sculpts the block . . . , and polishing and cleansing our spirit, forms Christ within us" *(In Psalmos* 2, 11: *PG* 44, 544b).

Gregory was anxious to explain: "In fact, this likeness to the divine is not our work at all; it is not the achievement of any faculty of man; it is the great gift of God bestowed upon our nature at the very moment of our birth" *(De Virginitate* 12, 2: *SC* 119, 408–10). For the soul, therefore, "it is not a question of knowing something about God but of having God within" *(De Beatitudinibus* 6: *PG* 44, 1269c). Moreover, as Gregory perceptively observes, "Divinity is purity, it is liberation from the passions and the removal of every evil: if all these things are in you, God is truly in you" *(De Beatitudinibus* 6: *PG* 44, 1272c).

When we have God in us, when one loves God, through that reciprocity which belongs to the law of love one wants what God himself wants (cf. *Homilia in Canticum* 9: *PG* 44, 956ac); hence, one cooperates with God in fashioning the divine image in oneself, so that "our spiritual birth is the result of a free choice, and we are in a certain way our own parents, creating ourselves as we ourselves wish to be, and through our will forming ourselves in accordance with the model that we choose" *(Vita Moysis* 2, 3: *SC* 1ff., 108). To ascend to God, one must be purified:

> The way that leads human nature to heaven is none other than detachment from the evils of this world. . . . Becoming like God means becoming righteous, holy and good. . . . If, therefore, according to Ecclesiastes (5:1), "God is in heaven'," and if, as the Prophet says, "You have made God your refuge' (Ps 73[72]:28), it necessarily follows that you must be where God is found, since you are united with him. Since he commanded you to call God "Father" when you pray, he tells you definitely to be likened to your Heavenly Father and to lead a life worthy of God, as the Lord orders us more clearly elsewhere, saying, "Be perfect as your Heavenly Father is perfect" (Mt 5:48). *(De Oratione Dominica* 2: *PG* 44, 1145ac)

In this journey of spiritual *ascesis*, Christ is the model and teacher; he shows us the beautiful image of God (cf. *De Perfectione Christiana: PG* 46, 272a). Each of us, looking at him, finds ourselves "the painter of our own life," who has the will to compose the work and the virtues as his colors (ibid.: *PG* 46, 272b). So, if man is deemed worthy of Christ's name, how should he behave? This is Gregory's answer: "[He must] always examine his own thoughts, his own words, and his own actions in his innermost depths to see whether they are oriented to Christ or are drifting away from him" (ibid.: *PG* 46, 284c). And this point is important because of the value it gives to the word *Christian*. A Christian is someone who bears Christ's name, who must therefore also liken his life to Christ. We Christians assume a great responsibility with baptism.

But Christ, Gregory says, is also present in the poor, which is why they must never be offended: "Do not despise them, those who lie idle, as if for this reason they were worth nothing. Consider who they are and you will discover wherein lies their dignity: they represent the person of the Savior. And this is how it is: for in his goodness, the Lord gives them his own person so that through it, those who are hard of heart and enemies of the poor may be moved to compassion" (*De Pauperibus Amandis: PG* 46, 460bc). Gregory, as we said, speaks of rising: rising to God in prayer through purity of heart, but also rising to God through love of neighbor. Love is the ladder that leads to God. Consequently, Gregory of Nyssa strongly recommends to all his listeners: "Be generous with these brothers and sisters, victims of misfortune. Give to the hungry from what you deprive your own stomach" (ibid.: *PG* 46, 457c).

Gregory recalls with great clarity that we all depend on God and therefore exclaims: "Do not think that everything belongs to you! There must also be a share for the poor, God's friends. In fact, the truth is that everything comes from God, the universal Father, and that we are brothers and sisters and belong to the same lineage" (ibid.: *PG*, 465b). The Christian should then examine oneself, Gregory insists further: "But what use is it to fast and abstain from eating meat if with your wickedness all you do is to gnaw at your brother? What do you gain in God's eyes from not eating your own food if later, acting unfairly, you snatch from their hands the food of the poor?"

Let us end our catechesis on the three great Cappadocian Fathers by recalling that important aspect of Gregory of Nyssa's spiritual doctrine, which is prayer. To progress on the journey to perfection and to welcome God within him, to bear the Spirit of God within him, the love of God, man must turn to God trustingly in prayer: "Through prayer we succeed in being with God. But anyone who is with God is far from the enemy. Prayer is a support and protection of charity, a brake on anger, an appeasement and the control of pride. Prayer is the custody of virginity, the protection of fidelity in marriage, the hope for those who are watching, an abundant harvest for farmers, certainty for sailors" (*De Oratione Dominica* 1: *PG* 44, 1124ab). The Christian always prays by drawing inspiration from the Lord's Prayer: "So if we want to pray for the kingdom of God to come, we must ask him for this with the power of the Word: that I may be distanced from corruption, delivered from death, freed from the chains of error; that death may never reign over me, that the tyranny of evil may never have power over us, that the adversary may never dominate me nor make me his prisoner through sin but that your kingdom may come to me so that the passions by which I am now ruled and governed may be distanced, or better still, blotted out" (ibid., 3: *PG* 44, 1156d–57a).

Having ended his earthly life, the Christian will thus be able to turn to God serenely. In speaking of this, St. Gregory remembered the death of his sister Macrina and wrote that she was praying this prayer to God while she lay dying: "You who on earth have the power to take away sins, 'forgive me, so that I may find refreshment' [cf. Ps 38:14], and so that I may be found without blemish in your sight at the time when I am emptied from my body [cf. Col 2:11], so that my spirit, holy and immaculate [cf. Eph 5:27], may be accepted into your hands 'like incense before you'" (Ps 141:[140]:2) (*Vita Macrinae* 24: *SC* 178, 224). This teaching of St. Gregory is always relevant: not only speaking of God but also carrying God within oneself. Let us do this by commitment to prayer and living in a spirit of love for all our brethren.

—29 August and 5 September 2007

ST. JOHN CHRYSOSTOM

The Years in Antioch

Recently we observed the sixteenth centenary of St. John Chrysostom's death (407–2007). It can be said that John of Antioch, nicknamed "Chrysostom," that is, "golden-mouthed," because of his eloquence, is also still alive today because of his works. An anonymous copyist left in writing that "they cross the whole globe like flashes of lightning."

Chrysostom's writings also enable us, as they did the faithful of his time whom his frequent exiles deprived of his presence, to live with his books, despite his absence. This is what he himself suggested in a letter when he was in exile (*To Olympias*, Letter 8, 45).

He was born in about the year 349. in Antioch, Syria (today Antakya in southern Turkey). He carried out his priestly ministry there for about eleven years, until 397, when, appointed bishop of Constantinople, he exercised his episcopal ministry in the capital of the empire prior to his two exiles, which succeeded one close upon the other, in 403 and 407.

He lost his father at a tender age and lived with Anthusa, his mother, who instilled in him exquisite human sensitivity and a deep Christian faith.

After completing his elementary and advanced studies, crowned by courses in philosophy and rhetoric, he had as his teacher Libanius, a pagan and the most famous rhetorician of that time. At his school, John became the greatest orator of late Greek antiquity.

He was baptized in 368 and trained for the ecclesiastical life by Bishop Meletius, who instituted him as lector in 371. This event marked Chrysostom's official entry into the ecclesiastical *cursus*. From 367 to 372, he attended the *Asceterius*, a sort of seminary in Antioch, together with a group of young men, some of whom later became bishops, under the guidance of the exegete Diodore of Tarsus, who initiated John into the literal and grammatical exegesis characteristic of Antiochene tradition.

He then withdrew for four years to the hermits on the neighboring Mount Silpius. He extended his retreat for a further two years, living alone in a cave under the guidance of an "old hermit." In that period, he dedicated himself unreservedly to meditating on "the laws of Christ," the Gospels, and especially the Letters of Paul. Having fallen ill, he found it impossible to care for himself unaided, and therefore had to return to the Christian community in Antioch (cf. Palladius, *Dialogue on the Life of St. John Chrysostom 5*).

The Lord, his biographer explains, intervened with the illness at the right moment to enable John to follow his true vocation. In fact, he himself was later to write that were he to choose between the troubles of Church government and the tranquility of monastic life, he would have preferred pastoral service a thousand times (cf. *On the Priesthood*, 6, 7): it was precisely to this that Chrysostom felt called.

It was here that he reached the crucial turning point in the story of his vocation: a full-time pastor of souls! Intimacy with the Word of God, cultivated in his years at the hermitage, had developed in him an irresistible urge to preach the gospel, to give to others what he himself had received in his years of meditation. The missionary ideal thus launched him into pastoral care, his heart on fire.

Between 378 and 379, he returned to the city. He was ordained a deacon in 381 and a priest in 386, and became a famous preacher in his city's churches. He preached homilies against the Arians, followed by homilies commemorating the Antiochene martyrs and other important liturgical celebrations: this was an important teaching of faith in Christ and also in the light of his saints.

The year 387 was John's "heroic year," that of the so-called revolt of the statues. As a sign of protest against levied taxes, the people destroyed the emperor's statues. It was in those days of Lent and the fear of the emperor's impending reprisal that Chrysostom gave his twenty-two vibrant *Homilies on the Statues*, whose aim was to induce repentance and conversion. This was followed by a period of serene pastoral care (387–397).

Chrysostom is among the most prolific of the Fathers: 17 treatises, more than 700 authentic homilies, commentaries on Matthew and on Paul (letters to the Romans, Corinthians, Ephesians, and Hebrews), and 241 letters are extant. He was not a speculative theologian. Nevertheless, he passed on the Church's tradition and reliable doctrine in an age of theological controversies, sparked above all by Arianism or, in other words, the denial of Christ's divinity. He is therefore a trustworthy witness of the dogmatic development achieved by the Church from the fourth to the fifth centuries.

His is a perfectly pastoral theology, in which there is constant concern for consistency between thought expressed via words and existential experience. It is this in particular that forms the main theme of the splendid catecheses with which he prepared catechumens to receive baptism.

On approaching death, he wrote that the value of the human being lies in "exact knowledge of true doctrine and in rectitude of life" (*Letter from Exile*). Both these things, knowledge of truth and rectitude of life, go hand in hand: knowledge has to be expressed in life. All his discourses aimed to develop in the faithful the use of intelligence, of true reason, in order to understand and to put into practice the moral and spiritual requirements of faith.

John Chrysostom was anxious to accompany his writings with the person's integral development in his physical, intellectual, and religious dimensions. The various phases of his growth are compared to as many seas in an immense ocean: "The first of these seas is childhood" (*Homily, 81, 5 on Matthew's Gospel*).

Indeed, "it is precisely at this early age that inclinations to vice or virtue are manifest." Thus, God's law must be impressed upon the soul from the outset "as on a wax tablet" (*Homily 3, 1 on John's Gospel*): This is indeed the most important age. We must bear in mind how fundamentally important it is that the great orientations which give a person a proper outlook on life truly enter in this first phase of life. Chrysostom therefore recommended: "From the tenderest age, arm children with spiritual weapons and teach them to make the sign of the Cross on their forehead with their hand" (*Homily 12, 7 on First Corinthians*).

Then come adolescence and youth: "Following childhood is the sea of adolescence, where violent winds blow . . . , for concupiscence . . . grows within us" (*Homily 81, 5 on Matthew's Gospel*).

Last comes engagement and marriage: "Youth is succeeded by the age of the mature person who assumes family commitments: this is the time to seek a wife" (ibid.).

He recalls the aims of marriage, enriching them—referring to virtue and temperance—with a rich fabric of personal relationships. Properly prepared spouses therefore bar the way to divorce: everything takes place with joy, and children can be educated in virtue. Then when the first child is born, the child is "like a bridge; the three become one flesh, because the child joins the two parts" (*Homily 12, 5 on the Letter to the Colossians*), and the three constitute "a family, a Church in miniature" (*Homily 20, 6 on the Letter to the Ephesians*).

Chrysostom's preaching usually took place during the liturgy, the "place" where the community is built with the Word and the eucharist. The assembly gathered here expresses the one Church (*Homily 8, 7 on the Letter to the Romans*), the same word is addressed everywhere to all (*Homily 24, 2 on First Corinthians*), and eucharistic communion becomes an effective sign of unity (*Homily 32, 7 on Matthew's Gospel*).

His pastoral project was incorporated into the Church's life, in which the lay faithful assume the priestly, royal, and prophetic office with baptism. To the lay faithful he said: "Baptism will also make you king, priest, and prophet" (*Homily 3, 5 on Second Corinthians*). From this stems the fundamental duty of mission, because each one is to some extent responsible for the salvation of others: "This is the principle of our social life not to be solely concerned with ourselves!" (*Homily 9, 2 on Genesis*). This all takes place between two poles: the great Church and the "Church in miniature," the family, in a reciprocal relationship.

As you can see, Chrysostom's lesson on the authentically Christian presence of the lay faithful in the family and in society is still more timely than ever today. Let us pray to the Lord to make us docile to the teachings of this great master of the faith.

The Years in Constantinople

After the period he spent in Antioch, in 397 John Chrysostom was appointed bishop of Constantinople, the capital of the Roman Empire of the East. John planned the reform of his Church from the outset: the austerity of the episcopal residence had to be an example for all—clergy, widows, monks, courtiers, and the rich. Unfortunately, many of those he criticized distanced themselves from him. Attentive to the poor, John was also called "the Almoner." Indeed, he was able as a careful administrator to establish highly appreciated charitable institutions. For some people, his initiatives in various fields made him a dangerous rival but as a true pastor, he treated everyone in a warm, fatherly way. In particular, he always spoke kindly to women and showed special concern for marriage and the family. He would invite the faithful to take part in liturgical life, which he made splendid and attractive with brilliant creativity.

Despite his kind heart, his life was far from peaceful. He was the pastor of the capital of the empire, and often found himself involved in political affairs and intrigues because of his ongoing relations with the authorities and civil institutions. Then, within the Church, having removed six bishops in Asia in 401 who had been improperly appointed, he was accused of having overstepped the boundaries of his own jurisdiction, and thus he easily became the target of accusations. Another accusation against him concerned the presence of some Egyptian monks, excommunicated by Patriarch Theophilus of Alexandria, who had sought refuge in Constantinople. A heated argument then flared up on account of Chrysostom's criticism of the Empress Eudoxia and her courtiers, who reacted by heaping slander and insults upon him. Thus, they proceeded to his removal during the synod organized by the same Patriarch Theophilus in 403, which led to his condemnation and his first, brief exile. After Chrysostom's return, the hostility he had instigated by his protests against the festivities in honor of the empress, which the bishop considered as sumptuous pagan celebrations, and by his expulsion of the priests responsible for the baptisms during the Easter Vigil in 404, marked the beginning of the persecution of Chrysostom and his followers, the so-called Johannites.

John then denounced the events in a letter to Innocent I, bishop of Rome, but it was already too late. In 406, he was once again forced into exile, this time to Cucusus in Armenia. The pope was convinced of his innocence but was powerless to help him. A council desired by Rome to establish peace between the two parts of the empire and among their churches could not take place. The gruelling journey from Cucusus to Pityus, a destination that he never reached, was meant to prevent the visits of the faithful and to break the resistance of the worn-out exile: his condemnation to exile was a true death sentence! The numerous letters from his exile in which John expressed his pastoral concern in tones of participation and sorrow at the persecution of his followers are moving. His journey toward death stopped at Comana in Ponto. Here, John, who was dying, was carried into the Chapel of the Martyr St. Basiliscus, where he gave up his spirit to God and was buried, one martyr next to the other (Palladius, *Dialogue on the Life of St. John Chrysostom* 119). It was 14 September 407, the Feast of the Triumph of the Holy Cross. He was rehabilitated in 438 through Theodosius II. The holy bishop's relics, which had been placed in the Church of the Apostles in Constantinople, were later, in 1204, translated to the first Constantinian Basilica in Rome, and now rest in the chapel of the Choir of the Canons in St. Peter's Basilica. On 24 August 2004, Pope John Paul II gave a large part of the saint's relics to Patriarch Bartholomew I of Constantinople. The saint's liturgical memorial is celebrated on 13 September. Blessed John XXIII proclaimed him Patron of the Second Vatican Council.

It is said of John Chrysostom that when he was seated upon the throne of the New Rome, that is, Constantinople, God caused him to be seen as a second Paul, a doctor of the universe. Indeed, there is in Chrysostom a substantial unity of thought and action, in Antioch as in Constantinople. It is only the role and situations that change. In his commentary on Genesis, in meditating on God's eight acts in the sequence of six days, Chrysostom desired to restore the faithful from the creation to the Creator: "It is a great good," he said, "to know the creature from the Creator." He shows us the beauty of the creation and God's transparency in his creation, which thus becomes, as it were, a "ladder" to ascend to God in order to know him. To this first step, however, is added a second: this God Creator is also the God of indulgence (*synkatabasis*). We are weak in "climbing"; our eyes grow dim. Thus, God becomes an indulgent God who sends to fallen man, foreign man, a letter, Sacred Scripture, so that the creation and Scripture may complete each another. We can decipher creation in the light of Scripture, the letter that God has given to us. God is called a "tender father" (*philostorgios*) (ibid.), a healer of souls (*Homily on Genesis* 40, 3), a mother (ibid.) and an affectionate friend (*On Providence* 8, 11–12). But in addition to this second step—first, the creation as a "ladder" to God, and then, the indulgence of God through a letter which he has given to us, Sacred Scripture—there is a third step. God does not only give us a letter: ultimately, he himself comes down to us, he takes flesh, becomes truly "God-with-us," our brother until his death on a cross. And to these three steps—God is visible in creation,

God gives us a letter, God descends and becomes one of us—a fourth is added at the end. In the Christian's life and action, the vital and dynamic principle is the Holy Spirit (*Pneuma*), who transforms the realities of the world. God enters our very existence through the Holy Spirit and transforms us from within our hearts.

Against this background, in Constantinople itself, John proposed in his continuing *Commentary on the Acts of the Apostles* the model of the primitive Church (Acts 4:32-37) as a pattern for society, developing a social "utopia" (almost an "ideal city"). In fact, it was a question of giving the city a soul and a Christian face. In other words, Chrysostom realized that it is not enough to give alms, to help the poor sporadically, but it is necessary to create a new structure, a new model of society; a model based on the outlook of the New Testament. It was this new society that was revealed in the newborn Church. John Chrysostom thus truly became one of the great Fathers of the Church's social doctrine: the old idea of the Greek *polis* gave way to the new idea of a city inspired by Christian faith. With Paul (cf. 1 Cor 8:11), Chrysostom upheld the primacy of the individual Christian, of the person as such, even of the slave and the poor person. His project thus corrected the traditional Greek vision of the *polis*, the city in which large sectors of the population had no access to the rights of citizenship, while in the Christian city all are brothers and sisters with equal rights. The primacy of the person is also a consequence of the fact that it is truly by starting with the person that the city is built, whereas in the Greek *polis* the homeland took precedence over the individual, who was totally subordinated to the city as a whole. So it was that a society built on the Christian conscience came into being with Chrysostom. And he tells us that our *polis* (city) is another, "our commonwealth is in heaven" (Phil 3:20), and our homeland, even on this earth, makes us all equal, brothers and sisters, and binds us to solidarity.

At the end of his life, from his exile on the borders of Armenia, "the most remote place in the world," John, linking up with his first preaching in 386, took up the theme of the plan for humanity that God pursues, which was so dear to him: it is an "indescribable and incomprehensible" plan, but certainly guided lovingly by God (cf. *On Providence* 2, 6). Of this we are certain. Even if we are unable to unravel the details of our personal and collective history, we know that God's plan is always inspired by his love. Thus, despite his suffering, Chrysostom reaffirmed the discovery that God loves each one of us with an infinite love and therefore desires salvation for us all. For his part, throughout his life the holy bishop cooperated generously in this salvation, never sparing himself. Indeed, he saw the ultimate end of his existence as that glory of God which—now dying—he left as his last testament: "Glory be to God for all things" (Palladius, *Dialogue on the Life of St. John Chrysostom* 11).

—*19 and 26 September 2007*

St. Cyril of Alexandria

CONTINUING OUR JOURNEY following the traces left by the Fathers of the Church, we meet an important figure: St. Cyril of Alexandria. Linked to the christological controversy that led to the Council of Ephesus in 431 and the last important representative of the Alexandrian tradition in the Greek Orient, Cyril was later defined as "the guardian of exactitude"—to be understood as guardian of the true faith—and even the "seal of the Fathers." These ancient descriptions express clearly a characteristic feature of Cyril: the bishop of Alexandria's constant reference to earlier ecclesiastical authors (including, in particular, Athanasius), for the purpose of showing the continuity with tradition of theology itself. He deliberately, explicitly inserted himself into the Church's tradition, which he recognized as guaranteeing continuity with the Apostles and with Christ himself. Venerated as a saint in both East and West, in 1882 St. Cyril was proclaimed a Doctor of the Church by Pope Leo XIII, who at the same time also attributed this title to another important exponent of Greek Patristics, St. Cyril of Jerusalem. Thus are revealed the attention and love for the Eastern Christian traditions of this pope, who later also chose to proclaim St. John Damascene a Doctor of the Church, thereby showing that both the Eastern and Western traditions express the doctrine of Christ's one Church.

We have almost no information on Cyril's life prior to his election to the important See of Alexandria. He was a nephew of Theophilus, who had governed the Diocese of Alexandria as bishop since 385, with a prestigious and iron hand. It is likely that Cyril was born in this Egyptian metropolis between 370 and 380, was initiated into ecclesiastical life while he was still very young, and received a good education, both culturally and theologically. In 403, he went to Constantinople in the retinue of his powerful uncle. It was here that he took part in the so-called Synod of the Oak, which deposed the bishop of the city, John (later known as "Chrysostom"), and thereby marked the triumph of the Alexandrian see over its traditional rival, the See of Constantinople, where the emperor resided. Upon his uncle Theophilus's death, the still-young Cyril was elected in 412 as bishop of the influential Church of Alexandria, which he governed energetically for thirty-two years, always seeking to affirm her primacy throughout the East, strong also because of her traditional bonds with Rome.

Two or three years later, in 417 or 418, the bishop of Alexandria showed himself to be realistic in mending the broken communion with Constantinople, which had lasted by then since 406 as a consequence of Chrysostom's deposition. But the old conflict with the Constantinople see flared up again about ten years later, when in 428 Nestorius was elected, a severe and authoritarian monk trained in Antioch. The new bishop of Constantinople, in fact, soon provoked opposition because he preferred to use as Mary's title in his preaching "Mother of Christ" (*Christotòkos*) instead of "Mother of God" (*Theotòkos*), already very dear to popular devotion. One reason for Bishop Nestorius's decision was his adherence to the Antiochene type of Christology, which, to safeguard the importance of Christ's humanity, ended by affirming the division of the divinity. Hence, the union between God and man in Christ could no longer be true, so naturally it was no longer possible to speak of the "Mother of God."

The reaction of Cyril—at that time the greatest exponent of Alexandrian Christology, who intended on the other hand to stress the unity of Christ's person—was almost immediate, and from 429 he left no stone unturned, even addressing several letters to Nestorius himself. In the second of Cyril's letters to Nestorius (*PG* 77, 44–49), written in February 430, we read a clear affirmation of the duty of pastors to preserve the faith of the people of God. This was his criterion, moreover, still valid today: the faith of the people of God is an expression of tradition; it is a guarantee of sound doctrine. This is what he wrote to Nestorius: "It is essential to explain the teaching and interpretation of the faith to the people in the most irreproachable way, and to remember that those who cause scandal even to only one of the little ones who believe in Christ will be subjected to an unbearable punishment."

In the same letter to Nestorius—a letter which later, in 451, was to be approved by the Council of Chalcedon, the Fourth Ecumenical Council—Cyril described his christological faith clearly: "Thus, we affirm that the natures are different that are united in one true unity, but from both has come only one Christ and Son; not because, due to their unity, the difference in their natures has been eliminated, but rather, because divinity and humanity, reunited in an ineffable and indescribable union, have produced for us one Lord and Christ and Son." And this is important: true humanity and true divinity are really united in only one person, our Lord Jesus Christ. Therefore, the bishop of Alexandria continued: "We will profess only one Christ and Lord, not in the sense that we worship the man together with the *Logos,* in order not to suggest the idea of separation by saying 'together,' but in the sense that we worship only one and the same, because he is not extraneous to the *Logos,* his body, with which he also sits at his Father's side, not as if "two sons" are sitting beside him but only one, united with his own flesh."

And soon the bishop of Alexandria, thanks to shrewd alliances, obtained the repeated condemnation of Nestorius: by the See of Rome, consequently with a series of twelve anathemas which he himself composed, and finally, by the Council held in Ephesus in 431, the Third

Ecumenical Council. The assembly, which went on with alternating and turbulent events, ended with the first great triumph of devotion to Mary and with the exile of the bishop of Constantinople, who had been reluctant to recognize the Blessed Virgin's right to the title of "Mother of God" because of an erroneous Christology that brought division to Christ himself. After thus prevailing against his rival and his doctrine, by 433 Cyril was nevertheless already able to achieve a theological formula of compromise and reconciliation with the Antiochenes. This is also significant: on the one hand is the clarity of the doctrine of faith, but in addition, on the other, the intense search for unity and reconciliation. In the following years, he devoted himself in every possible way to defending and explaining his theological stance, until his death on 27 June 444.

Cyril's writings—truly numerous and already widely disseminated in various Latin and Eastern translations in his own lifetime, attested to by their instant success—are of the utmost importance for the history of Christianity. His commentaries on many of the New and Old Testament books are important, including those on the entire Pentateuch, Isaiah, the Psalms, and the Gospels of John and Luke. Also important are his many doctrinal works, in which the defense of the Trinitarian faith against the Arian and Nestorian theses recurs. The basis of Cyril's teaching is the ecclesiastical tradition and in particular, as I mentioned, the writings of Athanasius, his great predecessor in the See of Alexandria. Among Cyril's other writings, the books *Against Julian* deserve mention. They were the last great response to the anti-Christian controversies, probably dictated by the bishop of Alexandria in the last years of his life to respond to the work *Against the Galileans,* composed many years earlier, in 363, by the emperor known as the "Apostate" for having abandoned the Christianity in which he was raised.

The Christian faith is first and foremost the encounter with Jesus, "a person, which gives life a new horizon" (*Deus Caritas Est,* n. 1). Saint Cyril of Alexandria was an unflagging, staunch witness of Jesus Christ, the Incarnate Word of God, emphasizing above all his unity, as he repeats in 433 in his first letter (*PG 77*, 228–37) to Bishop Successus: "Only one is the Son, only one the Lord Jesus Christ, both before the Incarnation and after the Incarnation. Indeed, the *Logos* born of God the Father was not one Son and the one born of the Blessed Virgin another; but we believe that the very One who was born before the ages was also born according to the flesh and of a woman." Over and above its doctrinal meaning, this assertion shows that faith in Jesus the *Logos* born of the Father is firmly rooted in history because, as St. Cyril affirms, this same Jesus came in time with his birth from Mary, the *Theotòkos,* and in accordance with his promise will always be with us. And this is important: God is eternal, he is born of a woman, and he stays with us every day. In this trust we live; in this trust we find the way for our life.

—*3 October 2007*

St. Hilary of Poitiers

I REFLECT NOW on a great Father of the Church of the West, St. Hilary of Poitiers, one of the important episcopal figures of the fourth century. In the controversy with the Arians, who considered Jesus the Son of God to be an excellent human creature but only human, Hilary devoted his whole life to defending faith in the divinity of Jesus Christ, Son of God, and God as the Father who generated him from eternity.

We have no reliable information on most of Hilary's life. Ancient sources say that he was born in Poitiers, probably in about the year 310. From a wealthy family, he received a solid literary education, which is clearly recognizable in his writings. It does not seem that he grew up in a Christian environment. He himself tells us of a quest for the truth which led him little by little to recognize God the Creator and the Incarnate God who died to give us eternal life. Baptized in about 345, he was elected bishop of his native city around 353–354. In the years that followed, Hilary wrote his first work, *Commentary on St. Matthew's Gospel*. It is the oldest extant commentary in Latin on this Gospel. In 356, Hilary took part as a bishop in the Synod of Béziers in the South of France, the "synod of false apostles," as he himself called it since the assembly was in the control of philo-Arian bishops, who denied the divinity of Jesus Christ. "These false apostles" asked the Emperor Constantius to have the bishop of Poitiers sentenced to exile. Thus, in the summer of 356, Hilary was forced to leave Gaul.

Banished to Phrygia, in present-day Turkey, Hilary found himself in contact with a religious context totally dominated by Arianism. Here too, his concern as a pastor impelled him to work strenuously to reestablish the unity of the Church on the basis of right faith as formulated by the Council of Nicaea. To this end, he began to draft his own best-known and most important dogmatic work: *De Trinitate (On the Trinity)*. Hilary explained in it his personal journey toward knowledge of God and took pains to show that not only in the New Testament but also in many Old Testament passages, in which Christ's mystery already appears, Scripture clearly testifies to the divinity of the Son and his equality with the Father. To the Arians, he insisted on the truth of the names of Father and Son, and developed his entire Trinitarian theology based on the formula of baptism given to us by the Lord himself: "In the name of the Father and of the Son and of the Holy Spirit."

The Father and the Son are of the same nature. And although several passages in the New Testament might make one think that the Son was inferior to the Father, Hilary offers precise rules to avoid misleading interpretations: some scriptural texts speak of Jesus as God, others highlight instead his humanity. Some refer to him in his preexistence with the Father; others take into consideration his state of emptying of self *(kenosis),* his descent to death; others, finally, contemplate him in the glory of the Resurrection. In the years of his exile, Hilary also wrote the *Book of Synods,* in which, for his brother bishops of Gaul, he reproduced confessions of faith and commented on them and on other documents of synods which met in the East in about the middle of the fourth century. Ever adamant in opposing the radical Arians, St. Hilary showed a conciliatory spirit to those who agreed to confess that the Son was essentially *similar* to the Father, seeking of course to lead them to the true faith, according to which there is not only a likeness but also a true equality of the Father and of the Son in divinity. This too seems to me to be characteristic: the spirit of reconciliation that seeks to understand those who have not yet arrived and helps them with great theological intelligence to reach full faith in the true divinity of the Lord Jesus Christ.

In 360 or 361, Hilary was finally able to return home from exile and immediately resumed pastoral activity in his Church, but the influence of his magisterium extended, in fact, far beyond its boundaries. A synod celebrated in Paris in 360 or 361 borrows the language of the Council of Nicaea. Several ancient authors believe that this anti-Arian turning point of the Gaul episcopate was largely due to the fortitude and docility of the bishop of Poitiers. This was precisely his gift: to combine strength in the faith and docility in interpersonal relations. In the last years of his life, he also composed the *Treatises on the Psalms,* a commentary on fifty-eight psalms interpreted according to the principle highlighted in the introduction to the work: "There is no doubt that all the things that are said in the Psalms should be understood in accordance with gospel proclamation, so that, whatever the voice with which the prophetic spirit has spoken, all may be referred nevertheless to the knowledge of the coming of our Lord Jesus Christ, the Incarnation, passion, and kingdom, and to the power and glory of our resurrection" *(Instructio Psalmorum 5).* He saw in all the Psalms this transparency of the mystery of Christ and of his Body, which is the Church. Hilary met St. Martin on various occasions: the future bishop of Tours founded a monastery right by Poitiers, which still exists today. Hilary died in 367. His liturgical memorial is celebrated on 13 January. In 1851, Blessed Pius IX proclaimed him a Doctor of the universal Church.

To sum up the essentials of his doctrine, Hilary found the starting point for his theological reflection in baptismal faith. In *De Trinitate,* Hilary writes that Jesus

> has commanded us to baptize *in the name of the Father and of the Son and of the Holy Spirit* [cf. Mt 28:19], that is, in the confession of

the Author, of the Only-Begotten One, and of the Gift. The Author of all things is one alone, for *one alone is God the Father, from whom all things proceed. And one alone is Our Lord Jesus Christ, through whom all things exist* [cf. 1 Cor 8:6], *and one alone is the Spirit* [cf. Eph 4:4], a gift in all. . . . In nothing can be found to be lacking so great a fullness, in which the immensity in the Eternal One, the revelation in the Image, joy in the Gift, converge in the Father, in the Son, and in the Holy Spirit. (*De Trinitate* 2, 1)

God the Father, being wholly love, is able to communicate his divinity to his Son in its fullness. I find particularly beautiful the following formula of St. Hilary: "God knows not how to be anything other than love; he knows not how to be anyone other than the Father. Those who love are not envious, and the one who is the Father is so in his totality. This name admits no compromise, as if God were father in some aspects and not in others" (ibid., 9, 61).

For this reason, the Son is fully God without any gaps or diminishment. "The One who comes from the perfect is perfect because he has all, he has given all" (ibid., 2, 8). Humanity finds salvation in Christ alone, Son of God and Son of man. In assuming our human nature, he has united himself with every man; "he has become the flesh of us all" (*Tractatus super Psalmos* 54, 9); "he took on himself the nature of all flesh and through it became true life; he has in himself the root of every vine shoot" (ibid., 51, 16). For this very reason, the way to Christ is open to all—because he has drawn all into his being as a man—even if personal conversion is always required: "Through the relationship with his flesh, access to Christ is open to all, on condition that they divest themselves of their former self [cf. Eph 4:22], nailing it to the Cross [cf. Col 2:14]; provided we give up our former way of life and convert in order to be buried with him in his baptism, in view of life [cf. Col 1:12; Rom 6:4]" (ibid., 91, 9).

Fidelity to God is a gift of his grace. Therefore, St. Hilary asks, at the end of his treatise on the Trinity, to be able to remain ever faithful to the baptismal faith. It is a feature of this book: reflection is transformed into prayer and prayer returns to reflection. The whole book is a dialogue with God. I end this catechesis with one of these prayers, which thus becomes our prayer: "Obtain, O Lord," St. Hilary recites with inspiration, "that I may keep ever faithful to what I have professed in the symbol of my regeneration, when I was baptized in the Father, in the Son, and in the Holy Spirit. That I may worship you, our Father, and with you, your Son; that I may deserve your Holy Spirit, who proceeds from you through your Only Begotten Son . . . Amen" (*De Trinitate* 12, 57).

St. Eusebius of Vercelli

I INVITE YOU TO REFLECT on St. Eusebius of Vercelli, the first bishop of northern Italy of whom we have reliable information. Born in Sardinia at the beginning of the fourth century, he moved to Rome with his family at a tender age. Later, he was instituted lector: he thus came to belong to the clergy of the city at a time when the Church was seriously troubled by the Arian heresy. The high esteem that developed around Eusebius explains his election in 345 to the episcopal See of Vercelli. The new bishop immediately began an intense process of evangelization in a region that was still largely pagan, especially in rural areas. Inspired by St. Athanasius—who had written the *Life of Anthony*, the father of monasticism in the East—he founded a priestly community in Vercelli that resembled a monastic community. This coenobium impressed upon the clergy of northern Italy a significant hallmark of apostolic holiness and inspired important episcopal figures such as Limenius and Honoratus, successors of Eusebius in Vercelli, Gaudentius in Novara, Exuperantius in Tortona, Eustasius in Aosta, Eulogius in Ivrea, and Maximus in Turin, all venerated by the Church as saints.

With his sound formation in the Nicene faith, Eusebius did his utmost to defend the full divinity of Jesus Christ, defined by the Nicene Creed as "of one being with the Father." To this end, he allied himself with the great Fathers of the fourth century—especially St. Athanasius, the standard-bearer of Nicene orthodoxy—against the philo-Arian policies of the emperor. For the emperor, the simpler Arian faith appeared politically more useful as the ideology of the empire. For him it was not truth that counted but rather political opportunism: he wanted to exploit religion as the bond of unity for the empire. But these great Fathers resisted him, defending the truth against political expediency. Eusebius was consequently condemned to exile, as were so many other bishops of the East and West: such as Athanasius himself, Hilary of Poitiers, of whom we spoke earlier, and Hosius of Cordoba. In Scythopolis, Palestine, to which he was exiled between 355 and 360, Eusebius wrote a marvelous account of his life. Here too, he founded a monastic community with a small group of disciples. It was also from here that he attended to his correspondence with his faithful in Piedmont, as can be seen in the second of the three *Letters* of Eusebius recognized as authentic. Later, after 360, Eusebius was exiled to Cappadocia and the Thebaid, where he suffered serious physical ill-treatment. After his death in 361, Constantius II was succeeded by the Emperor Julian, known as "the Apostate," who was not interested in making Christianity the religion of the empire but merely wished to restore paganism. He rescinded the banishment of these bishops and thereby also enabled Eusebius to be reinstated in his see. In 362, he was invited by Anastasius to take part in the Council of Alexandria, which decided to pardon the Arian bishops as long as they returned to the secular state. Eusebius was able to exercise his episcopal ministry for another ten years, until he died, creating an exemplary relationship with his city, which did not fail to inspire the pastoral service of other bishops of northern Italy, such as St. Ambrose of Milan and St. Maximus of Turin.

The bishop of Vercelli's relationship with his city is illustrated in particular by two testimonies in his correspondence. The first is found in the letter cited above, which Eusebius wrote from his exile in Scythopolis "to the beloved brothers and priests missed so much, as well as to the holy people with a firm faith of Vercelli, Novara, Ivrea, and Tortona" (*Second Letter: CCL 9*, 104). These first words, which demonstrate the deep emotion of the good pastor when he thought of his flock, are amply confirmed at the end of the letter, in his very warm fatherly greetings to each and every one of his children in Vercelli, with expressions overflowing with affection and love. One should note first of all the explicit relationship that bound the bishop to the *sanctae plebes*, not only of *Vercellae/*Vercelli—the first and subsequently for some years the only diocese in the Piedmont—but also of *Novaria/*Novara, *Eporedia/*Ivrea and *Dertona/*Tortona, that is, of the Christian communities in the same diocese, which had become quite numerous and acquired a certain consistency and autonomy. Another interesting element is provided by the farewell with which the letter concludes. Eusebius asked his sons and daughters to give his greeting "also to those who are outside the Church, yet deign to nourish feelings of love for us: *etiam hos, qui foris sunt et nos dignantur diligere.*" This is an obvious proof that the bishop's relationship with his city was not limited to the Christian population but also extended to those who, outside the Church, recognized in some way his spiritual authority and loved this exemplary man.

The second testimony of the bishop's special relationship with his city comes from the letter St. Ambrose of Milan wrote to the Vercellians in about 394, more than twenty years after Eusebius's death (*Ep. extra collecitonem* 14: *Maur. 63*). The Church of Vercelli was going through a difficult period: she was divided and lacked a bishop. Ambrose frankly declared that he hesitated to recognize these Vercellians as descending from "the lineage of the Holy fathers who approved of Eusebius as soon as they saw him, without ever having known him previously and even forgetting their own fellow citizens." In the same letter, the bishop of Milan attested to his esteem for Eusebius in the clearest possible way: "Such a great man," he wrote in peremptory tones, "well deserves to be elected by the whole of the Church." Ambrose's admiration for Eusebius was based above all on the fact that the bishop of Vercelli governed his diocese with the witness of his life: "With the austerity of fasting he governed his Church." Indeed, Ambrose was also fascinated, as he himself admits, with the monastic ideal of the contemplation of God which, in the footsteps of the Prophet Elijah, Eusebius had pursued. First of all, Ambrose commented, the bishop of Vercelli gathered his clergy in *vita communis* and educated its members in "the observance of the monastic rule, although they lived in the midst of the city." The bishop and his clergy were to share the problems of their fellow citizens and did so credibly, precisely by cultivating at the same time a different citizenship, that of heaven (cf. Heb 13:14). And thus, they really built true citizenship and true solidarity among all the citizens of Vercelli.

While Eusebius was adopting the cause of the *sancta plebs* of Vercelli, he lived a monk's life in the heart of the city, opening the city to God. This trait, though, in no way diminished his exemplary pastoral dynamism. It seems among other things that he set up parishes in Vercelli for an orderly and stable ecclesial service and promoted Marian shrines for the conversion of the pagan populations in the countryside. This "monastic feature," however, conferred a special dimension on the bishop's relationship with his hometown. Just like the Apostles, for whom Jesus prayed at his Last Supper, the pastors and faithful of the Church "are of the world" (Jn 17:11), but not "in the world." Therefore, pastors, Eusebius said, must urge the faithful not to consider the cities of the world as their permanent dwelling place but to seek the future city, the definitive heavenly Jerusalem. This "eschatological reserve" enables pastors and faithful to preserve the proper scale of values without ever submitting to the fashions of the moment and the unjust claims of the current political power. The authentic scale of values, Eusebius's whole life seems to say, does not come from emperors of the past or of today but from Jesus Christ, the perfect man, equal to the Father in divinity, yet a human like us. In referring to this scale of values, Eusebius never tired of "warmly recommending" his faithful "to jealously guard the faith, to preserve harmony, to be assiduous in prayer" (*Second Letter, CCL 9, 104*).

I too warmly recommend these perennial values to you, using the very words with which the holy Bishop Eusebius concluded his *Second Letter*: "I address you all, my holy brothers and sisters, sons and daughters, faithful of both sexes and of every age group, so that you may . . . bring our greeting also to those who are outside the Church, yet deign to nourish sentiments of love for us" (ibid.).

—*17 October 2007*

St. Ambrose of Milan

Holy Bishop Ambrose, about whom I now speak to you, died in Milan in the night between 3 and 4 April 397. It was dawn on Holy Saturday. The day before, at about five o'clock in the afternoon, he had settled down to pray, lying on his bed with his arms wide open in the form of a cross. Thus, he took part in the solemn Easter Triduum, in the death and Resurrection of the Lord. "We saw his lips moving," said Paulinus, the faithful deacon who wrote his *Life* at St. Augustine's suggestion, "but we could not hear his voice." The situation suddenly became dramatic. Honoratus, bishop of Vercelli, who was assisting Ambrose and was sleeping on the upper floor, was awoken by a voice saying again and again, "Get up quickly! Ambrose is dying." "Honoratus hurried downstairs," Paulinus continues, "and offered the saint the body of the Lord. As soon as he had received and swallowed it, Ambrose gave up his spirit, taking the good Viaticum with him. His soul, thus refreshed by the virtue of that food, now enjoys the company of Angels" (*Life* 47). On that Holy Friday 397, the wide open arms of the dying Ambrose expressed his mystical participation in the death and Resurrection of the Lord. This was his last catechesis: in the silence of the words, he continued to speak with the witness of his life.

Ambrose was not old when he died. He had not even reached the age of sixty, since he was born in about 340 in Treves, where his father was prefect of the Gauls. His family was Christian. Upon his father's death while he was still a boy, his mother took him to Rome and educated him for a civil career, assuring him a sound instruction in rhetoric and jurisprudence. In about 370, he was sent to govern the provinces of Emilia and Liguria, with headquarters in Milan. It was precisely there that the struggle between orthodox and Arians was raging and became particularly heated after the death of the Arian bishop Auxentius. Ambrose intervened to pacify the members of the two opposing factions; his authority was such that although he was merely a catechumen, the people acclaimed him bishop of Milan.

Until that moment, Ambrose had been the most senior magistrate of the empire in northern Italy. Culturally well-educated but at the same time ignorant of the Scriptures, the new bishop briskly began to study them. From the works of Origen, the indisputable master of the "Alexandrian School," he learned to know and to comment on the Bible. Thus, Ambrose transferred to the Latin environment the meditation on the Scriptures which Origen had begun, introducing in the West the practice of *lectio divina*. The method of *lectio* served to guide all of Ambrose's preaching and writings, which stemmed precisely from prayerful listening to the Word of God. The famous introduction of an Ambrosian catechesis shows clearly how the holy bishop applied the Old Testament to Christian life: "Every day, when we were reading about the lives of the Patriarchs and the maxims of the Proverbs, we addressed morality," the bishop of Milan said to his catechumens and neophytes, "so that formed and instructed by them you may become accustomed to taking the path of the Fathers and to following the route of obedience to the divine precepts" (*On the Mysteries* 1, 1). In other words, the neophytes and catechumens, in accordance with the bishop's decision, after having learned the art of a well-ordered life, could henceforth consider themselves prepared for Christ's great mysteries. Thus, Ambrose's preaching, which constitutes the structural nucleus of his immense literary opus, starts with the reading of the sacred books ("the Patriarchs" or the historical books and "Proverbs," or in other words, the Wisdom Books) in order to live in conformity with divine revelation.

It is obvious that the preacher's personal testimony and the level of exemplarity of the Christian community condition the effectiveness of the preaching. In this perspective, a passage from St. Augustine's *Confessions* is relevant. He had come to Milan as a teacher of rhetoric; he was a skeptic and not Christian. He was seeking the Christian truth but was not capable of truly finding it. What moved the heart of the young African rhetorician, skeptic and downhearted, and what impelled him to definitive conversion was not above all Ambrose's splendid homilies (although he deeply appreciated them). It was rather the testimony of the bishop and his Milanese Church that prayed and sang as one intact body. It was a Church that could resist the tyrannical ploys of the emperor and his mother, who in early 386 again demanded a church building for the Arians' celebrations. In the building that was to be requisitioned, Augustine relates, "the devout people watched, ready to die with their bishop." This testimony of the *Confessions* is precious because it points out that something was moving in Augustine, who continues, "We too, although spiritually tepid, shared in the excitement of the whole people" (*Confessions* 9, 7).

Augustine learned from the life and example of Bishop Ambrose to believe and to preach. We can refer to a famous sermon of the African, which centuries later merited citation in the conciliar constitution on divine revelation, *Dei Verbum*: "Therefore, all clerics, particularly priests of Christ and others who, as deacons or catechists, are officially engaged in the ministry of the Word," *Dei Verbum* recommends, "should immerse themselves in the Scriptures by constant sacred reading and diligent study. For it must not happen that anyone becomes"—and this is Augustine's citation—"'an empty preacher of the Word of God to others, not being a hearer of the Word in his own heart'" (n. 25). Augustine had learned precisely from Ambrose how to "hear in his own heart" this perseverance in reading Sacred Scripture with a prayerful approach, so as truly to absorb and assimilate the Word of God in one's heart.

I would like further to propose to you a sort of "Patristic icon," which, interpreted in the light of what we have said, effectively represents "the heart" of Ambrosian doctrine. In the sixth book of the *Confessions,* Augustine tells of his meeting with Ambrose, an encounter that was indisputably of great importance in the history of the Church. He writes in his text that whenever he went to see the bishop of Milan, he would regularly find him taken up with *catervae* of people full of problems for whose needs he did his utmost. There was always a long queue waiting to talk to Ambrose, seeking in him consolation and hope. When Ambrose was not with them, with the people (and this happened for the space of the briefest of moments), he was either restoring his body with the necessary food or nourishing his spirit with reading. Here Augustine marvels because Ambrose read the Scriptures with his mouth shut, only with his eyes (cf. *Confessions* 6, 3). Indeed, in the early Christian centuries, reading was conceived of strictly for proclamation, and reading aloud also facilitated the reader's understanding. That Ambrose could scan the pages with his eyes alone suggested to the admiring Augustine a rare ability for reading and familiarity with the Scriptures. Well, in that "reading under one's breath," where the heart is committed to achieving knowledge of the Word of God—this is the "icon" to which we are referring—one can glimpse the method of Ambrosian catechesis; it is Scripture itself, intimately assimilated, which suggests the content to proclaim that will lead to the conversion of hearts.

Thus, with regard to the magisterium of Ambrose and of Augustine, catechesis is inseparable from witness of life. What I wrote on the theologian in the *Introduction to Christianity* might also be useful to the catechist. An educator in the faith cannot risk appearing like a sort of clown who recites a part "by profession." Rather, to use an image dear to Origen, a writer who was particularly appreciated by Ambrose, he must be like the beloved disciple, who rested his head against his Master's heart and there learned the way to think, speak, and act. The true disciple is ultimately the one whose proclamation of the gospel is the most credible and effective.

Like the Apostle John, Bishop Ambrose, who never tired of saying: "*Omnia Christus est nobis!* To us Christ is all!" continues to be a genuine witness of the Lord. Let us thus conclude our catechesis with his same words, full of love for Jesus: "*Omnia Christus est nobis!* If you have a wound to heal, he is the doctor; if you are parched by fever, he is the spring; if you are oppressed by injustice, he is justice; if you are in need of help, he is strength; if you fear death, he is life; if you desire heaven, he is the way; if you are in the darkness, he is light. . . . Taste and see how good is the Lord: blessed is the man who hopes in him!" (*De Virginitate* 16, 99). Let us also hope in Christ. We shall thus be blessed and shall live in peace.

—24 October 2007

St. Maximus of Turin

BETWEEN THE END OF THE FOURTH CENTURY and the beginning of the fifth, another Father of the Church made a great contribution to the spread and consolidation of Christianity in northern Italy: St. Maximus, whom we come across in 398—a year after St. Ambrose's death—as bishop of Turin. Very little is known about him; in compensation, we have inherited a collection of about ninety of his sermons. It is possible to perceive in them the bishop's profound and vital bond with his city, which attests to an evident point of contact between the episcopal ministry of Ambrose and that of Maximus.

At that time, serious tensions were disturbing orderly civil coexistence. In this context, as pastor and teacher, Maximus succeeded in obtaining the Christian people's support. The city was threatened by various groups of barbarians. They entered by the eastern passes, which went as far as the western Alps. Turin was therefore permanently garrisoned by troops and at critical moments became a refuge for the populations fleeing from the countryside and urban centers where there was no protection. Maximus's interventions in the face of this situation testify to his commitment to respond to the civil degradation and disintegration. Although it is still difficult to determine the social composition of those for whom the sermons were intended, it would seem that Maximus's preaching—to avoid the risk of vagueness—was specifically addressed to a chosen nucleus of the Christian community of Turin, consisting of rich landowners who had property in the Turinese countryside and a house in the city. This was a clear-sighted pastoral decision by the bishop, who saw this type of preaching as the most effective way to preserve and strengthen his own ties with the people.

To illustrate this view of Maximus's ministry in his city, I point out, for example, *Sermons* 17 and 18, dedicated to an ever timely topic: wealth and poverty in Christian communities. In this context, too, the city was fraught with serious tensions. Riches were accumulated and hidden. "No one thinks about the needs of others," the bishop remarked bitterly in his seventeenth *Sermon*. "In fact, not only do many Christians not share their own possessions but they also rob others of theirs. Not only, I say, do they not bring the money they collect to the feet of the Apostles, but in addition, they drag from priests' feet their own brethren who are seeking help." And he concluded: "In our cities, there are many guests or pilgrims. Do what you have promised," adhering to faith, "so that what was said to Ananias will not be said to you as well: 'You have not lied to men, but to God'" (*Sermon* 17, 2–3).

In the next *Sermon*, the eighteenth, Maximus condemns the recurring forms of exploitation of others' misfortunes. "Tell me, Christian," the bishop reprimands his faithful, "tell me why you snatched the booty abandoned by the plunderers? Why did you take home 'ill-gotten gains' as you yourself think, torn apart and contaminated? But perhaps," he continues, "you say you have purchased them, and thereby believe you are avoiding the accusation of avarice. However, this is not the way to equate purchasing with selling. It is a good thing to make purchases, but that means what is sold freely in times of peace, not goods looted during the sack of a city. . . . So act as a Christian and a citizen who purchases in order to repay" (*Sermon* 18, 3). Without being too obvious, Maximus thus managed to preach a profound relationship between a Christian's and a citizen's duties. In his eyes, living a Christian life also meant assuming civil commitments. Vice versa, every Christian who, "despite being able to live by his own work, seizes the booty of others with the ferocity of wild beasts"; who "tricks his neighbor, who tries every day to nibble away at the boundaries of others, to gain possession of their produce," does not compare to a fox biting off the heads of chickens but rather to a wolf savaging pigs (*Sermon* 41, 4).

In comparison with the cautious, defensive attitude that Ambrose adopted to justify his famous project of redeeming prisoners of war, the historical changes that occurred in the relationship between the bishop and the municipal institutions are clearly evident. By now, sustained through legislation that invited Christians to redeem prisoners, Maximus, with the collapse of the civil authority of the Roman Empire, felt fully authorized to exercise true control over the city. This control was to become increasingly extensive and effective until it replaced the irresponsible evasion of the magistrates and civil institutions. In this context, Maximus not only strove to rekindle in the faithful the traditional love for their hometown, but he also proclaimed the precise duty to pay taxes, however burdensome and unpleasant they might appear (cf. *Sermon* 26, 2). In short, the tone and substance of the sermons imply an increased awareness of the bishop's political responsibility in the specific historical circumstances. He was "the lookout tower" posted in the city. Whoever could these watchmen be, Maximus wonders in *Sermon* 92, "other than the most blessed bishops set on a lofty rock of wisdom, so to speak, to defend the peoples and to warn them about the evils approaching in the distance?" And in *Sermon* 89, the bishop of Turin describes his tasks to his faithful, making a unique comparison between the bishop's function and the function of bees: "Like the bee," he said, bishops "observe bodily chastity; they offer the food of heavenly life using the sting of the law. They are pure in sanctifying, gentle in restoring, and severe in punishing." With these words, St. Maximus described the task of the bishop in his time.

In short, historical and literary analyses show an increasing awareness of the political responsibility of the ecclesiastical authority in a context in which it continued de facto to replace the civil authority. Indeed, the ministry of the bishop of northwest Italy—starting with Eusebius, who dwelled in his Vercelli "like a monk," to Maximus of Turin, positioned "like a sentinel" on the highest rock in the city—developed along these lines. It is obvious that the contemporary historical, cultural, and social context is profoundly different. Today's context is rather the context outlined by my venerable predecessor Pope John Paul II in the postsynodal apostolic exhortation *Ecclesia in Europa*, in which he offers an articulate analysis of the challenges and signs of hope for the Church in Europe today (nn. 6–22). In any case, on the basis of the changed conditions, the believer's duties to his city and his homeland still remain effective. The combination of the commitments of the "honest citizen" with those of the "good Christian" has not, in fact, disappeared.

In conclusion, to highlight one of the most important aspects of the unity of Christian life, I recall the words of the pastoral constitution *Gaudium et Spes*: consistency between faith and conduct, between gospel and culture. The council exhorts the faithful "to perform their duties faithfully in the spirit of the gospel. It is a mistake to think that, because we have here no lasting city, but seek the city which is to come, we are entitled to shirk our earthly responsibilities; this is to forget that by our faith we are bound all the more to fulfill these responsibilities according to the vocation of each one" (n. 43). In following the magisterium of St. Maximus and of many other Fathers, let us make our own the council's desire that the faithful may be increasingly eager to "carry out their earthly activity in such a way as to integrate human, domestic, professional, scientific, and technical enterprises with religious values, under whose supreme direction all things are ordered to the glory of God" (ibid.) and thus for humanity's good.

—31 October 2007

ST. JEROME

His Life and Work

We now turn our attention to St. Jerome, a Church Father who centered his life on the Bible: he translated it into Latin, commented on it in his works, and above all, strove to live it in practice throughout his long earthly life, despite the well-known difficult, hot-tempered character with which nature had endowed him.

Jerome was born into a Christian family in about 347 in Stridon. He was given a good education and was even sent to Rome to fine-tune his studies. As a young man, he was attracted by the worldly life (cf. *Ep.* 22, 7), but his desire for and interest in the Christian religion prevailed.

Jerome received baptism in about 366 and opted for the ascetic life. He went to Aquileia and joined a group of fervent Christians that had formed around Bishop Valerian and that he described as almost "a choir of blesseds" (*Chron. ad ann.* 374). He then left for the East and lived as a hermit in the Desert of Chalcis, south of Aleppo (*Ep.* 14, 10), devoting himself assiduously to study. He perfected his knowledge of Greek, began learning Hebrew (cf. *Ep.* 125, 12), and transcribed codices and Patristic writings (cf. *Ep.* 5, 2). Meditation, solitude, and contact with the Word of God helped his Christian sensibility to mature. He bitterly regretted the indiscretions of his youth (cf. *Ep.* 22, 7) and was keenly aware of the contrast between the pagan mentality and the Christian life: a contrast made famous by the dramatic and lively "vision," of which he has left us an account, in which it seemed to him that he was being scourged before God because he was "Ciceronian rather than Christian" (cf. *Ep.* 22, 30).

In 382, he moved to Rome: here, acquainted with his fame as an ascetic and his ability as a scholar, Pope Damasus engaged him as secretary and counselor; the pope encouraged him, for pastoral and cultural reasons, to embark on a new Latin translation of the biblical texts. Several members of the Roman aristocracy, especially such as noblewomen Paula, Marcella, Asella, Lea, and others, desirous of committing themselves to the way of Christian perfection and of deepening their knowledge of the Word of God, chose him as their spiritual guide and teacher in the methodical approach to the sacred texts. These noblewomen also learned Greek and Hebrew.

After the death of Pope Damasus, Jerome left Rome in 385 and went on pilgrimage, first to the Holy Land, a silent witness of Christ's earthly life, and then to Egypt, the favorite country of numerous monks (cf.

Contra Rufinum 3, 22; *Ep.* 108, 6–14). In 386, he stopped in Bethlehem, where male and female monasteries were built through the generosity of the noblewoman Paula, as well as a hospice for pilgrims bound for the Holy Land, "remembering Mary and Joseph, who had found no room there" (*Ep.* 108, 14). He stayed in Bethlehem until he died, continuing to do a prodigious amount of work: he commented on the Word of God; he defended the faith, vigorously opposing various heresies; he urged the monks on to perfection; he taught classical and Christian culture to young students; he welcomed with a pastor's heart pilgrims who were visiting the Holy Land. He died in his cell close to the Grotto of the Nativity on 30 September 419–420.

Jerome's literary studies and vast erudition enabled him to revise and translate many biblical texts: an invaluable undertaking for the Latin Church and for Western culture. On the basis of the original Greek and Hebrew texts, and thanks to the comparison with previous versions, he revised the four Gospels in Latin, then the Psalter and a large part of the Old Testament. Taking into account the original Hebrew and Greek texts of the Septuagint, the classical Greek version of the Old Testament that dates back to pre-Christian times, as well as the earlier Latin versions, Jerome was able, with the assistance later of other collaborators, to produce a better translation: this constitutes the so-called *Vulgate*, the "official" text of the Latin Church, which was recognized as such by the Council of Trent and which, after the recent revision, continues to be the "official" Latin text of the Church. It is interesting to point out the criteria which the great biblicist abided by in his work as a translator. He himself reveals them when he says that he respects even the order of the words of the Sacred Scriptures, for in them, he says, "the order of the words is also a mystery" (*Ep.* 57, 5), that is, a revelation. Furthermore, he reaffirms the need to refer to the original texts: "Should an argument on the New Testament arise between Latins because of interpretations of the manuscripts that fail to agree, let us turn to the original, that is, to the Greek text in which the New Testament was written. Likewise, with regard to the Old Testament, if there are divergences between the Greek and Latin texts, we should have recourse to the original Hebrew text; thus, we shall be able to find in the streams all that flows from the source" (*Ep.* 106, 2). Jerome also commented on many biblical texts. For him, the commentaries had to offer multiple opinions "so that the shrewd reader, after reading the different explanations and hearing many opinions—to be accepted or rejected—may judge which is the most reliable, and, like an expert moneychanger, may reject the false coin" (*Contra Rufinum* 1, 16).

Jerome refuted with energy and liveliness the heretics who contested the tradition and faith of the Church. He also demonstrated the importance and validity of Christian literature, which had by then become a real culture that deserved to be compared with classical literature: he did so by composing his *De Viris Illustribus*, a work in which Jerome presents the biographies of more than a hundred Christian authors. Further, he wrote biographies of monks, comparing among other things their spiritual itineraries as well as monastic ideal. In addition, he translated various works by Greek authors. Last, in the important *Epistulae*, a masterpiece of Latin literature, Jerome emerges with the profile of a man of culture, an ascetic, and a guide of souls.

What can we learn from St. Jerome? It seems to me, this above all to love the Word of God in Sacred Scripture. St. Jerome said: "Ignorance of the Scriptures is ignorance of Christ." It is therefore important that every Christian live in contact and in personal dialogue with the Word of God given to us in Sacred Scripture. This dialogue with Scripture must always have two dimensions: on the one hand, it must be a truly personal dialogue because God speaks with each one of us through Sacred Scripture and it has a message for each one. We must not read Sacred Scripture as a word of the past but as the Word of God that is also addressed to us, and we must try to understand what it is that the Lord wants to tell us. On the other hand, to avoid falling into individualism, we must bear in mind that the Word of God has been given to us precisely in order to build communion and to join forces in the truth on our journey toward God. Thus, although it is always a personal Word, it is also a Word that builds community; that builds the Church. We must therefore read it in communion with the living Church. The privileged place for reading and listening to the Word of God is the liturgy, in which, celebrating the Word and making Christ's body present in the sacrament, we actualize the Word in our lives and make it present among us. We must never forget that the Word of God transcends time. On the one hand, human opinions come and go. What is very modern today will be very antiquated tomorrow. On the other hand, the Word of God is the Word of eternal life, it bears within it eternity and is valid forever. By carrying the Word of God within us, we therefore carry within us eternity, eternal life.

I thus conclude this consideration on St. Jerome's life and work with a word he once addressed to St. Paulinus of Nola. In it the great exegete expressed this very reality, that is, in the Word of God we receive eternity, eternal life. St. Jerome said: "Seek to learn on earth those truths which will remain ever valid in heaven" (*Ep.* 53, 10).

Interpreter of Scripture

As we said, St. Jerome dedicated his life to studying the Bible, so much so that he was recognized by my predecessor Pope Benedict XV as "an outstanding doctor in the interpretation of Sacred Scripture." Jerome emphasized the joy and importance of being familiar with biblical texts: "Does one not seem to dwell, already here on earth, in the kingdom of heaven when one lives with these texts, when one meditates on them, when one does not know or seek anything else?" (*Ep.* 53, 10). In reality, to dialogue with God, with his Word, is in a certain sense a presence of heaven, a presence of God. To draw near to the biblical texts, above all the New Testament, is essential for the believer, because "ignorance of the Scriptures is ignorance of Christ." This is his famous phrase, cited also by the Second Vatican Council in the constitution *Dei Verbum* (n. 25).

Truly "in love" with the Word of God, he asked himself: "How could one live without the knowledge of Scripture, through which one learns to know Christ himself, who is the life of believers?" (*Ep.* 30, 7). The Bible, an instrument "by which God speaks every day to the faithful" (*Ep.* 133, 13), thus becomes a stimulus and source of Christian life for all situations and for each person. To read Scripture is to converse with God: "If you pray," he writes to a young Roman noblewoman, "you speak with the Spouse; if you read, it is he who speaks to you" (*Ep.* 22, 25). The study of and meditation on Scripture renders man wise and serene (cf. *In Eph.*, Prologue). Certainly, to penetrate the Word of God ever more profoundly, a constant and progressive application is needed. Hence, Jerome recommends to the priest Nepotian: "Read the divine Scriptures frequently; rather, may your hands never set the Holy Book down. Learn here what you must teach" (*Ep.* 52, 7). To the Roman matron Leta he gave this counsel for the Christian education of her daughter: "Ensure that each day she studies some Scripture passage. . . . After prayer, reading should follow, and after reading, prayer. . . . Instead of jewels and silk clothing, may she love the divine books" (*Ep.* 107, 9, 12). Through meditation on and knowledge of the Scriptures, one "maintains the equilibrium of the soul" (*Ad Eph.*, Prologue). Only a profound spirit of prayer and the Holy Spirit's help can introduce us to understanding the Bible: "In the interpretation of Sacred Scripture, we always need the help of the Holy Spirit" (*In Mich.* 1, 1, 10, 15).

A passionate love for Scripture therefore pervaded Jerome's whole life, a love that he always sought to deepen in the faithful too. He recommends to one of his spiritual daughters: "Love Sacred Scripture and wisdom will love you; love it tenderly, and it will protect you; honor it and you will receive its caresses. May it be for you as your necklaces and your earrings" (*Ep.* 130, 20). And again: "Love the science of Scripture, and you will not love the vices of the flesh" (*Ep.* 125, 11).

For Jerome, a fundamental criterion of the method for interpreting the Scriptures was harmony with the Church's magisterium. We should never read Scripture alone because we meet too many closed doors and could easily slip into error. The Bible has been written by the people of God and for the people of God under the inspiration of the Holy Spirit. Only in this communion with the people of God do we truly enter into the "we," into the nucleus of the truth that God himself wants to tell us. For him, an authentic interpretation of the Bible must always be in harmonious accord with the faith of the Catholic Church. It is not a question of an exegesis imposed on this book from without; the book is really the voice of the pilgrim people of God and only in the faith of this people are we "correctly attuned" to understand Sacred Scripture. Therefore, Jerome admonishes, "Remain firmly attached to the traditional doctrine that you have been taught, so that you can preach according to right doctrine and refute those who contradict it" (*Ep.* 52, 7). In particular, given that Jesus Christ founded his Church on Peter, every Christian, he concludes, must be in communion "with St. Peter's See. I know that on this rock the Church is built" (*Ep.* 15, 2). Consequently, without equivocation, he declared: "I am with whoever is united to the teaching of St. Peter" (*Ep.* 16).

Obviously, Jerome does not neglect the ethical aspect. Indeed, he often recalls the duty to harmonize one's life with the divine Word, and only by living it does one also find the capacity to understand it. This consistency is indispensable for every Christian, and particularly for the preacher, so that his actions may never contradict his discourses nor be an embarrassment to him. Thus, he exhorts the priest Nepotian: "May your actions never be unworthy of your words, may it not happen that, when you preach in church, someone might say to himself: 'Why does he therefore not act like this?' How could a teacher, on a full stomach, discuss fasting; even a thief can blame avarice; but in the priest of Christ the mind and words must harmonize" (*Ep.* 52, 7). In another epistle, Jerome repeats: "Even if we possess a splendid doctrine, the person who feels condemned by his own conscience remains disgraced" (*Ep.* 127, 4). Also on the theme of consistency, he observes: the gospel must translate into truly charitable behavior, because in each human being the person of Christ himself is present. For example, addressing the presbyter Paulinus (who then became bishop of Nola and a saint), Jerome counsels: "The true temple of Christ is the soul of the faithful: adorn it and beautify this shrine, place your offerings in it and receive Christ. What is the use of decorating the walls with precious stones if Christ dies of hunger in the person of the poor?" (*Ep.* 58, 7). Jerome concretizes the need "to clothe Christ in the poor, to visit him in the suffering, to nourish him in the hungry, to house him in the homeless" (*Ep.* 130, 14). The love of Christ, nourished with study and meditation, makes us rise above every difficulty: "Let us also love Jesus Christ, always seeking union with him: then even what is difficult will seem easy to us" (*Ep.* 22, 40).

Prosper of Aquitaine, who defined Jerome as a "model of conduct and teacher of the human race" (*Carmen de ingratis* 57), also left us a rich and varied teaching on Christian asceticism. He reminds us that a courageous commitment toward perfection requires constant vigilance, frequent mortifications, even if with moderation and prudence, and assiduous intellectual and manual labor to avoid idleness (cf. *Epp.* 125, 11; 130, 15), and above all obedience to God: "Nothing . . . pleases God as much as obedience . . . , which is the most excellent and sole virtue" (*Hom. de Oboedientia: CCL* 78, 552). The practice of pilgrimage can also be part of the ascetical journey. In particular, Jerome promoted pilgrimages to the Holy Land, where pilgrims were welcomed and housed in the lodgings that were built next to the monastery of Bethlehem, thanks to the generosity of the noblewoman Paula, a spiritual daughter of Jerome (cf. *Ep.* 108, 14).

Last, one cannot remain silent about the importance that Jerome gave to the matter of Christian pedagogy (cf. *Epp.* 107; 128). He proposed to form "one soul that must become the temple of the Lord" (*Ep.* 107, 4), a "very precious gem" in the eyes of God (*Ep.* 107, 13). With profound intuition, he advises to preserve oneself from evil and from the occasions of sin, and to exclude equivocal or dissipating friendships (cf. *Ep.* 107, 4, 8–9; also *Ep.* 128, 3–4). Above all, he exhorts parents to create a serene and joyful environment around their children, to stimulate them to study and work also through praise and emulation (cf. *Epp.* 107, 4; 128, 1), encouraging them to overcome difficulties, foster good habits, and avoid picking up bad habits, so that, and here he cites a phrase of Publius Siro which he heard at school, "it will be difficult for you to correct those things to which you are quietly habituating yourself" (*Ep.* 107, 8). Parents are the principal educators of their children, the first teachers of life. With great clarity, Jerome, addressing a young girl's mother and then mentioning her father, admonishes, almost expressing a fundamental duty of every human creature who comes into existence, "May she find in you her teacher, and may she look to you with the inexperienced wonder of childhood. Neither in you nor in her father should she ever see behavior that could lead to sin, as it could be copied. Remember that . . . you can educate her more by example than with words" (*Ep.* 107, 9). Among Jerome's principal intuitions as a pedagogue, one must emphasize the importance he attributed to a healthy and integral education beginning from early childhood, the particular responsibility belonging to parents, the urgency of a serious moral and religious formation, and the duty to study for a more complete human formation. Moreover, an aspect rather disregarded in ancient times but held vital by our author is the promotion of women, to whom he recognizes the right to a complete formation: human, scholastic, religious, professional. We see precisely today how the education of the personality in its totality, the education to responsibility before God and man, is the true condition of all progress, all peace, all reconciliation, and the exclusion of violence. Education before God and man: it is Sacred Scripture that offers us the guide for education and thus of true humanism.

We cannot conclude these quick notes on the great Father of the Church without mentioning his effective contribution to safeguarding the positive and valid elements of the ancient Hebrew, Greek, and Roman cultures for nascent Christian civilization. Jerome recognized and assimilated the artistic values of the richness of the sentiments and the harmony of the images present in the classics, which educate the heart and fantasy to noble sentiments. Above all, he put at the center of his life and activity the Word of God, which indicates the path of life to man and reveals the secrets of holiness to him. We cannot fail to be deeply grateful for all of this, even in our day.

—*7 and 14 November 2007*

Aphraates, "The Sage"

In our excursion into the world of the Fathers of the Church, I guide you today to a little-known part of this universe of faith, in the territories where the Semitic-language churches flourished, still uninfluenced by Greek thought. These churches developed throughout the fourth century in the Near East, from the Holy Land to Lebanon and to Mesopotamia. In that century, which was a period of formation on the ecclesial and literary level, these communities contributed to the ascetic-monastic phenomenon with autochthonous characteristics that did not come under Egyptian monastic influence. The Syriac communities of the fourth century, therefore, represent the Semitic world from which the Bible itself has come, and they are an expression of a Christianity whose theological formulation had not yet entered into contact with different cultural currents but lived in their own way of thinking. They are churches in which asceticism in its various hermitic forms (hermits in the desert, caverns, recluses, stylites) and monasticism in forms of community life, exert a role of vital importance in the development of theological and spiritual thought.

I introduce this world through the great figure of Aphraates, known also by the sobriquet "the Sage." He was one of the most important and at the same time most enigmatic personages of fourth-century Syriac Christianity. A native of the Nineveh-Mosul region, today in Iraq, he lived during the first half of the fourth century. We have little information about his life; he maintained, however, close ties with the ascetic-monastic environment of the Syriac-speaking Church, of which he has given us some information in his work and to which he dedicates part of his reflection. Indeed, according to some sources, he was the head of a monastery and later consecrated a bishop. He wrote twenty-three homilies, known as *Expositions* or *Demonstrations,* on various aspects of Christian life, such as faith, love, fasting, humility, prayer, the ascetic life, and also the relationship between Judaism and Christianity, between the Old and New Testaments. He wrote in a simple style, with short sentences and sometimes with contrasting parallelisms; nevertheless, he was able to weave consistent discourses with a well-articulated development of the various arguments he treated.

Aphraates was from an ecclesial community situated on the frontier between Judaism and Christianity. It was a community strongly linked to the mother Church of Jerusalem, and its bishops were traditionally chosen from among the so-called family of James, the "brother of the Lord" (cf. Mk 6:3). They were people linked by blood and by faith to the Church of Jerusalem. Aphraates's language was Syriac, therefore a Semitic language like the Hebrew of the Old Testament and like the Aramaic spoken by Jesus himself. Aphraates's ecclesial community was a community that sought to remain faithful to the Judeo-Christian tradition, of which it felt it was a daughter. It therefore maintained a close relationship with the Jewish world and its Sacred Books. Significantly, Aphraates defines himself as a "disciple of the Sacred Scripture" of the Old and New Testaments (*Expositions* 22, 26), which he considers as his only source of inspiration, having recourse to it in such abundance as to make it the center of his reflection.

Aphraates develops various arguments in his *Expositions*. Faithful to Syriac tradition, he often presents the salvation wrought by Christ as a healing and thus Christ himself as the physician. Sin, on the other hand, is seen as a wound that only penance can heal: "A man who has been wounded in battle," Aphraates said, "is not ashamed to place himself in the hands of a wise doctor . . . ; in the same way, the one who has been wounded by Satan must not be ashamed to recognize his fault and distance himself from it, asking for the medicine of penance" (*Expositions* 7, 3). Another important aspect in Aphraates's work is his teaching on prayer, and in a special way on Christ as the teacher of prayer. The Christian prays following Jesus' teaching and example of oration: "Our Savior taught people to pray like this, saying: "Pray in secret to the One who is hidden, but who sees all"; and again: "Go into your room and shut the door and pray to your Father who is in secret; and your Father who sees in secret will reward you' [Mt 6:6] . . . Our Savior wants to show that God knows the desires and thoughts of the heart" (*Expositions* 4, 10).

For Aphraates, the Christian life is centered on the imitation of Christ, in taking up his yoke and following him on the way of the gospel. One of the most useful virtues for Christ's disciple is humility. It is not a secondary aspect in the Christian's spiritual life: human nature is humble, and it is God who exalts it to his own glory. Aphraates observed that humility is not a negative value: "If man's roots are planted in the earth, his fruits ascend before the Lord of majesty" (*Expositions* 9, 14). By remaining humble in the earthly reality in which one lives, the Christian can enter into relationship with the Lord: "The humble man is humble, but his heart rises to lofty heights. The eyes of his face observe the earth and the eyes of his mind the lofty heights" (*Expositions* 9, 2).

Aphraates's vision of the human and the physical reality is very positive: the human body, in the example of the humble Christ, is called to beauty, joy, and light: "God draws near to the man who loves, and it is right to love humility and to remain in a humble state. The humble are simple, patient, loving, integral, upright, good, prudent, calm, wise, quiet, peaceful, merciful, ready to convert, benevolent, profound, thoughtful, beautiful, and attractive" (*Expositions* 9, 14). Aphraates often presented the Christian life in a clear ascetic and spiritual dimension: faith is the base, the foundation; it makes of persons a temple where Christ himself dwells. Faith, therefore, makes sincere charity possible, which expresses itself in love for God and neighbor. Another important aspect in Aphraates's thought is fasting, which he understood in a broad sense. He spoke of fasting from food as a necessary practice to be charitable and pure, of fasting understood as continence with a view to holiness, of fasting from vain or detestable words, of fasting from anger, of fasting from the possession of goods with a view to ministry, of fasting from sleep to be watchful in prayer.

To conclude, we return again to Aphraates's teaching on prayer. According to this ancient sage, prayer is achieved when Christ dwells in the Christian's heart and invites one to a coherent commitment to charity toward one's neighbor. In fact, he wrote:

> Give relief to those in distress, visit the ailing,
>   help the poor: this is prayer.
> Prayer is good, and its works are beautiful.
> Prayer is accepted when it gives relief to one's neighbor.
> Prayer is heard when it includes forgiveness of affronts.
> Prayer is strong
>   when it is full of God's strength. (*Expositions* 4, 14–16)

With these words, Aphraates invites us to a prayer that becomes Christian life, a fulfilled life, a life penetrated by faith, by openness to God, and therefore to love of neighbor.

—*21 November 2007*

St. Ephrem

COMMON OPINION TODAY supposes Christianity to be a European religion that subsequently exported the culture of this continent to other countries. But the reality is far more complex, since the roots of the Christian religion are found in the Old Testament, hence, in Jerusalem and the Semitic world. Christianity is still nourished by these Old Testament roots. Furthermore, its expansion in the first centuries was both toward the West—toward the Greco-Latin world, where it later inspired European culture—and in the direction of the East, as far as Persia and India. It thus contributed to creating a specific culture in Semitic languages with an identity of its own.

To demonstrate this cultural pluralism of the one Christian faith in its origins, I spoke in my last chapter of a representative of this other Christianity who is almost unknown to us: Aphraates, the Persian sage. Now, along the same lines, I talk about St. Ephrem the Syrian, who was born into a Christian family in Nisibis in about 306. He was Christianity's most important Syriac-speaking representative and uniquely succeeded in reconciling the vocations of theologian and poet. He was educated and grew up beside James, bishop of Nisibis (303–338), and with him founded the theological school in his city. He was ordained a deacon and was intensely active in local Christian community life until 363, the year when Nisibis fell into Persian hands. Ephrem then emigrated to Edessa, where he continued his activity as a preacher. He died in this city in 373, a victim of the disease he contracted while caring for those infected with the plague. It is not known for certain whether he was a monk, but we can be sure in any case that he remained a deacon throughout his life and embraced virginity and poverty. Thus, the common and fundamental Christian identity appears in the specificity of his own cultural expression: faith, hope—the hope which makes it possible to live poor and chaste in this world, placing every expectation in the Lord—and last, charity, to the point of giving his life through nursing those sick with the plague.

Saint Ephrem has left us an important theological inheritance. His substantial opus can be divided into four categories: works written in ordinary prose (his polemic works or biblical commentaries); works written in poetic prose; homilies in verse; and last, hymns, undoubtedly Ephrem's most abundant production. He is a rich and interesting author in many ways, but especially from the theological point of view. It is the fact that theology and poetry converge in his work which makes it so special. If we desire to approach his doctrine, we must insist on this from the outset: namely, on the fact that he produces theology in poetical form. Poetry enabled him to deepen his theological reflection through paradoxes and images. At the same time, his theology became liturgy, became music; indeed, he was a great composer, a musician. Theology, reflection on the faith, poetry, song, and praise of God go together; and it is precisely in this liturgical character that the divine truth emerges clearly in Ephrem's theology. In his search for God, in his theological activity, he employed the way of paradoxes and symbols. He made ample use of contrasting images because they served to emphasize the mystery of God.

I cannot present much of his writing here, partly because his poetry is difficult to translate, but to give at least some idea of his poetical theology I cite parts of two hymns. First of all, and also with a view to the approach of Advent, I shall propose to you several splendid images taken from his hymns *On the Nativity of Christ*. Ephrem expressed his wonder before the Virgin in inspired tones:

> The Lord entered her and became a servant; the Word entered her, and became silent within her; thunder entered her and his voice was still; the Shepherd of all entered her; he became a Lamb in her, and came forth bleating.
>
> The belly of your Mother changed the order of things, O you who order all! Rich he went in, he came out poor: the High One went into her [Mary], he came out lowly. Brightness went into her and clothed himself, and came forth a despised form. . . .
>
> He that gives food to all went in, and knew hunger. He who gives drink to all went in, and knew thirst. Naked and bare came forth from her the Clother of all things [in beauty]. (Hymn *De Nativitate* 11, 6–8)

To express the mystery of Christ, Ephrem uses a broad range of topics, expressions, and images. In one of his hymns, he effectively links Adam (in Paradise) to Christ (in the eucharist):

> It was by closing with the sword of the cherub that the path to the tree of life was closed. But for the peoples, the Lord of this tree gave himself as food in his (eucharistic) oblation.
>
> The trees of the Garden of Eden were given as food to the first Adam. For us, the gardener of the Garden in person made himself food for our souls. Indeed, we had all left Paradise together with Adam, who left it behind him.
>
> Now that the sword has been removed here below (on the Cross), replaced by the spear, we can return to it. (*Hymn* 49, 9–11)

To speak of the eucharist, Ephrem used two images, embers or burning coal and the pearl. The burning-coal theme was taken from the

Prophet Isaiah (cf. 6:6). It is the image of one of the seraphim who picks up a burning coal with tongs and simply touches the lips of the Prophet with it in order to purify them; the Christian, on the other hand, touches and consumes the Burning Coal which is Christ himself:

> In your bread hides the Spirit who cannot be consumed; in your wine is the fire that cannot be swallowed. The Spirit in your bread, fire in your wine: behold a wonder heard from our lips.
>
> The seraph could not bring himself to touch the glowing coal with his fingers, it was Isaiah's mouth alone that it touched; neither did the fingers grasp it nor the mouth swallow it; but the Lord has granted us to do both these things.
>
> The fire came down with anger to destroy sinners, but the fire of grace descends on the bread and settles in it. Instead of the fire that destroyed man, we have consumed the fire in the bread and have been invigorated. (Hymn *De Fide* 10, 8–10)

Here again is a final example of St. Ephrem's hymns, where he speaks of the pearl as a symbol of the riches and beauty of faith:

> I placed (the pearl), my brothers, on the palm of my hand, to be able to examine it. I began to look at it from one side and from the other: it looked the same from all sides. (Thus) is the search for the Son inscrutable, because it is all light. In its clarity I saw the Clear One who does not grow opaque; and in his purity, the great symbol of the Body of our Lord, which is pure. In his indivisibility I saw the truth which is indivisible. (Hymn *On the Pearl* 1:2–3)

The figure of Ephrem is still absolutely timely for the life of the various Christian churches. We discover him in the first place as a theologian who reflects poetically, on the basis of Holy Scripture, on the mystery of man's redemption brought about by Christ, the Word of God incarnate. His is a theological reflection expressed in images and symbols taken from nature, daily life, and the Bible. Ephrem gives his poetry and liturgical hymns a didactic and catechetical character: they are theological hymns yet at the same time suitable for recitation or liturgical song. On the occasion of liturgical feasts, Ephrem made use of these hymns to spread Church doctrine. Time has proven them to be an extremely effective catechetical instrument for the Christian community.

Ephrem's reflection on the theme of God the Creator is important: nothing in creation is isolated, and the world, next to Sacred Scripture, is a Bible of God. By using his freedom wrongly, man upsets the cosmic order. The role of women was important to Ephrem. The way he spoke of them was always inspired with sensitivity and respect: the dwelling place of Jesus in Mary's womb greatly increased women's dignity. Ephrem held that just as there is no redemption without Jesus, there is no Incarnation without Mary. The divine and human dimensions of the mystery of our redemption can already be found in Ephrem's texts; poetically and with fundamentally scriptural images, he anticipated the theological background and in some way the very language of the great christological definitions of the fifth-century councils.

Ephrem, honored by Christian tradition with the title "Harp of the Holy Spirit," remained a deacon of the Church throughout his life. It was a crucial and emblematic decision: he was a deacon, a servant, in his liturgical ministry and, more radically, in his love for Christ—whose praises he sang in an unparalleled way—and also in his love for his brethren, whom he introduced with rare skill to the knowledge of divine revelation.

—28 November 2007

St. Paulinus of Nola

THE FATHER OF THE CHURCH to whom we turn our attention now is St. Paulinus of Nola. Paulinus, a contemporary of St. Augustine to whom he was bound by a firm friendship, exercised his ministry at Nola in Campania, where he was a monk and later a priest and a bishop. However, he was originally from Aquitaine, in the south of France, to be precise, Bordeaux, where he was born into a high-ranking family. It was here, with the poet Ausonius as his teacher, that he received a fine literary education. He left his native region for the first time to follow his precocious political career, which was to see him rise while still young to the position of governor of Campania. In this public office, he attracted admiration for his gifts of wisdom and gentleness. It was during this period that grace caused the seed of conversion to grow in his heart. The incentive came from the simple and intense faith with which the people honored the tomb of a saint, Felix the Martyr, at the shrine of present-day Cimitile. As the head of public government, Paulinus took an interest in this shrine and had a hospice for the poor built and a road to facilitate access to it for the many pilgrims.

While he was doing his best to build the city on earth, he continued discovering the way to the city in heaven. The encounter with Christ was the destination of a laborious journey, strewn with ordeals. Difficult circumstances which resulted from his loss of favor with the political authorities made the transience of things tangible to him. Once he had arrived at faith, he was to write: "The man without Christ is dust and shadow" (*Carm.* 10, 289). Eager to shed light on the meaning of life, he went to Milan to attend the school of Ambrose. He then completed his Christian formation in his native land, where he was baptized by Bishop Delphinus of Bordeaux. Marriage was also a landmark on his journey of faith. Indeed, he married Therasia, a devout noblewoman from Barcelona, with whom he had a son. He would have continued to live as a good lay Christian had not the infant's death after only a few days intervened to rouse him, showing him that God had other plans for his life. Indeed, he felt called to consecrate himself to Christ in a rigorous ascetic life.

In full agreement with his wife Therasia, he sold his possessions for the benefit of the poor and, with her, left Aquitaine for Nola. Here, the husband and wife settled beside the basilica of the patron saint, Felix, living henceforth in chaste brotherhood according to a form of life which also attracted others. The community's routine was typically monastic, but Paulinus, who had been ordained a priest in Barcelona, took it upon himself despite his priestly status to care for pilgrims. This won him the liking and trust of the Christian community, which chose Paulinus, upon the death of the bishop in about 409, as his successor in the See of Nola. Paulinus intensified his pastoral activity, distinguished by special attention to the poor. He has bequeathed to us the image of an authentic pastor of charity, as St. Gregory the Great described him in chapter 3 of his *Dialogues*, in which he depicts Paulinus in the heroic gesture of offering himself as a prisoner in the place of a widow's son. The historical truth of this episode is disputed, but the figure of a bishop with a great heart who knew how to make himself close to his people in the sorrowful trials of the barbarian invasions lives on.

Paulinus's conversion impressed his contemporaries. His teacher Ausonius, a pagan poet, felt "betrayed" and addressed bitter words to him, reproaching him on the one hand for his "contempt," considered insane, of material goods, and on the other for abandoning his literary vocation. Paulinus replied that giving to the poor did not mean contempt for earthly possessions but rather an appreciation of them for the loftiest aim of charity. As for literary commitments, what Paulinus had taken leave of was not his poetic talent, which he was to continue to cultivate, but poetic forms inspired by mythology and pagan ideals. A new aesthetic now governed his sensibility: the beauty of God incarnate, crucified and risen, whose praises he now sang. Actually, he had not abandoned poetry but was henceforth to find his inspiration in the gospel, as he says in this verse: "To my mind the only art is the faith, and Christ is my poetry" (*At nobis ars una fides, et musica Christus: Carm*. 20, 32).

Paulinus's poems are songs of faith and love in which the daily history of small and great events is seen as a history of salvation, a history of God with us. Many of these compositions, the so-called *Carmina natalicia,* are linked to the annual feast of Felix the Martyr, whom he had chosen as his heavenly patron. Remembering St. Felix, Paulinus desired to glorify Christ himself, convinced as he was that the saint's intercession had obtained the grace of conversion for him: "In your light, joyful, I loved Christ" (*Carm*. 21, 373). He desired to express this very concept by enlarging the shrine with a new basilica, which he had decorated in such a way that the paintings, described by suitable captions, would constitute a visual catechesis for pilgrims. Thus, he explained his project in a poem dedicated to another great catechist, St. Nicetas of Remesiana, as he accompanied him on a visit to his basilicas: "I now want you to contemplate the paintings that unfold in a long series on the walls of the painted porticos. . . . It seemed to us useful to portray sacred themes in painting throughout the house of Felix, in the hope that when the peasants see the painted figure, these images will awaken interest in their astonished minds" (*Carm*. 27, 511, 580–83). Today, it is still possible to admire the remains of these works which rightly place the saint of Nola among the figures with a Christian archaeological reference.

Life, in accordance with the ascetic discipline of Cimitile, was spent in poverty and prayer and was wholly immersed in *lectio divina*. Scripture, read, meditated upon, and assimilated, was the light in whose brightness the saint of Nola examined his soul as he strove for perfection. He told those who were struck by his decision to give up material goods that this act was very far from representing total conversion. "The relinquishment or sale of temporal goods possessed in this world is not the completion but only the beginning of the race in the stadium; it is not, so to speak, the goal, but only the starting point. In fact, the athlete does not win because he strips himself, for he undresses precisely in order to begin the contest, whereas he only deserves to be crowned as victorious when he has fought properly" (cf. *Ep.* 24, 7 to Sulpicius Severus).

After the ascetic life and the Word of God came charity; the poor were at home in the monastic community. Paulinus did not limit himself to distributing alms to them: he welcomed them as though they were Christ himself. He reserved a part of the monastery for them and by so doing, it seemed to him that he was not so much giving as receiving, in the exchange of gifts between the hospitality offered and the prayerful gratitude of those assisted. He called the poor his "masters" (cf. *Ep.* 13, 11 to Pammachius) and, remarking that they were housed on the lower floor, liked to say that their prayers constituted the foundations of his house (cf. *Carm.* 26, 393–94).

Saint Paulinus did not write theological treatises, but his poems and ample correspondence are rich in a lived theology, woven from God's Word, constantly examined as a light for life. The sense of the Church as a mystery of unity emerges in particular from them. Paulinus lived communion above all through a pronounced practice of spiritual friendship. He was truly a master in this, making his life a crossroads of elect spirits: from Martin of Tours to Jerome, from Ambrose to Augustine, from Delphinus of Bordeaux to Nicetas of Remesiana, from Victricius of Rouen to Rufinus of Aquileia, from Pammachius to Sulpicius Severus, and many others more or less well known. It was in this atmosphere that the intense pages written to Augustine came into being. Over and above the content of the individual letters, one is impressed by the warmth with which the saint of Nola sings of friendship itself as a manifestation of the one body of Christ, enlivened by the Holy Spirit. Here is an important passage that comes at the beginning of the correspondence between the two friends: "It is not surprising if, despite being far apart, we are present to each other and, without being acquainted, know each other, because we are members of one body, we have one head, we are steeped in one grace, we live on one loaf, we walk on one road, and we dwell in the same house" (*Ep.* 6, 2). As can be seen, this is a very beautiful description of what it means to be Christian, to be the body of Christ, to live within the Church's communion. The theology of our time has found the key to approaching the mystery of the Church precisely in the concept of communion. The witness of St. Paulinus of Nola helps us to perceive the Church, as she is presented to us by the Second Vatican Council, as a sacrament of intimate union with God, hence, of unity among all of us and, last, among the whole human race (cf. *Lumen Gentium*, n. 1).

—*12 December 2007*

St. Augustine of Hippo

His Life

We speak now of the greatest Father of the Latin Church, St. Augustine. This man of passion and faith, of the highest intelligence and tireless in his pastoral care, a great saint and Doctor of the Church, is often known, at least by hearsay, even by those who ignore Christianity or who are not familiar with it, because he left a very deep mark on the cultural life of the West and on the whole world. Because of his special importance, St. Augustine's influence was widespread. It could be said on the one hand that all the roads of Latin Christian literature led to Hippo (today Annaba, on the coast of Algeria), the place where he was bishop from 395 to his death in 430, and, on the other, that from this city of Roman Africa, many other roads of later Christianity and of Western culture itself branched out.

A civilization has seldom encountered such a great spirit who was able to assimilate Christianity's values and exalt its intrinsic wealth, inventing ideas and forms that were to nourish the future generations, as Paul VI also stressed: "It may be said that all the thought-currents of the past meet in his works and form the source which provides the whole doctrinal tradition of succeeding ages" (Inaugural *Address* at the Patristic Institute of the "Augustinianum," 4 May 1970; *L'Osservatore Romano*, English edition, 21 May 1970, 8). Augustine is also the Father of the Church who left the greatest number of works. Possidius, his biographer, said that it seemed impossible that one man could have written so many things in his lifetime. We shall speak of these different works after focusing first on his life, which is easy to reconstruct from his writings, in particular the *Confessions,* his extraordinary spiritual autobiography written in praise of God. This is his most famous work; and rightly so, since it is precisely Augustine's *Confessions*, with their focus on interiority and psychology, that constitute a unique model in Western (and not only Western) literature—including non-religious literature—up to modern times. This attention to the spiritual life, to the mystery of the "I," to the mystery of God who is concealed in the "I," is something quite extraordinary, without precedent, and remains for ever, as it were, a spiritual "peak."

But to come back to his life: Augustine was born in Tagaste, in the Roman province of Numidia, Africa, on 13 November 354 to Patricius, a pagan who later became a catechumen, and Monica, a fervent Christian.

This passionate woman, venerated as a saint, exercised an enormous influence on her son and raised him in the Christian faith. Augustine had also received the salt, a sign of acceptance in the catechumenate, and was always fascinated by the figure of Jesus Christ; indeed, he said that he had always loved Jesus but had drifted further and further away from ecclesial faith and practice, as also happens to many young people today.

Augustine also had a brother, Navigius, and a sister whose name is unknown to us and who, after being widowed subsequently became the head of a monastery for women. As a boy with a very keen intelligence, Augustine received a good education, although he was not always an exemplary student. However, he learned grammar well, first in his native town and then in Madaura, and from 370, he studied rhetoric in Carthage, the capital of Roman Africa. He mastered Latin perfectly but was not quite as successful with Greek and did not learn Punic, spoken by his contemporaries. It was in Carthage itself that for the first time Augustine read the *Hortensius,* a writing by Cicero later lost, an event that can be placed at the beginning of his journey toward conversion. In fact, Cicero's text awoke within him love for wisdom, as, by then a bishop, he was to write in his *Confessions:* "The book changed my feelings," to the extent that "every vain hope became empty to me, and I longed for the immortality of wisdom with an incredible ardour in my heart" (3, 4, 7).

However, since he was convinced that without Jesus the truth cannot be said effectively to have been found and since Jesus' name was not mentioned in this book, immediately after he read it he began to read Scripture, the Bible. But it disappointed him. This was not only because the Latin style of the translation of the Sacred Scriptures was inadequate but also because to him their content itself did not seem satisfying. In the scriptural narratives of wars and other human vicissitudes, he discovered neither the loftiness of philosophy nor the splendor of the search for the truth which is part of it. Yet he did not want to live without God and thus sought a religion which corresponded to his desire for the truth and also with his desire to draw close to Jesus. Thus, he fell into the net of the Manichaeans, who presented themselves as Christians and promised a totally rational religion. They said that the world was divided into two principles: good and evil. And in this way, the whole complexity of human history can be explained. Their dualistic morals also pleased Augustine, because it included a very high morality for the elect: and those like him who adhered to it could live a life better suited to the situation of the time, especially for a young man. He therefore became a Manichaean, convinced at that time that he had found the synthesis between rationality and the search for the truth and love of Jesus Christ. Manichaeanism also offered him a concrete advantage in life: joining the Manichaeans facilitated the prospects of a career. By belonging to that religion, which included so many influential figures, he was able to continue his relationship with a woman and to advance in his career. By this woman he had a son, Adeodatus, who was very dear to him and very intelligent, who was later to be present during the preparation for baptism near Lake Como, taking part in those dialogues, which St. Augustine has passed down to us. The boy unfortunately died prematurely. Having been a grammar teacher since his twenties in the city of his birth, Augustine soon returned to Carthage, where he became a brilliant and famous teacher of rhetoric. However, with time Augustine began to distance himself from the faith of the Manichaeans. They disappointed him precisely from the intellectual viewpoint since they proved incapable of dispelling his doubts. He moved to Rome and then to Milan, where the imperial court resided at that time and where he obtained a prestigious post through the good offices and recommendations of the prefect of Rome, Symmacus, a pagan hostile to St. Ambrose, bishop of Milan.

In Milan, Augustine acquired the habit of listening, at first for the purpose of enriching his rhetorical baggage, to the eloquent preaching of Bishop Ambrose, who had been a representative of the emperor for northern Italy. The African rhetorician was fascinated by the words of the great Milanese prelate; and not only by his rhetoric. It was above all the content that increasingly touched Augustine's heart. The great difficulty with the Old Testament, because of its lack of rhetorical beauty and lofty philosophy, was resolved in St. Ambrose's preaching through his typological interpretation of the Old Testament: Augustine realized that the whole of the Old Testament was a journey toward Jesus Christ. Thus, he found the key to understanding the beauty and even the philosophical depth of the Old Testament and grasped the whole unity of the mystery of Christ in history, as well as the synthesis between philosophy, rationality, and faith in the *Logos*, in Christ, the Eternal Word, who was made flesh.

Augustine soon realized that the allegorical interpretation of Scripture and the Neoplatonic philosophy practiced by the bishop of Milan enabled him to solve the intellectual difficulties which, when he was younger during his first approach to the biblical texts, had seemed insurmountable to him.

Thus, Augustine followed his reading of the philosophers' writings by reading Scripture anew, especially the Pauline Letters. His conversion to Christianity on 15 August 386 therefore came at the end of a long and tormented inner journey—of which we shall speak in another catechesis—and the African moved to the countryside, north of Milan by Lake Como, with his mother, Monica, his son, Adeodatus, and a small group of friends—to prepare himself for baptism. So it was that at the age of thirty-two, Augustine was baptized by Ambrose in the Cathedral of Milan on 24 April 387, during the Easter Vigil.

After his baptism, Augustine decided to return to Africa with his friends, with the idea of living a community life of the monastic kind at the service of God. However, while awaiting their departure in Ostia, his mother fell ill unexpectedly and died shortly afterward, breaking her son's heart. Having returned to his homeland at last, the convert settled in Hippo for the very purpose of founding a monastery. In this city on the African coast, he was ordained a priest in 391, despite his reticence, and with a few companions began the monastic life which had long been in his mind, dividing his time between prayer, study, and preaching. All he wanted was to be at the service of the truth. He did not feel he had a vocation to pastoral life but realized later that God was calling him to be a pastor among others and thus to offer people the gift of the truth. He was ordained a bishop in Hippo four years later, in 395. Augustine continued to deepen his study of Scripture and of the texts of the Christian tradition and was an exemplary bishop in his tireless pastoral commitment: he preached several times a week to his faithful, supported the poor and orphans, and supervised the formation of the clergy and the organization of mens' and womens' monasteries. In short, the former rhetorician asserted himself as one of the most important exponents of Christianity of that time. He was very active in the government of his diocese—with remarkable, even civil, implications—in the more than thirty-five years of his episcopate, and the bishop of Hippo actually exercised a vast influence in his guidance of the Catholic Church in Roman Africa and, more generally, in the Christianity of his time, coping with religious tendencies and tenacious, disruptive heresies such as Manichaeism, Donatism, and Pelagianism, which endangered the Christian faith in the one God, rich in mercy.

And Augustine entrusted himself to God every day until the very end of his life: smitten by fever, while for almost three months his Hippo was being besieged by vandal invaders, the bishop, his friend Possidius recounts in his *Vita Augustini*, asked that the penitential psalms be transcribed in large characters, "and that the sheets be attached to the wall, so that while he was bedridden during his illness he could see and read them and he shed constant hot tears" (31, 2). This is how Augustine spent the last days of his life. He died on 28 August 430, when he was not yet seventy-six. We will devote our next encounters to his work, his message, and his inner experience.

Last Days at Hippo

Augustine chose to appoint his successor four years before he died. Thus, on 26 September 426, he gathered the people in the Basilica of Peace at Hippo to present to the faithful the one he had designated for this task. He said:

In this life we are all mortal, and the day which shall be the last of life on earth is to every man at all times uncertain; but in infancy there is hope of entering boyhood looking forward from boyhood to youth, from youth to manhood, and from manhood to old age; whether these hopes may be realized or not is uncertain, but there is in each case something which may be hoped for. But old age has no other period of this life to look forward to with expectation: in any case, how long old age may be prolonged is uncertain. . . . I came to this town, for such was the will of God, when I was in the prime of life. I was young then, but now I am old. (*Ep.* 213, 1)

At this point, Augustine named the person he had chosen as his successor, the presbyter Heraclius. The assembly burst into applause of approval, shouting twenty-three times, "To God be thanks! To Christ be praise!" With other acclamations, the faithful also approved what Augustine proposed for his future: he wanted to dedicate the years that were left to him to a more intense study of Sacred Scripture (cf. *Ep.* 213, 6).

Indeed, what followed were four years of extraordinary intellectual activity: he brought important works to conclusion, he embarked on others, equally demanding, held public debates with heretics—he was always seeking dialogue—and intervened to foster peace in the African provinces threatened by barbarian southern tribes. He wrote about this to Count Darius, who had come to Africa to settle the disagreement between Boniface and the imperial court which the tribes of Mauritania were exploiting for their incursions: "It is a higher glory still," he said in his letter, "to stay war itself with a word than to slay men with the sword, and to procure or maintain peace by peace, not by war. For those who fight, if they are good men, doubtlessly seek peace; nevertheless, it is through blood. Your mission, however, is to prevent the shedding of blood" (*Ep.* 229, 2). Unfortunately, the hope of pacification in the African territories was disappointed; in May 429, the Vandals, whom out of spite Boniface had invited to Africa, passed the straits of Gibraltar and streamed into Mauritania. The invasion rapidly reached the other rich African provinces. In May or June 430, "the destroyers of the Roman Empire," as Possidius described these barbarians (*Vita* 30, 1), were surrounding and besieging Hippo.

Boniface had also sought refuge in the city. Having been reconciled with the court too late, he was now trying in vain to block the invaders' entry. Possidius, Augustine's biographer, describes Augustine's sorrow: "More tears than usual were his bread, night and day, and when he had reached the very end of his life, his old age caused him, more than others, grief and mourning" (*Vita* 28, 6). And he explains: "Indeed, that man of God saw the massacres and the destruction of the city; houses in the countryside were pulled down and the inhabitants killed by the enemy or put to flight and dispersed. Private churches belonging to priests and ministers were demolished, sacred virgins and religious scattered on every side; some died under torture, others were killed by the sword, still others taken prisoner, losing the integrity of their soul and body and even their faith, reduced by their enemies to a long, drawn-out, and painful slavery" (ibid., 28, 8).

Despite being old and weary, Augustine stood in the breach, comforting himself and others with prayer and meditation on the mysterious designs of providence. In this regard, he spoke of the "old age of the world"—and this Roman world was truly old—he spoke of this old age as years earlier he had spoken to comfort the refugees from Italy when Alaric's Goths had invaded the city of Rome in 410. In old age, he said, ailments proliferate: coughs, catarrh, bleary eyes, anxiety, and exhaustion. Yet, if the world grows old, Christ is perpetually young; hence, the invitation: "Do not refuse to be rejuvenated united to Christ, even in the old world. He tells you: Do not fear, *your youth will be renewed like that of the eagle*" (cf. *Serm.* 81, 8). Thus, the Christian must not lose heart, even in difficult situations, but rather he must spare no effort to help those in need. This is what the great doctor suggested in his response to Honoratus, bishop of Tiabe, who had asked him whether a bishop or a priest or any man of the Church with the barbarians hot on his heels could flee to save his life: "When danger is common to all, that is, for bishops, clerics, and laypeople, may those who need others not be abandoned by the people whom they need. In this case, either let all depart together to safe places or let those who must remain not be deserted by those through whom, in things pertaining to the Church, their necessities must be provided for; and so let them share life in common, or share in common that which the Father of their family appoints them to suffer" (*Ep.* 228, 2). And he concluded: "Such conduct is especially the proof of love" (ibid., 3). How can we fail to recognize in these words the heroic message that so many priests down the centuries have welcomed and made their own?

In the meantime, the city of Hippo resisted. Augustine's monastery-home had opened its doors to welcome episcopal colleagues who were asking for hospitality. Also of this number was Possidius, a former disciple of Augustine; he was able to leave us his direct testimony of those last dramatic days. "In the third month of that siege," Possidius recounts, "Augustine took to his bed with a fever: it was his last illness" (*Vita* 29, 3). The holy old man made the most of that period when he was at last free to dedicate himself with greater intensity to prayer. He was in the habit of saying that no one, bishop, religious, or layman, however irreprehensible his conduct might seem, can face death without adequate repentance. For this reason, he ceaselessly repeated between his tears the penitential psalms he had so often recited with his people (cf. ibid., 31, 2).

The worse his illness became, the more the dying bishop felt the need for solitude and prayer: "In order that no one might disturb him in his recollection, about ten days before leaving his body, he asked those of us present not to let anyone into his room outside the hours in which the doctors came to visit him or when his meals were brought. His desire was minutely complied with and in all that time he devoted himself to prayer" (ibid., 31, 3). He breathed his last on 28 August 430: his great heart rested at last in God.

"For the last rites of his body," Possidius informs us, "the sacrifice in which we took part was offered to God and then he was buried" (*Vita* 31, 5). His body on an unknown date was translated to Sardinia, and from here, in about 725, to the Basilica of San Pietro in Ciel d'Oro in Pavia, where it still rests today. His first biographer has this final opinion of him: "He bequeathed to his Church a very numerous clergy and also monasteries of men and women full of people who had taken vows of chastity under the obedience of their superiors, as well as libraries containing his books and discourses and those of other saints, from which one learns what, through the grace of God, were his merits and greatness in the Church, where the faithful always find him alive" (Possidius, *Vita* 31, 8). This is an opinion in which we can share. We too "find him alive" in his writings. When I read St. Augustine's writings, I do not get the impression that he is a man who died more or less sixteen hundred years ago; I feel he is like a man of today: a friend, a contemporary who speaks to me, who speaks to us with his fresh and timely faith. In St. Augustine who talks to us, talks to me in his writings, we see the everlasting timeliness of his faith; of the faith that comes from Christ, the Eternal Incarnate Word, Son of God and Son of Man. And we can see that this faith is not of the past, although it was preached yesterday; it is still timely today, for Christ is truly yesterday, today, and forever. He is the Way, the Truth, and the Life. Thus, St. Augustine encourages us to entrust ourselves to this ever-living Christ and in this way find the path of life.

Faith and Reason

In 1986, the sixteenth centenary of Augustine's conversion, my beloved predecessor John Paul II dedicated a long, full document to him, the Apostolic Letter *Augustinum Hipponensem*. The pope himself chose to describe this text as "a thanksgiving to God for the gift that he has made to the Church, and through her to the whole human race." I will return to the topic of conversion at another time. It is a fundamental theme not only for Augustine's personal life but also for ours. In the Gospel, the Lord himself summed up his preaching with the word: "Repent." By following in St. Augustine's footsteps, we will be able to meditate on what this conversion is: it is something definitive, decisive, but the fundamental decision must develop, be brought about throughout our life.

This catechesis, however, is dedicated to the subject of faith and reason, a crucial, or better, the crucial theme for St. Augustine's biography. As a child, he learned the Catholic faith from Monica, his mother. But he abandoned this faith as an adolescent because he could no longer discern its reasonableness and rejected a religion that was not, to his mind, also an expression of reason, that is, of the truth. His thirst for truth was radical and therefore led him to drift away from the Catholic faith. Yet his radicalism was such that he could not be satisfied with philosophies that did not go to the truth itself, that did not go to God and to a God who was not only the ultimate cosmological hypothesis but also the true God, the God who gives life and enters into our lives.

Thus, Augustine's entire intellectual and spiritual development is also a valid model today in the relationship between faith and reason, a subject not only for believers but for every person who seeks the truth, a central theme for the balance and destiny of every human being. These two dimensions, faith and reason, should not be separated or placed in opposition; rather, they must always go hand in hand. As Augustine himself wrote after his conversion, faith and reason are "the two forces that lead us to knowledge" (*Contra Academicos* 3, 20, 43). In this regard, through the two rightly famous Augustinian formulas (cf. *Sermones* 43, 9) that express this coherent synthesis of faith and reason: *crede ut intelligas* ("I believe in order to understand")—believing paves the way to crossing the threshold of the truth—but also, and inseparably, *intellige ut credas* ("I understand, the better to believe"), the believer scrutinizes the truth to be able to find God and to believe.

Augustine's two affirmations express with effective immediacy and as much corresponding depth the synthesis of this problem in which the Catholic Church sees her own journey expressed. This synthesis had been acquiring its form in history even before Christ's coming, in the encounter between the Hebrew faith and Greek thought in Hellenistic Judaism. At a later period, this synthesis was taken up and developed by many Christian thinkers. The harmony between faith and reason means above all that God is not remote: he is not far from our reason and our life; he is close to every human being, close to our hearts and to our reason, if we truly set out on the journey.

Augustine felt this closeness of God to human beings with extraordinary intensity. God's presence in the human is profound and at the same time mysterious, but he can recognize and discover it deep down inside himself. "Do not go outside," the convert says, but "return to within yourself; truth dwells in the inner man; and if you find that your nature is changeable, transcend yourself. But remember, when you transcend yourself, you are transcending a soul that reasons. Reach, therefore, to where the light of reason is lit" (*De vera religione* 39, 72). It is just like what he himself stresses with a very famous statement at the beginning of the *Confessions*, a spiritual biography which he wrote in praise of God: "You have made us for yourself, and our heart is restless until it rests in you" (1, 1, 1).

God's remoteness is therefore equivalent to remoteness from oneself: "But," Augustine admitted (*Confessions*, 3, 6, 11), addressing God directly, "you were more inward than my most inward part and higher than the highest element within me," *interior intimo meo et superior summo meo*; so that, as he adds in another passage remembering the period before his conversion, "you were there before me, but I had departed from myself. I could not even find myself, much less you" (*Confessions*, 5, 2, 2). Precisely because Augustine lived this intellectual and spiritual journey in the first person, he could portray it in his works with such immediacy, depth, and wisdom, recognizing in two other famous passages from the *Confessions* (4, 4, 9 and 14, 22), that the human is "a great enigma" (*magna quaestio*) and "a great abyss" (*grande profundum*), an enigma and an abyss that only Christ can illuminate and save us from. This is important: a human who is distant from God is also distant from oneself, alienated from oneself, and can only find oneself by encountering God. In this way, one will come back to oneself, to one's true self, to one's true identity.

The human being, Augustine stresses later in *De Civitate Dei* (12, 27), is social by nature but antisocial by vice and is saved by Christ, the one Mediator between God and humanity and the "universal way of liberty and salvation," as my predecessor John Paul II said (*Augustinum Hipponensem*, n. 3). Outside this way, "which has never been lacking for the human race," St. Augustine says further, "no one has been set free; no one will be set free" (*De Civitate Dei*, 10, 32, 2). As the one mediator of salvation, Christ is head of the Church and mystically united with her to the point that Augustine could say, "We have become Christ. For, if he is the head, we, the members; he and we together are the whole man" (*In Iohannis evangelium tractatus* 21, 8).

People of God and House of God: the Church in Augustine's vision is therefore closely bound to the concept of the Body of Christ, founded on the christological reinterpretation of the Old Testament and on the sacramental life centered on the eucharist, in which the Lord gives us his body and transforms us into his body. It is then fundamental that the Church, the People of God in a christological and not a sociological sense, be truly inserted into Christ, who, as Augustine says in a beautiful passage, "prays for us, prays in us, and prays by us; he prays for us as our priest, he prays in us as our head, and he prays by us as our God: let us therefore recognize him as our voice and ourselves as his" (*Enarrationes in Psalmos* 85, 1).

At the end of the Apostolic Letter *Augustinum Hipponensem*, John Paul II wished to ask the saint himself what he would have to say to the people of today and answers first of all with the words Augustine entrusted to a letter dictated shortly after his conversion: "It seems to me that the hope of finding the truth must be restored to humankind" (*Epistulae* 1, 1); that truth which is Christ himself, true God, to whom is addressed one of the most beautiful prayers and most famous of the *Confessions* (10, 27, 38):

> Late have I loved you, beauty so old and so new: late have I loved you. And see, you were within and I was in the external world and sought you there, and in my unlovely state I plunged into those lovely created things which you made. You were with me, and I was not with you. The lovely things kept me far from you, though if they did not have their existence in you, they had no existence at all. You called and cried aloud and shattered my deafness. You were radiant and resplendent; you put to flight my blindness. You were fragrant, and I drew in my breath and now pant after you. I tasted you, and I feel but hunger and thirst for you. You touched me, and I am set on fire to attain the peace which is yours.

Here then, Augustine encountered God and throughout his life experienced him to the point that this reality—which is primarily his meeting with a person, Jesus—changed his life, as it changes the lives of everyone, men and women, who in every age have the grace to encounter him. Let us pray that the Lord will grant us this grace and thereby enable us to find his peace.

Chief Works

Augustine is the Father of the Church who left us the greatest number of works. Some of Augustine's writings were of major importance, not only for the history of Christianity but also for the formation of the whole of Western culture. The clearest example is the *Confessions*, undoubtedly one of the most widely read books of Christian antiquity. Like various Fathers of the Church in the first centuries but on an incomparably larger scale, the bishop of Hippo, in fact, exercised an extensive and persistent influence, as already appears from the superabundant manuscript transcriptions of his works, which are indeed extremely numerous.

He reviewed them himself in the *Retractationum* several years before he died, and shortly after his death they were correctly recorded in the *Indiculus* ("list") added by his faithful friend Possidius to his biography of St. Augustine, *Vita Augustini*. The list of Augustine's works was drafted with the explicit intention of keeping their memory alive while the Vandal invasion was sweeping through all of Roman Africa, and it included at least 1,030 writings numbered by their author, with others "that cannot be numbered because he did not give them any number." Possidius, the bishop of a neighboring city, dictated these words in Hippo itself, where he had taken refuge and where he witnessed his friend's death, and it is almost certain that he based his list on the catalog of Augustine's personal library. Today, more than 300 letters of the bishop of Hippo and almost 600 homilies are extant, but originally there were far more, perhaps even as many as between 3,000 and 4,000, the result of forty years of preaching by the former rhetorician who had chosen to follow Jesus and no longer to speak to important figures of the imperial court, but rather, to the simple populace of Hippo.

And in recent years, the discoveries of a collection of letters and several homilies have further enriched our knowledge of this great Father of the Church. "He wrote and published many books," Possidius wrote, "many sermons were delivered in church, transcribed and corrected, both to refute the various heresies and to interpret the Sacred Scriptures for the edification of the holy children of the Church. These works," his bishop-friend emphasized, "are so numerous that a scholar would find it difficult to read them all and learn to know them" (*Vita Augustini* 18, 9).

In the literary corpus of Augustine—more than a thousand publications divided into philosophical, apologetic, doctrinal, moral, monastic, exegetical, and antiheretical writings, in addition precisely to the letters and homilies—certain exceptional works of immense theological and philosophical breadth stand out. First of all, it is essential to remember the *Confessions*, mentioned above, written in thirteen books between 397 and 400 in praise of God. They are a sort of autobiography in the form of a dialogue with God. This literary genre actually mirrors St. Augustine's life, which was not one closed in on self, dispersed in many things, but was lived substantially as a dialogue with God, hence, a life with others. The title *Confessions* indicates the specific nature of this autobiography. In Christian Latin, this word *confessiones* developed from the tradition of the psalms and has two meanings that are nevertheless interwoven. In the first place, *confessiones* means the confession of our own faults, of the wretchedness of sin; but at the same time, *confessiones* also means praise of God, thanksgiving to God. Seeing our own wretchedness in the light of God becomes praise to God and thanksgiving, for God loves and accepts us, transforms us and raises us to himself. Of these *Confessions*, which met with great success during his lifetime, St. Augustine wrote: "They exercised such an influence on me while I was writing them and still exercise it when I reread them. Many brothers like these works" (*Retractationum*, 2, 6); and I can say that I am one of these "brothers." Thanks to the *Confessions*, moreover, we can follow step by step the inner journey of this extraordinary and passionate man of God. A less well-known but equally original and very important text is the *Retractationum*, composed in two books in about 427, in which St. Augustine, by then elderly, set down a "revision" *(retractatio)* of his entire opus, thereby bequeathing to us a unique and very precious literary document but also a teaching of sincerity and intellectual humility.

De Civitate Dei, an impressive work crucial to the development of Western political thought and the Christian theology of history, was written between 413 and 426 in twenty-two books. The occasion was the sack of Rome by the Goths in 410. Numerous pagans still alive and even many Christians said: Rome has fallen; the Christian God and the Apostles can now no longer protect the city. While the pagan divinities were present, Rome was the *caput mundi,* the great capital, and no one could have imagined that it would fall into enemy hands. Now, with the Christian God, this great city no longer seemed safe. Therefore, the God of the Christians did not protect; he could not be the God to whom to entrust oneself. Saint Augustine answered this objection, which also touched Christian hearts profoundly, with this impressive work, *De Civitate Dei*, explaining what we should and should not expect of God, and what the relationship is between the political sphere and the sphere of faith, of the Church. This book is also today a source for defining clearly between true secularism and the Church's competence, the great true hope that the faith gives to us.

This important book presents the history of humanity governed by divine providence but currently divided by two loves. This is the fundamental plan, its interpretation of history, which is the struggle between two loves: love of self, "to the point of indifference to God," and love of God, "to the point of indifference to the self" (*De Civitate Dei* 14, 28), to full freedom from the self for others in the light of God. This, therefore, is perhaps St. Augustine's greatest book and is of lasting importance. Equally important is the *De Trinitate*, a work in fifteen books on the central core of the Christian faith, faith in the Trinitarian God. It was written in two phases: the first twelve books between 399 and 412, published without the knowledge of Augustine, who in about 420 completed and revised the entire work. Here he reflects on the face of God and seeks to understand this mystery of God who is unique, the one Creator of the world, of us all, and yet this one God is precisely Trinitarian, a circle of love. He seeks to understand the unfathomable mystery: the actual Trinitarian being, in three persons, is the most real and profound unity of the one God. *De Doctrina Christiana* is instead a true and proper cultural introduction to the interpretation of the Bible and ultimately of Christianity itself, which had a crucial importance in the formation of Western culture.

Despite all his humility, Augustine must certainly have been aware of his own intellectual stature. Yet it was far more important to him to take the Christian message to the simple than to write lofty theological works. This deepest intention of his that guided his entire life appears in a letter written to his colleague Evodius, in which he informs him of his decision to suspend the dictation of the books of *De Trinitate* for the time being, "because they are too demanding and I think that few can understand them; it is therefore urgent to have more texts which we hope will be useful to many" (*Epistulae* 169, 1, 1). Thus, it served his purpose better to communicate the faith in a manner that all could understand rather than to write great theological works. The responsibility he felt acutely with regard to the popularization of the Christian message was later to become the origin of writings such as *De Catechizandis Rudibus*, a theory and also a method of catechesis, or the *Psalmus contra Partem Donati.*

The Donatists were the great problem of St. Augustine's Africa, a deliberately African schism. They said: true Christianity is African Christianity. They opposed Church unity. The great bishop fought against this schism all his life, seeking to convince the Donatists that only in unity could "Africanness" also be true. And to make himself understood by the simple, who could not understand the difficult Latin of the rhetorician, he said: I must even write with grammatical errors, in a very simplified Latin. And he did so, especially in this *Psalmus,* a sort of simple poem against the Donatists, in order to help all the people understand that it is only through Church unity that our relationship with God may be truly fulfilled for all and that peace may grow in the world.

The mass of homilies that he would often deliver "off the cuff," transcribed by tachygraphers during his preaching and immediately circulated, had a special importance in this production destined for a wider public. The very beautiful *Enarrationes in Psalmos,* read widely in the Middle Ages, stand out among them. The practice of publishing Augustine's thousands of homilies, often without the author's control, precisely explains their dissemination and later dispersion but also their vitality. In fact, because of the author's fame, the bishop of Hippo's sermons became very sought-after texts and, adapted to ever new contexts, also served as models for other bishops and priests.

A fresco in the Lateran that dates back to the fourth century shows that the iconographical tradition already depicted St. Augustine with a book in his hand, suggesting, of course, his literary opus, which had such a strong influence on the Christian mentality and Christian thought. But it also suggests his love for books and reading, as well as his knowledge of the great culture of the past. At his death, he left nothing, Possidius recounts, but "recommended that the library of the church with all the codes be kept carefully for future generations," especially those of his own works. In these, Possidius stresses, Augustine is "ever alive" and benefits his readers, although "I believe that those who were able to see and listen to him were able to draw greater benefit from being in touch with him when he himself was speaking in church, and especially those who experienced his daily life among the people" (*Vita Augustini* 31). Yes, for us too it would have been beautiful to be able to hear him speaking. Nonetheless, he is truly alive in his writings and present in us, and so we too see the enduring vitality of the faith to which he devoted his entire life.

A Journey of Conversions

After having dwelt on his life, works, and some aspects of his thought, I conclude the presentation of the figure of St. Augustine by returning to his inner experience, which made him one of Christian history's greatest converts.

In 2007, during my pilgrimage to Pavia to venerate the mortal remains of this Father of the Church, I particularly dedicated my reflection to this experience of his. By doing so, I wished to express to him the homage of the entire Catholic Church but also to manifest my personal devotion and gratitude in regard to a figure to whom I feel very linked for the role he has had in my life as a theologian, priest, and pastor.

Today, it is still possible to trace St. Augustine's experiences, thanks above all to the *Confessions,* which were written to praise God and which are at the origin of one of the most specific literary forms of the West, the autobiography or personal expression of one's self-knowledge. Anyone who encounters this extraordinary and fascinating book, still widely read today, soon realizes that Augustine's conversion was not sudden or fully accomplished at the beginning but can be defined, rather, as a true and proper journey that remains a model for each one of us. This itinerary certainly culminated with his conversion and then with baptism, but it was not concluded in that Easter Vigil of the year 387, when the African rhetorician was baptized in Milan by Bishop Ambrose. Augustine's journey of conversion, in fact, humbly continued to the very end of his life, so much so that one can truly say that his various steps—three can be easily distinguished—are one single great conversion.

St. Augustine was a passionate seeker of truth: he was from the beginning and then throughout his life. The first step of his conversion journey was accomplished exactly in his progressive nearing to Christianity. Actually, he had received from his mother, Monica, to whom he would always remain very closely bound, a Christian education, and even though he lived an errant life during the years of his youth, he always felt a deep attraction to Christ, having drunk in with his mother's milk the love for the Lord's name, as he himself emphasizes (cf. *Confessions,*

3, 4, 8). But also philosophy, especially that of a Platonic stamp, led him even closer to Christ, revealing to him the existence of the *Logos* or creative reason. Philosophy books showed him the existence of reason, from which the whole world came, but they could not tell him how to reach this *Logos*, which seemed so distant. Only by reading St. Paul's epistles within the faith of the Catholic Church was the truth fully revealed to him. This experience was summarized by Augustine in one of the most famous passages of the *Confessions*: he recounts that, in the torment of his reflections, withdrawing to a garden, he suddenly heard a child's voice chanting a rhyme never heard before: *tolle, lege, tolle, lege,* "pick up and read, pick up and read" (8, 12, 29). He then remembered the conversion of Anthony, the Father of Monasticism, and carefully returned to the Pauline codex that he had recently read, opened it, and his glance fell on the passage of the Epistle to the Romans where the Apostle exhorts to abandon the works of the flesh and to be clothed with Christ (cf. 13:13–14). He understood that those words in that moment were addressed personally to him; they came from God through the Apostle and indicated to him what he had to do at that time. Thus, he felt the darkness of doubt clearing and he finally found himself free to give himself entirely to Christ: he described it as "your converting me to yourself" (*Confessions* 8, 12, 30). This was the first and decisive conversion.

The African rhetorician reached this fundamental step in his long journey thanks to his passion for man and for the truth, a passion that led him to seek God, the great and inaccessible One. Faith in Christ made him understand that God, apparently so distant, in reality was not that at all. He, in fact, made himself near to us, becoming one of us. In this sense, faith in Christ brought Augustine's long search on the journey to truth to completion. Only a God who made himself "tangible," one of us, was finally a God to whom he could pray, for whom and with whom he could live. This is the way to take with courage and at the same time with humility, open to a permanent purification which each of us always needs. But with the Easter Vigil of 387, as we have said, Augustine's journey was not finished. He returned to Africa and founded a small monastery, where he retreated with a few friends to dedicate himself to the contemplative life and study. This was his life's dream. Now he was called to live totally for the truth, with the truth, in friendship with Christ, who is Truth: a beautiful dream that lasted three years, until he was, against his will, ordained a priest at Hippo and destined to serve the faithful, continuing, yes, to live with Christ and for Christ, but at the service of all. This was very difficult for him, but he understood from the beginning that only by living for others, and not simply for his private contemplation, could he really live with Christ and for Christ.

Thus, renouncing a life solely of meditation, Augustine learned, often with difficulty, to make the fruit of his intelligence available to others.

He learned to communicate his faith to simple people and thus learned to live for them in what became his hometown, tirelessly carrying out a generous and onerous activity which he describes in one of his most beautiful sermons: "To preach continuously, discuss, reiterate, edify, be at the disposal of everyone—it is an enormous responsibility, a great weight, an immense effort" (*Sermon* 339, 4). But he took this weight upon himself, understanding that it was exactly in this way that he could be closer to Christ. To understand that one reaches others with simplicity and humility was his true second conversion.

But there is a last step to Augustine's journey, a third conversion that brought him every day of his life to ask God for pardon. Initially, he thought that once he was baptized, in the life of communion with Christ, in the sacraments, in the eucharistic celebration, he would attain the life proposed in the Sermon on the Mount: the perfection bestowed by baptism and reconfirmed in the eucharist. During the last part of his life, he understood that what he had concluded at the beginning about the Sermon on the Mount—that is, now that we are Christians, we live this ideal permanently—was mistaken. Only Christ himself truly and completely accomplishes the Sermon on the Mount. We always need to be washed by Christ, who washes our feet, and be renewed by him. We need permanent conversion. Until the end, we need this humility that recognizes that we are sinners journeying along, until the Lord gives us his hand definitively and introduces us into eternal life. It was in this final attitude of humility, lived day after day, that Augustine died.

This attitude of profound humility before the only Lord Jesus led him also to experience an intellectual humility. Augustine, in fact, who is one of the great figures in the history of thought, in the last years of his life wanted to submit all his numerous works to a clear, critical examination. This was the origin of the *Retractationum* ("Revision"), which placed his truly great theological thought within the humble and holy faith that he simply refers to by the name *Catholic,* that is, of the Church. He wrote in this truly original book: "I understood that only one is truly perfect, and that the words of the Sermon on the Mount are completely realized in only one—in Jesus Christ himself. The whole Church, instead—all of us, including the Apostles—must pray everyday: Forgive us our sins as we forgive those who sin against us" (*De Sermone Domini in Monte* 1, 19, 1–3).

Augustine converted to Christ, who is Truth and love, followed him throughout his life, and became a model for every human being, for all of us in search of God. This is why I wanted to ideally conclude my pilgrimage to Pavia by consigning to the Church and to the world, before the tomb of this great lover of God, my first encyclical, titled *Deus Caritas Est*. I owe much, in fact, especially in the first part, to Augustine's thought. Even today, as in his time, humanity needs to know and above all to live this fundamental reality: God is love, and the encounter with God is the only response to the restlessness of the human heart; a heart inhabited by hope, still perhaps obscure and unconscious in many of our contemporaries but which already today opens us Christians to the future, so much so that St. Paul wrote that "in this hope we were saved" (Rom 8:24). I wished to devote my second encyclical to hope, *Spe Salvi*, and it is also largely indebted to Augustine and his encounter with God.

In a beautiful passage, St. Augustine defines prayer as the expression of desire and affirms that God responds by moving our hearts toward him. On our part, we must purify our desires and our hopes to welcome the sweetness of God (cf. *In I Ioannis* 4, 6). Indeed, only this opening of ourselves to others saves us. Let us pray, therefore, that we can follow the example of this great convert every day of our lives, and in every moment of our life encounter the Lord Jesus, the only One who saves us, purifies us, and gives us true joy, true life.

—*9, 16, and 30 January*
   20 and 27 February 2008

St. Leo the Great

CONTINUING OUR JOURNEY through the Fathers of the Church, true stars that shine in the distance, we next encounter a pope who, in 1754, Benedict XIV proclaimed a Doctor of the Church: St. Leo the Great. As the nickname soon attributed to him by tradition suggests, he was truly one of the greatest pontiffs to have honored the Roman See and made a very important contribution to strengthening its authority and prestige. He was the first bishop of Rome to have been called Leo, a name used subsequently by another twelve supreme pontiffs, and was also the first pope whose preaching to the people who gathered round him during celebrations has come down to us. We spontaneously think of him also in the context of today's Wednesday general audiences, which over the decades have become a customary meeting of the bishop of Rome with the faithful and the many visitors from every part of the world.

Leo was a Tuscan native. In about the year 430, he became a deacon of the Church of Rome, in which he acquired over time a very important position. In the year 440, his prominent role induced Galla Placidia, who then ruled the empire of the West, to send him to Gaul to heal a difficult situation. But in the summer of that year, Pope Sixtus III, whose name is associated with the magnificent mosaics in St. Mary Major's, died, and it was Leo who was elected to succeed him. Leo heard the news precisely while he was carrying out his peace mission in Gaul. Having returned to Rome, the new pope was consecrated on 29 September 440. This is how his pontificate began. It lasted more than twenty-one years and was undoubtedly one of the most important in the Church's history. Pope Leo died on 10 November 461 and was buried near the tomb of St. Peter. Today, his relics are preserved in one of the altars in the Vatican Basilica.

The times in which Pope Leo lived were very difficult: constant barbarian invasions, the gradual weakening of imperial authority in the West, and the long, drawn-out social crisis forced the bishop of Rome— as was to happen even more obviously a century and a half later during the pontificate of Gregory the Great—to play an important role in civil and political events. This, naturally, could only add to the importance and prestige of the Roman See. The fame of one particular episode in Leo's life has endured. It dates back to 452, when the pope, together with a Roman delegation, met Attila, chief of the Huns, in Mantua and dissuaded him from continuing the war of invasion by which he had already devastated the northeastern regions of Italy. Thus, he saved the rest of the peninsula. This important event soon became memorable and lives on as an emblematic sign of the pontiff's action for peace. Unfortunately, the outcome of another papal initiative three years later was not as success-ful, yet it was a sign of courage that still amazes us: in the spring of 455, Leo did not manage to prevent Genseric's Vandals, who had reached the gates of Rome, from invading the undefended city that they plundered for two weeks. This gesture of the pope, who, defenseless and surrounded by his clergy, went forth to meet the invader to implore him to desist, nevertheless prevented Rome from being burned and assured that the Basilicas of St. Peter, St. Paul, and St. John—in which part of the terrified population sought refuge—were spared.

We are familiar with Pope Leo's action thanks to his most beauti-ful sermons—almost 100 in a splendid and clear Latin have been pre-served—and thanks to his approximately 150 letters. In these texts, the pontiff appears in all his greatness, devoted to the service of truth in charity through an assiduous exercise of the Word which shows him to us as both theologian and pastor. Leo the Great, constantly thoughtful of his faithful and of the people of Rome but also of communion between the different churches and of their needs, was a tireless champion and upholder of the Roman primacy, presenting himself as the Apostle Peter's authentic heir: the many bishops who gathered at the Council of Chalce-don, the majority of whom came from the East, were well aware of this.

This council, held in 451 and in which 350 bishops took part, was the most important assembly ever to have been celebrated in the history of the Church. Chalcedon represents the sure goal of the Christology of the three previous Ecumenical Councils: Nicaea in 325, Constantinople in 381, and Ephesus in 431. By the sixth century, these four councils that sum up the faith of the ancient Church were already being compared to the four Gospels. This is what Gregory the Great affirms in a famous let-ter (1, 24): "I confess that I receive and revere, as the four books of the Gospel, so also the four Councils," because on them, Gregory explains further, "as on a four-square stone, rises the structure of the holy faith." The Council of Chalcedon, which rejected the heresy of Eutyches, who denied the true human nature of the Son of God, affirmed the union in his one person, without confusion and without separation, of his two natures, human and divine.

The pope asserted this faith in Jesus Christ, true God and true man, in an important doctrinal text addressed to the bishop of Constantinople, the so-called *Tome to Flavian*, which, read at Chalcedon, was received by the bishops present with an eloquent acclamation. Information on it has been preserved in the proceedings of the council: "Peter has spoken through the mouth of Leo," the Council Fathers announced in unison. From this intervention in particular, but also from others made during the christological controversy in those years, it is clear that the pope felt with special urgency his responsibilities as successor of Peter, whose role in the Church is unique since "to one Apostle alone was entrusted what was communicated to all the Apostles," as Leo said in one of his sermons for the Feast of Sts. Peter and Paul (83, 2). And the pontiff was able to exercise these responsibilities, in the West as in the East, intervening in various circumstances with caution, firmness, and lucidity through his writings and legates. In this manner, he showed how exercising the Roman primacy was as necessary then as it is today to effectively serve communion, a characteristic of Christ's one Church.

Aware of the historical period in which he lived and of the change that was taking place—from pagan Rome to Christian Rome—in a period of profound crisis, Leo the Great knew how to make himself close to the people and the faithful with his pastoral action and his preaching. He enlivened charity in a Rome tried by famines, an influx of refugees, injustice, and poverty. He opposed pagan superstitions and the actions of Manichaean groups. He associated the liturgy with the daily life of Christians: for example, by combining the practice of fasting with charity and almsgiving above all on the occasion of the *Quattro tempora*, which in the course of the year marked the change of seasons. In particular, Leo the Great taught his faithful, and his words still apply for us today, that the Christian liturgy is not the memory of past events, but the actualization of invisible realities which act in the lives of each one of us. This is what he stressed in a sermon (cf. 64, 1–2) on Easter, to be celebrated in every season of the year "not so much as something of the past as rather an event of the present." All this fits into a precise project, the holy pontiff insisted: just as, in fact, the Creator enlivened with the breath of rational life man formed from the dust of the ground, after the original sin, he sent his Son into the world to restore to man his lost dignity and to destroy the dominion of the devil through the new life of grace.

This is the christological mystery to which St. Leo the Great, with his Letter to the Council of Ephesus, made an effective and essential contribution, confirming for all time, through this council, what St. Peter said at Caesarea Philippi. With Peter and as Peter, he professed: "You are the Christ, the Son of the living God." And so it is that God and man together "are not foreign to the human race but alien to sin" (cf. *Serm.* 64). Through the force of this christological faith, he was a great messenger of peace and love. He thus shows us the way: in faith we learn charity. Let us therefore learn with St. Leo the Great to believe in Christ, true God and true man, and to implement this faith every day in action for peace and love of neighbor.

—*5 March 2008*

BOETHIUS AND CASSIODORUS

I NOW DISCUSS TWO ECCLESIASTICAL WRITERS, Boethius and Cassiodorus, who lived in some of the most turbulent years in the Christian West and in the Italian peninsula in particular. Odoacer, King of the Rugians, a Germanic race, had rebelled, putting an end to the Western Roman Empire (476), but it was not long before he was killed by Theodoric's Ostrogoths, who had controlled the Italian Peninsula for some decades. Boethius, born in Rome in about 480 from the noble Anicius lineage, entered public life when he was still young and by age twenty-five was already a senator. Faithful to his family's tradition, he devoted himself to politics, convinced that it would be possible to temper the fundamental structure of Roman society with the values of the new peoples. And in this new time of cultural encounter, he considered it his role to reconcile and bring together these two cultures, the classical Roman and the nascent Ostrogoth culture. Thus, he was also politically active under Theodoric, who at the outset held him in high esteem. In spite of this public activity, Boethius did not neglect his studies and dedicated himself in particular to acquiring a deep knowledge of philosophical and religious subjects. However, he also wrote manuals on arithmetic, geometry, music, and astronomy, all with the intention of passing on the great Greco-Roman culture to the new generations, to the new times. In this context, in his commitment to fostering the encounter of cultures, he used the categories of Greek philosophy to present the Christian faith, here too seeking a synthesis between the Hellenistic-Roman heritage and the gospel message. For this very reason, Boethius was described as the last representative of ancient Roman culture and the first of the medieval intellectuals.

Boethius's most famous work is undoubtedly *De Consolatione Philosophiae,* which he wrote in prison to help explain his unjust detention. In fact, he had been accused of plotting against King Theodoric for having taken the side of his friend Senator Albinus in a court case. But this was a pretext. Actually, Theodoric, an Arian and a barbarian, suspected that Boethius was sympathizing with the Byzantine Emperor Justinian. Boethius was tried and sentenced to death. He was executed on 23 October 524, when he was only forty-four years old. It is precisely because of his tragic end that he can also speak from the heart of his own experience to contemporary man, and especially to the multitudes who suffer the same fate because of the injustice inherent in so much of "human justice." Through this work, *De Consolatione Philosophiae,* he sought consolation, enlightenment, and wisdom in prison. And he said that precisely in this situation he knew how to distinguish between apparent goods, which disappear in prison, and true goods such as genuine friendship, which even in prison do not disappear. The loftiest good is God: Boethius, and he teaches us this, learned not to sink into a fatalism that extinguishes hope. He teaches us that it is not the event but providence that governs, and providence has a face. It is possible to speak to providence because providence is God. Thus, even in prison, he was left with the possibility of prayer, of dialogue with the One who saves us. At the same time, even in this situation, he retained his sense of the beauty of culture and remembered the teaching of the great ancient Greek and Roman philosophers such as Plato, Aristotle—he had begun to translate these Greeks into Latin—Cicero, Seneca, and also poets such as Tibullus and Virgil.

Boethius held that philosophy, in the sense of the quest for true wisdom, was the true medicine of the soul (bk. 1). On the other hand, one can only experience authentic happiness within one's own interiority (bk. 2). Boethius thus succeeded in finding meaning by thinking of his own personal tragedy in the light of a sapiential text of the Old Testament (Wis 7:30—8:1), which he cites: "Against wisdom evil does not prevail. She reaches mightily from one end of the earth to the other, and she orders all things well" (bk. 3, 12: *PL* 63, col. 780). The so-called prosperity of the wicked is therefore proven to be false (bk. 4), and the providential nature of *adversa fortuna* is highlighted. Life's difficulties not only reveal how transient and short-lived life is, but are even shown to serve for identifying and preserving authentic relations among human beings. *Adversa fortuna,* in fact, makes it possible to discern false friends from true and makes one realize that nothing is more precious to the human being than a true friendship. The fatalistic acceptance of a condition of suffering is nothing short of perilous, the believer Boethius added, because "it eliminates at its roots the very possibility of prayer and of theological hope, which form the basis of man's relationship with God" (bk. 5, 3: *PL* 63, col. 842).

The final peroration of *De Consolatione Philosophiae* can be considered a synthesis of the entire teaching that Boethius addressed to himself and all who might find themselves in his same condition. Thus, in prison he wrote: "So combat vices: dedicate yourselves to a virtuous life oriented by hope, which draws the heart upwards until it reaches heaven with prayers nourished by humility. Should you refuse to lie, the imposition you have suffered can change into the enormous advantage of always having before your eyes the supreme judge, who sees and knows how things truly are" (bk. 5, 6: *PL* 63, col. 862). Every prisoner, regardless of the reason why he ended up in prison, senses how burdensome this particular human condition is, especially when it is brutalized, as it was for Boethius, by recourse to torture. Then particularly absurd is the condition of those like Boethius, whom the city of Pavia recognizes and celebrates in the liturgy as a martyr of the faith, who are tortured to death for no other reason than their own ideals and political and religious convictions. Boethius, the symbol of an immense number of people unjustly imprisoned in all ages and on all latitudes, is, in fact, an objective entrance way that gives access to contemplation of the mysterious Crucified One of Golgotha.

Marcus Aurelius Cassiodorus was a contemporary of Boethius, a Calabrian who was born in Scyllacium in about 485 and who died at a very advanced age in Vivarium in 580. Cassiodorus, a man with a privileged social status, likewise devoted himself to political life and cultural commitment as few others in the Roman West of his time. Perhaps the only men who could stand on an equal footing in this twofold interest were Boethius, whom we have mentioned, and Gregory the Great, the future pope of Rome (590–604). Aware of the need to prevent all the human and humanist patrimony accumulated in the golden age of the Roman Empire from vanishing into oblivion, Cassiodorus collaborated generously, and with the highest degree of political responsibility, with the new peoples who had crossed the boundaries of the empire and settled in Italy. He too was a model of cultural encounter, of dialogue, of reconciliation. Historical events did not permit him to make his political and cultural dreams come true; he wanted to create a synthesis between the Roman and Christian traditions of Italy and the new culture of the Goths. These same events, however, convinced him of the providentiality of the monastic movement that was putting down roots in Christian lands. He decided to support it and gave it all his material wealth and spiritual energy.

Cassiodorus conceived the idea of entrusting to the monks the task of recovering, preserving, and transmitting to those to come the immense cultural patrimony of the ancients so that it would not be lost. For this reason, he founded *Vivarium,* a cenobitic community in which everything was organized in such a way that the monk's intellectual work was esteemed as precious and indispensable. He arranged that even those monks who had no academic training must not be involved solely in physical labor and farming but also in transcribing manuscripts and thus helping to transmit the great culture to future generations. And this was by no means at the expense of monastic and Christian spiritual dedication or of charitable activity for the poor. In his teaching, expounded in various works but especially in the treatise *De Anima* and in the *Institutiones Divinarum Litterarum* (cf. *PL* 69, col. 1108), prayer nourished by Sacred Scripture and particularly by assiduous recourse to the Psalms (cf. *PL* 69, 1149) always has a central place as the essential sustenance for all. Thus, for example, this most learned Calabrian introduced his *Expositio in Psalterium*: "Having rejected and abandoned in Ravenna the demands of a political career marked by the disgusting taste of worldly concerns, having enjoyed the Psalter, a book that came from heaven, as true honey of the soul, I dived into it avidly, thirsting to examine it without a pause, to steep myself in that salutary sweetness, having had enough of the countless disappointments of active life" (*PL* 70, col. 10). The search for God, the aspiration to contemplate God, Cassiodorus notes, continues to be the permanent goal of monastic life (cf. *PL* 69, col. 1107). Nonetheless, he adds that with the help of divine grace (cf. *PL* 69, col. 1131, 1142), greater profit can be attained from the revealed Word with the use of scientific discoveries and the "profane" cultural means that were possessed in the past by the Greeks and Romans (cf. *PL* 69, col. 1140). Personally, Cassiodorus dedicated himself to philosophical, theological, and exegetical studies without any special creativity, but was attentive to the insights he considered valid in others. He read Jerome and Augustine in particular with respect and devotion. Of the latter he said: "In Augustine there is such a great wealth of writings that it seems to me impossible to find anything that has not already been abundantly treated by him" (cf. *PL* 70, col. 10). Citing Jerome, on the other hand, he urged the monks of *Vivarium*: "It is not only those who fight to the point of bloodshed or who live in virginity who win the palm of victory but also all who, with God's help, triumph over physical vices and preserve their upright faith. But in order that you may always, with God's help, more easily overcome the world's pressures and enticements while remaining in it as pilgrims constantly journeying forward, seek first to guarantee for yourselves the salutary help suggested by the first Psalm, which recommends meditation night and day on the law of the Lord. Indeed, the enemy will not find any gap through which to assault you if all your attention is taken up by Christ" (*De Institutione Divinarum Scripturarum* 32: *PL* 70, col. 1147). This is a recommendation we can also accept as valid. In fact, we live in a time of intercultural encounter, of the danger of violence that destroys cultures, and of the necessary commitment to pass on important values and to teach the new generations the path of reconciliation and peace. We find this path by turning to the God with the human face, the God who revealed himself to us in Christ.

—*12 March 2008*

St. Benedict of Nursia

BENEDICT, THE FOUNDER OF WESTERN MONASTICISM, is also the patron of my pontificate. I begin with words that St. Gregory the Great wrote about St. Benedict: "The man of God who shone on this earth among so many miracles was just as brilliant in the eloquent exposition of his teaching" (cf. *Dialogues 2, 36*). The great pope wrote these words in 592. The holy monk, who had died barely fifty years earlier, lived on in people's memories and especially in the flourishing religious order he had founded.

Saint Benedict of Nursia, with his life and his work, had a fundamental influence on the development of European civilization and culture. The most important source on Benedict's life is the second book of St. Gregory the Great's *Dialogues*. It is not a biography in the classical sense. In accordance with the ideas of his time, by giving the example of a real man, St. Benedict in this case, Gregory wished to illustrate the ascent to the peak of contemplation which can be achieved by those who abandon themselves to God. He therefore gives us a model for human life in the climb toward the summit of perfection. Saint Gregory the Great also tells in this book of the *Dialogues* of many miracles worked by the saint. Here too he does not merely wish to recount something curious but rather to show how God, by admonishing, helping, and even punishing, intervenes in the practical situations of man's life. Gregory's aim was to demonstrate that God is not a distant hypothesis placed at the origin of the world but is present in the life of man, of every man.

This perspective of the "biographer" is also explained in light of the general context of his time: straddling the fifth and sixth centuries, "the world was overturned by a tremendous crisis of values and institutions caused by the collapse of the Roman Empire, the invasion of new peoples, and the decay of morals." But in this terrible situation, here, in this very city of Rome, Gregory presented St. Benedict as a "luminous star" in order to point the way out of the "black night of history" (cf. John Paul II, 18 May 1979). In fact, the saint's work and particularly his *Rule* were to prove heralds of an authentic spiritual leaven which, in the course of the centuries, far beyond the boundaries of his country and time, changed the face of Europe following the fall of the political unity created by the Roman Empire, inspiring a new spiritual and cultural unity, that of the Christian faith shared by the peoples of the Continent. This is how the reality we call "Europe" came into being.

Saint Benedict was born around the year 480. As St. Gregory said, he came *ex provincia Nursiae*—from the province of Nursia. His well-to-do parents sent him to study in Rome. However, he did not stay long in the

Eternal City. As a fully plausible explanation, Gregory mentions that the young Benedict was put off by the dissolute lifestyle of many of his fellow students and did not wish to make the same mistakes. He wanted only to please God: *soli Deo placere desiderans (II Dialogues,* Prologue 1). Thus, even before he finished his studies, Benedict left Rome and withdrew to the solitude of the mountains east of Rome. After a short stay in the village of Enfide (today, Affile), where for a time he lived with a "religious community" of monks, he became a hermit in the neighboring locality of Subiaco. He lived there completely alone for three years in a cave, which has been the heart of a Benedictine monastery called the "Sacro Speco" (Holy Grotto) since the early Middle Ages. The period in Subiaco, a time of solitude with God, was a time of maturation for Benedict. It was here that he bore and overcame the three fundamental temptations of every human being: the temptation of self-affirmation and the desire to put oneself at the center, the temptation of sensuality, and, last, the temptation of anger and revenge. In fact, Benedict was convinced that only after overcoming these temptations would he be able to say a useful word to others about their own situations of neediness. Thus, having tranquilized his soul, he could be in full control of the drive of his ego and thus create peace around him. Only then did he decide to found his first monasteries in the Valley of the Anio, near Subiaco.

In the year 529, Benedict left Subiaco and settled in Monte Cassino. Some have explained this move as an escape from the intrigues of an envious local cleric. However, this attempt at an explanation hardly proved convincing since the latter's sudden death did not induce Benedict to return (*II Dialogues* 8). In fact, this decision was called for because he had entered a new phase of inner maturity and monastic experience. According to Gregory the Great, Benedict's exodus from the remote Valley of the Anio to Monte Cassio, a plateau dominating the vast surrounding plain, which can be seen from afar, has a symbolic character: a hidden monastic life has its own raison d'être, but a monastery also has its public purpose in the life of the Church and of society, and it must give visibility to the faith as a force of life. Indeed, when Benedict's earthly life ended on 21 March 547, he bequeathed with his *Rule* and the Benedictine family he founded a heritage that bore fruit in the passing centuries and is still bearing fruit throughout the world.

Throughout the second book of his *Dialogues,* Gregory shows us how St. Benedict's life was steeped in an atmosphere of prayer, the foundation of his existence. Without prayer, there is no experience of God. Yet Benedict's spirituality was not an interiority removed from reality. In the anxiety and confusion of his day, he lived under God's gaze and in this very way never lost sight of the duties of daily life and of man with his practical needs. Seeing God, he understood the reality of man and his mission. In his *Rule,* he describes monastic life as "a school for the service of the Lord" (Prologue 45) and advises his monks, "Let nothing be preferred to the Work of God" (that is, the Divine Office or the Liturgy of the Hours) (43, 3). However, Benedict states that in the first place prayer is an act of listening (Prologue 9–11), which must then be expressed in action. "The Lord is waiting every day for us to respond to his holy admonitions by our deeds" (Prologue 35). Thus, the monk's life becomes a fruitful symbiosis between action and contemplation, "so that God may be glorified in all things" (57, 9). In contrast with a facile and egocentric self-fulfilment, today often exalted, the first and indispensable commitment of a disciple of St. Benedict is the sincere search for God (58, 7) on the path mapped out by the humble and obedient Christ (5, 13), whose love he must put before all else (4, 21; 72, 11), and in this way, in the service of the other, he becomes a man of service and peace. In the exercise of obedience practiced by faith inspired by love (5, 2), the monk achieves humility (5, 1), to which the *Rule* dedicates an entire chapter (7). In this way, one conforms ever more to Christ and attains true self-fulfillment as a creature in the image and likeness of God.

The obedience of the disciple must correspond with the wisdom of the abbot who, in the monastery, "is believed to hold the place of Christ" (2, 2; 63, 13). The figure of the abbot, which is described above all in chapter 2 of the *Rule* with a profile of spiritual beauty and demanding commitment, can be considered a self-portrait of Benedict, since, as St. Gregory the Great wrote, "The holy man could not teach otherwise than as he himself lived" (cf. *Dialogues* 2, 36). The abbot must be at the same time a tender father and a strict teacher (cf. 2, 24), a true educator. Inflexible against vices, he is nevertheless called above all to imitate the tenderness of the Good Shepherd (27, 8), to "serve rather than to rule" (64, 8) in order "to show them all what is good and holy by his deeds more than by his words" and "illustrate the divine precepts by his example" (2, 12). To be able to decide responsibly, the abbot must also be a person who listens to "the brethren's views" (3, 2), because "the Lord often reveals to the youngest what is best" (3, 3). This provision makes a *Rule* written almost fifteen centuries ago surprisingly modern! A person with public responsibility even in small circles must always be one who can listen and learn from what he hears.

Benedict describes the *Rule* he wrote as "minimal, just an initial outline" (cf. 73, 8); in fact, however, he offers useful guidelines not only for monks but for all who seek guidance on their journey toward God. For its moderation, humanity, and sober discernment between the essential and the secondary in spiritual life, his *Rule* has retained its illuminating power even today. By proclaiming St. Benedict Patron of Europe on 24 October 1964, Paul VI intended to recognize the marvelous work the saint achieved with his *Rule* for the formation of the civilization and culture of Europe. Having recently emerged from a century that was deeply wounded by two world wars and the collapse of the great ideologies, now revealed as tragic utopias, Europe today is in search of its own identity. Of course, in order to create new and lasting unity, political, economic, and juridical instruments are important; but it is also necessary to awaken an ethical and spiritual renewal that draws on the Christian roots of the continent. Otherwise, a new Europe cannot be built. Without this vital sap, man is exposed to the danger of succumbing to the ancient temptation of seeking to redeem himself by himself—a utopia which in different ways in twentieth-century Europe, as Pope John Paul II pointed out, has caused "a regression without precedent in the tormented history of humanity" (*Address to the Pontifical Council for Culture*, 12 January 1990). Today, in seeking true progress, let us also listen to the *Rule* of St. Benedict as a guiding light on our journey. The great monk is still a true master at whose school we can learn to become proficient in true humanism.

—*9 April 2008*

Pseudo-Dionysius the Areopagite

In the course of my catechesis on the Fathers of the Church, I speak next of a rather mysterious figure: a sixth-century theologian whose name is unknown and who wrote under the pseudonym of Dionysius the Areopagite. With this pseudonym, he was alluding to the passage of Scripture, the event recounted by St. Luke in chapter 17 of the Acts of the Apostles, where he tells how Paul preached in Athens at the Areopagus to an elite group of the important Greek intellectual world. In the end, the majority of his listeners proved not to be interested and went away jeering at him. Yet some, St. Luke says a few, approached Paul and opened themselves to the faith. The evangelist gives us two names: Dionysius, a member of the Areopagus, and a woman named Damaris.

If five centuries later the author of these books chose the pseudonym "Dionysius the Areopagite," it means that his intention was to put Greek wisdom at the service of the Gospel, to foster the encounter of Greek culture and intelligence with the proclamation of Christ; he wanted to do what this Dionysius had intended, that is, to make Greek thought converge with St. Paul's proclamation; being a Greek, he wanted to become a disciple of St. Paul, hence a disciple of Christ.

Why did he hide his name and choose this pseudonym? One part of the answer I have already given: he wanted, precisely, to express this fundamental intention of his thought. But there are two hypotheses concerning this anonymity and pseudonym. The first hypothesis says that it was a deliberate falsification by which, in dating his works back to the first century, to the time of St. Paul, he wished to give his literary opus a quasi-apostolic authority. But there is another, better hypothesis than this, which seems to me barely credible: namely, that he himself desired to make an act of humility; he did not want to glorify his own name; he did not want to build a monument to himself with his work but rather truly to serve the gospel, to create an ecclesial theology, neither individual nor based on himself. Actually, he succeeded in elaborating a theology which, of course, we can date to the sixth century but cannot attribute to any of the figures of that period: it is a somewhat "deindividualized" theology, that is, a theology that expresses a common thought and language. It was a period of fierce polemics following the Council of Chalcedon; indeed, he said in his *Seventh Epistle*: "I do not wish to spark polemics; I simply speak of the truth; I seek the truth." And the light of truth by itself causes errors to fall away and makes what is good shine forth. And with this principle, he purified Greek thought and related it to the gospel. This principle, which he affirms in his seventh letter, is also the expression of a true spirit of dialogue: it is not about seeking the things that separate but seeking the truth in Truth itself. This then radiates and causes errors to fade away.

Therefore, although this author's theology is, so to speak, "suprapersonal," truly ecclesial, we can place it in the sixth century. Why? The Greek spirit, which he placed at the service of the gospel, he encountered in the books of Proclus, who died in Athens in 485. Proclus belonged to late Platonism, a current of thought that had transformed Plato's philosophy into a sort of religion, whose ultimate purpose was to create a great apologetic for Greek polytheism and return, following Christianity's success, to the ancient Greek religion. He wanted to demonstrate that in reality, the divinities were the active forces in the cosmos. The consequence to be drawn from this was that polytheism must be considered truer than monotheism, with its single Creator God. What Proclus was demonstrating was a great cosmic system of divinity, of mysterious forces, through which, in this deified cosmos, one could find access to the divinity. However, he made a distinction between paths for the simple, who were incapable of rising to the heights of truth—certain rites could suffice for them—and paths for the wise, who were to purify themselves to arrive at the pure light.

As can be seen, this thought is profoundly anti-Christian. It is a late reaction to the triumph of Christianity, an anti-Christian use of Plato, whereas a Christian interpretation of the great philosopher was already in course. It is interesting that this Pseudo-Dionysius dared to avail himself of this very thought to demonstrate the truth of Christ; to transform this polytheistic universe into a cosmos created by God, into the harmony of God's cosmos, where every force is praise of God, and to show this great harmony, this symphony of the cosmos that goes from the seraphim to the angels and archangels, to humans and to all the creatures which, together, reflect God's beauty and are praise of God. He thus transformed the polytheistic image into a praise of the Creator and his creature. In this way, we can discover the essential characteristics of his thought: first and foremost, it is cosmic praise. All creation speaks of God and is praise of God. Since the creature is praise of God, Pseudo-Dionysius's theology became a liturgical theology: God is found above all in praising him, not only in reflection; and the liturgy is not something made by us, something invented in order to have a religious experience for a certain period of time; it is singing with the choir of creatures and entering into cosmic reality itself. And in this very way, the liturgy, apparently only ecclesiastical, becomes expansive and great; it becomes our union with the language of all creatures. He says: God cannot be spoken of in an abstract way; speaking of God is always, he says using a Greek word, a *hymnein*, singing for God with the great hymn of the creatures, which is reflected and made concrete in liturgical praise. Yet, although his theology is cosmic, ecclesial, and liturgical, it is also profoundly personal.

He created the first great mystical theology. Indeed, with him the word "mystic" acquires a new meaning. Until then for Christians such a word was equivalent to the word "sacramental," that is, what pertains to the *mysterion,* to the sacrament. With him the word *mystic* becomes more personal, more intimate: it expresses the soul's journey toward God. And how can God be found? Here we note once again an important element in his dialogue between Greek philosophy and Christianity, and in particular biblical faith. Apparently what Plato says and what the great philosophy on God says is far loftier, far truer; the Bible appears somewhat "barbaric," simple or precritical one might say today; but he remarks that precisely this is necessary, so that in this way we can understand that the loftiest concepts on God never reach his true grandeur: they always fall short of it. In fact, these images enable us to understand that God is above every concept; in the simplicity of the images, we find more truth than in great concepts. The face of God is our inability to express truly what he is. In this way, one speaks, and Pseudo-Dionysius himself speaks, of a "negative theology." It is easier for us to say what God is not rather than to say what he truly is. Only through these images can we intuit his true face; moreover, this face of God is very concrete: it is Jesus Christ.

Although Dionysius shows us, following Proclus, the harmony of the heavenly choirs in such a way that it seems that they all depend on one another, it is true that on our journey toward God we are still very far from him. Pseudo-Dionysius shows that in the end the journey to God is God himself, who makes himself close to us in Jesus Christ. Thus, a great and mysterious theology also becomes very concrete, both in the interpretation of the liturgy and in the discourse on Jesus Christ: with all this, Dionysius the Areopagite exerted a strong influence on all medieval theology and on all mystical theology, both in the East and in the West. He was virtually rediscovered in the thirteenth century, especially by St. Bonaventure, the great Franciscan theologian who in this mystical theology found the conceptual instrument for reinterpreting the heritage, so simple and profound, of St. Francis. Together with Dionysius, the "Poverello" tells us that in the end love sees more than reason. Where the light of love shines, the shadows of reason are dispelled; love sees, love is an eye, and experience gives us more than reflection. Bonaventure saw in St. Francis what this experience is: it is the experience of a very humble, very realistic journey, day by day; it is walking with Christ, accepting his cross. In this poverty and in this humility, in the humility that is also lived in ecclesiality, is an experience of God that is loftier than that attained by reflection. In it we really touch God's heart.

Today Dionysius the Areopagite has a new relevance: he appears as a great mediator in the modern dialogue between Christianity and the mystical theologies of Asia, whose characteristic feature is the conviction that it is impossible to say who God is, that only indirect things can be said about him; that God can only be spoken of with the "not," and that it is only possible to reach him by entering into this indirect experience of "not." And here a similarity can be seen between the thought of the Areopagite and that of Asian religions; he can be a mediator today as he was between the Greek spirit and the gospel.

In this context, it can be seen that dialogue does not accept superficiality. It is precisely when one enters into the depths of the encounter with Christ that an ample space for dialogue also opens. When one encounters the light of truth, one realizes that it is a light for everyone; polemics disappear, and it is possible to understand one another, or at least to speak to one another, to come closer. The path of dialogue consists precisely in being close to God in Christ, in a deep encounter with him, in the experience of the truth which opens us to the light and helps us reach out to others with the light of truth, the light of love. And in the end, he tells us: take the path of experience, the humble experience of faith, every day. Then the heart is enlarged and can see and also illumine reason so that it perceives God's beauty. Let us pray to the Lord to help us today too to place the wisdom of our day at the service of the gospel, discovering ever anew the beauty of faith, the encounter with God in Christ.

—*14 May 2008*

St. Romanus the Melodist

A LITTLE-KNOWN FIGURE, ROMANUS THE MELODIST, was born in about 490 in Emesa (today Homs), in Syria. Theologian, poet, and composer, he belonged to the great ranks of theologians who transformed theology into poetry. Let us think of his compatriot, St. Ephrem the Syrian, who lived two hundred years before him. However, we can also think of Western theologians, such as St. Ambrose, whose hymns are still part of our liturgy and still move hearts; or of a theologian, a very vigorous thinker such as St. Thomas, who gave us hymns for the Feast of Corpus Christi; we think of St. John of the Cross and of so many others. Faith is love and therefore creates poetry and music. Faith is joy, therefore it creates beauty.

Thus, Romanus the Melodist is one of these, a poet theologian and composer. Having acquired the rudiments of Greek and Syrian culture in his native town, he moved to Berytus (Beirut), perfecting there his classical education and his knowledge of rhetoric. After being ordained a permanent deacon (c. 515), he was a preacher there for three years. He then moved to Constantinople toward the end of the reign of Anastasius I (c. 518) and settled there in the monastery adjacent to the Church of the *Theotokos*, the Mother of God. It was here that the key episode of his life occurred: the *Synaxarion* (The Lives of the Orthodox saints) informs us of the apparition of the Mother of God in a dream, and of the gift of the poetic charism. In fact, Mary enjoined him to swallow a scroll. On awakening the following morning, it was the Feast of the Nativity of the Lord, Romanus began declaiming from the ambo, "Today the Virgin gives birth to the Transcendent" (Hymn *"On the Nativity" I, Proemio*). So it was that he became a homilist-cantor until his death (after 555).

Romanus lives on in history as one of the most representative authors of liturgical hymns. At that time, the homily was virtually the only opportunity for catechetical instruction afforded to the faithful. Thus, Romanus is an eminent witness of the religious feeling of his epoch, but also of a lively and original catechesis. In his compositions, we can appreciate the creativity of this form of catechesis, the creativity of the theological thought and aesthetics and sacred hymnography of that time. The place in which Romanus preached was a sanctuary on the outskirts of Constantinople: he would mount the ambo that stood in the center of the church and speak to the community utilizing a somewhat extravagant technique: he referred to the mural depictions or icons arranged on the ambo, and even made use of dialogue. He sung his homilies in metric verse known as *kontakia*. The term *kontakion,* "little rod," would seem to refer to the staff around which a liturgical or other manuscript was wound. Eighty-nine *kontakia* bearing Romanus's name have come down to us, but tradition attributes a thousand to him.

In the works of Romanus, every *kontakion* is composed of strophes, the majority of which go from eighteen to twenty-four, with an equal number of syllables, structured on the model of the first strophe, the *irmo*. The rhythmic accents in the verses of all the strophes are modeled on those of the *irmo*. Each strophe ends with a refrain (*efimnio*), which is usually identical in order to create poetic unity. Furthermore, the initial letter of each stanza spell the author's name (*acrostic*), and are often preceded by the adjective "humble." A prayer referring to the events celebrated or evoked concludes the hymn. After the biblical reading, Romanus sang the *Proemium*, usually in the form of a prayer or supplication. Thus he announced the topic of the sermon and explained the *refrain* to be repeated in chorus at the end of each stanza, which he delivered in rhythmic prose.

An important example is offered to us by the *kontakion* for Good Friday: it is a dramatic dialogue between Mary and her son that takes place on the Way of the Cross. Mary says: "Where are you going, my Child? For whose sake are you finishing this swift race? I never thought I would see you, my Son, in such necessity, nor did I ever believe that the lawless would rage so, and unjustly stretch out their hands against you." Jesus answers: "Why, mother, do you weep? . . . Lest I suffer? Lest I die? How then should I save Adam?" Mary's son consoles his mother, but reminds her of her role in the history of salvation: "Put aside your grief, mother, put it aside; mourning is not right for you who have been called 'Full of Grace'" (*Mary at the Foot of the Cross* 1–2; 4–5). Then in the hymn on Abraham's sacrifice, Sarah claims for herself the decision on Isaac's life. Abraham says: "When Sarah hears, my Lord, all your words, upon knowing your will, she will say to me: If the one who has given it desires to repossess it, why did he give it? . . . O watchful one, leave me my son, and when he who called you wants him, it is to me that he must speak" (cf. *The Sacrifice of Abraham* 7).

Romanus did not use the solemn Byzantine Greek of the imperial court but the simple Greek that was close to the language of the populace. I cite here an example of the lively and highly personal manner in which he speaks about the Lord Jesus: he calls him the "source that is never consumed by fire and the light against the darkness," and says: "I long to hold you in my hand like a lamp; indeed, anyone who carries an oil lamp among men and women is illuminated without being burned. Illuminate me, then, You who are the light that never burns out" (*The Presentation* or *Feast of Encounter* 8). The force of conviction in his preaching was based on the close consistency between his words and his life. In one prayer, he says: "Make my language clear, my Savior; open my mouth and, after filling it, penetrate my heart so that my acts may correspond to my words" (*Mission of the Apostles* 2).

Let us now examine some of his main themes. A fundamental subject that recurs in his preaching is the unity of God's action in history, the unity between creation and the history of salvation, the unity between the Old and New Testaments. Another important theme is pneumatology, the teaching on the Holy Spirit. On the Feast of Pentecost, Romanus stressed the continuity that exists between Christ, ascended into heaven, and the Apostles, that is, the Church, and he exalts missionary action in the world: "With divine virtue they conquered all men; they took up the cross of Christ as a pen; they used words like 'fishing nets' and set them to 'catch' the world; they used the Word of God as a sharp hook and as bait they used the flesh of the Sovereign One of the universe" (*Pentecost* 2, 18).

Another central theme is, of course, Christology. Romanus did not involve himself in the difficult theological concepts, hotly debated at that time, which lacerated not only the unity of theologians but also the unity of Christians in the Church. He preached a simple but fundamental Christology, the Christology of the great councils. Above all, however, Romanus was close to popular piety—moreover, the ideas of the councils were inspired by popular piety and knowledge of the human heart— and in this way, Romanus emphasized that Christ is true man and true God, and in being the true man-God, he is only one person, the synthesis between creation and the Creator, in whose human words we hear the voice of the Word of God himself. He said: "Christ was a man, but he was also God, yet he was not divided in two: He is One, the Son of a Father who is One alone" (*The Passion* 19). With regard to Mariology, grateful to the Virgin for his gift of a poetic talent, Romanus mentions her at the end of almost all his hymns and dedicated to her some of his most beautiful *kontakia*: *The Nativity of Christ, The Annunciation, The Divine Motherhood, The New Eve*.

Last, his moral teachings refer to the Last Judgment (*The Ten Virgins* [2]). He takes us toward this moment of truth in our lives, the appearance before the just Judge, and therefore exhorts us to conversion with penance and fasting. The positive aspect is that the Christian must practice charity and almsgiving. Romanus accentuated the primacy of charity over continence in two hymns, *The Wedding at Cana* and *The Ten Virgins*.

Charity is the greatest of the virtues: "Ten virgins possessed the virtue of virginity intact, but for five of them the difficult practice proved unfruitful. The others shone with their lamps of love for humanity, and for this reason the bridegroom invited them in" (*The Ten Virgins* 1). Vibrant humanity, the ardor of faith, and profound humility pervade the hymns of Romanus the Melodist. This great poet and composer reminds us of the whole treasure of Christian culture, born of faith, born of the heart that has encountered Christ, the Son of God. Culture, the whole of our great Christian culture, is born from this contact of the heart with the Truth, who is Love. Nor, if faith stays alive, will this cultural inheritance die; rather, it will remain alive and present. To this day, images still speak to the hearts of believers; they are not relics of the past. Cathedrals are not medieval monuments but rather houses of life in which we feel "at home" and where we meet God and one another. Nor is great music—Gregorian chant, Bach, or Mozart—something of the past; rather, it lives on in the vitality of the liturgy and in our faith. If faith is alive, Christian culture can never become "obsolete" but on the contrary will remain alive and present. And if faith is alive, today too we can respond to the imperative that is ceaselessly repeated in the Psalms: "O Sing to the Lord a new song" (Ps 98[97]:1). Creativity, innovation, a new song, a new culture, and the presence of the entire cultural heritage are not mutually exclusive but form one reality: they are the presence of God's beauty and the joy of being God's children.

—*21 May 2008*

Part Three

Monks and Missionaries

St. Gregory the Great

A *Life during Crisis*

One of the greatest Fathers in the history of the Church, one of four Doctors of the West, Pope St. Gregory was bishop of Rome from 590 to 604. He earned the traditional title of *Magnus*, the Great.

Gregory was truly a great pope and a great Doctor of the Church. He was born in Rome about 540 into a rich patrician family of the *gens Anicia*, who were distinguished not only for their noble blood but also for their adherence to the Christian faith and for their service to the Apostolic See. Two popes came from this family: Felix III (483–492), the great-great grandfather of Gregory, and Agapetus (535–536). The house in which Gregory grew up stood on the Clivus Scauri, surrounded by majestic buildings that attested to the greatness of ancient Rome and the spiritual strength of Christianity. The example of his parents, Gordian and Sylvia, both venerated as saints, and those of his father's sisters, Aemiliana and Tharsilla, who lived in their own home as consecrated virgins following a path of prayer and self-denial, inspired lofty Christian sentiments in him.

In the footsteps of his father, Gregory entered early into an administrative career that reached its climax in 572, when he became prefect of the city. This office, complicated by the sorry times, allowed him to apply himself on a vast range to every type of administrative problem, drawing light for future duties from them. In particular, he retained a deep sense of order and discipline: having become pope, he advised bishops to take as a model for the management of ecclesial affairs the diligence and respect for the law like civil functionaries. Yet this life could not have satisfied him since shortly after, he decided to leave every civil assignment in order to withdraw to his home to begin the monastic life, transforming his family home into the monastery of St. Andrew on the Coelian Hill. This period of monastic life, the life of permanent dialogue with the Lord in listening to his word, generated a perennial nostalgia which he referred to ever anew and ever more in his homilies. In the midst of the pressure of pastoral worries, he often recalled it in his writings as a happy time of recollection in God, dedication to prayer, and peaceful immersion in study. Thus, he could acquire that deep understanding of Sacred Scripture and of the Fathers of the Church that later served him in his work.

But Gregory's cloistered withdrawal did not last long. The precious experience that he gained in civil administration during a period marked by serious problems, the relationships he had had in this post with the Byzantines, and the universal respect that he acquired induced Pope Pelagius to appoint him deacon and to send him to Constantinople as his "apocrisarius"—today one would say "Apostolic Nuncio"—in order to help overcome the last traces of the Monophysite controversy and above all to obtain the emperor's support in the effort to check the Lombard invaders. The stay at Constantinople, where he resumed monastic life with a group of monks, was very important for Gregory, since it permitted him to acquire direct experience of the Byzantine world, as well as to approach the problem of the Lombards, who would later put his ability and energy to the test during the years of his pontificate. After some years, he was recalled to Rome by the pope, who appointed him his secretary. They were difficult years: continual rain, flooding due to overflowing rivers, famine that afflicted many regions of Italy as well as Rome. Finally, even the plague broke out, which claimed numerous victims, among whom was also Pope Pelagius II. The clergy, people, and senate were unanimous in choosing Gregory as his successor to the See of Peter. He tried to resist, even attempting to flee, but to no avail: finally, he had to yield. The year was 590.

Recognizing the will of God in what had happened, the new pontiff immediately and enthusiastically set to work. From the beginning, he showed a singularly enlightened vision of realty with which he had to deal, an extraordinary capacity for work confronting both ecclesial and civil affairs, a constant and even balance in making decisions, at times with courage, imposed on him by his office.

Abundant documentation has been preserved from his governance thanks to the register of his letters (approximately 800), reflecting the complex questions that arrived on his desk on a daily basis. They were questions that came from bishops, abbots, clergy, and even from civil authorities of every order and rank. Among the problems that afflicted Italy and Rome at that time was one of special importance both in the civil and ecclesial spheres: the Lombard question. The pope dedicated every possible energy to it in view of a truly peaceful solution. Contrary to the Byzantine emperor, who assumed that the Lombards were only uncouth individuals and predators to be defeated or exterminated, St. Gregory saw this people with the eyes of a good pastor. He was concerned with proclaiming the word of salvation to them, establishing fraternal relationships with them in view of a future peace founded on mutual respect and peaceful coexistence between Italians, imperials, and Lombards. He was concerned with the conversion of the young people and the new civil structure of Europe: the Visigoths of Spain, the Franks, the Saxons, the immigrants in Britain, and the Lombards were the privileged recipients of his evangelizing mission. Each year, for example, we celebrate the liturgical memorial of St. Augustine of Canterbury, the leader of a group of monks Gregory assigned to go to Britain to evangelize England.

The pope, who was a true peacemaker, deeply committed himself to establish an effective peace in Rome and in Italy by undertaking intense negotiations with Agilulf, the Lombard king. This negotiation led to a period of truce that lasted for about three years (598–601), after which, in 603, it was possible to stipulate a more stable armistice. This positive result was obtained also thanks to the parallel contacts that, meanwhile, the pope undertook with Queen Theodolinda, a Bavarian princess who, unlike the leaders of other Germanic peoples, was deeply Catholic. A series of letters from Pope Gregory to this queen has been preserved in which he reveals his respect and friendship for her. Theodolinda, little by little, was able to guide the king to Catholicism, thus preparing the way to peace. The pope also was careful to send her relics for the Basilica of St. John the Baptist, which she had had built in Monza, and did not fail to send his congratulations and precious gifts for the same Cathedral of Monza on the occasion of the birth and baptism of her son, Adaloald. The series of events concerning this queen constitutes a beautiful testimony to the importance of women in the history of the Church. Gregory constantly focused on three basic objectives: to limit the Lombard expansion in Italy; to preserve Queen Theodolinda from the influence of schismatics and to strengthen the Catholic faith; and to mediate between the Lombards and the Byzantines in view of an accord that guaranteed peace in the peninsula and at the same time permitted the evangelization of the Lombards themselves. Therefore, in the complex situation, his scope was constantly twofold: to promote understanding on the diplomatic-political level and to spread the proclamation of the true faith among the peoples.

Along with his purely spiritual and pastoral action, Pope Gregory also became an active protagonist in multifaceted social activities. With the revenues from the Roman See's substantial patrimony in Italy, especially in Sicily, he bought and distributed grain; assisted those in need; helped priests, monks, and nuns who lived in poverty; paid the ransom for citizens held captive by the Lombards; and purchased armistices and truces. Moreover, whether in Rome or other parts of Italy, he carefully carried out the administrative reorganization, giving precise instructions so that the goods of the Church, useful for her sustenance and evangelizing work in the world, were managed with absolute rectitude and according to the rules of justice and mercy. He demanded that the tenants on Church territory be protected from dishonest agents, and, in cases of fraud, tenants were to be quickly compensated so that the face of the bride of Christ was not soiled with dishonest profits.

Gregory carried out this intense activity notwithstanding his poor health, which often forced him to remain in bed for days on end. The fasts practiced during the years of monastic life had caused him serious digestive problems. Furthermore, his voice was so feeble that he was often obliged to entrust the reading of his homilies to the deacon, so that the faithful present in the Roman basilicas could hear him. On feast days, he did his best to celebrate the *Missarum solemnia,* that is, the solemn Mass, and then he met personally with the people of God, who were very fond of him, because they saw in him the authoritative reference from whom to draw security: not by chance was the title *consul Dei* quickly attributed to him. Notwithstanding the very difficult conditions in which he had to work, he gained the faithful's trust, thanks to his holiness of life and rich humanity, achieving truly magnificent results for his time and for the future. He was a man immersed in God: his desire for God was always alive in the depths of his soul, and precisely because of this he was always close to his neighbor, to the needy people of his time. Indeed, during a desperate period of havoc, he was able to create peace and give hope. This man of God shows us the true sources of peace, from which true hope comes. Thus, he becomes a guide also for us today.

Teacher and Guide

Notwithstanding the many duties connected to his office as the bishop of Rome, Gregory left to us numerous works, from which the Church in successive centuries has drawn with both hands. Besides the important correspondence—in my earlier catechesis, I cited the *Register* that contains over eight hundred letters—first of all, he left us writings of an exegetical character, among which his *Morals,* a commentary on Job (known under the Latin title *Moralia in Iob),* the *Homilies on Ezekiel,* and the *Homilies on the Gospel* stand out. Then there is an important work of a hagiographical character, the *Dialogues,* written by Gregory for the edification of the Lombard Queen Theodolinda. The primary and best-known work is undoubtedly the *Regula pastoralis* ("pastoral rule"), which the pope published at the beginning of his pontificate with clearly programmatic goals.

Wanting to review these works quickly, we must first of all note that, in his writings, Gregory never sought to delineate "his own" doctrine, his own originality. Rather, he intended to echo the traditional teaching of the Church. He simply wanted to be the mouthpiece of Christ and of the Church on the way that must be taken to reach God. His exegetical commentaries are models of this approach. He was a passionate reader of the Bible, which he approached not simply with a speculative purpose: from Sacred Scripture, he thought, the Christian must draw not theoretical understanding so much as the daily nourishment for his soul, for his life as man in this world. For example, in the *Homilies on Ezekiel,* he emphasized this function of the sacred text: to approach the Scripture simply to satisfy one's own desire for knowledge means to succumb to the temptation of pride and thus to expose oneself to the risk of sliding into heresy. Intellectual humility is the primary rule for one who searches to penetrate the supernatural realities beginning from the sacred book. Obviously, humility does not exclude serious study; but to ensure that the results are spiritually beneficial, facilitating true entry into the depth of the text, humility remains indispensable. Only with this interior attitude can one really listen to and eventually perceive the voice of God. On the other hand, when it is a question of the Word of God, understanding it means nothing if it does not lead to action. In these *Homilies on Ezekiel* is also found that beautiful expression according to which "the preacher must dip his pen into the blood of his heart; then he can also reach the ear of his neighbor." Reading his homilies, one sees that Gregory truly wrote with his lifeblood, and therefore he still speaks to us today.

Gregory also developed this discourse in the *Book of Morals,* a commentary on Job. Following the Patristic tradition, he examined the sacred text in the three dimensions of its meaning: the literal dimension, the allegorical dimension, and the moral dimension, which are dimensions of the unique sense of Sacred Scripture. Nevertheless, Gregory gave a clear prevalence to the moral sense. In this perspective, he proposed his thought by way of some dual meanings—*to know-to do, to speak-to live, to know-to act*—in which he evokes the two aspects of human life that should be complementary, but which often end by being antithetical. The moral ideal, he comments, always consists in realizing a harmonious integration between word and action, thought and deed, prayer and dedication to the duties of one's state: this is the way to realize that synthesis thanks to which the divine descends to man and man is lifted up until he becomes one with God. Thus, the great pope marks out a complete plan of life for the authentic believer; for this reason the *Book of Morals,* a commentary on Job, would constitute in the course of the Middle Ages a kind of *summa* of Christian morality.

Of notable importance and beauty are also the *Homilies on the Gospel.* The first of these was given in St. Peter's Basilica in 590 during the Advent season, hence only a few months after Gregory's election to the papacy; the last was delivered in St. Lawrence's Basilica on the second Sunday after Pentecost in 593. The pope preached to the people in the churches where the "stations" were celebrated—special prayer ceremonies during the important seasons of the liturgical year—or the feasts of titular martyrs. The guiding principle, which links the different homilies, is captured in the word *preacher:* not only the minister of God, but also every Christian, has the duty "to preach" of what he has experienced in his innermost being, following the example of Christ, who was made man to bring to all the good news of salvation. The horizon of this commitment is eschatological: the expectation of the fulfillment of all things in Christ was a constant thought of the great pontiff and ended by becoming the guiding reason of his every thought and activity. From here sprang his incessant reminders to be vigilant and to perform good works. Probably the most systematic text of Gregory the Great is the *Pastoral Rule*, written in the first years of his pontificate. In it Gregory proposed to treat the figure of the ideal bishop, the teacher and guide of his flock. To this end, he illustrated the seriousness of the office of pastor of the Church and its inherent duties. Therefore, those who were not called to this office may not seek it with superficiality; instead, those who assumed it without due reflection necessarily feel trepidation rise within their soul. Taking up again a favorite theme, he affirmed that the bishop is above all the "preacher" par excellence; for this reason, he must be above all an example for others, so that his behavior may be a point of reference for all. Efficacious pastoral action requires that he know his audience and adapt his words to the situation of each person: here Gregory paused to illustrate the various categories of the faithful with acute and precise annotations, which can justify the evaluation of those who have also seen in this work a treatise on psychology. From this, one understands that he really knew his flock and spoke of all things with the people of his time and his city.

Nevertheless, the great pontiff insisted on the pastor's duty to recognize daily his own unworthiness in the eyes of the Supreme Judge, so that pride did not negate the good accomplished. For this, the final chapter of the *Rule* is dedicated to humility: "When one is pleased to have achieved many virtues, it is well to reflect on one's own inadequacies and to humble oneself: instead of considering the good accomplished, it is necessary to consider what was neglected." All these precious indications demonstrate the lofty concept that St. Gregory had for the care of souls, which he defined as the *ars artium*, the art of arts. The *Rule* had such great, and the rather rare, good fortune to have been quickly translated into Greek and Anglo-Saxon.

Another significant work is the *Dialogues*. In this work, addressed to his friend Peter the deacon who was convinced that customs were so corrupt as to impede the rise of saints as in times past, Gregory demonstrated just the opposite: holiness is always possible, even in difficult times. He proved it by narrating the life of contemporaries or those who had died recently, who could well be considered saints, even if not canonized. The narration was accompanied by theological and mystical reflections that make the book a singular hagiographical text, capable of enchanting entire generations of readers. The material was drawn from the living traditions of the people and intended to edify and form, attracting the attention of the reader to a series of questions regarding the meaning of miracles, the interpretation of Scripture, the immortality of the soul, the existence of hell, the representation of the next world—all themes that require fitting clarification. Book 2 is wholly dedicated to the figure of Benedict of Nursia and is the only ancient witness to the life of the holy monk, whose spiritual beauty the text highlights fully. In the theological plan that Gregory develops regarding his works, the past, present, and future are compared. What counted for him more than anything was the entire arch of salvation history that continues to unfold in the obscure meanderings of time. In this perspective, it is significant that he inserted the news of the conversion of the angels in the middle of his *Book of Morals*, a commentary on Job: to his eyes, the event constituted a furthering of the kingdom of God which the Scripture treats. Therefore, it could rightly be mentioned in the commentary on a holy book. According to him, the leaders of Christian communities must commit themselves to reread events in the light of the Word of God: in this sense, the great pontiff felt he had the duty to orient pastors and the faithful on the spiritual itinerary of an enlightened and correct *lectio divina*, placed in the context of one's own life.

Before concluding, it is necessary to say a word on the relationship that Pope Gregory nurtured with the patriarchs of Antioch, of Alexandria, and of Constantinople itself. He always concerned himself with recognizing and respecting rights, protecting them from every interference that would limit legitimate autonomy. Still, if St. Gregory, in the context of the historical situation, was opposed to the title "ecumenical" on the part of the patriarch of Constantinople, it was not to limit or negate this legitimate authority but rather because he was concerned about the fraternal unity of the universal Church. Above all, he was profoundly convinced that humility should be the fundamental virtue for every bishop, even more so for the patriarch. Gregory remained a simple monk in his heart and therefore was decisively contrary to great titles. He wanted to be, and this is his expression, *servus servorum Dei*. Coined by him, this phrase was not just a pious formula on his lips but a true manifestation of his way of living and acting. He was intimately struck by the humility of God, who in Christ made himself our servant. He washed and washes our dirty feet. Therefore, Gregory was convinced that a bishop, above all, should imitate this humility of God and follow Christ in this way. His desire was to live truly as a monk, in permanent contact with the Word of God, but for love of God he knew how to make himself the servant of all in a time full of tribulation and suffering. He knew how to make himself the "servant of the servants." Precisely because he was this, he is great and also shows us the measure of true greatness.

—28 May and 4 June 2008

St. Columban

THE HOLY ABBOT COLUMBAN was the best-known Irishman of the early Middle Ages. Since he worked as a monk, missionary, and writer in various countries of western Europe with good reason he can be called a "European" saint. With the Irish of his time, he had a sense of Europe's cultural unity. The expression *totius Europae*—"of all Europe," with reference to the Church's presence on the continent, is found for the first time in one of his letters, written around the year 600, addressed to Pope Gregory the Great (cf. *Epistula* 1, 1).

Columban was born c. 543 in the province of Leinster, in southeast Ireland. He was educated at home by excellent tutors who introduced him to the study of liberal arts. He was then entrusted to the guidance of Abbot Sinell of the community of Cleenish in Northern Ireland, where he was able to deepen his study of Sacred Scripture. At the age of about twenty, he entered the monastery of Bangor, in the northeast of the island, whose abbot Comgall was a monk well known for his virtue and ascetic rigor. In full agreement with his abbot, Columban zealously practiced the severe discipline of the monastery, leading a life of prayer, *ascesis*, and study. While there, he was also ordained a priest. His life at Bangor and the abbot's example influenced the conception of monasticism that developed in Columban over time and that he subsequently spread in the course of his life.

When he was approximately fifty years old, following the characteristically Irish ascetic ideal of the *peregrinatio pro Christo,* namely, making oneself a pilgrim for the sake of Christ, Columban left his island with twelve companions to engage in missionary work on the European continent. We should, in fact, bear in mind that the migration of people from the North and the East had caused whole areas, previously Christianized, to revert to paganism. Around the year 590, the small group of missionaries landed on the Breton coast. Welcomed kindly by the king of the Franks of Austrasia (present-day France), they asked only for a small piece of uncultivated land. They were given the ancient Roman fortress of Annegray, totally ruined and abandoned and covered by forest. Accustomed to a life of extreme hardship, in the span of a few months the monks managed to build the first hermitage on the ruins. Thus their re-evangelization began, in the first place, through the witness of their lives. With the new cultivation of the land, they also began a new cultivation of souls. The fame of those foreign religious who, living on prayer and in great austerity, built houses and worked the land spread rapidly, attracting pilgrims and penitents. In particular, many young men asked to be accepted by the monastic community in order to live, like them, this exemplary life which was renewing the cultivation of the land and of souls. It was not long before the foundation of a second monastery was required. It was built a few kilometres away on the ruins of an ancient spa, Luxeuil. This monastery was to become the center of the traditional Irish monastic and missionary outreach on the European continent. A third monastery was erected at Fontaine, an hour's walk further north.

Columban lived at Luxeuil for almost twenty years. Here the saint wrote for his followers the *Regula monachorum*, for a while more widespread in Europe than Benedict's *Rule*, which portrayed the ideal image of the monk. It is the only ancient Irish monastic rule in our possession today. Columban integrated it with the *Regula coenobialis*, a sort of penal code for the offenses committed by monks, with punishments that are somewhat surprising to our modern sensibility and can only be explained by the mentality and environment of that time. With another famous work, titled *De poenitentiarum misura taxanda,* also written at Luxeuil, Columban introduced confession and private and frequent penance on the Continent. It was known as "tariffed" penance because of the proportion established between the gravity of the sin and the type of penance imposed by the confessor. These innovations roused the suspicion of local bishops, a suspicion that became hostile when Columban had the courage to rebuke them openly for the practices of some of them. The controversy over the date of Easter was an opportunity to demonstrate their opposition: Ireland, in fact, followed the Eastern rather than the Roman tradition. The Irish monk was convoked in 603 to account to a synod at Chalon-sur-Saône for his practices regarding penance and Easter. Instead of presenting himself before the Synod, he sent a letter in which he minimized the issue, inviting the synod fathers not only to discuss the problem of the date of Easter, in his opinion a negligible problem, "but also all the necessary canonical norms that, something more serious, are disregarded by many" (cf. *Epistula* 2, 1). At the same time, he wrote to Pope Boniface IV, just as several years earlier he had turned to Pope Gregory the Great (cf. *Epistula* 1), asking him to defend the Irish tradition (cf. *Epistula* 3).

Intransigent as he was in every moral matter, Columban then came into conflict with the royal house for having harshly reprimanded King Theuderic for his adulterous relations. This created a whole network of personal, religious, and political intrigues and maneuvers which, in 610, culminated in a decree of expulsion banishing Columban and all the monks of Irish origin from Luxeuil and condemning them to definitive exile. They were escorted to the sea and, at the expense of the court, boarded a ship bound for Ireland. However, not far from shore, the ship ran aground and the captain, who saw this as a sign from heaven, abandoned the voyage and, for fear of being cursed by God, brought the monks back to dry land. Instead of returning to Luxeuil, they decided to begin a new work of evangelization. Thus, they embarked on a Rhine boat and traveled up the river.

After a first stop in Tuggen, near Lake Zurich, they went to the region of Bregenz, near Lake Constance, to evangelize the Alemanni.

However, soon afterward, because of political events unfavorable to his work, Columban decided to cross the Alps with the majority of his disciples. Only one monk, whose name was Gallus, stayed behind; it was from his hermitage that the famous abbey of St. Gall in Switzerland subsequently developed. Having arrived in Italy, Columban met with a warm welcome at the Lombard royal court but was immediately faced with considerable difficulties: the life of the Church was torn apart by the Arian heresy, still prevalent among the Lombards, and by a schism which had detached most of the Church in northern Italy from communion with the bishop of Rome. Columban entered authoritatively into this context, writing a satirical pamphlet against Arianism and a letter to Boniface IV to convince him to take some decisive steps with a view to reestablishing unity (cf. *Epistula 5*). When, in 612 or 613, the king of the Lombards allocated to him a plot of land in Bobbio, in the Trebbia Valley, Columban founded a new monastery there which was later to become a cultural center on a par with the famous monastery of Monte Cassino. Here he came to the end of his days: he died on 23 November 615 and to this day is commemorated on this date in the Roman rite.

Saint Columban's message is concentrated in a firm appeal to conversion and detachment from earthly goods, with a view to the eternal inheritance. With his ascetic life and conduct free from compromises when he faced the corruption of the powerful, he is reminiscent of the severe figure of St. John the Baptist. His austerity, however, was never an end in itself but merely the means with which to open himself freely to God's love and to correspond with his whole being to the gifts received from him, thereby restoring in himself the image of God, while at the same time cultivating the earth and renewing human society. I quote from his *Instructiones*: "If man makes a correct use of those faculties that God has conceded to his soul, he will be likened to God. Let us remember that we must restore to him all those gifts which he deposited in us when we were in our original condition. He has taught us the way with his commandments. The first of them tells us to love the Lord with all our heart, because he loved us first, from the beginning of time, even before we came into the light of this world" (cf. *Instructiones* 11). The Irish saint truly incarnated these words in his own life. A man of great culture, he also wrote poetry in Latin and a grammar book; he proved rich in gifts of grace. He was a tireless builder of monasteries as well as an intransigent penitential preacher who spent every ounce of his energy on nurturing the Christian roots of Europe, which was coming into existence. With his spiritual energy, with his faith, with his love for God and neighbor, he truly became one of the fathers of Europe. He shows us even today the roots from which our Europe can be reborn.

—*11 June 2008*

St. Isidore of Seville

Saint Isidore of Seville was a younger brother of Leander, archbishop of Seville, and a great friend of Pope Gregory the Great. Pointing this out is important because it enables us to bear in mind a cultural and spiritual approach that is indispensable for understanding Isidore's personality. Indeed, he owed much to Leander, an exacting, studious, and austere person who created around his younger brother a family context marked by the ascetic requirements proper to a monk, and from the work pace demanded by a serious dedication to study. Furthermore, Leander was concerned to have the wherewithal to confront the political and social situation of that time: in those decades, in fact, the Visigoths, barbarians, and Arians had invaded the Iberian peninsula and taken possession of territories that belonged to the Roman Empire. It was essential to regain them for the Roman world and for Catholicism. Leander and Isidore's home was furnished with a library richly endowed with classical, pagan, and Christian works. Isidore, who felt simultaneously attracted to both, was therefore taught under the responsibility of his elder brother to develop a very strong discipline, in devoting himself to study with discretion and discernment.

Thus, a calm and open atmosphere prevailed in the episcopal residence in Seville. We can deduce this from Isidore's cultural and spiritual interests, as they emerge from his works themselves, which include an encyclopedic knowledge of pagan classical culture and a thorough knowledge of Christian culture. This explains the eclecticism characteristic of Isidore's literary opus; he glided with the greatest of ease from Martial to Augustine or from Cicero to Gregory the Great. The inner strife that the young Isidore had to contend with, having succeeded his brother Leander on the episcopal throne of Seville in 599, was by no means unimportant. The impression of excessive voluntarism that strikes one on reading the works of this great author, considered to be the last of the Christian Fathers of antiquity, may, perhaps, actually be due to this constant struggle with himself. A few years after his death in 636, the Council of Toledo in 653 described him as "an illustrious teacher of our time and the glory of the Catholic Church."

Isidore was without a doubt a man of accentuated dialectical antitheses. Moreover, he experienced a permanent inner conflict in his personal life, similar to that which Gregory the Great and St. Augustine had experienced earlier, between a desire for solitude to dedicate himself solely to meditation on the Word of God, and the demands of charity to his brethren for whose salvation, as bishop, he felt responsible. He wrote, for example, with regard to Church leaders: "The man responsible for a Church (*vir ecclesiasticus*) must on the one hand allow himself to be crucified to the world with the mortification of his flesh, and on the other, accept the decision of the ecclesiastical order—when it comes from God's will—to devote himself humbly to government, even if he does not wish to" (*Sententiarum liber* 3, 33, 1: PL 83, col 705b). Just a paragraph later he adds: "Men of God (*sancti viri*) do not, in fact, desire to dedicate themselves to things of the world and groan when by some mysterious design of God they are charged with certain responsibilities. . . . They do their utmost to avoid them but accept what they would like to shun and do what they would have preferred to avoid. Indeed, they enter into the secrecy of the heart and seek there to understand what God's mysterious will is asking of them. And when they realize that they must submit to God's plans, they bend their hearts to the yoke of the divine decision" (*Sententiarum liber* 3, 33, 3: PL 83, coll. 705–6).

To understand Isidore better, it is first of all necessary to recall the complexity of the political situations in his time to which I have already referred: during the years of his boyhood, he was obliged to experience the bitterness of exile. He was nevertheless pervaded with apostolic enthusiasm. He experienced the rapture of contributing to the formation of a people that was at last rediscovering its unity, both political and religious, with the providential conversion of Hermenegild, the heir to the Visigoth throne, from Arianism to the Catholic faith. Yet we must not underestimate the enormous difficulty of coming to grips with such very serious problems as were the relations with heretics and with the Jews. There was a whole series of problems which appear very concrete to us today too, especially if we consider what is happening in certain regions in which we seem almost to be witnessing the recurrence of situations very similar to those that existed on the Iberian Peninsula in the sixth century. The wealth of cultural knowledge that Isidore had assimilated enabled him to constantly compare the Christian newness with the Greco-Roman cultural heritage; however, rather than the precious gift of synthesis, it would seem that he possessed the gift of *collatio*, that is, of collecting, which he expressed in an extraordinary personal erudition, although it was not always ordered as might have been desired.

In any case, his nagging worry not to overlook anything that human experience had produced in the history of his homeland and of the whole world is admirable. Isidore did not want to lose anything that man had acquired in the epochs of antiquity, regardless of whether they had been pagan, Jewish, or Christian. Hence, it should not come as a surprise if, in pursuing this goal, he did not always manage to filter the knowledge he possessed sufficiently in the purifying waters of the Christian faith as he would have wished. The point is, however, that in Isidore's intentions, the proposals he made were always in tune with the Catholic faith, which he staunchly upheld. In the discussion of the various theological problems, he showed that he perceived their complexity and often astutely suggested solutions that summarize and express the complete Christian truth. This has enabled believers through the ages and to our times to profit with gratitude from his definitions. A significant example of this is offered by Isidore's teaching on the relations between active and contemplative life. He wrote: "Those who seek to attain repose in contemplation must first train in the stadium of active life; and then, free from the dross of sin, they will be able to display that pure heart which alone makes the vision of God possible" (*Differentiarum Lib.* 2, 34, 133: PL 83, col. 91a). Nonetheless, the realism of a true pastor convinced him of the risk the faithful run of reducing themselves to one dimension. He therefore added: "The middle way, consisting of both of these forms of life, normally turns out to be more useful in resolving those tensions which are often aggravated by the choice of a single way of life and are instead better tempered by an alternation of the two forms" (*Differentiarum Lib.* 2, 34, 134; ibid., col 91b).

Isidore sought in Christ's example the definitive confirmation of a just orientation of life and said: "The Savior Jesus offers us the example of active life when during the day he devoted himself to working signs and miracles in the town, but he showed the contemplative life when he withdrew to the mountain and spent the night in prayer" (*Differentiarum Lib.* 2, 34, 134: ibid.). In the light of this example of the divine teacher, Isidore can conclude with this precise moral teaching: "Therefore, let the servant of God, imitating Christ, dedicate himself to contemplation without denying himself active life. Behaving otherwise would not be right. Indeed, just as we must love God in contemplation, so we must love our neighbor with action. It is therefore impossible to live without the presence of both the one and the other form of life; nor can we live without experiencing both the one and the other" (*Differentiarum Lib.* 2, 34, 135; ibid. col 91c). I consider that this is the synthesis of a life that seeks contemplation of God, dialogue with God in prayer and in the reading of Sacred Scripture, as well as action at the service of the human community and of our neighbor. This synthesis is the lesson that the great bishop of Seville has bequeathed to us, Christians of today, called to witness to Christ at the beginning of a new millennium.

—*18 June 2008*

St. Maximus the Confessor

ONE OF THE GREAT FATHERS of the Eastern Church in later times was a monk, St. Maximus. His fearless courage in witnessing to—"confessing"—even while suffering, the integrity of his faith in Jesus Christ, true God and true man, savior of the world, earned him Christian tradition's title of *Confessor*. Maximus was born in Palestine, the land of the Lord, in about 580. As a boy, he was initiated to the monastic life and the study of the Scriptures through the works of Origen, the great teacher who by the third century had already "established" the exegetical tradition of Alexandria.

Maximus moved from Jerusalem to Constantinople and from there, because of the barbarian invasions, sought refuge in Africa. Here he was distinguished by his extreme courage in the defense of orthodoxy. Maximus refused to accept any reduction of Christ's humanity. A theory had come into being which held that there was only one will in Christ, the divine will. To defend the oneness of Christ's person, people denied that he had his own true and proper human will. And, at first sight, it might seem to be a good thing that Christ had only one will. But St. Maximus immediately realized that this would destroy the mystery of salvation, for humanity without a will, a man without a will, is not a real man but an amputated man. Had this been so, the man Jesus Christ would not have been a true man; he would not have experienced the drama of being human, which consists, precisely, of conforming our will with the great truth of being. Thus, St. Maximus declared with great determination: Sacred Scripture does not portray to us an amputated man with no will but rather true and complete man: God, in Jesus Christ, really assumed the totality of being human—obviously with the exception of sin—hence also a human will. And said like this, his point is clear: Christ either is or is not a man. If he is a man, he also has a will. But here the problem arises: do we not end up with a sort of dualism? Do we not reach the point of affirming two complete personalities: reason, will, sentiment? How is it possible to overcome dualism, to keep the completeness of the human being and yet succeed in preserving the unity of the person of Christ who was not schizophrenic?

St. Maximus demonstrates that man does not find his unity, the integration of himself or his totality within himself but by surpassing himself, by coming out of himself. Thus, also in Christ, by coming out of himself, man finds himself in God, in the Son of God. It is not necessary to amputate man to explain the Incarnation; all that is required is to understand the dynamism of the human being who is fulfilled only by coming out of himself; it is in God alone that we find ourselves, our totality, and our completeness. Hence, we see that the person who withdraws into oneself is not a complete person but the person who is open, who comes out of oneself, becomes complete and finds oneself, finds one's true humanity, precisely in the Son of God. For St. Maximus, this vision did not remain a philosophical speculation; he saw it realized in Jesus' actual life, especially in the drama of Gethsemane. In this drama of Jesus' agony, of the anguish of death, of the opposition between the human will not to die and the divine will which offers itself to death, in this drama of Gethsemane the whole human drama is played out, the drama of our redemption. Saint Maximus tells us that, and we know that this is true, Adam (and we ourselves are Adam) thought that the no was the peak of freedom. He thought that only a person who can say no is truly free; that if he is truly to achieve his freedom, man must say no to God; only in this way he believed he could at last be himself, that he had reached the heights of freedom. This tendency also carried within it the human nature of Christ, but went beyond it, for Jesus saw that it was not the no that was the height of freedom. The height of freedom is the yes, in conformity with God's will. It is only in the yes that the human person truly becomes oneself; only in the great openness of the yes, in the unification of one's will with the divine, that the human becomes immensely open, becomes "divine." What Adam wanted was to be like God, that is, to be completely free. But the person who withdraws into oneself is not divine, is not completely free; the person is freed by emerging from oneself; it is in the yes that one becomes free; and this is the drama of Gethsemane: not my will but yours. It is by transferring the human will to the divine will that the real person is born; it is in this way that we are redeemed. This, in a few brief words, is the fundamental point of what St. Maximus wanted to say, and here we see that the whole human being is truly at issue; the entire question of our life lies here. In Africa, St. Maximus was already having problems defending this vision of man and of God. He was then summoned to Rome. In 649, he took an active part in the Lateran Council, convoked by Pope Martin I to defend the two wills of Christ against the imperial edict which, *pro bono pacis*, forbade discussion of this matter. Pope Martin was made to pay dearly for his courage. Although he was in a precarious state of health, he was arrested and taken to Constantinople. Tried and condemned to death, Pope Martin I obtained the commutation of his sentence into permanent exile in the Crimea, where he died on 16 September 655, after two long years of humiliation and torment.

It was Maximus's turn shortly afterward, in 662, as he too opposed the emperor, repeating: "It cannot be said that Christ has a single will!" (cf. *PG* 91, cols. 268–69). Thus, together with his two disciples, both called Anastasius, Maximus was subjected to an exhausting trial, although he was then over eighty years of age. The emperor's tribunal condemned him with the accusation of heresy, sentencing him to the cruel mutilation of his tongue and his right hand—the two organs through which, by words and writing, Maximus had fought the erroneous doctrine of the single will of Christ. In the end, thus mutilated, the holy monk was finally exiled to the region of Colchis on the Black Sea, where he died, worn out by the suffering he had endured, at the age of eighty-two, on 13 August that same year, 662.

In speaking of Maximus's life, we mentioned his literary opus in defense of orthodoxy. We referred in particular to the *Disputation with Pyrrhus,* formerly patriarch of Constantinople: in this debate, he succeeded in persuading his adversary of his errors. With great honesty, in fact, Pyrrhus concluded the *Disputation* with these words: "I ask forgiveness for myself and for those who have preceded me: by ignorance we arrived at these absurd ideas and arguments; and I ask that a way may be found to cancel these absurdities, saving the memory of those who erred" (*PG* 91, col. 352). Several dozen important works have also been handed down to us, among which the *Mystagogia* is outstanding. This is one of St. Maximus's most important writings, which gathers his theological thought in a well-structured synthesis.

St. Maximus's thought was never merely theological, speculative, or introverted because its target was always the practical reality of the world and its salvation. In this context in which he had to suffer, he could not escape into purely theoretical and philosophical affirmations. He had to seek the meaning of life, asking himself: Who am I? What is the world? God entrusted to man, created in his image and likeness, the mission of unifying the cosmos. And just as Christ unified the human being in himself, the Creator unified the cosmos in man. He showed us how to unify the cosmos in the communion of Christ and thus truly arrived at a redeemed world. Hans Urs von Balthasar, one of the greatest theologians of the twentieth century, referred to this powerful saving vision when, "relaunching" Maximus—he defined his thought with the vivid expression *Kosmische Liturgie,* "cosmic liturgy." Jesus, the one Savior of the world, is always at the center of this solemn "liturgy." The efficacy of his saving action, which definitively unified the cosmos, is guaranteed by the fact that in spite of being God in all things, he is also integrally a man and has the "energy" and will of a man.

The life and thought of Maximus were powerfully illumined by his immense courage in witnessing to the integral reality of Christ without any reduction or compromise. And thus, who man really is and how we should live in order to respond to our vocation appears. We must live united to God in order to be united to ourselves and to the cosmos, giving the cosmos itself and humanity their proper form. Christ's universal yes also shows us clearly how to put all the other values in the right place. We think of values that are justly defended today such as tolerance, freedom, and dialogue. But a tolerance that no longer distinguishes between good and evil would become chaotic and self-destructive, just as a freedom that did not respect the freedom of others or find the common measure of our respective liberties would become anarchy and destroy authority. Dialogue that no longer knows what to discuss becomes empty chatter. All these values are important and fundamental but can only remain true values if they have the point of reference that unites them and gives them true authenticity. This reference point is the synthesis between God and the cosmos, the figure of Christ in which we learn the truth about ourselves and thus where to rank all other values, because we discover their authentic meaning. Jesus Christ is the reference point that gives light to all other values. This was the conclusion of the great Confessor's witness. And it is in this way, ultimately, that Christ indicates that the cosmos must become a liturgy, the glory of God, and that worship is the beginning of true transformation, of the true renewal of the world.

Therefore, I conclude with a fundamental passage from one of St. Maximus's works: "We adore one Son together with the Father and the Holy Spirit, as it was in the beginning before all time, is now and ever shall be, for all time and for the time after time. Amen!" (*PG* 91, col. 269).

—*25 June 2008*

John Climacus

In presenting the great writers of the Church of the East and West in the Middle Age, I include the figure of John, known as Climacus. His name is a Latin transliteration of the Greek term *klimakos*, which means "of the ladder" (*klimax*). This is the title of his most important work, in which he describes the ladder of human life ascending toward God. He was born in about 575. He lived, therefore, during the years in which Byzantium, the capital of the Roman Empire of the East, experienced the greatest crisis in its history. The geographical situation of the empire suddenly changed, and the torrent of barbarian invasions swept away all its structures. Only the structure of the Church withstood them, continuing in these difficult times to carry out her missionary, human, social, and cultural action, especially through the network of monasteries in which great religious figures such as, precisely, John Climacus were active.

John lived and told of his spiritual experiences in the mountains of Sinai, where Moses encountered God, and Elijah heard his voice. Information on him has been preserved in a brief *Life* (*PG* 88, 596–608), written by a monk, Daniel of Raithu. At the age of sixteen, John, who had become a monk on Mount Sinai, made himself a disciple of Abba Martyr, an "elder," that is, a "wise man." At about twenty years of age, he chose to live as a hermit in a grotto at the foot of the mountain in the locality of Tola, eight kilometres from the present-day St. Catherine's monastery. Solitude, however, did not prevent him from meeting people eager for spiritual direction, or from paying visits to several monasteries near Alexandria. In fact, far from being an escape from the world and human reality, his eremitical retreat led to ardent love for others (*Life 5*) and for God (ibid., 7). After forty years of life as a hermit lived in love for God and for neighbor, years in which he wept, prayed, and fought with demons, he was appointed hegumen of the large monastery on Mount Sinai and thus returned to cenobitic life in a monastery. However, several years before his death, nostalgic for the eremitical life, he handed over the government of the community to his brother, a monk in the same monastery.

John died after the year 650. He lived his life between two mountains, Sinai and Tabor, and one can truly say that he radiated the light which Moses saw on Sinai and which was contemplated by the three Apostles on Mount Tabor!

He became famous, as I have already said, through his work titled *The Climax*, in the West known as the *Ladder of Divine Ascent* (*PG* 88, 632–1164). Composed at the insistent request of the hegumen of the

neighboring monastery of Raithu in Sinai, the *Ladder* is a complete treatise of spiritual life in which John describes the monk's journey from
renunciation of the world to the perfection of love. This journey according to his book covers thirty steps, each one of which is linked to the
next. The journey may be summarized in three consecutive stages: the
first is expressed in renunciation of the world in order to return to a
state of evangelical childhood. Thus, the essential is not the renunciation but rather the connection with what Jesus said, that is, the return to
true childhood in the spiritual sense, becoming like children. John comments: "A good foundation of three layers and three pillars is: innocence,
fasting, and temperance. Let all babes in Christ [cf. 1 Cor 3:1] begin
with these virtues, taking as their model the natural babes" (1, 20; 636).
Voluntary detachment from beloved people and places permits the soul
to enter into deeper communion with God. This renunciation leads to
obedience which is the way to humility through humiliations which will
never be absent on the part of the brethren. John comments: "Blessed is
he who has mortified his will to the very end and has entrusted the care
of himself to his teacher in the Lord: indeed, he will be placed on the
right hand of the Crucified One!" (4, 37; 704).

The second stage of the journey consists in spiritual combat against
the passions. Every step of the ladder is linked to a principal passion
that is defined and diagnosed, with an indication of the treatment and
a proposal of the corresponding virtue. Altogether, these steps of the
ladder undoubtedly constitute the most important treatise of spiritual
strategy that we possess. The struggle against the passions, however, is
steeped in the positive. It does not remain as something negative, thanks
to the image of the "fire" of the Holy Spirit: that "all those who enter
upon the good fight [cf. 1 Tim 6:12], which is hard and narrow, . . . may
realize that they must leap into the fire if they really expect the celestial
fire to dwell in them" (1, 18; 636). The fire of the Holy Spirit is the fire
of love and truth. The power of the Holy Spirit alone guarantees victory.
However, according to John Climacus, it is important to be aware that
the passions are not evil in themselves; they become so through human
freedom's wrong use of them. If they are purified, the passions reveal to
man the path toward God with energy unified by *ascesis* and grace and,
"if they have received from the Creator an order and a beginning . . . , the
limit of virtue is boundless" (26/2, 37; 1068).

The last stage of the journey is Christian perfection, which is developed in the last seven steps of the *Ladder*. These are the highest stages of
spiritual life, which can be experienced by the "Hesychasts": the solitar-
ies, those who have attained quiet and inner peace; but these stages are
also accessible to the more fervent cenobites. Of the first three, simplicity,
humility, and discernment, John, in line with the Desert Fathers, considered the ability to discern the most important. Every type of behavior

must be subject to discernment; everything, in fact, depends on one's deepest motivations, which need to be closely examined. Here one enters into the soul of the person; and it is a question of reawakening in the hermit, in the Christian, spiritual sensitivity and a "feeling heart," which are gifts from God: "After God, we ought to follow our conscience as a rule and guide in everything," (26/1, 5; 1013). In this way, one reaches tranquillity of soul, *hesychia,* by means of which the soul may gaze upon the abyss of the divine mysteries.

The state of quiet, of inner peace, prepares the Hesychast for prayer, which in John is twofold: "corporeal prayer" and "prayer of the heart." The former is proper to those who need the help of bodily movement: stretching out the hands, uttering groans, beating the breast, and so on. (15, 26; 900). The latter is spontaneous, because it is an effect of the reawakening of spiritual sensitivity, a gift of God to those who devote themselves to corporeal prayer. In John, this takes the name "Jesus prayer" (*Iesou euche*), and is constituted in the invocation of solely Jesus' name, an invocation that is continuous, like breathing: "May your remembrance of Jesus become one with your breathing, and you will then know the usefulness of *hesychia,* inner peace" (27/2, 26; 1112). At the end, the prayer becomes very simple: the word *Jesus* simply becomes one with the breath.

The last step of the ladder (30), suffused with "the sober inebriation of the spirit," is dedicated to the supreme "trinity of virtues": faith, hope, and above all charity. John also speaks of charity as *eros* (human love), a symbol of the matrimonial union of the soul with God, and once again chooses the image of fire to express the fervor, light, and purification of love for God. The power of human love can be reoriented to God, just as a cultivated olive may be grafted on to a wild olive tree (cf. Rom 11:24) (cf. 15, 66; 893). John is convinced that an intense experience of this *eros* will help the soul to advance far more than the harsh struggle against the passions, because of its great power. Thus, in our journey, the positive aspect prevails. Yet charity is also seen in close relation to hope: "Hope is the power that drives love. Thanks to hope, we can look forward to the reward of charity. . . . Hope is the doorway of love. . . . The absence of hope destroys charity: our efforts are bound to it, our labors are sustained by it, and through it we are enveloped by the mercy of God" (30, 16; 1157). The conclusion of the *Ladder* contains the synthesis of the work in words that the author has God himself utter: "May this ladder teach you the spiritual disposition of the virtues. I am at the summit of the ladder, and as my great initiate (St. Paul) said: 'So faith, hope, love abide, these three; but the greatest of these is love' [1 Cor 13:13]!" (30, 18; 1160).

At this point, a last question must be asked: can the *Ladder,* a work written by a hermit monk who lived fourteen hundred years ago, say something to us today? Can the existential journey of a man who lived his entire life on Mount Sinai in such a distant time be relevant to us? At first glance, it would seem that the answer must be no, because John Climacus is too remote from us. But if we look a little closer, we see that the monastic life is only a great symbol of baptismal life, of Christian life. It shows, so to speak, in capital letters what we write day after day in small letters. It is a prophetic symbol that reveals what the life of the baptized person is, in communion with Christ, with his death and resurrection. The fact that the top of the "ladder," the final steps, are at the same time the fundamental, initial, and most simple virtues is particularly important to me: faith, hope, and charity. These are not virtues accessible only to moral heroes; rather, they are gifts of God to all the baptized: in them our life develops too. The beginning is also the end; the starting point is also the point of arrival: the whole journey toward an ever more radical realization of faith, hope, and charity. The whole ascent is present in these virtues. Faith is fundamental, because this virtue implies that I renounce my arrogance, my thought, and the claim to judge by myself without entrusting myself to others. This journey toward humility, toward spiritual childhood is essential.

It is necessary to overcome the attitude of arrogance that makes one say: I know better, in this my time of the twenty-first century, than what people could have known then. Instead, it is necessary to entrust oneself to Sacred Scripture alone, to the Word of the Lord, to look out on the horizon of faith with humility, in order to enter into the enormous immensity of the universal world, of the world of God. In this way, our soul grows; the sensitivity of the heart grows toward God. Rightly, John Climacus says that hope alone renders us capable of living charity; hope is how we transcend the things of every day. We do not expect success in our earthly days, but we look forward to the revelation of God himself at last. It is only in this extension of our soul, in this self-transcendence, that our life becomes great and that we are able to bear the effort and disappointments of every day, that we can be kind to others without expecting any reward. Only if there is God, this great hope to which I aspire, can I take the small steps of my life and thus learn charity. The mystery of prayer, of the personal knowledge of Jesus, is concealed in charity: simple prayer that strives only to move the divine teacher's heart. So it is that one's own heart opens, one learns from him his own kindness, his love. Let us therefore use this "ascent" of faith, hope, and charity. In this way, we will arrive at true life.

—*11 February 2009*

BEDE THE VENERABLE

THE SAINT WE ARE APPROACHING NOW is called Bede and was born in the northeast of England; to be exact, Northumbria, in the year 672 or 673. He himself recounts that when he was seven years old his parents entrusted him to the abbot of the neighboring Benedictine monastery to be educated, "spending all the remaining time of my life a dweller in that monastery." He recalls, "I wholly applied myself to the study of Scripture; and amid the observance of the monastic rule and the daily charge of singing in church, I always took delight in learning, or teaching, or writing" (*Historia eccl. Anglorum*, 5, 24). In fact, Bede became one of the most outstanding erudite figures of the early Middle Ages since he was able to avail himself of many precious manuscripts which his abbots would bring him on their return from frequent journeys to the Continent and to Rome. His teaching and the fame of his writings occasioned his friendships with many of the most important figures of his time, who encouraged him to persevere in his work, from which so many were to benefit. When Bede fell ill, he did not stop working, always preserving an inner joy that he expressed in prayer and song. He ended his most important work, the *Historia Ecclesiastica gentis Anglorum,* with this invocation: "I beseech you, O good Jesus, that to the one to whom you have graciously granted sweetly to drink in the words of your knowledge, you will also vouchsafe in your loving-kindness that he may one day come to you, the Fountain of all wisdom, and appear for ever before your face." Death took him on 26 May 737; it was the Ascension.

Sacred Scripture was the constant source of Bede's theological reflection. After a critical study of the text (a copy of the monumental *Codex Amiatinus* of the Vulgate on which Bede worked has come down to us), he comments on the Bible, interpreting it in a christological key, that is, combining two things: on the one hand, he listens to exactly what the text says, he really seeks to hear and understand the text itself; on the other, he is convinced that the key to understanding Sacred Scripture as the one Word of God is Christ, and with Christ, in his light, one understands the Old and New Testaments as "one" Sacred Scripture. The events of the Old and New Testaments go together; they are the way to Christ, although expressed in different signs and institutions. (This is what he calls the *concordia sacramentorum.*) For example, the tent of the covenant that Moses pitched in the desert and the first and second Temple of Jerusalem are images of the Church, the new temple built on Christ and on the Apostles with living stones, held together by the love of the Spirit. And just as pagan peoples also contributed to building the ancient temple by making available valuable materials and the technical experience of their master builders, so too contributing to the construction of the Church there were Apostles and teachers, not only from ancient Jewish, Greek, and Latin lineage, but also from the new peoples, among whom Bede was pleased to list the Irish Celts and Anglo-Saxons. Saint Bede saw the growth of the universal dimension of the Church, which is not restricted to one specific culture but is composed of all the cultures of the world that must be open to Christ and find in him their goal.

Another of Bede's favorite topics is the history of the Church. After studying the period described in the Acts of the Apostles, he reviews the history of the Fathers and the councils, convinced that the work of the Holy Spirit continues in history. In the *Chronica Maiora*, Bede outlines a chronology that was to become the basis of the universal calendar *ab incarnatione Domini*. In his day, time was calculated from the foundation of the city of Rome. Realizing that the true reference point, the center of history, is the birth of Christ, Bede gave us this calendar that interprets history starting from the Incarnation of the Lord. Bede records the first six Ecumenical Councils and their developments, faithfully presenting Christian doctrine, both Mariological and soteriological, and denouncing the Monophysite and Monothelite, iconoclastic and neo-Pelagian heresies. Last, he compiled with documentary rigor and literary expertise the *Ecclesiastical History of the English Peoples*, mentioned above, which earned him recognition as "the father of English historiography." The characteristic features of the Church that Bede sought to emphasize are first, *catholicity*, seen as faithfulness to tradition while remaining open to historical developments, and as the quest for unity in multiplicity, in historical and cultural diversity according to the directives Pope Gregory the Great had given to Augustine of Canterbury, the Apostle of England. Second, *apostolicity and Roman traditions*: in this regard, he deemed it of prime importance to convince all the Irish, Celtic, and Pict churches to have one celebration for Easter in accordance with the Roman calendar. The *Computo*, which he worked out scientifically to establish the exact date of the Easter celebration, hence the entire cycle of the liturgical year, became the reference text for the whole Catholic Church.

Bede was also an eminent teacher of liturgical theology. In his homilies on the Gospels for Sundays and feast days, he achieves a true mystagogy, teaching the faithful to celebrate the mysteries of the faith joyfully and to reproduce them coherently in life, while awaiting their full manifestation with the return of Christ, when, with our glorified bodies, we shall be admitted to the offertory procession in the eternal liturgy of God in heaven. Following the "realism" of the catecheses of Cyril, Ambrose, and Augustine, Bede teaches that the sacraments of Christian initiation make every faithful person "not only a Christian but Christ." Indeed, every time that a faithful soul lovingly accepts and preserves the Word of

God, in imitation of Mary, he conceives and generates Christ anew. And every time that a group of neophytes receives the Easter sacraments, the Church "reproduces herself" or, to use a more daring term, the Church becomes "Mother of God," participating in the generation of her children through the action of the Holy Spirit.

Through his way of creating theology, interweaving the Bible, liturgy, and history, Bede has a timely message for the different "states of life." For scholars (*doctores ac doctrices*), he recalls two essential tasks: to examine the marvels of the Word of God in order to present them in an attractive form to the faithful and to explain the dogmatic truths, avoiding heretical complications and keeping to "Catholic simplicity," with the attitude of the lowly and humble to whom God is pleased to reveal the mysteries of the kingdom. Pastors, for their part, must give priority to preaching, not only through verbal or hagiographic language but also by giving importance to icons, processions, and pilgrimages. Bede recommends that they use the Vulgate as he himself does, explaining the Our Father and the creed in Northumbrian and continuing, until the last day of his life, his commentary on the Gospel of John in the Vulgate. Bede recommends to consecrated people who devote themselves to the Divine Office, living in the joy of fraternal communion and progressing in the spiritual life by means of *ascesis* and contemplation, that they attend to the apostolate—no one possesses the Gospel for oneself alone but must perceive it as a gift for others too—both by collaborating with bishops in pastoral activities of various kinds for the young Christian communities and by offering themselves for the evangelizing mission among the pagans, outside their own country, as *peregrini pro amore Dei*.

Making this viewpoint his own, in his commentary on the Song of Songs, Bede presents the synagogue and the Church as collaborators in the dissemination of God's Word. Christ the bridegroom wants a hardworking Church, "weathered by the efforts of evangelization." There is a clear reference to the word in the Song of Songs (1:5), where the bride says, *Nigra sum sed formosa* ("I am very dark, but comely"), intent on tilling other fields or vineyards and in establishing among the new peoples "not a temporary hut but a permanent dwelling place." In other words, Bede is intent on integrating the gospel into their social fabric and cultural institutions. From this perspective, the holy doctor urges lay faithful to be diligent in religious instruction, imitating those "insatiable crowds of the Gospel who did not even allow the Apostles time to take a mouthful." He teaches them how to pray ceaselessly, "reproducing in life what they celebrate in the liturgy," offering all their actions as a spiritual sacrifice in union with Christ. He explains to parents that in their small domestic circle too they can exercise "the priestly office as pastors and guides," giving their children a Christian upbringing. He also affirms that he knows many of the faithful (men and women, married and single) "capable of irreproachable conduct who, if appropriately guided, will be able every day to receive eucharistic communion" (*Epist. ad Ecgberctum,* ed. Plummer, 419). The fame of holiness and wisdom that Bede already enjoyed in his lifetime earned him the title of "Venerable." Pope Sergius I called him this when he wrote to his abbot in 701 asking him to allow him to come to Rome temporarily to give advice on matters of universal interest. After his death, Bede's writings were widely disseminated in his homeland and on the European continent. Bishop St. Boniface, the great missionary of Germany (d. 754), asked the archbishop of York and the abbot of Wearmouth several times to have some of his works transcribed and sent to him so that he and his companions might also enjoy the spiritual light that shone from them. A century later, Notker Balbulus, abbot of Sankt Gallen (d. 912), noting the extraordinary influence of Bede, compared him to a new sun that God had caused to rise, not in the East but in the West, to illuminate the world. Apart from the rhetorical emphasis, it is a fact that with his works Bede made an effective contribution to building a Christian Europe in which the various peoples and cultures amalgamated with one another, thereby giving them a single physiognomy, inspired by the Christian faith. Let us pray that today too there may be figures of Bede's stature, to keep the whole continent united; let us pray that we may all be willing to rediscover our common roots, in order to be builders of a profoundly human and authentically Christian Europe.

—*18 February 2009*

ST. BONIFACE, APOSTLE
OF THE GERMANS

WE REFLECT HERE ON A GREAT EIGHTH-CENTURY MISSIONARY who spread Christianity in central Europe—indeed, also in my own country: St. Boniface, who has gone down in history as "the Apostle of the Germans."

We have a fair amount of information on Boniface's life, thanks to the diligence of his biographers. He was born into an Anglo-Saxon family in Wessex in about 675 and was baptized with the name of Winfrid. He entered the monastery at a very early age, attracted by the monastic ideal. Since he possessed considerable intellectual ability, he seemed destined for a peaceful and brilliant academic career. He became a teacher of Latin grammar, wrote several treatises, and even composed various poems in Latin. He was ordained a priest at the age of about thirty and felt called to an apostolate among the pagans on the Continent. His country, Great Britain, which had been evangelized barely a hundred years earlier by Benedictines led by St. Augustine, at the time showed such sound faith and ardent charity that it could send missionaries to central Europe to proclaim the gospel there. In 716, Winfrid went to Frisia (today Holland) with a few companions, but he encountered the opposition of the local chieftain, and his attempt at evangelization failed. Having returned home, he did not lose heart and two years later traveled to Rome to speak to Pope Gregory II and receive his instructions. One biographer recounts that the pope welcomed him "with a smile and a look full of kindliness," and had "important conversations" with him in the following days (Willibaldo [Willibald of Mainz], *Vita S. Bonifatii*, ed. Levison, 13–14), and last, after conferring upon him the new name of Boniface, assigned to him, in official letters, the mission of preaching the gospel among the German peoples.

Comforted and sustained by the pope's support, Boniface embarked on the preaching of the gospel in those regions, fighting against pagan worship and reinforcing the foundations of human and Christian morality. With a deep sense of duty, he wrote in one of his letters: "We are united in the fight on the Lord's Day, because days of affliction and wretchedness have come. . . . We are not mute dogs or taciturn observers or mercenaries fleeing from wolves! On the contrary, we are diligent pastors who watch over Christ's flock, who proclaim God's will to the leaders and ordinary folk, to the rich and the poor in season and out of season" (cf. *Epistulae* 3, 352, 354). With his tireless activity and his gift for organization, Boniface, adaptable and friendly yet firm, obtained great results. The pope then "declared that he wished to confer upon him the episcopal dignity so that he might thus with greater determination correct and lead back to the path of truth those who had strayed, feeling supported by the greater authority of the apostolic dignity and being much more readily accepted by all in the office of preacher, the clearer it was that this was why he had been ordained by the apostolic bishop" (Othlo, *Vita S. Bonifatii,* ed. Levison, lib. 1, 127).

The supreme pontiff himself consecrated Boniface "regional bishop," that is, for the whole of Germany. Boniface then resumed his apostolic labors in the territories assigned to him and extended his action also to the Church of the Gauls: with great caution, he restored discipline in the Church, convoked various synods to guarantee the authority of the sacred canons, and strengthened the necessary communion with the Roman pontiff, a point that he had very much at heart. The successors of Pope Gregory II also held him in the highest esteem. Gregory III appointed him archbishop of all the Germanic tribes, sent him the pallium, and granted him the faculties to organize the ecclesiastical hierarchy in those regions (cf. *Epist.* 28: *S. Bonifatii Epistulae,* ed. Tangl [Berolini, 1916]. Pope Zacchary confirmed him in his office and praised his dedication (cf. *Epist.* 51, 57, 58, 60, 68, 77, 80, 86, 87, 89); Pope Stephen III, newly elected, received a letter from him in which he expressed his filial respect (cf. *Epist.* 108: *S. Bonifatii Epistulae,* ed. Tangl [Berolini, 1916]).

In addition to this work of evangelization and organization of the Church through the founding of dioceses and the celebration of synods, this great bishop did not omit to encourage the foundation of various male and female monasteries so that they would become like beacons, so as to radiate human and Christian culture and the faith in the territory. He summoned monks and nuns from the Benedictine monastic communities in his homeland who gave him a most effective and invaluable help in proclaiming the gospel and in disseminating the humanities and the arts among the population. Indeed, he rightly considered that work for the gospel must also be work for a true human culture. Above all, the monastery of Fulda, founded in about 743, was the heart and center of outreach of religious spirituality and culture: there the monks, in prayer, work, and penance, strove to achieve holiness; there they trained in the study of the sacred and profane disciplines and prepared themselves for the proclamation of the gospel in order to be missionaries. Thus, it was to the credit of Boniface, of his monks and nuns (for women too had a very important role in this work of evangelization) that human culture, which is inseparable from faith and reveals its beauty, flourished.

Boniface himself has left us an important intellectual corpus. First of all is his copious correspondence, in which pastoral letters alternate with official letters and others private in nature, which record social events but above all reveal his richly human temperament and profound faith.

In addition, he composed a treatise on the *Ars grammatica*, in which he explained the declinations, verbs, and syntax of the Latin language but which also became for him a means of spreading culture and the faith. An *Ars metrica*, that is, an introduction on how to write poetry, as well as various poetic compositions, and, last, a collection of fifteen sermons are also attributed to him.

Although he was getting on in years (he was almost eighty), Boniface prepared himself for a new evangelizing mission: with about fifty monks, he returned to Frisia, where he had begun his work. Almost as a prediction of his imminent death, in alluding to the journey of life, he wrote to Bishop Lull, his disciple and successor in the see of Mainz: "I wish to bring to a conclusion the purpose of this journey; in no way can I renounce my desire to set out. The day of my end is near and the time of my death is approaching; having shed my mortal body, I shall rise to the eternal reward. May you, my dear son, ceaselessly call the people from the maze of error, complete the building of the Basilica of Fulda that has already been begun, and in it lay my body, worn out by the long years of life" (Willibald, *Vita S. Bonifatii* 46). While he was beginning the celebration of Mass at Dokkum (in what today is northern Holland) on 5 June 754, he was assaulted by a band of pagans. Advancing with a serene expression, he "forbade his followers from fighting, saying, "Cease, my sons, from fighting, give up warfare, for the witness of Scripture recommends that we do not give an eye for an eye but rather good for evil. Here is the long awaited day, the time of our end has now come; courage in the Lord!"" (ibid., 49–50). These were his last words before he fell under the blows of his aggressors. The mortal remains of the martyr bishop were then taken to the monastery of Fulda, where they received a fitting burial. One of his first biographers had already made this judgment of him: "The holy Bishop Boniface can call himself father of all the inhabitants of Germany, for it was he who first brought them forth in Christ with the words of his holy preaching; he strengthened them with his example, and last, he gave his life for them; no greater love than this can be shown" (Othlo, *Vita S. Bonifatii, ed. cit.*, lib. 1, 158).

Centuries later, what message can we gather today from the teaching and marvelous activity of this great missionary and martyr? For those who approach Boniface, an initial fact stands out: *the centrality of the Word of God,* lived and interpreted in the faith of the Church, a word that he lived, preached, and witnessed to until he gave the supreme gift of himself in martyrdom. He was so passionate about the Word of God that he felt the urgent need and duty to communicate it to others, even at his own personal risk. This word was the pillar of the faith, which he had committed himself to spreading at the moment of his episcopal ordination: "I profess integrally the purity of the holy Catholic faith and with the help of God I desire to remain in the unity of this faith, in which there is no doubt that the salvation of Christians lies" (*Epist.* 12, in *S. Bonifatii Epistolae* 29). The second most important proof that emerges from the life of Boniface is his *faithful communion with the Apostolic See,* which was a firm and central reference point of his missionary work; he always preserved this communion as a rule of his mission and left it, as it were, as his will. In a letter to Pope Zachary, he said: "I never cease to invite and to submit to obedience to the Apostolic See those who desire to remain in the Catholic faith and in the unity of the Roman Church and all those whom God grants to me as listeners and disciples in my mission" (*Epist.* 50: in ibid., 81). One result of this commitment was the steadfast spirit of cohesion around the successor of Peter, which Boniface transmitted to the Church in his mission territory, uniting England, Germany, and France with Rome and thereby effectively contributing to planting those Christian roots of Europe which were to produce abundant fruit in the centuries to come. Boniface also deserves our attention for a third characteristic: he encouraged *the encounter between the Christian-Roman culture and the Germanic culture.* Indeed, he knew that humanizing and evangelizing culture was an integral part of his mission as bishop. In passing on the ancient patrimony of Christian values, he grafted onto the Germanic populations a new, more human lifestyle, thanks to which the inalienable rights of the person were more widely respected. As a true son of St. Benedict, he was able to combine prayer and labor (manual and intellectual), pen and plough.

Boniface's courageous witness is an invitation to us all to welcome God's word into our lives as an essential reference point, to love the Church passionately, to feel co-responsible for her future, to seek her unity around the successor of Peter. At the same time, he reminds us that Christianity, by encouraging the dissemination of culture, furthers human progress. It is now up to us to be equal to such a prestigious patrimony and to make it fruitful for the benefit of the generations to come.

His ardent zeal for the gospel never fails to impress me. At the age of forty-one, he left a beautiful and fruitful monastic life, the life of a monk and teacher, in order to proclaim the gospel to the simple, to barbarians. Once again, at the age of eighty, he went to a region in which he foresaw his martyrdom. By comparing his ardent faith, this zeal for the gospel, with our own often lukewarm and bureaucratized faith, we see what we must do and how to renew our faith, in order to give the precious pearl of the gospel as a gift to our time.

—*11 March 2009*

GERMANUS OF CONSTANTINOPLE

PATRIARCH GERMANUS OF CONSTANTINOPLE does not belong among the most representative figures of the Greek-speaking world of Eastern Christianity. Yet his name appears with a certain solemnity in the list of the great champions of sacred images drafted by the Second Council of Nicaea, the Seventh Ecumenical Council (787). The Greek Church celebrates his feast in the liturgy of 12 May. He played an important role in the overall history of the controversy over images during the "Iconoclastic Crisis": he was able to resist effectively the pressures of an Iconoclast emperor, in other words opposed to icons, such as Leo III.

During the patriarchate of Germanus (715–730), the capital of the Byzantine Empire, Constantinople, was subjected to a dangerous siege by the Saracens. On that occasion (717–718), a solemn procession was organized in the city displaying the image of the Mother of God, the *Theotokos*, and the relic of the True Cross, to invoke protection for the city from on high. In fact, Constantinople was liberated from the siege. The enemy decided to desist forever from the idea of establishing their capital in the city that was the symbol of the Christian empire, and the people were extremely grateful for the divine help.

After that event, Patriarch Germanus was convinced that God's intervention must be considered as obvious approval of the devotion shown by the people for the holy icons. However, the Emperor Leo III was of the absolute opposite opinion; that very year (717), he was enthroned as the undisputed emperor in the capital, over which he reigned until 741. After the liberation of Constantinople and after a series of other victories, the Christian emperor began to show more and more openly his conviction that the consolidation of the empire must begin precisely with a reordering of the manifestations of faith, with particular reference to the risk of idolatry to which, in his opinion, the people were prone because of their excessive worship of icons.

Patriarch Germanus's appeals to the tradition of the Church and to the efficacy of certain images—unanimously recognized as "miraculous"—were to no avail. The emperor more and more stubbornly applied his restoration project, which provided for the elimination of icons. At a public meeting on 7 January 730, when he openly took a stance against the worship of images, Germanus was in no way ready to comply with the emperor's will on matters he himself deemed crucial for the Orthodox faith, of which he believed worship and love for images were part. As a consequence, Germanus was forced to resign from the office of patriarch, condemning himself to exile in a monastery where he died forgotten by almost all. His name reappeared on the occasion of the Second Council of Nicaea (787), when the Orthodox Fathers decided in favor of icons, recognizing the merits of Germanus.

Patriarch Germanus took great care of the liturgical celebrations and, for a certain time, was also believed to have introduced the feast of the *Akathistos*. As is well known, the *Akathistos* is a famous ancient hymn to the *Theotokos*, the Mother of God, which came into being in the Byzantine context. Despite the fact that from the theological viewpoint Germanus cannot be described as a great thinker, some of his works had a certain resonance, especially on account of some of his insights concerning Mariology. In fact, various of his homilies on Marian topics are extant, and some of them profoundly marked the piety of entire generations of faithful, both in the East and in the West. His splendid *Homilies on the Presentation of Mary at the Temple* are still living testimony of the unwritten tradition of the Christian Churches. Generations of nuns and monks and the members of a great number of institutes of consecrated life continue still today to find in these texts the most precious pearls of spirituality.

Some of Germanus's Mariological texts still give rise to wonder today. They are part of the homilies he gave *In SS. Deiparae dormitionem,* a celebration that corresponds with our Feast of the Assumption. Among these texts, Pope Pius XII picked out one that he set like a pearl in his Apostolic Constitution *Munificentissimus Deus* (1950), with which he declared Mary's Assumption a dogma of faith. Pope Pius XII cited this text in the above-mentioned constitution, presenting it as one of the arguments in favor of the permanent faith of the Church concerning the bodily Assumption of Mary into heaven. Germanus wrote:

> May it never happen, Most Holy Mother of God, that heaven and earth, honored by your presence, and you, with your departure, leave men and women without your protection. No. It is impossible to think of such things. In fact, just as when you were in the world you did not feel foreign to the realities of heaven, so too after you had emigrated from this world, you were not foreign to the possibility of communicating in spirit with mankind. . . . You did not at all abandon those to whom you had guaranteed salvation . . . in fact, your spirit lives in eternity nor did your flesh suffer the corruption of the tomb. You, O Mother, are close to all and protect all, and although our eyes are unable to see you, we know, O Most Holy One, that you dwell among all of us and make yourself present in the most varied ways. . . . You (Mary) reveal your whole self, as is written, in your beauty. Your virginal body is entirely holy, entirely chaste, entirely the dwelling place of God so that, even for this reason, it is absolutely incorruptible. It is unchangeable since what was human in it has been taken up in incorruptibility, remaining

alive and absolutely glorious, undamaged, and sharing in perfect life. Indeed, it was impossible that the one who had become the vase of God and the living temple of the most holy divinity of the Only Begotten One be enclosed in the sepulcher of the dead. On the other hand, we believe with certainty that you continue to walk with us. (*PG* 98, col. 344b–46b, passim)

It has been said that for the Byzantines the decorum of the rhetorical form in preaching and especially in hymns or in the poetic compositions that they call *troparia* is equally important in the liturgical celebration as the beauty of the sacred building in which it takes place. Patriarch Germanus was recognized, in that tradition, as one who made a great contribution to keeping this conviction alive, that is, that the beauty of the words and language must coincide with the beauty of the building and the music. I quote the inspired words with which Germanus described the Church at the beginning of his small masterpiece:

The Church is the temple of God, a sacred space, a house of prayer, the convocation of people, the body of Christ. . . . She is heaven on earth, where the transcendent God dwells as if in his own home and passes through, but she is also an impression made (*antitypos*) of the crucifixion, the tomb, and the resurrection. . . . The Church is God's house in which the life-giving mystical sacrifice is celebrated, at the same time the most intimate part of the shrine and sacred grotto. Within her, in fact, the sepulcher and the table are found, nourishment for the soul and a guarantee of life. In her, last, are found those true and proper precious pearls which are the divine dogmas of teaching that the Lord offered directly to this disciples. (*PG* 98, col. 384b–85a)

Last, the question remains: what does this saint chronologically and also culturally rather distant from us have to tell us today? I am thinking mainly of three things. The first: there is a certain visibility of God in the world, in the Church, that we must learn to perceive. God has created man in his image, but this image was covered with the scum of so much sin that God almost no longer shines through it. Thus, the Son of God was made true man, a perfect image of God: thus, in Christ we may also contemplate the face of God and learn to be true men ourselves, true images of God. Christ invites us to imitate him, to become similar to him, so in every person the face of God shines out anew. To tell the truth, in the Ten Commandments God forbade the making of images of God, but this was because of the temptations to idolatry to which the believer might be exposed in a context of paganism. Yet when God made himself visible in Christ through the Incarnation, it became legitimate to reproduce the face of Christ. The holy images teach us to see God represented in the face of Christ. After the Incarnation of the Son of God, it therefore became possible to see God in images of Christ and also in the faces of the saints, in the faces of all people in whom God's holiness shines out.

The second thing is the beauty and dignity of the liturgy. To celebrate the liturgy in the awareness of God's presence, with that dignity and beauty which make a little of his splendor visible, is the commitment of every Christian trained in his faith.

The third thing is to love the Church. Precisely with regard to the Church, we men and women are prompted to see above all the sins and the negative side, but with the help of faith, which enables us to see in an authentic way, today and always we can rediscover the divine beauty in her. It is in the Church that God is present, offers himself to us in the holy eucharist, and remains present for adoration. In the Church, God speaks to us; in the Church, God "walks beside us," as St. Germanus said. In the Church, we receive God's forgiveness and learn to forgive.

Let us pray God to teach us to see his presence and his beauty in the Church, to see his presence in the world, and to help us too to be transparent to his light.

—*29 April 2009*

JOHN DAMASCENE

JOHN DAMASCENE WAS A PERSONAGE OF PRIME IMPORTANCE in the history of Byzantine theology and a great doctor in the history of the universal Church. Above all, he was an eyewitness of the passage from the Greek and Syrian Christian cultures shared by the Eastern part of the Byzantine Empire to the Islamic culture, which spread through its military conquests in the territory commonly known as the Middle or Near East.

John, born into a wealthy Christian family, at an early age assumed the role, perhaps already held by his father, of treasurer of the caliphate. Very soon, however, dissatisfied with life at court, he decided on a monastic life and entered the monastery of Mar Saba, near Jerusalem. This was around the year 700. He never again left the monastery but dedicated all his energy to *ascesis* and literary work, not disdaining a certain amount of pastoral activity, as is shown by his numerous homilies. His liturgical commemoration is on the 4 December. Pope Leo XIII proclaimed him Doctor of the Universal Church in 1890.

In the East, his best-remembered works are the three *Discourses against Those Who Calumniate the Holy Images,* which were condemned after his death by the iconoclastic Council of Hieria (754). These discourses, however, were also the fundamental grounds for his rehabilitation and canonization on the part of the Orthodox Fathers summoned to the Council of Nicaea (787), the Seventh Ecumenical Council. In these texts, it is possible to trace the first important theological attempts to legitimize the veneration of sacred images, relating them to the mystery of the Incarnation of the Son of God in the womb of the Virgin Mary.

John Damascene was also among the first to distinguish, in the cult, both public and private, of the Christians, between worship (*latreia*) and veneration (*proskynesis*): the first can only be offered to God, spiritual above all else; the second, however, can make use of an image to address the one whom the image represents. Obviously, the saint can in no way be identified with the material of which the icon is composed. This distinction was immediately seen to be very important in finding an answer in Christian terms to those who considered universal and eternal the strict Old Testament prohibition against the use of cult images. This was also a matter of great debate in the Islamic world, which accepts the Jewish tradition of the total exclusion of cult images. Christians, on the other hand, in this context, have discussed the problem and found a justification for the veneration of images. John Damascene writes:

In other ages, God had not been represented in images, being incorporate and faceless. But since God has now been seen in the flesh, and lived among men, I represent that part of God which is visible. I do not venerate matter, but the Creator of matter, who became matter for my sake and deigned to live in matter and bring about my salvation through matter. I will not cease therefore to venerate that matter through which my salvation was achieved. But I do not venerate it in absolute terms as God! How could that which, from non-existence, has been given existence, be God? . . . But I also venerate and respect all the rest of matter which has brought me salvation, since it is full of energy and holy graces. Is not the wood of the cross, three times blessed, matter? . . . And the ink, and the most holy book of the Gospels, are they not matter? The redeeming altar which dispenses the bread of life, is it not matter? . . . And, before all else, are not the flesh and blood of our Lord matter? Either we must suppress the sacred nature of all these things, or we must concede to the tradition of the Church the veneration of the images of God and that of the friends of God who are sanctified by the name they bear, and for this reason are possessed by the grace of the Holy Spirit. Do not, therefore, offend matter: it is not contemptible, because nothing that God has made is contemptible. (cf. *Contra imaginum calumniatores* 1, 16, ed. Kotter, 89–90)

We see that as a result of the Incarnation, matter is seen to have become divine, is seen as the habitation of God. It is a new vision of the world and of material reality. God became flesh, and flesh became truly the habitation of God, whose glory shines in the human face of Christ. Thus, the arguments of the Doctor of the East are still extremely relevant today, considering the very great dignity that matter has acquired through the Incarnation, capable of becoming, through faith, a sign and a sacrament, efficacious in the meeting of man with God. John Damascene remains, therefore, a privileged witness of the cult of icons, which would come to be one of the most distinctive aspects of Eastern spirituality up to the present day. It is, however, a form of cult that belongs simply to the Christian faith, to the faith in that God who became flesh and was made visible. The teaching of St. John Damascene thus finds its place in the tradition of the universal Church, whose sacramental doctrine foresees that material elements taken from nature can become vehicles of grace by virtue of the invocation (*epiclesis*) of the Holy Spirit, accompanied by the confession of the true faith.

John Damascene extends these fundamental ideas to the veneration of the relics of saints, on the basis of the conviction that the Christian saints, having become partakers of the Resurrection of Christ, cannot be considered simply "dead." Numbering, for example, those whose relics or images are worthy of veneration, John states in his third discourse in defense of images: "First of all (let us venerate) those among whom God reposed, he alone holy, who reposes among the saints [cf. Is 57:15], such as the Mother of God and all the saints. These are those who, as far as possible, have made themselves similar to God by their own will; and by God's presence in them, and his help, they are really called gods [cf. Ps 82(81):6], not by their nature, but by contingency, just as the red-hot iron is called fire, not by its nature, but by contingency and its participation in the fire. He says, in fact: you shall be holy, because I am holy (cf. Lev 19:2)" (3, 33, col. 1352a). After a series of references of this kind, John Damascene was able serenely to deduce:

> God, who is good, and greater than any goodness, was not content with the contemplation of himself, but desired that there should be beings benefited by him, who might share in his goodness: therefore he created from nothing all things, visible and invisible, including man, a reality visible and invisible. And he created him envisaging him and creating him as a being capable of thought (*ennoema ergon*), enriched with the word (*logo[i] symploroumenon*), and oriented toward the spirit (*pneumati teleioumenon*). (2, 2: PG 94, col. 865a)

And to clarify this thought further, he adds:

> We must allow ourselves to be filled with wonder (*thaumazein*) at all the works of providence (*tes pronoias erga*), to accept and praise them all, overcoming any temptation to identify in them aspects which to many may seem unjust or iniquitous (*adika*), and admitting instead that the project of God (*pronoia*) goes beyond man's capacity to know or to understand (*agnoston kai akatalepton*), while on the contrary only he may know our thoughts, our actions, and even our future. (2, 29: PG 94, col. 964c)

Plato, in fact, had said already that all philosophy begins with wonder. Our faith, too, begins with wonder at the very fact of the creation, and at the beauty of God who makes himself visible.

The optimism of the contemplation of nature (*physike theoria*), of seeing in the visible creation the good, the beautiful, the true, this Christian optimism, is not ingenuous: it takes account of the wound inflicted on human nature by the freedom of choice desired by God and misused by humans, with all the consequences of widespread discord which have derived from it. From this derives the need, clearly perceived by John Damascene, that nature, in which the goodness and beauty of God are reflected, wounded by our fault, "should be strengthened and renewed" by the descent of the Son of God in the flesh, after God had tried in many ways and on many occasions to show that he had created man so that he might exist not only in "being," but also in "well-being" (cf. *The Orthodox Faith*, 2, 1: PG 94, col. 981). With passionate eagerness, John explains: "It was necessary for nature to be strengthened and renewed, and for the path of virtue to be indicated and effectively taught (*didachthenai aretes hodòn*), the path that leads away from corruption and toward eternal life. . . . So there appeared on the horizon of history the great sea of love that God bears toward man (*philanthropias pelagos*)." It is a fine expression. We see on one side the beauty of creation, and on the other the destruction wrought by the fault of man. But we see in the Son of God, who descends to renew nature, the sea of love that God has for man. John Damascene continues: "He himself, the Creator and the Lord, fought for his creation, transmitting to it his teaching by example. . . . And so the Son of God, while still remaining in the form of God, lowered the skies and descended . . . to his servants . . . achieving the newest thing of all, the only thing really new under the sun, through which he manifested the infinite power of God" (3, 1, PG 94, col. 981c–84b).

We may imagine the comfort and joy which these words, so rich in fascinating images, poured into the hearts of the faithful. We listen to them today, sharing the same feelings with the Christians of those far-off days: God desires to repose in us; God wishes to renew nature through our conversion; God wants to allow us to share in his divinity. May the Lord help us to make these words the substance of our lives.

—*6 May 2009*

St. Theodore the Studite

THE SAINT WE MEET NOW, ST. THEODORE THE STUDITE, brings us to the middle of the medieval Byzantine period, in a somewhat turbulent period from the religious and political perspectives.

Theodore was born in 759 into a devout noble family: his mother, Theoctista, and an uncle, Plato, abbot of the monastery of Saccudium in Bithynia, are venerated as saints. Indeed, it was his uncle who guided him toward monastic life, which he embraced at the age of twenty-two. He was ordained a priest by Patriarch Tarasius but soon ended his relationship with him because of the toleration the patriarch showed in the case of the adulterous marriage of the Emperor Constantine VI. This led to Theodore's exile in 796 to Thessalonica. He was reconciled with the imperial authority the following year under the Empress Irene, whose benevolence induced Theodore and Plato to transfer to the urban monastery of Studios, together with a large portion of the community of the monks of Saccudium, in order to avoid the Saracen incursions. So it was that the important "Studite Reform" began.

Theodore's personal life, however, continued to be eventful. With his usual energy, he became the leader of the resistance against the iconoclasm of Leo V, the Armenian who once again opposed the existence of images and icons in the Church. The procession of icons organized by the monks of Studios evoked a reaction from the police. Between 815 and 821, Theodore was scourged, imprisoned, and exiled to various places in Asia Minor. In the end, he was able to return to Constantinople but not to his own monastery. He therefore settled with his monks on the other side of the Bosporus. He is believed to have died in Prinkipo on 11 November 826, the day on which he is commemorated in the Byzantine calendar.

Theodore distinguished himself within Church history as one of the great reformers of monastic life and as a defender of the veneration of sacred images, beside St. Nicephorus, patriarch of Constantinople, in the second phase of the iconoclasm. Theodore had realized that the issue of the veneration of icons was calling into question the truth of the Incarnation itself. In his three books, the *Antirretikoi* (*Confutations*), Theodore makes a comparison between eternal intra-Trinitarian relations, in which the existence of each of the divine persons does not destroy their unity, and the relations between Christ's two natures, which do not jeopardize in him the one person of the *Logos*. He also argues: abolishing veneration of the icon of Christ would mean repudiating his redeeming work, given that, in assuming human nature, the invisible eternal Word appeared in visible human flesh and in so doing sanctified the entire visible cosmos.

Theodore and his monks, courageous witnesses in the period of the iconoclastic persecutions, were inseparably bound to the reform of cenobitic life in the Byzantine world. Their importance was notable if only for an external circumstance: their number. Whereas the number of monks in monasteries of that time did not exceed thirty or forty, we know from the *Life of Theodore* of the existence of more than one thousand Studite monks overall. Theodore himself tells us of the presence in his monastery of about three hundred monks; thus, we see the enthusiasm of faith that was born within the context of this man's being truly informed and formed by faith itself. However, more influential than these numbers was the new spirit the founder impressed on cenobitic life. In his writings, he insists on the urgent need for a conscious return to the teaching of the Fathers, especially to St. Basil, the first legislator of monastic life, and to St. Dorotheus of Gaza, a famous spiritual father of the Palestinian desert. Theodore's characteristic contribution consists in insistence on the need for order and submission on the monks' part. During the persecutions, they had scattered, and each one had grown accustomed to living according to his own judgment. Then, as it was possible to reestablish community life, it was necessary to do the utmost to make the monastery once again an organic community, a true family, or, as St. Theodore said, a true "body of Christ." In such a community, the reality of the Church as a whole is realized concretely.

Another of St. Theodore's basic convictions was this: monks, differently from lay people, take on the commitment to observe the Christian duties with greater strictness and intensity. For this reason, they make a special profession which belongs to the *hagiasmata (consecrations)*, and it is, as it were, a "new baptism," symbolized by their taking the habit. Characteristic of monks in comparison with laypeople, then, is the commitment to poverty, chastity, and obedience. In addressing his monks, Theodore spoke in a practical, at times picturesque manner about poverty, but poverty in the following of Christ is from the start an essential element of monasticism and also points out a way for all of us. The renunciation of private property, this freedom from material things, as well as moderation and simplicity, apply in a radical form only to monks, but the spirit of this renouncement is equal for all. Indeed, we must not depend on material possessions but instead must learn renunciation, simplicity, austerity, and moderation. Only in this way can a supportive society develop and the great problem of poverty in this world be overcome. Therefore, in this regard, the monks' radical poverty is essentially also a path for us all. Then, when he explains the temptations against chastity, Theodore does not conceal his own experience and indicates the way of inner combat to find self-control and hence respect for one's own body and for the body of the other as a temple of God.

However, the most important renunciations in his opinion are those required by obedience, because each one of the monks has his own way of living, and fitting into the large community of three hundred monks truly involves a new way of life which he describes as the "martyrdom of submission." Here too the monks' example serves to show us how necessary this is for us, because, after original sin, man has tended to do what he likes. The first principle is for the life of the world; all the rest must be subjected to it. However, in this way, if each person is self-centered, the social structure cannot function. Only by learning to fit into the common freedom, to share and to submit to it, learning legality, that is, submission and obedience to the rules of the common good and life in common, can society be healed, as well as the *self*, of the pride of being the center of the world. Thus, St. Theodore, with fine introspection, helped his monks and ultimately also helps us to understand true life, to resist the temptation to set up our own will as the supreme rule of life, and to preserve our true personal identity, which is always an identity shared with others and peace of heart.

For Theodore the Studite, an important virtue on a par with obedience and humility is *philergia,* that is, the love of work, in which he sees a criterion by which to judge the quality of personal devotion: the person who is fervent and works hard in material concerns, he argues, will be the same in those of the spirit. Therefore, he does not permit the monk to dispense with work, including manual work, under the pretext of prayer and contemplation; for work to his mind and in the whole monastic tradition is actually a means of finding God. Theodore is not afraid to speak of work as the "sacrifice of the monk," as his "liturgy," even as a sort of mass through which monastic life becomes angelic life. And it is precisely in this way that the world of work must be humanized, and man, through work, becomes more himself and closer to God. One consequence of this unusual vision is worth remembering: precisely because it is the fruit of a form of "liturgy," the riches obtained from common work must not serve for the monks' comfort but must be earmarked for assistance to the poor. Here we can all understand the need for the proceeds of work to be a good for all. Obviously, the Studites work was not only manual: they had great importance in the religious and cultural development of the Byzantine civilization as calligraphers, painters, poets, educators of youth, school teachers, and librarians.

Although he exercised external activities on a truly vast scale, Theodore did not let himself be distracted from what he considered closely relevant to his role as superior: being the spiritual father of his monks. He knew what a crucial influence both his good mother and his holy uncle Plato, whom he described with the significant title "father" had had on his life. Thus, he himself provided spiritual direction for the monks. Every day, his biographer says, after evening prayer he would place himself in front of the iconostasis to listen to the confidences of all. He also gave spiritual advice to many people outside the monastery. The *Spiritual Testament* and the *Letters* highlight his open and affectionate character, and show that true spiritual friendships were born from his fatherhood both in the monastic context and outside it.

The *Rule*, known by the name of *Hypotyposis,* codified shortly after Theodore's death, was adopted, with a few modifications, on Mount Athos when in 962 St. Athanasius Anthonite founded the Great Laura there, and in the Kievan Rus's, when at the beginning of the second millennium St. Theodosius introduced it into the Laura of the Grottos. Understood in its genuine meaning, the *Rule* has proven to be unusually up to date. Numerous trends today threaten the unity of the common faith and impel people toward a sort of dangerous spiritual individualism and spiritual pride. It is necessary to strive to defend and to increase the perfect unity of the Body of Christ, in which the peace of order and sincere personal relations in the Spirit can be harmoniously composed.

It may be useful to return at the end to some of the main elements of Theodore's spiritual doctrine: love for the Lord incarnate and for his visibility in the liturgy and in icons; fidelity to baptism and the commitment to live in communion with the Body of Christ, also understood as the communion of Christians with each other; a spirit of poverty, moderation, and renunciation; chastity, self-control, humility, and obedience against the primacy of one's own will that destroys the social fabric and the peace of souls; love for physical and spiritual work; spiritual love born from the purification of one's own conscience, one's own soul, one's own life. Let us seek to comply with these teachings that really do show us the path of true life.

—*27 May 2009*

RABANUS MAURUS

A TRULY EXTRAORDINARY FIGURE OF THE LATIN WEST, Rabanus Maurus was an exceptional and prolific monk. Together with men such as Isidore of Seville and the Venerable Bede and Ambrose Autpert, two of whom I have spoken previously, during the centuries of the so-called Middle Ages, he was able to preserve the contact with the great culture of the ancient scholars and of the Christian Fathers. Often remembered as the *praeceptor Germaniae*, Rabanus Maurus was extraordinarily prolific. With his absolutely exceptional capacity for work, he perhaps made a greater contribution than anyone else to keeping alive that theological, exegetical, and spiritual culture on which successive centuries were to draw. He was referred to by great figures belonging to the monastic world, such as Peter Damian, Peter the Venerable, and Bernard of Clairvaux, as well as by an ever increasing number of "clerics" of the secular clergy who gave life to one of the most beautiful periods of the fruitful flourishing of human thought in the twelfth and thirteenth centuries.

Born in Mainz in about 780, Rabanus entered the monastery at a very early age. He was nicknamed "Maurus" after the young St. Maur who, according to *Book 2 of the Dialogues* of St. Gregory the Great, was entrusted by his parents, Roman nobles, to the Abbot Benedict of Nursia. Alone this precocious insertion of Rabanus as *puer oblatus* in the Benedictine monastic world and the benefits he drew from it for his own human, cultural, and spiritual growth were to provide an interesting glimpse not only of the life of monks and of the Church but also of the whole of society of his time, usually described as "Carolingian." About them or perhaps about himself, Rabanus Maurus wrote: "There are some who have had the good fortune to be introduced to the knowledge of Scripture from a tender age (*a cunabulis suis*) and who were so well-nourished with the food offered to them by Holy Church as to be fit for promotion, with the appropriate training, to the highest of sacred orders" (*PL* 107, col. 419bc).

The extraordinary culture for which Rabanus Maurus was distinguished soon brought him to the attention of the great of his time. He became the advisor of princes. He strove to guarantee the unity of the empire and, at a broader cultural level, never refused to give those who questioned him a carefully considered reply, which he found preferably in the Bible or in the texts of the Holy Fathers. First elected abbot of the famous monastery of Fulda and then appointed archbishop of Mainz, his native city, this did not stop him from pursuing his studies, showing by the example of his life that it is possible to be at the same time available to others without depriving oneself of the appropriate time for reflection, study, and meditation.

Rabanus Maurus was exegete, philosopher, poet, pastor, and man of God. The Dioceses of Fulda, Mainz, Limburg, and Breslau (Wrocław) venerate him as a saint or blessed. His works fill at least six volumes of Migne's *Patrologia Latina*. It is likely that we are indebted to him for one of the most beautiful hymns known to the Latin Church, the *Veni Creator Spiritus*, an extraordinary synthesis of Christian pneumatology. In fact, Rabanus's first theological work is expressed in the form of poetry and had as its subject the mystery of the Holy Cross in a book titled: *De laudibus Sanctae Crucis*, conceived in such a way as to suggest not only a conceptual content but also more exquisitely artistic stimuli, by the use of both poetic and pictorial forms within the same manuscript codex. Suggesting the image of the crucified Christ between the lines of his writing, he says, for example, "This is the image of the Savior who, with the position of his limbs, makes sacred for us the most salubrious, gentle, and loving form of the cross, so that by believing in his name and obeying his commandments we may obtain eternal life thanks to his passion. However, every time we raise our eyes to the cross, let us remember the one who died for us to save us from the powers of darkness, accepting death to make us heirs to eternal life" (*Lib.* 1, fig. 1: *PL* 107 col. 151c).

This method of combining all the arts, the intellect, the heart, and the senses, which came from the East, was to experience a great development in the West, reaching unparalleled heights in the miniature codices of the Bible and in other works of faith and art that flourished in Europe until the invention of printing and beyond. In Rabanus Maurus, in any case, is shown an extraordinary awareness of the need to involve, in the experience of faith, not only the mind and the heart but also the senses through those other aspects of aesthetic taste and human sensitivity that lead man to benefit from the truth with his whole self, "mind, soul, and body." This is important: faith is not only thought but also touches the whole of our being. Since God became human in flesh and blood, since he entered the tangible world, we must seek and encounter God in all the dimensions of our being. Thus, the reality of God, through faith, penetrates our being and transforms it. This is why Rabanus Maurus focused his attention above all on the liturgy as a synthesis of all the dimensions of our perception of reality. This intuition of Rabanus Maurus makes it extraordinarily up to date. Also famous among his opus are the *Hymns*, suggested for use especially in liturgical celebrations. In fact, since Rabanus was primarily a monk, his interest in the liturgical celebration was taken for granted. However, he did not devote himself to the art of poetry as an end in itself but, rather, used art and every other form of erudition as a means for deepening knowledge of the Word of God. He therefore sought with great application and rigor to introduce his contemporaries, especially ministers (bishops, priests, and deacons), to an understanding of the profoundly theological and spiritual meaning of all the elements of the liturgical celebration.

He thus sought to understand and to present to others the theological meanings concealed in the rites, drawing from the Bible and from the tradition of the Fathers. For the sake of honesty and to give greater weight to his explanations, he did not hesitate to indicate the Patristic sources to which he owed his knowledge. Nevertheless, he used them with freedom and with careful discernment, continuing the development of Patristic thought. At the end of the *Epistola prima*, addressed to a "chorbishop" of the Diocese of Mainz, for example, after answering the requests for clarification concerning the behavior to adopt in the exercise of pastoral responsibility, he continues, "We have written all these things for you as we deduced them from the Sacred Scriptures and the canons of the Fathers. Yet, most holy man, may you take your decisions as you think best, case by case, seeking to temper your evaluation in such a way as to guarantee discretion in all things because it is the mother of all the virtues" (*Epistulae*, 1, *PL* 112, col. 1510c). Thus, the continuity of the Christian faith, which originates in the Word of God, becomes visible; yet it is always alive, develops, and is expressed in new ways, ever consistent with the whole construction, with the whole edifice of faith.

Since an integral part of liturgical celebration is the Word of God, Rabanus Maurus dedicated himself to it with the greatest commitment throughout his life. He produced appropriate exegetical explanations for almost all the biblical books of the Old and New Testaments, with clearly pastoral intentions that he justified with words such as these: "I have written these things . . . summing up the explanations and suggestions of many others, not only in order to offer a service to the poor reader, who may not have many books at his disposal, but also to make it easier for those who in many things do not succeed in entering in depth into an understanding of the meanings discovered by the Fathers" (*Commentariorum in Matthaeum praefatio, PL* 107, col. 727d). In fact, in commenting on the biblical texts, he drew amply from the ancient Fathers, with special preference for Jerome, Ambrose, Augustine, and Gregory the Great.

His outstanding pastoral sensitivity later led him to occupy himself above all with one of the problems most acutely felt by the faithful and sacred ministers of his time: that of penance. Indeed, he compiled the *Penitenziari*, as he called them, in which, according to the sensibility of his day, sins and the corresponding penances were listed, using as far as possible reasons found in the Bible, in the decisions of the councils and in papal decretals. The Carolingians also used these texts in their attempt to reform the Church and society. Corresponding with the same pastoral intentions were works such as *De disciplina ecclesiastica* and *De institutione clericorum*, in which, drawing above all from Augustine, Rabanus explained to the simple and to the clergy of his diocese the basic elements of the Christian faith: they were like little catechisms.

I end the presentation of this great churchman by quoting some of his words in which his basic conviction is clearly reflected:

> Those who are negligent in contemplation (*qui vacare Deo negligit*) deprive themselves of the vision of God's light; then those who let themselves be indiscreetly invaded by worries and allow their thoughts to be overwhelmed by the tumult of worldly things condemn themselves to the absolute impossibility of penetrating the secrets of the invisible God. (*Lib* 1: *PL* 112, col. 1263a)

I think that Rabanus Maurus is also addressing these words to us today: in periods of work, with its frenetic pace, and in holiday periods we must reserve moments for God. We must open our lives to him, addressing to him a thought, a reflection, a brief prayer, and above all we must not forget Sunday as the Lord's Day, the day of the liturgy, in order to perceive God's beauty itself in the beauty of our churches, in our sacred music, and in the Word of God, letting him enter our being. Only in this way does our life become great, become true life.

—*3 June 2009*

John Scotus Erigena

THOUGH A NOTEWORTHY THINKER OF THE CHRISTIAN WEST, John Scotus Erigena's origins are nonetheless obscure. He certainly came from Ireland, where he was born at the beginning of the ninth century. But we do not know when he left his island to cross the channel and thus fully enter that cultural world which was coming into being around the Carolingians, and in particular around Charles the Bald, in ninth-century France. Just as we are not certain of the date of his birth, likewise we do not know the year of his death; but, according to the experts, it must have been in about the year 870.

John Scotus Erigena had a Patristic culture, both Greek and Latin, at firsthand. Indeed, he had direct knowledge of the writings of both the Latin and the Greek Fathers. He was well acquainted with, among others, the works of Augustine, Ambrose, Gregory the Great, and the important Fathers of the Christian West. But he was just as familiar with the thought of Origen, Gregory of Nyssa, John Chrysostom, and other Christian Fathers of the East who were equally important. He was an exceptional man who in that period had also mastered the Greek language. He devoted very special attention to St. Maximus the Confessor and above all to Dionysius the Areopagite. This pseudonym conceals a fifth-century ecclesiastical writer, but throughout the Middle Ages people, including John Scotus Erigena, were convinced that this author could be identified with a direct disciple of St. Paul who is mentioned in the Acts of the Apostles (17:34). Scotus Erigena, convinced of the apostolicity of Dionysius's writings, described him as a "divine author" par excellence; Dionysius's writings were therefore an eminent source of his thought. John Scotus translated his works into Latin. The great medieval theologians, such as St. Bonaventure, became acquainted with Dionysius's works through this translation. Throughout his life, John Scotus devoted himself to deepening his knowledge and developing his thought, drawing on these writings to the point that still today it can sometimes be difficult to distinguish where we are dealing with Scotus Erigena's thought and where, instead, he is merely proposing anew the thought of Pseudo-Dionysius.

The theological opus of John Scotus truly did not meet with much favor. Not only did the end of the Carolingian era cause his works to be forgotten; but a censure on the part of the Church authorities also cast a shadow over him. In fact, John Scotus represents a radical Platonism that sometimes seems to approach a pantheistic vision, even though his personal subjective intentions were always orthodox. Some of John Scotus Erigena's works have come down to us, among which the following in particular deserve mention: the reatise *On the Division of Nature* and the expositions on *The Heavenly Hierarchy* of St. Dionysius. In them, he continues to develop stimulating theological and spiritual reflections which could suggest an interesting furthering of knowledge also to contemporary theologians. I refer, for example, to what he wrote on the duty of exercising an appropriate discernment on what is presented as *auctoritas vera,* or on the commitment to continue the quest for the truth until one achieves some experience of it in the silent adoration of God.

Our author says: *Salus nostra ex fide inchoat*—our salvation begins with faith; in other words, we cannot speak of God starting with our own inventions but rather with what God says of himself in the Sacred Scriptures. Since, however, God tells only the truth, Scotus Erigena is convinced that authority and reason can never contradict each other; he is convinced that true religion and true philosophy coincide. In this perspective, he writes: "Any type of authority that is not confirmed by true reason must be considered weak. . . . Indeed, there is no true authority other than that which coincides with the truth, discovered by virtue of reason, even should one be dealing with an authority recommended and handed down for the use of the successors of the Holy Fathers" (1: *PL* 122, col. 513bc). Consequently, he warns: "Let no authority intimidate you or distract you from what makes you understand the conviction obtained through correct rational contemplation. Indeed, authentic authority never contradicts right reason, nor can the latter ever contradict a true authority. The one and the other both come indisputably from the same source, which is divine wisdom" (1: *PL* 122, col. 511b). We see here a brave affirmation of the value of reason, founded on the certainty that the true authority is reasonable, because God is creative reason.

According to Erigena, Scripture itself does not escape the need to be approached with the same criterion of discernment. In fact, although Scripture comes from God, the Irish theologian maintains, proposing anew a reflection made earlier by John Chrysostom, it would not be necessary had the human being not sinned. It must therefore be deduced that Scripture was given by God with a pedagogical intention and with indulgence so that man might remember all that had been impressed within his heart from the moment of his creation, "in the image and likeness of God" (cf. Gen 1:26) and that the fall of man had caused him to forget. Erigena writes in his *Expositiones*: "It is not man who was created for Scripture, which he would not have needed had he not sinned, but rather it is Scripture, interwoven with doctrine and symbols, which was given to man. Thanks to Scripture, in fact, our rational nature may be introduced to the secrets of authentic and pure contemplation of God" (2: *PL* 122, col. 146c). The words of Sacred Scripture purify our somewhat blind reason and help us to recover the memory of what we, as the image of God, carry in our hearts, unfortunately wounded by sin.

From this derive certain hermeneutical consequences concerning the way to interpret Scripture that still today can point out the right approach for a correct reading of Sacred Scripture. In fact, it is a question of discovering the hidden meaning in the sacred text, and this implies a special inner exercise through which reason is open to the sure road to the truth. This exercise consists in cultivating constant readiness for conversion. Indeed, to acquire an in-depth vision of the text, it is necessary to progress at the same time in conversion of the heart and in the conceptual analysis of the biblical passage, whether it is of a cosmic, historical, or doctrinal character. Indeed, it is only by means of a constant purification of both the eye of the heart and the eye of the mind that it is possible to arrive at an exact understanding.

This arduous, demanding, and exciting journey, which consists of continuous achievements and the relativization of human knowledge, leads the intelligent creature to the threshold of the divine mystery, where all notions admit of their own weakness and inability and thus, with the simple free and sweet power of the truth, make it obligatory ceaselessly to surpass all that is progressively achieved. Worshipful and silent recognition of the mystery which flows into unifying communion is therefore revealed as the only path to a relationship with the truth that is at the same time the most intimate possible and the most scrupulously respectful of otherness. John Scotus, here too using terminology dear to the Christian tradition of the Greek language, called this experience for which we strive *theosis*, or divinization, with such daring affirmations that he might be suspected of heterodox pantheism. Yet even today, one cannot but be strongly moved by texts such as the following, in which with recourse to the ancient metaphor of the smelting of iron he writes: "just as all red-hot iron is liquified to the point that it seems nothing but fire and yet the substances remain distinct from one another, so it must be accepted that after the end of this world all nature, both the corporeal and the incorporeal, will show forth God alone and yet remain integral so that God can in a certain way be comprehended while remaining incomprehensible and that the creature itself may be transformed, with ineffable wonder, and reunited with God" (5: PL 122, col. 451b).

In fact, the entire theological thought of John Scotus is the most evident demonstration of the attempt to express the expressible of the inexpressible God, based solely upon the mystery of the Word made flesh in Jesus of Nazareth. The numerous metaphors John Scotus used to point out this ineffable reality show how aware he was of the absolute inadequacy of the terms in which we speak of these things. And yet, the enchantment and that aura of authentic mystical experience, which every now and then one can feel tangibly in his texts, endures. As proof of this, it suffices to cite a passage from *De divisione naturae* which touches in depth even our mind as believers of the twenty-first century: "We should desire nothing," he writes, "other than the joy of the truth that is Christ, avoid nothing other than his absence. The greatest torment of a rational creature consists in the deprivation or absence of Christ. Indeed, this must be considered the one cause of total and eternal sorrow. Take Christ from me and I am left with no good thing, nor will anything terrify me so much as his absence. The greatest torments of a rational creature are the deprivation and absence of him" (5: *PL* 122, col. 989a). These are words that we can make our own, translating them into a prayer to the One for whom our hearts long.

—*10 June 2009*

STS. CYRIL AND METHODIUS

SAINTS CYRIL AND METHODIUS WERE BROTHERS by blood and in the faith, the so-called Apostles to the Slavs. Cyril was born in Thessalonica to Leo, an imperial magistrate, in 826 or 827. He was the youngest of seven. As a child, he learned the Slavonic language. When he was fourteen years old, he was sent to Constantinople to be educated and was companion to the young emperor, Michael III. In those years, Cyril was introduced to the various university disciplines, including dialectics, and his teacher was Photius. After refusing a brilliant marriage, he decided to receive holy orders and became "librarian" at the patriarchate. Shortly afterward, wishing to retire in solitude, he went into hiding at a monastery but was soon discovered and entrusted with teaching the sacred and profane sciences. He carried out this office so well that he earned the nickname of "Philosopher." In the meantime, his brother Michael (born in about 815) left the world after an administrative career in Macedonia and withdrew to a monastic life on Mount Olympus in Bithynia, where he was given the name "Methodius" (a monk's monastic name had to begin with the same letter as his baptismal name) and became hegumen of the monastery of Polychron.

Attracted by his brother's example, Cyril too decided to give up teaching and go to Mount Olympus to meditate and pray. A few years later (in about 861), the imperial government sent him on a mission to the Khazars on the Sea of Azov, who had asked for a scholar to be sent to them who could converse with both Jews and Saracens. Cyril, accompanied by his brother Methodius, stayed for a long time in Crimea, where he learned Hebrew and sought the body of Pope Clement I, who had been exiled there. Cyril found Pope Clement's tomb, and when he made the return journey with his brother, he took Clement's precious relics with him. Having arrived in Constantinople, the two brothers were sent to Moravia by the Emperor Michael III, who had received a specific request from Prince Ratislav of Moravia: "Since our people rejected paganism," Ratislav wrote to Michael, "they have embraced the Christian law; but we do not have a teacher who can explain the true faith to us in our own language." The mission was soon unusually successful. By translating the liturgy into the Slavonic language, the two brothers earned immense popularity.

However, this gave rise to hostility among the Frankish clergy, who had arrived in Moravia before the brothers and considered the territory to be under their ecclesiastical jurisdiction. In order to justify themselves, in 867 the two brothers traveled to Rome. On the way, they stopped in

Venice, where they had a heated discussion with the champions of the so-called trilingual heresy, who claimed that there were only three languages in which it was lawful to praise God: Hebrew, Greek, and Latin. The two brothers obviously forcefully opposed this claim. In Rome, Cyril and Methodius were received by Pope Adrian II, who led a procession to meet them in order to give a dignified welcome to St. Clement's relics. The pope had also realized the great importance of their exceptional mission. Since the middle of the first millennium, in fact, thousands of Slavs had settled in those territories located between the two parts of the Roman Empire, the East and the West, whose relations were fraught with tension. The pope perceived that the Slavic peoples would be able to serve as a bridge and thereby help to preserve the union between the Christians of both parts of the empire. Thus, he did not hesitate to approve the mission of the two brothers in Great Moravia, accepting and approving the use of the Slavonic language in the liturgy. The Slavonic books were laid on the altar of St. Mary of Phatmé (St. Mary Major), and the liturgy in the Slavonic tongue was celebrated in the Basilicas of St. Peter, St. Andrew, and St. Paul.

Unfortunately, Cyril fell seriously ill in Rome. Feeling that his death was at hand, he wanted to consecrate himself totally to God as a monk in one of the Greek monasteries of the city (probably Santa Prassede) and took the monastic name of Cyril. (His baptismal name was Constantine.) He then insistently begged his brother Methodius, who in the meantime had been ordained a bishop, not to abandon their mission in Moravia and to return to the peoples there. He addressed this prayer to God: "Lord, my God . . . hear my prayers and keep the flock you have entrusted to me faithful. . . . Free them from the heresy of the three languages, gather them all in unity, and make the people you have chosen agree in the true faith and confession." He died on 14 February 869.

Faithful to the pledge he had made with his brother, Methodius returned to Moravia and Pannonia (today, Hungary) the following year, 870, where once again he encountered the violent aversion of the Frankish missionaries, who took him prisoner. He did not lose heart, and when he was released in 873, he worked hard to organize the Church and train a group of disciples. It was to the merit of these disciples that it was possible to survive the crisis unleashed after the death of Methodius on 6 April 885: persecuted and imprisoned, some of them were sold as slaves and taken to Venice, where they were redeemed by a Constantinopolitan official who allowed them to return to the countries of the Slavonic Balkans. Welcomed in Bulgaria, they were able to continue the mission that Methodius had begun and to disseminate the gospel in the "Land of the Rus." God with his mysterious providence thus availed himself of their persecution to save the work of the holy brothers. Literary documentation of their work is extant. It suffices to think of texts such as the *Evangeliarium* (liturgical passages of the New Testament), the *Psalter*, various liturgical texts in Slavonic, on which both the brothers had worked. Indeed, after Cyril's death, it is to Methodius and to his disciples that we owe the translation of the entire Sacred Scriptures, the *Nomocanone* and the *Book of the Fathers*.

To sum up concisely the profile of the two brothers, we first recall the enthusiasm with which Cyril approached the writings of St. Gregory of Nazianzus, learning from him the value of language in the transmission of the revelation. Saint Gregory had expressed the wish that Christ would speak through him: "I am a servant of the Word, so I put myself at the service of the Word." Desirous of imitating Gregory in this service, Cyril asked Christ to deign to speak in Slavonic through him. He introduced his work of translation with the solemn invocation: "Listen, O all of you Slav peoples, listen to the word that comes from God, the word that nourishes souls, the word that leads to the knowledge of God." In fact, a few years before the Prince of Moravia had asked the Emperor Michael III to send missionaries to his country, it seems that Cyril and his brother Methodius, surrounded by a group of disciples, were already working on the project of collecting the Christian dogmas in books written in Slavonic. The need for new graphic characters closer to the language spoken was therefore clearly apparent: so it was that the Glagolitic alphabet came into being. Subsequently modified, it was later designated by the name "Cyrillic," in honor of the man who inspired it. It was a crucial event for the development of the Slav civilization in general. Cyril and Methodius were convinced that the individual peoples could not claim to have received revelation fully unless they had heard it in their own language and read it in the characters proper to their own alphabet.

Methodius had the merit of ensuring that the work begun by his brother was not suddenly interrupted. While Cyril, the "philosopher," was more inclined to contemplation, Methodius, on the other hand, had a leaning for the active life. Thanks to this, he was able to lay the foundations of the successive affirmation of what we might call the "Cyrillian-Methodian idea": it accompanied the Slav peoples in the different periods of their history, encouraging their cultural, national, and religious development. This was already recognized by Pope Pius XI in his apostolic letter *Quod Sanctum Cyrillum,* in which he described the two brothers: "Sons of the East, with a Byzantine homeland, of Greek origin, for the Roman missions to reap Slav apostolic fruit" (*AAS* 19 [1927] 93–96). The historic role they played was later officially proclaimed by Pope John Paul II who, with his apostolic letter *Egregiae Virtutis*, declared them co-patrons of Europe, together with St. Benedict (31 December 1980; *L'Osservatore Romano*, English edition, 19 January 1981, 3).

Cyril and Methodius are, in fact, a classic example of what today is meant by the term *enculturation*: every people must integrate the revealed message into its own culture and express its saving truth in its own language. This implies a very demanding effort of "translation" because it requires the identification of the appropriate words to present anew, without distortion, the riches of the revealed word. The two holy brothers have left us a most important testimony of this, to which the Church also looks today in order to draw from it inspiration and guidance.

—*17 June 2009*

ST. ODO OF CLUNY

WE RESUME THE PRESENTATION of important writers of the Eastern and Western Church in the Middle Ages because in their lives and writings we see, as in a mirror, what it means to be Christian. One such luminous figure is St. Odo, abbot of Cluny.

Odo fits into that period of medieval monasticism which saw the surprising success in Europe of the life and spirituality inspired by the Rule of St. Benedict. In those centuries, there was a wonderful increase in the number of cloisters that sprang up and branched out over the continent, spreading the Christian spirit and sensibility far and wide. Saint Odo takes us back in particular to Cluny, one of the most illustrious and famous monasteries in the Middle Ages that still today reveals to us, through its majestic ruins, the signs of a past rendered glorious by intense dedication to *ascesis*, study, and, in a special way, to divine worship endowed with decorum and beauty.

Odo was the second abbot of Cluny. He was born in about 880, on the boundary between the Maine and the Touraine regions of France. Odo's father consecrated him to the holy Bishop Martin of Tours, in whose beneficent shadow and memory he was to spend his entire life, which he ended close to St. Martin's tomb. His choice of religious consecration was preceded by the inner experience of a special moment of grace, of which he himself spoke to another monk, John the Italian, who later became his biographer. Odo was still an adolescent, about sixteen years old, when one Christmas Eve he felt this prayer to the Virgin rise spontaneously to his lips: "My Lady, Mother of Mercy, who on this night gave birth to the Savior, pray for me. May your glorious and unique experience of childbirth, O Most Devout Mother, be my refuge" (*Vita sancti Odonis* 1, 9: PL 133, 747). The name "Mother of Mercy" with which young Odo then invoked the Virgin was to be the title by which he always subsequently liked to address Mary. He also called her "the one Hope of the world . . . thanks to whom the gates of heaven were opened to us" (*In veneratione S. Mariae Magdalenae*: PL 133, 721). At that time, Odo chanced to come across the Rule of St. Benedict and to comment on it, "bearing, while not yet a monk, the light yoke of monks" (ibid., 1, 14: PL 133, 50). In one of his sermons, Odo was to celebrate Benedict as the "lamp that shines in the dark period of life" (*De sancto Benedicto abbate*: PL 133, 725) and to describe him as "a teacher of spiritual discipline" (ibid.: PL 133, 727). He was to point out with affection that Christian piety, "with the liveliest gentleness commemorates him" in the knowledge that God raised him "among the supreme and elect Fathers of Holy Church" (ibid.: PL 133, 722).

Fascinated by the Benedictine ideal, Odo left Tours and entered the Benedictine abbey of Baume as a monk; he later moved to Cluny, of which in 927 he became abbot. From that center of spiritual life, he was able to exercise a vast influence over the monasteries on the continent. Various monasteries or coenobiums were able to benefit from his guidance and reform, including that of St. Paul Outside-the-Walls. More than once Odo visited Rome, and he even went as far as Subiaco, Monte Cassino, and Salerno. He actually fell ill in Rome in the summer of 942. Feeling that he was nearing his end, he was determined, and made every effort, to return to St. Martin in Tours, where he died, in the octave of the saint's feast, on 18 November 942. His biographer, stressing the "virtue of patience" that Odo possessed, gives a long list of his other virtues that include contempt of the world, zeal for souls, and the commitment to peace in the churches. Abbot Odo's great aspirations were concord between kings and princes, the observance of the commandments, attention to the poor, the correction of youth, and respect for the elderly (cf. *Vita sancti Odonis* 1, 17: *PL* 133, 49).

Odo loved the cell in which he dwelled, "removed from the eyes of all, eager to please God alone" (ibid., 1, 14: *PL* 133, 49). However, he did not fail also to exercise, as a "superabundant source," the ministry of the word and to set an example, "regretting the immense wretchedness of this world" (ibid., 1, 17: *PL* 133, 51). In a single monk, his biographer comments, were combined the different virtues that exist, which are found to be few and far between in other monasteries: "Jesus, in his goodness, drawing on the various gardens of monks, in a small space created a paradise, in order to water the hearts of the faithful from its fountains" (ibid., 1, 14: *PL* 133, 49). In a passage from a sermon in honor of Mary of Magdala, the abbot of Cluny reveals to us how he conceived of monastic life:

> Mary, who, seated at the Lord's feet, listened attentively to his words, is the symbol of the sweetness of contemplative life; the more its savor is tasted, the more it induces the mind to be detached from visible things and the tumult of the world's preoccupations. (*In ven. S. Mariae Magd.*: *PL* 133, 717)

Odo strengthened and developed this conception in his other writings. From them transpire his love for interiority, a vision of the world as a brittle, precarious reality from which to uproot oneself, a constant inclination to detachment from things felt to be sources of anxiety, an acute sensitivity to the presence of evil in the various types of people, and a deep eschatological aspiration. This vision of the world may appear rather distant from our own; yet Odo's conception of it, his perception of the fragility of the world, values an inner life that is open to the other, to the love of one's neighbor, and in this very way transforms life and opens the world to God's light.

The devotion to the body and blood of Christ which Odo in the face of a widespread neglect of them, which he himself deeply deplored, always cultivated with conviction deserves special mention. Odo was, in fact, firmly convinced of the real presence, under the eucharistic species, of the body and blood of the Lord, by virtue of the conversion of the "substance" of the bread, and the wine. He wrote: "God, Creator of all things, took the bread, saying that this was his body and that he would offer it for the world, and he distributed the wine, calling it his blood"; now, "it is a law of nature that the change should come about in accordance with the Creator's command," and thus "nature immediately changes its usual condition: the bread instantly becomes flesh, and the wine becomes blood"; at the Lord's order, "the substance changes" (*Odonis Abb. Cluniac. occupatio*, ed. A. Swoboda [Leipzig 1900], 121). Unfortunately, our abbot notes, this "sacrosanct mystery of the Lord's body, in whom the whole salvation of the world consists" (*Collationes*, 28: *PL* 133, 572), is celebrated carelessly. "Priests," he warns, "who approach the altar unworthily, stain the bread, that is, the body of Christ" (ibid.: *PL* 133, 572–73). Only those who are spiritually united to Christ may worthily participate in his eucharistic body: should the contrary be the case, to eat his flesh and to drink his blood would not be beneficial but rather a condemnation (cf. ibid., 30: *PL* 133, 575). All this invites us to believe the truth of the Lord's presence with new force and depth. The presence in our midst of the Creator, who gives himself into our hands and transforms us as he transforms the bread and the wine, thus transforms the world.

Saint Odo was a true spiritual guide both for the monks and for the faithful of his time. In the face of the "immensity of the vices" widespread in society, the remedy he strongly advised was that of a radical change of life, based on humility, austerity, detachment from ephemeral things, and adherence to those that are eternal (cf. *Collationes* 30: *PL* 133, 613). In spite of the realism of his diagnosis on the situation of his time, Odo does not indulge in pessimism: "We do not say this," he explains, "in order to plunge those who wish to convert into despair. Divine mercy is always available; it awaits the hour of our conversion" (ibid.: *PL* 133, 563). And he exclaims: "O ineffable depths of divine piety! God pursues wrongs and yet protects sinners" (ibid.: *PL* 133, 592). Sustained by this conviction, the abbot of Cluny used to like to pause to contemplate the mercy of Christ, the Savior whom he describes evocatively as "a lover of men": *amator hominum Christus* (ibid., 53: *PL* 133, 637). He observes, "Jesus took upon himself the scourging that would have been our due in order to save the creature he formed and loves (cf. ibid.: *PL* 133, 638).

Here, a trait of the holy abbot appears that at first sight is almost hidden beneath the rigor of his austerity as a reformer: his deep, heartfelt kindness. He was austere, but above all he was good, a man of great goodness, a goodness that comes from contact with the divine goodness. Thus Odo, his peers tell us, spread around him his overflowing joy. His biographer testifies that he never heard "such mellifluous words" on human lips (ibid., 1, 17: *PL* 133, 31). His biographer also records that he was in the habit of asking the children he met along the way to sing and that he would then give them some small token, and he adds: "Abbot Odo's words were full of joy . . . his merriment instilled in our hearts deep joy" (ibid., 2, 5: *PL* 133, 63). In this way, the energetic yet at the same time lovable medieval abbot, enthusiastic about reform, with incisive action nourished in his monks, as well as in the lay faithful of his time, the resolution to progress swiftly on the path of Christian perfection.

Let us hope that his goodness, the joy that comes from faith, together with austerity and opposition to the world's vices, may also move our hearts, so that we too may find the source of the joy that flows from God's goodness.

—*2 September 2009*

St. Peter Damian

ONE OF THE MOST SIGNIFICANT FIGURES of the eleventh century, St. Peter Damian, was a monk, a lover of solitude, and at the same time a fearless man of the Church. He was also committed personally to the task of reform, initiated by the popes of the time.

Peter was born in Ravenna in 1007, into a noble family but in straitened circumstances. He was left an orphan, and his childhood was not exempt from hardships and suffering, although his sister Roselinda tried to be a mother to him; and his elder brother, Damian, adopted him as his son. For this very reason, he was to be called Piero di Damiano, Pier Damiani (Peter of Damian, Peter Damian). He was educated first at Faenza and then at Parma where, already at the age of twenty-five, we find him involved in teaching. As well as a good grounding in the field of law, he acquired a refined expertise in the art of writing the *ars scribendi* and, thanks to his knowledge of the great Latin classics, became "one of the most accomplished Latinists of his time, one of the greatest writers of medieval Latin" (J. Leclercq, *Pierre Damien, ermite et homme d'Église* [Rome, 1960], 172).

Peter distinguished himself in the widest range of literary forms: from letters to sermons, from hagiographies to prayers, from poems to epigrams. His sensitivity to beauty led him to poetic contemplation of the world. Peter Damian conceived of the universe as a never-ending "parable" and a sequence of symbols on which to base the interpretation of inner life and divine and supranatural reality. In this perspective, in about the year 1034, contemplation of the absolute God impelled him gradually to detach himself from the world and from its transient realties and to withdraw to the monastery of Fonte Avellana. It had been founded only a few decades earlier but was already celebrated for its austerity. For the monks' edification he wrote the *Life* of the founder, St. Romuald of Ravenna, and at the same time strove to deepen their spirituality, expounding on his ideal of eremitic monasticism.

One detail should be immediately emphasized: the hermitage at Fonte Avellana was dedicated to the holy cross, and the Cross was the Christian mystery that was to fascinate Peter Damian more than all the others. "Those who do not love the Cross of Christ do not love Christ," he said (*Sermo 18*, 11, 117); and he described himself as *Petrus crucis Christi servorum famulu*—Peter, servant of the servants of the cross of Christ" (*Ep. 9*, 1). Peter Damian addressed the most beautiful prayers to the Cross, in which he reveals a vision of this mystery that has cosmic dimensions, for it embraces the entire history of salvation: "O blessed

Cross," he exclaimed, "You are venerated, preached, and honored by the faith of the patriarchs, the predictions of the prophets, the senate that judges the Apostles, the victorious army of martyrs, and the throngs of all the saints" (*Sermo 47*, 14, 304). May the example of St. Peter Damian spur us too to look always to the Cross as to the supreme act God's love for humankind of God, who has given us salvation.

This great monk compiled a Rule for eremitical life in which he heavily stressed the "rigor of the hermit": in the silence of the cloister, the monk is called to spend a life of prayer, by day and by night, with prolonged and strict fasting; he must put into practice generous brotherly charity in ever prompt and willing obedience to the prior. In study and in the daily meditation on Sacred Scripture, Peter Damian discovered the mystical meaning of the Word of God, finding in it nourishment for his spiritual life. In this regard, he described the hermit's cell as the "parlor in which God converses with men." For him, living as a hermit was the peak of Christian existence, "the loftiest of the states of life" because the monk, now free from the bonds of worldly life and of his own self, receives "a dowry from the Holy Spirit and his happy soul is united with its heavenly Spouse" (*Ep.* 18, 17; cf. *Ep.* 28, 43ff.). This is important for us today too, even though we are not monks: to know how to make silence within us to listen to God's voice, to seek, as it were, a "parlor" in which God speaks with us: learning the word of God in prayer and in meditation is the path to life.

Saint Peter Damian, who was essentially a man of prayer, meditation, and contemplation, was also a fine theologian: his reflection on various doctrinal themes led him to important conclusions for life. Thus, for example, he expresses with clarity and liveliness the Trinitarian doctrine, already using, under the guidance of biblical and Patristic texts, the three fundamental terms which were subsequently to become crucial also for the philosophy of the West: *processio, relatio,* and *persona* (cf. *Opusc.* 38: *PL 145*, 633–42; and *Opusc.* 2 and 3: ibid., 41ff. and 58ff). However, because theological analysis of the mystery led him to contemplate the intimate life of God and the dialogue of ineffable love between the three divine persons, he drew ascetic conclusions from them for community life and even for relations between Latin and Greek Christians, divided on this topic. His meditation on the figure of Christ is significantly reflected in practical life, since the whole of Scripture is centered on him. The "Jews," St. Peter Damian notes, "through the pages of Sacred Scripture, bore Christ on their shoulders, as it were" (*Sermo 46*, 15). Therefore, Christ, he adds, must be the center of the monk's life: "May Christ be heard in our language; may Christ be seen in our life; may he be perceived in our hearts" (*Sermo 8*, 5). Intimate union with Christ engages not only monks but all the baptized. Here we find a strong appeal for us too, not to let ourselves be totally absorbed by the activities, problems, and preoccupations of every day, forgetting that Jesus must truly be the center of our life.

Communion with Christ creates among Christians a unity of love. In *Letter* 28, which is a brilliant ecclesiological treatise, Peter Damian develops a profound theology of the Church as communion. "Christ's Church," he writes, is united by the bond of charity to the point that just as she has many members so is she, mystically, entirely contained in a single member in such a way that the whole universal Church is rightly called the one bride of Christ in the singular, and each chosen soul, through the sacramental mystery, is considered fully Church." This is important: not only that the whole universal Church should be united but also that the Church should be present in her totality in each one of us. Thus, the service of the individual becomes "an expression of universality" (*Ep.* 28, 9–23). However, the ideal image of "Holy Church" illustrated by Peter Damian does not correspond, as he knew well, to the reality of his time. For this reason, he did not fear to denounce the state of corruption that existed in the monasteries and among the clergy because, above all, of the practice of the conferral by the lay authorities of ecclesiastical offices; various bishops and abbots were behaving as the rulers of their subjects rather than as pastors of souls. Their moral life frequently left much to be desired. For this reason, in 1057 Peter Damian left his monastery with great reluctance and sorrow and accepted, if unwillingly, his appointment as cardinal bishop of Ostia. So it was that he entered fully into collaboration with the popes in the difficult task of Church reform. He saw that to make his own contribution of helping in the work of the Church's renewal, contemplation did not suffice. He thus relinquished the beauty of the hermitage and courageously undertook numerous journeys and missions.

Because of his love for monastic life, ten years later, in 1067, he obtained permission to return to Fonte Avellana and resigned from the Diocese of Ostia. However, the tranquillity he had longed for did not last long: two years later, he was sent to Frankfurt in an endeavor to prevent the divorce of Henry IV from his wife Bertha. And again, two years later, in 1071, he went to Monte Cassino for the consecration of the abbey church and at the beginning of 1072, to Ravenna, to reestablish peace with the local archbishop, who had supported the antipope, bringing interdiction upon the city. On the journey home to his hermitage, an unexpected illness obliged him to stop at the Benedictine monastery of Santa Maria Vecchia Fuori Porta in Faenza, where he died in the night between 22 and 23 February 1072.

It is a great grace that the Lord should have raised up in the life of the Church a figure as exuberant, rich, and complex as St. Peter Damian. Moreover, it is rare to find theological works and spirituality as keen and vibrant as those of the hermitage at Fonte Avellana. Saint Peter Damian was a monk through and through, with forms of austerity which to us today might even seem excessive. Yet in that way, he made monastic life an eloquent testimony of God's primacy and an appeal to all to walk toward holiness, free from any compromise with evil. He spent himself, with lucid consistency and great severity, for the reform of the Church of his time. He gave all his spiritual and physical energies to Christ and to the Church, but always remained, as he liked to describe himself, *Petrus ultimus monachorum servus*—Peter, the lowliest servant of the monks.

—*9 September 2009*

SYMEON THE NEW THEOLOGIAN

ALSO BEARING REFLECTION from this period is an Eastern monk, Symeon the New Theologian, whose writings have had a notable influence on the theology and spirituality of the East, in particular with regard to the experience of mystical union with God.

Symeon the New Theologian was born in 949 in Galatai, Paphlagonia, in Asia Minor, into a provincial noble family. While he was still young he moved to Constantinople to complete his education and enter the emperor's service. However, he did not feel attracted by the civil career that awaited him. Under the influence of the inner illumination he was experiencing, he set out in search of someone who would guide him in the period of doubt and perplexity he was living through and help him advance on the path of union with God. He found this spiritual guide in Symeon the Pious (*Eulabes*), a simple monk of the Studios in Constantinople who advised him to read Mark the Monk's treatise *The Spiritual Law*. Symeon the New Theologian found in this text a teaching that made a deep impression on him: "If you seek spiritual healing, be attentive to your conscience," he read in it. "Do all that it tells you and you will find what serves you." From that very moment, he himself says, he never went to sleep without first asking himself whether his conscience had anything with which to reproach him.

Symeon entered the Studite monastery where, however, his mystical experiences and extraordinary devotion to his spiritual father caused him some difficulty. He moved to the small convent of St. Mamas, also in Constantinople, of which three years later he became abbot, or *hegumen*. There he embarked on an intense quest for spiritual union with Christ, which gave him great authority. It is interesting to note that he was given the title "New Theologian," in spite of the tradition that reserved this title for two figures, John the Evangelist and Gregory of Nazianzus. Symeon suffered misunderstandings and exile but was rehabilitated by Patriarch Sergius II of Constantinople.

Symeon the New Theologian spent the last stage of his life at the monastery of St. Marina, where he wrote a large part of his opus, becoming ever more famous for his teaching and his miracles. He died on 12 March 1022.

The best known of his disciples, Niceta Stethatos, who collected and copied Symeon's writings, compiled a posthumous edition of them and subsequently wrote his biography. Symeon's opus consists of nine volumes that are divided into theological, gnostic, and practical chapters; three books of catecheses addressed to monks; two books of theological and ethical treatises; and one of hymns. Moreover, his numerous letters should not be forgotten. All these works have had an important place in the Eastern monastic tradition to our day.

Symeon focused his reflection on the Holy Spirit's presence in the baptized and on the awareness they must have of this spiritual reality. "Christian life," he emphasized, "is intimate, personal communion with God; divine grace illumines the believer's heart and leads him to a mystical vision of the Lord." Along these lines, Symeon the New Theologian insisted that true knowledge of God does not come from books but rather from spiritual experience, from spiritual life. Knowledge of God is born from a process of inner purification that begins with conversion of heart through the power of faith and love. It passes through profound repentance and sincere sorrow for one's sins to attain union with Christ, the source of joy and peace, suffused with the light of his presence within us. For Symeon, this experience of divine grace did not constitute an exceptional gift for a few mystics but rather was the fruit of baptism in the life of every seriously committed believer.

This holy Eastern monk calls us all to pay attention to our spiritual life, to the hidden presence of God within us, to the sincerity of the conscience and to purification, to conversion of heart, so that the Holy Spirit may really become present in us and guide us. Indeed, if rightly we are concerned to care for our physical, human, and intellectual development, it is even more important not to neglect our inner growth. This consists in the knowledge of God, in true knowledge, not only learned from books but also from within and in communion with God, to experience his help at every moment and in every circumstance. Basically, it is this that Symeon describes when he recounts his own mystical experience.

Already as a young man, before entering the monastery, while at home one night immersed in prayer and invoking God's help to fight temptations, he saw the room fill with light. Later, when he entered the monastery, he was given spiritual books for instruction but reading them did not procure for him the peace that he sought. He felt, he himself says, as if he were a poor little bird without wings. He humbly accepted this situation without rebelling, and it was then that his visions of light began once again to increase. Wishing to assure himself of their authenticity, Symeon asked Christ directly: "Lord, is it truly you who are here?" He heard the affirmative answer resonating in his heart and was supremely comforted. "That, Lord," he was to write later, "was the first time that you considered me, a prodigal son, worthy of hearing your voice." However, not even this revelation left him entirely at peace. He wondered, rather, whether he ought to consider that experience an illusion.

At last, one day an event occurred that was crucial to his mystical experience. He began to feel like "a poor man who loves his brethren" (*ptochós philádelphos*). Around him, he saw hordes of enemies bent on ensnaring him and doing him harm, yet he felt within an intense surge of love for them. How can this be explained? Obviously, such great love could not come from within him but must well up from another source. Symeon realized that it was coming from Christ present within him, and everything became clear: he had a sure proof that the source of love in him was Christ's presence. He was certain that having in ourselves a love that exceeds our personal intentions suggests that the source of love is in us. Thus, we can say on the one hand that if we are without a certain openness to love, Christ does not enter us and on the other, that Christ becomes a source of love and transforms us.

This experience remains particularly important for us today if we are to find the criteria that tell us whether we are truly close to God, whether God exists and dwells in us. God's love develops in us if we stay united to him with prayer and with listening to his word with an open heart. Divine love alone prompts us to open our hearts to others and makes us sensitive to their needs, bringing us to consider everyone as brothers and sisters and inviting us to respond to hatred with love and to offense with forgiveness.

In thinking about this figure of Symeon the New Theologian, we may note a further element of his spirituality. On the path of ascetic life which he proposed and took, the monk's intense attention and concentration on the inner experience conferred an essential importance on the spiritual father of the monastery. The same young Symeon, as has been said, had found a spiritual director who gave him substantial help and whom he continued to hold in the greatest esteem such as to profess veneration for him, even in public, after his death. And the invitation to have recourse to a good spiritual father who can guide every individual to profound knowledge of himself and lead him to union with the Lord so that his life may be in ever closer conformity with the Gospel still applies for all priests, consecrated and laypeople, and especially youth. To go toward the Lord, we always need a guide, a dialogue. We cannot do it with our thoughts alone. And this is also the meaning of the ecclesiality of our faith, of finding this guide.

To conclude, we may sum up the teaching and mystical experience of Symeon the New Theologian in these words: in his ceaseless quest for God, even amid the difficulties he encountered and the criticism of which he was the object, in the end he let himself be guided by love. He himself was able to live and teach his monks that for every disciple of Jesus the essential is to grow in love; thus we grow in the knowledge of Christ himself, to be able to say with St. Paul: "It is no longer I who live, but Christ who lives in me" (Gal 2:20).

—*16 September 2009*

PART FOUR

Mystics, Mendicants, and Scholastics

St. Anselm

The Benedictine abbey of Sant'Anselmo (St. Anselm) is located on the Aventine Hill in Rome. As the headquarters of an academic institute of higher studies and of the abbot primate of the Confederated Benedictines, it is a place that unites within it prayer, study, and governance, the same three activities that were a feature of the life of the saint to whom it is dedicated: Anselm of Aosta, the ninth centenary of whose death occurred in 2009. The many initiatives promoted for this happy event, especially by the Diocese of Aosta, highlighted the interest that this medieval thinker continues to rouse. He is also known as Anselm of Bec and Anselm of Canterbury because of the cities with which he was associated.

Who is this figure to whom three places, distant from one another and located in three different nations—Italy, France, England—feel particularly bound? A monk with an intense spiritual life, an excellent teacher of the young, a theologian with an extraordinary capacity for speculation, a wise man of governance, and an intransigent defender of *libertas ecclesiae,* of the Church's freedom, Anselm is one of the eminent figures of the Middle Ages who was able to harmonize all these qualities, thanks to the profound mystical experience that always guided his thought and his action.

Saint Anselm was born in 1033 (or at the beginning of 1034) in Aosta, the first child of a noble family. His father was a coarse man, dedicated to the pleasures of life, who squandered his possessions. On the other hand, Anselm's mother was a profoundly religious woman of high moral standing (cf. Eadmer, *Vita Sancti Anselmi*: PL 159, col. 49). It was she, his mother, who saw to the first human and religious formation of her son whom she subsequently entrusted to the Benedictines at a priory in Aosta.

Anselm, who since childhood, as his biographer recounts, imagined that the good Lord dwelled among the towering, snow-capped peaks of the Alps, dreamed one night that he had been invited to this splendid kingdom by God himself, who had a long and affable conversation with him and then gave him to eat "a very white bread roll" (ibid., col. 51). This dream left him with the conviction that he was called to carry out a lofty mission. At the age of fifteen, he asked to be admitted to the Benedictine order, but his father brought the full force of his authority to bear against him and did not even give way when his son, seriously ill and feeling close to death, begged for the religious habit as a supreme comfort.

After his recovery and the premature death of his mother, Anselm went through a period of moral dissipation. He neglected his studies and, consumed by earthly passions, grew deaf to God's call. He left home and began to wander through France in search of new experiences. Three years later, having arrived in Normandy, he went to the Benedictine abbey of Bec, attracted by the fame of Lanfranc of Pavia, the prior. For him this was a providential meeting, crucial to the rest of his life. Under Lanfranc's guidance, Anselm energetically resumed his studies, and it was not long before he became not only the favorite pupil but also the teacher's confidante. His monastic vocation was rekindled and, after an attentive evaluation, at the age of twenty-seven he entered the monastic order and was ordained a priest. *Ascesis* and study unfolded new horizons before him, enabling him to rediscover at a far higher level the same familiarity with God which he had had as a child.

When Lanfranc became abbot of Caen in 1063, Anselm, after barely three years of monastic life, was named prior of the monastery of Bec and teacher of the cloister school, showing his gifts as a refined educator. He was not keen on authoritarian methods; he compared young people to small plants that develop better if they are not enclosed in greenhouses and if granted a "healthy" freedom. He was very demanding with himself and with others in monastic observance, but rather than imposing his discipline he strove to have it followed by persuasion.

Upon the death of Abbot Herluin, the founder of the abbey of Bec, Anselm was unanimously elected to succeed him; it was February 1079. In the meantime, numerous monks had been summoned to Canterbury to bring to their brethren on the other side of the channel the renewal that was being brought about on the Continent. Their work was so well received that Lanfranc of Pavia, abbot of Caen, became the new archbishop of Canterbury. He asked Anselm to spend a certain period with him in order to instruct the monks and to help him in the difficult plight in which his ecclesiastical community had been left after the Norman Conquest. Anselm's stay turned out to be very fruitful; he won such popularity and esteem that when Lanfranc died he was chosen to succeed him in the archiepiscopal See of Canterbury. He received his solemn episcopal consecration in December 1093.

Anselm immediately became involved in a strenuous struggle for the Church's freedom, valiantly supporting the independence of the spiritual power from the temporal. Anselm defended the Church from undue interference by political authorities, especially King William Rufus and Henry I, finding encouragement and support in the Roman pontiff, to whom he always showed courageous and cordial adherence. In 1103, this fidelity even cost him the bitterness of exile from his See of Canterbury. Moreover, it was only in 1106, when King Henry I renounced his right to the conferral of ecclesiastical offices, as well as to the collection of taxes and the confiscation of Church properties, that Anselm could return to England, where he was festively welcomed by the clergy and the people.

Thus, the long battle he had fought with the weapons of perseverance, pride, and goodness ended happily.

This holy archbishop, who roused such deep admiration around him wherever he went, dedicated the last years of his life to the moral formation of the clergy and to intellectual research into theological topics. He died on 21 April 1109, accompanied by the words of the Gospel proclaimed in holy mass on that day: "You are those who have continued with me in my trials; as my Father appointed a kingdom for me, so do I appoint for you that you may eat and drink at my table in my kingdom." . . . (Lk 22:28-30). So it was that the dream of the mysterious banquet he had had as a small boy, at the very beginning of his spiritual journey, found fulfillment. Jesus, who had invited him to sit at his table, welcomed Anselm upon his death into the eternal kingdom of the Father.

"I pray, O God, to know you, to love you, that I may rejoice in you. And if I cannot attain to full joy in this life, may I at least advance from day to day, until that joy shall come to the full" (*Proslogion* 14). This prayer enables us to understand the mystical soul of this great saint of the Middle Ages, the founder of scholastic theology, to whom Christian tradition has given the title "Magnificent Doctor," because he fostered an intense desire to deepen his knowledge of the divine mysteries but in the full awareness that the quest for God is never ending, at least on this earth. The clarity and logical rigor of his thought always aimed at "raising the mind to contemplation of God" (ibid., *Proemium*). He states clearly that whoever intends to study theology cannot rely on his intelligence alone but must cultivate at the same time a profound experience of faith. The theologian's activity, according to St. Anselm, thus develops in three stages: *faith,* a gift God freely offers, to be received with humility; *experience,* which consists in incarnating God's Word in one's own daily life; and therefore true *knowledge,* which is never the fruit of ascetic reasoning but rather of contemplative intuition. In this regard, his famous words remain more useful than ever, even today, for healthy theological research and for anyone who wishes to deepen his knowledge of the truths of faith:

> I do not endeavor, O Lord, to penetrate your sublimity, for in no wise do I compare my understanding with that; but I long to understand in some degree your truth, which my heart believes and loves. For I do not seek to understand that I may believe, but I believe in order to understand. For this also I believe, that unless I believed, I should not understand. (ibid., 1)

May the love of the truth and the constant thirst for God that marked St. Anselm's entire existence be an incentive to every Christian to seek tirelessly an evermore intimate union with Christ, the Way, the Truth,

and the Life. In addition, may the zeal full of courage that distinguished
his pastoral action and occasionally brought him misunderstanding, sorrow, and even exile be an encouragement for pastors, for consecrated
people, and for all the faithful to love Christ's Church, to pray, to work,
and to suffer for her without ever abandoning or betraying her. May the
Virgin Mother of God, for whom St. Anselm had a tender, filial devotion,
obtain this grace for us. "Mary, it is you whom my heart yearns to love,"
St. Anselm wrote. "It is you whom my tongue ardently desires to praise."

—*23 September 2009*

PETER THE VENERABLE

PETER THE VENERABLE TAKES US BACK to the famous abbey of Cluny, to its *decor* ("decorum") and *nitor* ("clarity"), to use terms that recur in the Cluny texts—a decorum and splendor that were admired especially in the beauty of the liturgy, a privileged way for reaching God. Even more than these aspects, however, Peter's personality recalls the holiness of the great abbots of Cluny, in Cluny, "there was not a single abbot who was not a saint," Pope Gregory VII said in 1080.

These holy men include Peter the Venerable, who possessed more or less all the virtues of his predecessors although, under him, in comparison with the new orders such as Cîteaux, Cluny began to feel some symptoms of crisis. Peter is a wonderful example of an ascetic strict with himself and understanding of others. He was born in about 1094 in the French region of Auvergne, he entered the monastery of Sauxillanges as a child, and became a monk there and then prior. In 1122, he was elected abbot of Cluny and remained in this office until he died, on Christmas day 1156, as he had wished. "A lover of peace," his biographer Rudolph wrote, "he obtained peace in the glory of God on the day of peace" (*Vita* 1, 17: *PL* 189, 28).

All who knew him praised his refined meekness, his serene equilibrium, rectitude, loyalty, reasonableness, and his special approach to mediation. "It is in my nature," he wrote, "to be particularly inclined to indulgence; I am urged to this by my habit of forgiveness. I am accustomed to toleration and forgiveness" (*Ep.* 192: in *The Letters of Peter the Venerable* [Harvard University Press, 1967], 446). He said further: "With those who hate peace let us always seek to be peacemakers" (*Ep.* 100: *Letters of Peter,* 261). And he wrote of himself: "I am not the type who is discontented with his lot . . . whose mind is always tormented by anxiety or doubt and who complains that everyone else is resting while they are the only ones working" (*Ep.* 182: *Letters of Peter,* 425).

With a sensitive and affectionate nature, he could combine love for the Lord with tenderness to his family members, especially his mother, and to his friends. He cultivated friendship, especially with his monks, who used to confide in him, certain that they would be heard and understood. According to his biographer's testimony: "He did not look down on anyone and never turned anyone away" (*Vita* 1, 3: *PL* 189, 19); "he appeared friendly to all; in his innate goodness he was open to all" (ibid., 1, 1: *PL* 189, 17).

We could say that this holy abbot also sets an example to the monks and Christians of our day, marked by a frenetic pace, when episodes of intolerance, incommunicability, division, and conflict are common. His testimony invites us to be able to combine love of God with love of neighbor and not to tire of building relations of brotherhood and reconciliation. Effectively, Peter the Venerable acted in this way. He found himself in charge of the monastery of Cluny in years that were far from tranquil for various reasons, both within the abbey and outside it, and managed to be at the same time both strict and profoundly human. He used to say: "One may obtain more from a man by tolerating him than by irritating him with reproach" (*Ep.* 172, *PL* 189, 409).

By virtue of his office, he had to undertake frequent journeys to Italy, England, Germany, and Spain. He found it hard to be wrenched from the quiet of contemplation. He confessed: "I go from one place to the next, I hurry, I am anxious, I am tormented, dragged here and there: my mind now on my own affairs and now on those of others, not without great mental agitation" (*Ep.* 91, *PL* 189, 233). Although he was obliged to navigate between the powers and nobles who surrounded Cluny, he succeeded in preserving his habitual calm, thanks to his sense of measure, magnanimity, and realism. Among the important figures with whom he came into contact was Bernard of Clairvaux, with whom he maintained a relationship of increasing friendship, despite the differences of their temperaments and approaches. Bernard described him as "an important man, occupied with important affairs" and held him in high esteem (*Ep.* 147, ed. *Scriptorium Claravallense* [Milan, 1986], 6/1, 658–60), while Peter the Venerable described Bernard as a "lamp of the Church" (*Ep.* 164, 396), and a "strong and splendid pillar of the monastic order and of the whole Church" (*Ep.* 175, 418).

With a lively sense of church, Peter the Venerable affirmed that the vicissitudes of the Christian people must be felt in the "depths of the heart" by those who will be numbered "among the members of Christ's body" (*Ep.* 164: ibid., 397). And he added: "Those who do not smart from the wounds of Christ's body are not nourished by the Spirit of Christ," wherever they may be produced (ibid.). In addition, he also showed care and concern for people outside the Church, in particular Jews and Muslims: to increase knowledge of the latter, he provided for the translation of the Qur'an. A historian recently remarked on this subject: "In the midst of the intransigence of medieval people, even the greatest among them, we admire here a sublime example of the sensitivity to which Christian charity leads" (J. Leclercq, *Pietro il Venerabile* [Jaca Book, 1991], 189).

Other aspects of Christian life dear to him were love for the eucharist and devotion to the Virgin Mary. On the blessed sacrament, he has left passages that constitute "one of the masterpieces of eucharistic literature of all time" (ibid., 267), and on the Mother of God, he wrote illuminating reflections, contemplating her, ever closely related to Jesus the Redeemer and his work of salvation. It suffices to present his inspired prayer:

Hail, Blessed Virgin, who put execration to flight. Hail, Mother of the Most High, Bride of the meekest Lamb. You have defeated the serpent; you crushed its head, when the God you bore destroyed it. . . . Shining Star of the East who dispelled the shadows of the west. Dawn who precedes the sun, day that knows no night. . . . Pray God who was born of you to dissolve our sin and, after pardoning it, to grant us his grace and his glory. (*Carmina*: PL 189, 1018–19)

Peter the Venerable also had a predilection for literary activity and a gift for it. He employed his reflections, persuaded of the importance of using the pen as if it were a plough, "to scatter the seed of the Word on paper" (*Ep.* 20, 38). Although he was not a systematic theologian, he was a great investigator of God's mystery. His theology is rooted in prayer, especially in liturgical prayer, and among the mysteries of Christ he preferred the Transfiguration, which prefigures the Resurrection. It was Peter himself who introduced this feast at Cluny, composing a special office for it that mirrors the characteristic theological devotion of Peter and of the Cluniac order, which was focused entirely on contemplation of the glorious face (*gloriosa facies*) of Christ, finding in it the reasons for that ardent joy which marked his spirit and shone out in the monastery's liturgy.

This holy monk is certainly a great example of monastic holiness, nourished from the sources of the Benedictine tradition. For him, the ideal of the monk consists in "adhering tenaciously to Christ" (*Ep.* 53: PL 189, 161), in a cloistered life distinguished by "monastic humility" (ibid.) and hard work (*Ep.* 77: PL 189, 211), as well as an atmosphere of silent contemplation and constant praise of God. The first and most important occupation of the monk, according to Peter of Cluny, is the solemn celebration of the Divine Office, "a heavenly action and the most useful of all" (*Statutes* 1, 1026) to be accompanied by reading, meditation, personal prayer, and penance observed with discretion (cf. *Ep.* 20: PL 189, 40). In this way, the whole of life is pervaded by profound love of God and love of others, a love that is expressed in sincere openness to neighbor, in forgiveness, and in the quest for peace.

We might say, to conclude, that if this lifestyle, combined with daily work, was the monk's ideal for St. Benedict, it also concerns all of us and can be to a large extent the lifestyle of the Christian who wants to become an authentic disciple of Christ, characterized precisely by tenacious adherence to him and by humility, diligence, and the capacity for forgiveness and peace.

—*14 October 2009*

St. Bernard of Clairvaux

St. Bernard of Clairvaux is often called "the last of the Fathers" of the Church because once again in the twelfth century he renewed and brought to the fore the important theology of the Fathers. We do not know in any detail about the years of Bernard's childhood; however, we know that he was born in 1090 in Fontaines, France, into a large and fairly well-to-do family. As a very young man, he devoted himself to the study of the so-called liberal arts, especially grammar, rhetoric, and dialectics, at the school of the canons of the Church of Saint-Vorles at Châtillon-sur-Seine; and the decision to enter religious life slowly matured within him.

At the age of about twenty, he entered Cîteaux, a new monastic foundation that was more flexible in comparison with the ancient and venerable monasteries of the period while at the same time stricter in the practice of the evangelical counsels. A few years later, in 1115, Bernard was sent by Stephen Harding, the third abbot of Cîteaux, to found the monastery of Clairvaux. Here the young abbot—he was only twenty-five years old—was able to define his conception of monastic life and set about putting it into practice. In looking at the discipline of other monasteries, Bernard firmly recalled the need for a sober and measured life, at table as in clothing and monastic buildings, and recommended the support and care of the poor. In the meantime, the community of Clairvaux became ever more numerous, and its foundations multiplied.

In those same years before 1130, Bernard started a prolific correspondence with many people of both important and modest social status. To the many *Epistolae* of this period must be added numerous *Sermones*, as well as *Sententiae* and *Tractatus*. Bernard's great friendships with William, abbot of Saint-Thierry, and with William of Champeaux, among the most important figures of the twelfth century, also date to this period.

From 1130, Bernard began to concern himself with many serious matters of the Holy See and of the Church. For this reason, he was obliged to leave his monastery ever more frequently, and he sometimes also traveled outside France. He founded several women's monasteries and was the protagonist of a lively correspondence with Peter the Venerable, abbot of Cluny, whom I discussed in the previous chapter.

In his polemical writings, he targeted in particular Abelard, a great thinker who had conceived of a new approach to theology, introducing above all the dialectic and philosophical method in the construction of theological thought. On another front, Bernard combated the heresy of the Cathars, who despised matter and the human body and consequently despised the Creator. On the other hand, he felt it was his duty to defend the Jews, and condemned the ever more widespread outbursts of anti-Semitism. With regard to this aspect of his apostolic action, several decades later Rabbi Ephraim of Bonn addressed a vibrant tribute to Bernard. In the same period, the holy abbot wrote his most famous works, such as the celebrated *Sermons on the Song of Songs* [*In Canticum Sermones*]. In the last years of his life—he died in 1153—Bernard was obliged to curtail his journeys but did not entirely stop traveling. He made the most of this time to review definitively the whole collection of his *Letters, Sermons,* and *Treatises.* Worthy of mention is a quite unusual book that he completed in this same period, in 1145, when Bernardo Pignatelli, a pupil of his, was elected pope with the name of Eugene III. On this occasion, Bernard, as his spiritual father, dedicated to his spiritual son the text *De Consideratione* (*Five Books on Consideration*), which contains teachings on how to be a good pope. In this book, which is still appropriate reading for the popes of all times, Bernard did not only suggest how to be a good pope but also expressed a profound vision of the mystery of the Church and of the mystery of Christ, which is ultimately resolved in contemplation of the mystery of the Triune God. "The search for this God who is not yet sufficiently sought must be continued," the holy abbot wrote, "yet it may be easier to search for him and find him in prayer rather than in discussion. So let us end the book here, but not the search" (14, 32: *PL* 182, 808) journeying on toward God.

I reflect here on only two of the main aspects of Bernard's rich doctrine: they concern Jesus Christ and Mary Most Holy, his mother. His concern for the Christian's intimate and vital participation in God's love in Jesus Christ brings no new guidelines to the scientific status of theology. However, in a more decisive manner than ever, the abbot of Clairvaux embodies the theologian, the contemplative, and the mystic. Jesus alone—Bernard insists in the face of the complex dialectical reasoning of his time—is "honey in the mouth, song to the ear, jubilation in the heart [*mel in ore, in aure melos, in corde iubilum*]." The title *Doctor Mellifluus,* attributed to Bernard by tradition, stems precisely from this; indeed, his praise of Jesus Christ "flowed like honey."

In the extenuating battles between Nominalists and Realists, two philosophical currents of the time, the abbot of Clairvaux never tired of repeating that only one name counts, that of Jesus of Nazareth. "All food of the soul is dry," he professed, "unless it is moistened with this oil; insipid, unless it is seasoned with this salt. What you write has no savor for me unless I have read *Jesus* in it" (*In Canticum Sermones* 15, 6: *PL* 183, 847). For Bernard, in fact, true knowledge of God consisted in a personal, profound experience of Jesus Christ and of his love. And this is true for every Christian: faith is first and foremost a personal, intimate encounter with Jesus; it is having an experience of his closeness, his friendship, and his love. It is in this way that we learn to know him ever better, to love him and to follow him more and more. May this happen to each one of us!

In another famous sermon, *Sermon on the Sunday in the Octave of the Assumption,* the holy abbot described with passionate words Mary's intimate participation in the redeeming sacrifice of her Son. "O Blessed Mother," he exclaimed, "a sword has truly pierced your soul! . . . So deeply has the violence of pain pierced your soul, that we may rightly call you more than a martyr, for in you participation in the passion of the Son by far surpasses in intensity the physical sufferings of martyrdom" (14: PL 183, 437–38). Bernard had no doubts: *per Mariam ad Iesum,* "through Mary we are led to Jesus." He testifies clearly to Mary's subordination to Jesus, in accordance with the foundation of traditional Mariology. Yet the text of the *Sermone* also documents the Virgin's privileged place in the economy of salvation, subsequent to the mother's most particular participation (*compassio*) in the sacrifice of the Son. It is not for nothing that a century and a half after Bernard's death, Dante Alighieri, in the last canticle of the *Divine Comedy,* was to put on the lips of the *Doctor Mellifluus* the sublime prayer to Mary: "Virgin Mother, daughter of your own Son, humble and exalted more than any creature, fixed term of the eternal counsel" (*Paradise* 33, 1ff.).

These reflections, characteristic of a person in love with Jesus and Mary as was Bernard, are still a salutary stimulus not only to theologians but to all believers. Some claim to have solved the fundamental questions on God, on being human, and on the world with the power of reason alone. Saint Bernard, on the other hand, solidly founded on the Bible and on the Fathers of the Church, reminds us that without a profound faith in God, nourished by prayer and contemplation, by an intimate relationship with the Lord, our reflections on the divine mysteries risk becoming an empty intellectual exercise and losing their credibility. Theology refers us back to the "knowledge of the saints," to their intuition of the mysteries of the living God, and to their wisdom, a gift of the Holy Spirit, which becomes a reference point for theological thought. Together with Bernard of Clairvaux, we too must recognize that one seeks God better and finds him more easily "in prayer than in discussion." In the end, the truest figure of a theologian and of every evangelizer remains the Apostle John, who laid his head on the teacher's breast.

I conclude these reflections on St. Bernard with the invocations to Mary that we read in one of his beautiful homilies. "In danger, in distress, in uncertainty," he says, "think of Mary, call upon Mary. She never leaves your lips; she never departs from your heart; and so that you may obtain the help of her prayers, never forget the example of her life. If you follow her, you cannot falter; if you pray to her, you cannot despair; if you think of her, you cannot err. If she sustains you, you will not stumble; if she protects you, you have nothing to fear; if she guides you, you will never flag; if she is favorable to you, you will attain your goal" (*Hom. 2 super Missus est,* 17: PL 183, 70–71).

—21 October 2009

BERNARD AND PETER ABELARD: TWO CONTRASTING THEOLOGICAL MODELS

IN MY LAST CHAPTER, I presented the main features of twelfth-century monastic theology and scholastic theology which, in a certain sense, we might call respectively "theology of the heart" and "theology of reason." Among the exponents of both these theological currents, a broad and at times heated discussion developed, symbolically represented by the controversy between St. Bernard of Clairvaux and Peter Abelard.

To understand this confrontation between the two great teachers, it helps to remember that theology is the search for a rational understanding, as far as this is possible, of the mysteries of Christian revelation, believed through faith: *fides quaerens intellectum*—faith seeks understanding—to borrow a traditional, concise, and effective definition. Now, whereas St. Bernard, a staunch representative of monastic theology, puts the accent on the first part of the definition, namely on *fides*, on faith, Abelard, who was a scholastic, insists on the second part, that is, on the *intellectus*, on understanding through reason.

For Bernard, faith itself is endowed with a deep certitude based on the testimony of Scripture and on the teaching of the Church Fathers. Faith, moreover, is reinforced by the witness of the saints and by the inspiration of the Holy Spirit in the individual believer's soul. In cases of doubt and ambiguity, faith is protected and illumined by the exercise of the magisterium of the Church. So it was that Bernard had difficulty in reaching agreement with Abelard and, more in general, with those who submitted the truths of faith to the critical examination of the intellect; an examination that in his opinion entailed a serious danger, that is, intellectualism, the relativization of truth, the questioning of the actual truths of faith. In this approach, Bernard saw audacity taken to the point of unscrupulousness, a product of the pride of human intelligence that claims to "grasp" the mystery of God. In a letter, he writes with regret:

> Human ingenuity takes possession of everything, leaving nothing to faith. It confronts what is above and beyond it, scrutinizes what is superior to it, bursts into the world of God, alters rather than illumines the mysteries of faith; it does not open what is closed and sealed but rather uproots it, and what it does not find viable in itself it considers as nothing and refuses to believe in it. (*Epistola 188*, 1: *PL* 182, 1, 353)

217

Theology for Bernard had a single purpose: to encourage the intense and profound experience of God. Theology is therefore an aid to loving the Lord ever more and ever better, as the title of his *Treatise on the Duty to Love God* says (*Liber de diligendo Deo*). On this journey, there are various stages that Bernard describes in detail, which lead to the crowning experience when the believer's soul becomes inebriated in ineffable love. Already on earth, the human soul can attain this mystical union with the divine Word, a union that the *Doctor Mellifluus* describes as "spiritual nuptials." The divine Word visits the soul, eliminates the last traces of resistance, illuminates, inflames, and transforms it. In this mystical union, the soul enjoys great serenity and sweetness and sings a hymn of joy to its Bridegroom. As I mentioned in the catechesis on the life and doctrine of St. Bernard, theology for him could not but be nourished by contemplative prayer, in other words by the affective union of the heart and the mind with God.

On the other hand, Peter Abelard, who among other things was the very person who introduced the term *theology* in the sense in which we understand it today, puts himself in a different perspective. Born in Brittany, France, this famous teacher of the twelfth century was endowed with a keen intelligence, and his vocation was to study. He first concerned himself with philosophy and then applied the results he achieved in that discipline to theology, which he taught in Paris, the most cultured city of the time, and later in the monasteries in which he lived.

Abelard was a brilliant orator: literally crowds of students attended his lectures. He had a religious spirit but a restless personality, and his life was full of dramatic events: he contested his teachers, and he had a son by Héloïse, a cultured and intelligent woman. He often argued with his theological colleagues and also underwent ecclesiastical condemnations, although he died in full communion with the Church, submitting to her authority with a spirit of faith.

Actually, St. Bernard contributed to condemning certain teachings of Abelard at the Provincial Synod of Sens in 1140 and went so far as to request Pope Innocent II's intervention. The abbot of Clairvaux contested, as we have seen, the excessively intellectualistic method of Abelard, who in his eyes reduced faith to mere opinion, detached from the revealed truth. Bernard's fears were not unfounded and were, moreover, shared by other great thinkers of his time.

Indeed, an excessive use of philosophy dangerously weakened Abelard's Trinitarian teaching, hence also his idea of God. In the moral field, his teaching was not devoid of ambiguity: he insisted on considering the intention of the subject as the sole source for defining the goodness or evil of moral acts, thereby neglecting the objective significance and moral value of the actions: a dangerous subjectivism. This, as we know, is a very timely aspect for our epoch, in which all too often culture seems to be marked by a growing tendency to ethical relativism; the self alone decides what is good for it, for oneself, at this moment. However, the great merits of Abelard, who had many disciples and made a crucial contribution to the development of scholastic theology—destined to be expressed in a more mature and fruitful manner in the following century—should not be forgotten. Nor should some of his insights be underestimated, such as, for example, his affirmation that non-Christian religious traditions already contain a preparation for the acceptance of Christ, the divine Word.

What can we learn today from the confrontation, frequently in very heated tones, between Bernard and Abelard and, in general, between monastic theology and scholastic theology? First, I believe that it demonstrates the usefulness and need for healthy theological discussion within the Church, especially when the questions under discussion are not defined by the magisterium—which, nevertheless, remains an ineluctable reference point. Saint Bernard, but also Abelard himself, always recognized her authority unhesitatingly. Furthermore, Abelard's condemnation on various occasions reminds us that in the theological field there must be a balance between what we may call the architectural principles given to us by revelation—which, therefore, always retain their priority importance—and the principles for interpretation suggested by philosophy, that is, by reason—which have an important but exclusively practical role. When this balance between the architecture and the instruments for interpretation is lacking, theological reflection risks being distorted by errors. It is then the task of the magisterium to exercise that necessary service to the truth that belongs to it. It must be emphasized, in addition, that among the reasons that induced Bernard to "take sides" against Abelard and to call for the intervention of the magisterium was also his concern to safeguard simple and humble believers, who must be defended when they risk becoming confused or misled by excessively personal opinions or by anticonformist theological argumentation that might endanger their faith.

Last, I recall that the theological confrontation between Bernard and Abelard ended with their complete reconciliation, thanks to the mediation of a common friend, Peter the Venerable, the abbot of Cluny, of whom I have spoken in a prior chapter. Abelard showed humility in recognizing his errors; Bernard used great benevolence. They both upheld the most important value in a theological controversy: to preserve the Church's faith and to make the truth in charity triumph. Today, too, may this be the attitude with which we confront one another in the Church, having as our goal the constant quest for truth.

—*4 November 2009*

Hugh and Richard of Saint-Victor

I HAVE BEEN PRESENTING EXEMPLARY FIGURES of believers dedicated to showing the harmony between reason and faith and to witnessing with their lives to the proclamation of the gospel. Hugh and Richard of Saint-Victor were among those philosophers and theologians known as "Victorines" because they lived and taught at the abbey of Saint-Victor in Paris, founded at the beginning of the twelfth century by William of Champeaux. William himself was a well-known teacher who succeeded in giving his abbey a solid cultural identity. Indeed, a school for the formation of the monks, also open to external students, was founded at Saint-Victor, where a felicitous synthesis was achieved between the two theological models of which I have spoken in previous Catecheses. These are monastic theology, primarily oriented to contemplation of the mysteries of the faith in Scripture, and scholastic theology, which aimed to use reason to scrutinize these mysteries with innovative methods in order to create a theological system.

A "Second St. Augustine"

We have little information about the life of Hugh of Saint-Victor. The date and place of his birth are uncertain; he may have been born in Saxony or in Flanders. It is known that having arrived in Paris—the European cultural capital at that time—he spent the rest of his days at the abbey of Saint-Victor, where he was first a disciple and subsequently a teacher. Even before his death in 1141, he earned great fame and esteem, to the point that he was called a "second St. Augustine."

Like Augustine, in fact, Hugh of Saint-Victor meditated deeply on the relationship between faith and reason, between the secular sciences and theology. According to Hugh, in addition to being useful for understanding the Scriptures, all the branches of knowledge have intrinsic value and must be cultivated in order to broaden human knowledge, as well as to answer the human longing to know the truth. This healthy intellectual curiosity led him to counsel students always to give free reign to their desire to learn. In his treatise on the methodology of knowledge and pedagogy, titled significantly *Didascalicon (On Teaching)* his recommendation was: "Learn willingly what you do not know from everyone. The person who has sought to learn something from everyone will be wiser than them all. The person who receives something from everyone ends by becoming the richest of all" (*Eruditiones Didascalicae* 3, 14: PL 176, 774).

The knowledge with which the philosophers and theologians known as Victorines were concerned in particular was theology, which requires first and foremost the loving study of Sacred Scripture. In fact, in order to know God, one cannot but begin with what God himself has chosen to reveal of himself in the Scriptures. In this regard, Hugh of Saint-Victor is a typical representative of monastic theology, based entirely on biblical exegesis. To interpret Scripture, he suggests the traditional Patristic and medieval structure, namely, the literal and historical sense first of all, then the allegorical and anagogical, and last, the moral. These are four dimensions of the meaning of Scripture that are being rediscovered even today. For this reason, one sees that in the text and in the proposed narrative a more profound meaning is concealed: the thread of faith that leads us heavenward and guides us on this earth, teaching us how to live.

Yet, while respecting these four dimensions of the meaning of Scripture, in an original way in comparison with his contemporaries, Hugh of Saint-Victor insists—and this is something new—on the importance of the historical and literal meaning. In other words, before discovering the symbolic value, the deeper dimensions of the biblical text, it is necessary to know and to examine the meaning of the event as it is told in Scripture. Otherwise, he warns, using an effective comparison, one risks being like grammarians who do not know the elementary rules.

To those who know the meaning of history as described in the Bible, human events appear marked by divine providence, in accordance with a clearly ordained plan. Thus, for Hugh of Saint-Victor, history is neither the outcome of a blind destiny nor as meaningless as it might seem. On the contrary, the Holy Spirit is at work in human history and inspires the marvelous dialogue of human beings with God, their friend. This theological view of history highlights the astonishing and salvific intervention of God, who truly enters and acts in history. It is almost as if he takes part in our history while ever preserving and respecting the human being's freedom and responsibility.

Hugh considered that the study of Sacred Scripture and its historical and literal meaning makes possible true and proper theology, that is, the systematic illustration of truths, knowledge of their structure, the illustration of the dogmas of the faith. He presents these in a solid synthesis in his treatise *De Sacramentis Christianae Fidei* (*The Sacraments of the Christian Faith*). Among other things, he provides a definition of *sacrament* which, further perfected by other theologians, contains ideas that are still very interesting today.

"The sacrament is a corporeal or material element proposed in an external and tangible way," he writes, "which by its likeness *makes present* an invisible and spiritual grace; it *signifies* it, because it was instituted to this end, and *contains* it, because it is capable of sanctifying" (9, 2: *PL* 176, 317). On the one hand is the visibility in the symbol, the "corporeity" of the gift of God. On the other hand, however, in it is concealed the divine grace that comes from the history of Jesus Christ, who himself created the fundamental symbols. Therefore, there are three elements that contribute to the definition of a sacrament, according to Hugh of Saint-Victor: the institution by Christ; the communication of grace; and the analogy between the visible or material element and the invisible element: the divine gifts.

This vision is very close to our contemporary understanding, because the sacraments are presented with a language interwoven with symbols and images capable of speaking directly to the human heart. Today too it is important that liturgical planners, and priests in particular, with pastoral wisdom, give due weight to the signs proper to sacramental rites to this visibility and tangibility of grace. They should pay special attention to catechesis, to ensure that all the faithful experience every celebration of the sacraments with devotion, intensity, and spiritual joy.

A Worthy Disciple

Richard, who came from Scotland, was Hugh of Saint-Victor's worthy disciple. He was prior of the abbey of Saint-Victor from 1162 to 1173, the year of his death. Richard too, of course, assigned a fundamental role to the study of the Bible but, unlike his master, gave priority to the allegorical sense, the symbolic meaning of Scripture. This is what he uses, for example, in his interpretation of the Old Testament figure of Benjamin, the son of Jacob, as a model of contemplation and the epitome of the spiritual life. Richard addresses this topic in two texts, *Benjamin Minor* and *Benjamin Maior*. In these, he proposes to the faithful a spiritual journey which is primarily an invitation to exercise the various virtues, learning to discipline and to control with reason the sentiments and the inner affective and emotional impulses. Only when the human being has attained balance and human maturity in this area is he or she ready to approach contemplation, which Richard defines as "a profound and pure gaze of the soul, fixed on the marvels of wisdom, combined with an ecstatic sense of wonder and admiration" (*Benjamin Maior* 1, 4: PL 196, 67).

Contemplation is therefore the destination, the result of an arduous journey that involves dialogue between faith and reason, that is, once again, a theological discourse. Theology stems from truths that are the subject of faith but seeks to deepen knowledge of them by the use of reason, taking into account the gift of faith.

This application of reason to the comprehension of faith is presented convincingly in Richard's masterpiece, one of the great books of history, the *De Trinitate* (*The Trinity*). In the six volumes of which it is composed, he reflects perspicaciously on the mystery of the Triune God. According to Richard, since God is love, the one divine substance includes communication, oblation, and love between the two persons, the Father and the Son, who are placed in a reciprocal, eternal exchange of love. However, the perfection of happiness and goodness admits of no exclusivism or closure. On the contrary, it requires the eternal presence of a third person, the Holy Spirit. Trinitarian love is participatory, harmonious, and includes a superabundance of delight, enjoyment, and ceaseless joy. Richard, in other words, supposes that God is love, analyzes the essence of love and what the reality love entails, and thereby arrives at the Trinity of the persons, which really is the logical expression of the fact that God is love.

Yet Richard is aware that love, although it reveals to us the essence of God, although it makes us "understand" the mystery of the Trinity, is nevertheless always an analogy that serves to speak of a mystery that surpasses the human mind. Being the poet and mystic that he is, Richard also has recourse to other images. For example, he compares divinity to a river, to a loving wave which originates in the Father and ebbs and flows in the Son, to be subsequently spread with joy through the Holy Spirit.

Authors such as Hugh and Richard of Saint-Victor raise our minds to contemplation of the divine realities. At the same time, the immense joy we feel at the thought, admiration, and praise of the Blessed Trinity supports and sustains the practical commitment to be inspired by this perfect model of communion in love in order to build our daily human relationships. The Trinity is truly perfect communion! How the world would change if relations were always lived in families, in parishes, and in every other community by following the example of the three divine persons in whom each lives not only *with* the other but *for* the other and *in* the other! A few months ago at the Angelus, I recalled: "Love alone makes us happy because we live in a relationship, and we live to love and to be loved" (*Angelus*, Trinity Sunday, 7 June 2009). It is love that works this ceaseless miracle. As in the life of the Blessed Trinity, plurality is recomposed in unity, where all is kindness and joy. With St. Augustine, held in great honor by the Victorines, we too may exclaim: "*Vides Trinitatem, si caritatem vides*—you contemplate the Trinity, if you see charity" (*De Trinitate* 8, 8, 12).

—*25 November 2009*

WILLIAM OF SAINT-THIERRY

THE BIOGRAPHER OF BERNARD OF CLAIRVEAUX, and a friend who esteemed him, was William of Saint-Thierry, on whom I reflect in this chapter.

William was born in Liège between 1075 and 1080. He came from a noble family, was endowed with a keen intelligence and an innate love of study. He attended famous schools of the time, such as those in his native city and in Rheims, France. He also came into personal contact with Peter Abelard, the teacher who applied philosophy to theology in such an original way as to give rise to great perplexity and opposition. William also expressed his own reservations, pressing his friend Bernard to take a stance concerning Abelard.

Responding to God's mysterious and irresistible call, which is the vocation to the consecrated life, William entered the Benedictine monastery of Saint-Nicasius in Rheims in 1113. A few years later, he became abbot of the monastery of Saint-Thierry in the Diocese of Rheims. In that period, there was a widespread need for the purification and renewal of monastic life to make it authentically evangelical. William worked on doing this in his own monastery and in general in the Benedictine order. However, he met with great resistance to his attempts at reform, and thus, although his friend Bernard advised him against it, in 1135 he left the Benedictine abbey and exchanged his black habit for a white one in order to join the Cistercians of Signy. From that time, until his death in 1148, he devoted himself to prayerful contemplation of God's mysteries, ever the subject of his deepest desires, and to the composition of spiritual literature, important writings in the history of monastic theology.

One of his first works is titled *De natura et dignitate amoris (The Nature and Dignity of Love)*. In it, William expressed one of his basic ideas, which is also valid for us. The principal energy that moves the human soul, he said, is love. Human nature, in its deepest essence, consists in loving. Ultimately, a single task is entrusted to every human being: to learn to like and to love, sincerely, authentically, and freely. However, it is only from God's teaching that this task is learned and that the human being may reach the end for which he was created. Indeed, William wrote: "The art of arts is the art of love. . . . Love is inspired by the Creator of nature. Love is a force of the soul that leads it as by a natural weight to its own place and end" (*De natura et dignitate amoris* 1: PL 184, 379).

Learning to love is a long and demanding process that is structured by William in four stages, corresponding to the ages of the human being: childhood, youth, maturity, and old age. On this journey, the person must impose upon himself an effective *ascesis*, firm self-control to eliminate every irregular affection, every capitulation to selfishness, and to unify his own life in God, the source, goal, and force of love, until he reaches the summit of spiritual life, which William calls "wisdom." At the end of this ascetic process, the person feels deep serenity and sweetness. All the human being's faculties—intelligence, will, affection—rest in God, known and loved in Christ.

In other works too, William speaks of this radical vocation to love for God, which is the secret of a successful and happy life and which he describes as a ceaseless, growing desire, inspired by God himself in the human heart. In a meditation, he says "that the object of this love is Love" with a capital L—namely, God. It is he who pours himself out into the hearts of those who love him and prepares them to receive him. "God gives himself until the person is sated and in such a way that the desire is never lacking. This impetus of love is the fulfillment of the human being" (*De Contemplando Deo* 6, *passim*: SC 61 bis, 79–83). The considerable importance that William gives to the emotional dimension is striking. Basically, our hearts are made of flesh and blood, and when we love God, who is Love itself, how can we fail to express in this relationship with the Lord our most human feelings, such as tenderness, sensitivity, and delicacy? In becoming human, the Lord himself wanted to love us with a heart of flesh!

Moreover, according to William, love has another important quality: it illuminates the mind and enables one to know God better and more profoundly and, in God, people and events. The knowledge that proceeds from the senses and the intelligence reduces but does not eliminate the distance between the subject and the object, between the "I" and the "you." Love, on the other hand, gives rise to attraction and communion, to the point that transformation and assimilation take place between the subject who loves and the beloved object. This reciprocity of affection and liking subsequently permits a far deeper knowledge than that which is brought by reason alone. A famous saying of William expresses it: *Amor ipse intellectus est*—love in itself is already the beginning of knowledge. Let us ask ourselves: is not our life just like this? Is it not perhaps true that we only truly know *who* and *what* we love? Without a certain affection, one knows no one and nothing! And this applies first of all to the knowledge of God and his mysteries that exceed our mental capacity to understand: God is known if he is loved!

A synthesis of William of Saint-Thierry's thought is contained in a long letter addressed to the Carthusians of Mont-Dieu, whom he visited and wished to encourage and console. Already in 1690, the learned Benedictine Jean Mabillon gave this letter a meaningful title: *Epistola Aurea* (*Golden Epistle*). In fact, the teachings on spiritual life that it contains are invaluable for all those who wish to increase in communion with God and in holiness. In this treatise, William proposes an itinerary in three stages. It is necessary, he says, to move on from the "animal" being to the "rational" one, in order to attain to the "spiritual."

What does he mean by these three terms? To start with, a person accepts the vision of life inspired by faith with an act of obedience and trust. Then, with a process of interiorization—in which the reason and the will play an important role—faith in Christ is received with profound conviction and one feels a harmonious correspondence between what is believed and what is hoped, and the most secret aspirations of the soul, our reason, our affections. One therefore arrives at the perfection of spiritual life, when the realities of faith are a source of deep joy and real and satisfying communion with God. One lives only in love and for love.

William based this process on a solid vision of the human being inspired by the ancient Greek Fathers, especially Origen, who, with bold language, taught that the human being's vocation was to become like God, who created him in his image and likeness. The image of God present in us impels us toward likeness, that is, toward an ever fuller identity between one's own will and the divine will. One does not attain this perfection, which William calls "unity of spirit," by one's own efforts, even if they are sincere and generous, because something else is necessary. This perfection is reached through the action of the Holy Spirit, who takes up his abode in the soul and purifies, absorbs, and transforms into charity every impulse and desire of love that is present in the human being. "Then there is a further likeness to God," we read in the *Epistola Aurea*, "which is no longer called 'likeness' but 'unity of spirit,' when the person becomes one with God, one in spirit, not only because of the unity of an identical desire but through being unable to desire anything else. In this way, the human being deserves to become not God but what God is: man becomes through grace what God is by nature" (*Epistola Aurea* 262–63: SC 223, 353–55).

This author, whom we might describe as the "Singer of Charity, of Love," teaches us to make the basic decision in our lives that gives meaning and value to all our other decisions: to love God and, through love of him, to love our neighbor. Only in this manner shall we be able to find true joy, an anticipation of eternal beatitude. Let us learn from the saints in order to learn to love authentically and totally, to set our being on this journey. Together with a young saint, a Doctor of the Church, Thérèse of the Child Jesus, let us tell the Lord that we too want to live of love. And I conclude with a prayer precisely by this saint:

> You know I love you, Jesus Christ, my Own! Your Spirit's fire of love enkindles me. By loving you, I draw the Father here, down to my heart, to stay with me always. Blessed Trinity! You are my prisoner dear, of love, today. . . . To live of love, 'tis without stint to give. And never count the cost, nor ask reward. . . . O Heart Divine, o'erflowing with tenderness, How swift I run, who all to You has given! Naught but your love I need, my life to bless.

—*2 December 2009*

St. Hildegard of Bingen

Prophetess and Visionary

In 1988, on the occasion of the Marian Year, Venerable John Paul II wrote an apostolic letter titled *Mulieris Dignitatem* on the precious role that women have played and play in the life of the Church. "The Church," one reads in it, "gives thanks for all the manifestations of the *feminine* 'genius' which have appeared in the course of history, in the midst of all peoples and nations; she gives thanks for all the charisms that the Holy Spirit distributes to women in the history of the People of God, for all the victories which she owes to their faith, hope, and charity: she gives thanks for all the fruits of feminine holiness" (n. 31).

Various female figures stand out for the holiness of their lives and the wealth of their teaching, even in those centuries of history that we usually call the Middle Ages, among them St. Hildegard of Bingen, who lived in Germany in the twelfth century. She was born in 1098, probably at Bermersheim, Rhineland, not far from Alzey, and died in 1179 at the age of eighty-one, in spite of having always been in poor health.

Hildegard belonged to a large noble family, and her parents dedicated her to God from birth for his service. At the age of eight, she was offered for the religious state (in accordance with the *Rule of St. Benedict 59*), and, to ensure that she received an appropriate human and Christian formation, she was entrusted to the care of the consecrated widow Uda of Gölklheim and then to Jutta of Spanheim, who had taken the veil at the Benedictine monastery of St. Disibodenberg. A small cloistered women's monastery was developing there that followed the Rule of St. Benedict.

Hildegard was clothed by Bishop Otto of Bamberg and in 1136, upon the death of Mother Jutta, who had become the community *magistra* (prioress), the sisters chose Hildegard to succeed her. She fulfilled this office making the most of her gifts as a woman of culture and of lofty spirituality, capable of dealing competently with the organizational aspects of cloistered life. A few years later, partly because of the increasing number of young women who were knocking at the monastery door, Hildegard broke away from the dominating male monastery of St. Disibodenburg. She took her community to Bingen, calling it after St. Rupert, and here she spent the rest of her days. Her manner of exercising the ministry of authority is an example for every religious community: she inspired holy emulation in the practice of good to such an extent that, as time was to tell, both the mother and her daughters competed in mutual esteem and in serving each other.

During the years when she was superior of the monastery of St. Disibodenberg, Hildegard began to dictate the mystical visions that she had been receiving for some time to the monk Volmar, her spiritual director, and to Richardis di Strade, her secretary, a sister of whom she was very fond. As always happens in the life of true mystics, Hildegard too wanted to put herself under the authority of wise people to discern the origin of her visions, fearing that they were the product of illusions and did not come from God. She thus turned to a person who was most highly esteemed in the Church in those times: St. Bernard of Clairvaux, of whom I have already spoken in several catecheses. He calmed and encouraged Hildegard. However, in 1147 she received a further, very important approval. Pope Eugene III, who was presiding at a synod in Trier, read a text dictated by Hildegard presented to him by Archbishop Henry of Mainz. The pope authorized the mystic to write down her visions and to speak in public. From that moment, Hildegard's spiritual prestige continued to grow so that her contemporaries called her the "Teutonic prophetess."

This is the seal of an authentic experience of the Holy Spirit, the source of every charism: the person endowed with supernatural gifts never boasts of them, never flaunts them, and, above all, shows complete obedience to the ecclesial authority. Every gift bestowed by the Holy Spirit is in fact intended for the edification of the Church, and the Church, through her pastors, recognizes its authenticity.

This great woman, this *prophetess*, also speaks with great timeliness to us today, with her courageous ability to discern the signs of the times, her love for creation, her medicine, her poetry, her music, which today has been reconstructed, her love for Christ and for his Church—which was suffering in that period too, wounded also in that time by the sins of both priests and laypeople, and far better loved as the Body of Christ.

Theologian

Saint Hildegard of Bingen truly was an important female figure of the Middle Ages who was distinguished for her spiritual wisdom and the holiness of her life. Hildegard's mystical visions resemble those of the Old Testament prophets: expressing herself in the cultural and religious categories of her time, she interpreted the Sacred Scriptures in the light of God, applying them to the various circumstances of life. Thus, all those who heard her felt the need to live a consistent and committed Christian lifestyle. In a letter to St. Bernard, the mystic from the Rhineland confesses:

The vision fascinates my whole being: I do not see with the eyes of the body, but it appears to me in the spirit of the mysteries. . . . I recognize the deep meaning of what is expounded on in the Psalter, in the Gospels, and in other books, which have been shown to me in the vision. This vision burns like a flame in my breast and in my soul and teaches me to understand the text profoundly. (*Epistolarium pars prima 1–90: CCCM 91*)

Hildegard's mystical visions have a rich theological content. They refer to the principal events of salvation history and use a language for the most part poetic and symbolic. For example, in her best-known work, titled *Scivias*, that is, "You know the ways," she sums up in thirty-five visions the events of the history of salvation from the creation of the world to the end of time. With the characteristic traits of feminine sensitivity, Hildegard develops at the very heart of her work the theme of the mysterious marriage between God and humanity that is brought about in the Incarnation. On the tree of the Cross take place the nuptials of the Son of God with the Church, his bride, filled with grace and the ability to give new children to God, in the love of the Holy Spirit (cf. *Visio tertia: PL 197*, 453c).

From these brief references, we already see that theology too can receive a special contribution from women because they are able to talk about God and the mysteries of faith using their own particular intelligence and sensitivity. I therefore encourage all those who carry out this service to do it with a profound ecclesial spirit, nourishing their own reflection with prayer and looking to the great riches, not yet fully explored, of the medieval mystic tradition, especially that represented by luminous models such as Hildegard of Bingen.

The Rhenish mystic is also the author of other writings, two of which are particularly important since, like *Scivias,* they record her mystical visions: they are the *Liber vitae meritorum* (*Book of the Merits of Life*) and the *Liber divinorum operum* (*Book of the Divine Works*), also called *De operatione Dei.* In the former, she describes a unique and powerful vision of God, who gives life to the cosmos with his power and his light. Hildegard stresses the deep relationship that exists between humanity and God and reminds us that the whole creation, of which humanity is the summit, receives life from the Trinity. The work is centered on the relationship between virtue and vice, which is why human beings must face the daily challenge of vice, which distances them on their way toward God, and of virtue, which benefits them. The invitation is to distance themselves from evil in order to glorify God and, after a virtuous existence, enter the life that consists "wholly of joy." In her second work—which many consider her masterpiece—she once again describes creation in its relationship with God and the centrality of the human being, expressing a strong Christocentrism with a biblical-Patristic flavor. The saint, who presents five visions inspired by the Prologue of the Gospel according to St. John, cites the words of the Son to the Father: "The whole task that you wanted and entrusted to me I have carried out successfully, and so here I am in you and you in me and we are one" (*Pars 3, Visio 10: PL* 197, 1025a).

Finally, in other writings, Hildegard manifests the versatility of interests and cultural vivacity of the women's monasteries of the Middle Ages in a manner contrary to the prejudices that still weighed on that period. Hildegard took an interest in medicine and in the natural sciences as well as in music, since she was endowed with artistic talent. Thus, she composed hymns, antiphons, and songs, gathered under the title: *Symphonia Harmoniae Caelestium Revelationum* (*Symphony of the Harmony of Heavenly Revelations*), which were performed joyously in her monasteries, spreading an atmosphere of tranquility and which have also come down to us. For her, the entire creation is a symphony of the Holy Spirit, who is in himself joy and jubilation.

The popularity that surrounded Hildegard impelled many people to seek her advice. It is for this reason that we have so many of her letters at our disposal. Many male and female monastic communities turned to her, as well as bishops and abbots. And many of her answers still apply for us. For instance, Hildegard wrote these words to a community of women religious:

> The spiritual life must be tended with great dedication. At first the effort is burdensome because it demands the renunciation of caprices of the pleasures of the flesh and of other such things. But if she lets herself be enthralled by holiness, a holy soul will find even contempt for the world sweet and lovable. All that is needed is to take care that the soul does not shrivel. (E. Gronau, *Hildegard. Vita di una donna profetica alle origini dell'età moderna* [Milan 1996], 402)

And when the Emperor Frederic Barbarossa caused a schism in the Church by supporting at least three anti-popes against Alexander III, the legitimate pope, Hildegard did not hesitate, inspired by her visions, to remind him that even he, the emperor, was subject to God's judgment. With fearlessness, a feature of every prophet, she wrote to the emperor these words as spoken by God: "You will be sorry for this wicked conduct of the godless who despise me! Listen, O king, if you wish to live! Otherwise my sword will pierce you!" (ibid., 412).

With the spiritual authority with which she was endowed, in the last years of her life Hildegard set out on journeys, despite her advanced age and the uncomfortable conditions of travel, in order to speak to the People of God. They all listened willingly, even when she spoke severely: they considered her a messenger sent by God. She called above all the monastic communities and the clergy to a life in conformity with their vocation. In a special way, Hildegard countered the movement of German *cátari* (Cathars). They—*cátari* means literally "pure"—advocated a radical reform of the Church, especially to combat the abuses of the clergy. She harshly reprimanded them for seeking to subvert the very nature of the Church, reminding them that a true renewal of the ecclesial community is obtained with a sincere spirit of repentance and a demanding process of conversion, rather than with a change of structures. This is a message that we should never forget. Let us always invoke the Holy Spirit, so that he may inspire in the Church holy and courageous women, like St. Hildegard of Bingen, who, developing the gifts they have received from God, make their own special and valuable contribution to the spiritual development of our communities and of the Church in our time.

—*1 and 8 September 2010*

JOHN OF SALISBURY

WE SHALL BECOME ACQUAINTED here with John of Salisbury, who belonged to one of the most important schools of philosophy and theology of the Middle Ages, that of the Cathedral of Chartres in France. Like the theologians of whom I have spoken in the past few chapters, John too helps us understand that faith, in harmony with the just aspirations of reason, impels thought toward the revealed truth in which is found the true good of the human being.

John was born in Salisbury, England, between 1100 and 1120. In reading his works, and especially the large collection of his letters, we learn about the most important events in his life. For about twelve years, from 1136 to 1148, he devoted himself to study, attending the best schools of his day, where he heard the lectures of famous teachers. He went to Paris and then to Chartres, the environment that made the greatest impression on his formation and from which he assimilated his great cultural openness, his interest in speculative problems, and his appreciation of literature.

As often happened in that time, the most brilliant students were chosen by prelates and sovereigns to be their close collaborators. This also happened to John of Salisbury, who was introduced to Theobald, archbishop of Canterbury, the Primatial See of England, by a great friend of his, Bernard of Clairvaux. Theobald was glad to welcome John among his clergy. For eleven years, from 1150 to 1161, John was the secretary and chaplain of the elderly archbishop.

With unflagging zeal, he continued to devote himself to study; he carried out intense diplomatic activity, going to Italy ten times for the explicit purpose of fostering relations between the kingdom and Church of England and the Roman pontiff. The pope in those years was Adrian IV, an Englishman who was a close friend of John of Salisbury. In the years following Adrian IV's death, in 1159, a situation of serious tension arose in England between the Church and the kingdom. In fact, King Henry II wished to impose his authority on the internal life of the Church, curtailing her freedom. This stance provoked John of Salisbury to react and, in particular, prompted the valiant resistance of St. Thomas Becket, Theobald's successor on the episcopal throne of Canterbury, who, for this reason, was exiled to France. John of Salisbury accompanied him and remained in his service, working ceaselessly for reconciliation.

In 1170, when both John and Thomas Becket had returned to England, Thomas was attacked and murdered in his cathedral. He died a martyr and was immediately venerated as such by the people. John continued to serve faithfully the successor of Thomas as well, until he was appointed bishop of Chartres, where he lived from 1176 until 1180, the year of his death.

Two of John of Salisbury's works—both bearing elegant Greek titles—are considered his masterpieces: *Metalogicon* (*In Defense of Logic*) and *Policraticus* (*The Man of Government*). In the first of these works, not without that fine irony that is a feature of many scholars, he rejects the position of those who had a reductionist conception of culture, which they saw as empty eloquence and vain words. John, on the contrary, praises culture, authentic philosophy, that is, the encounter between rigorous thought and communication, effective words. He writes:

> Indeed, just as eloquence that is not illuminated by reason is not only rash but blind, so wisdom that does not profit from the use of words is not only weak but in a certain way is mutilated. Indeed, although, at times, wisdom without words might serve to square the individual with his own conscience, it is of rare or little profit to society. (*Metalogicon* 1, 1: *PL* 199, 327)

This is a very timely teaching. Today, what John described as "eloquence," that is, the possibility of communicating with increasingly elaborate and widespread means, has increased enormously. Yet the need to communicate messages endowed with "wisdom," which is inspired by truth, goodness, and beauty, is more urgent than ever. This is a great responsibility that calls into question in particular the people who work in the multiform and complex world of culture, of communications, of the media. And this is a realm in which the gospel can be proclaimed with missionary zeal.

In the *Metalogicon* John treats the problems of logic, in his day a subject of great interest, and asks himself a fundamental question: What can human reason know? To what point can it correspond with the aspiration that exists in every person, namely, to seek the truth? John of Salisbury adopts a moderate position, based on the teaching of certain treatises of Aristotle and Cicero. In his opinion, human reason normally attains knowledge that is not indisputable but probable and arguable. Human knowledge—this is his conclusion—is imperfect, because it is subject to finiteness, to human limitations. Nevertheless, it grows and is perfected, thanks to the experience and elaboration of correct and consistent reasoning, able to make connections between concepts and the reality, through discussion, exchanges, and knowledge that is enriched from one generation to the next. Only in God is there perfect knowledge, which is communicated to the human being, at least partially, by means of revelation received in faith, which is why the knowledge of faith, theology, unfolds the potential of reason and makes it possible to advance with humility in the knowledge of God's mysteries.

The believer and the theologian who deepen the treasure of faith also open themselves to a practical knowledge that guides our daily activity, in other words, moral law and the exercise of the virtues. John of Salisbury writes:

> God's clemency has granted us his law, which establishes what it is useful for us to know and points out to us what it is legitimate for us to know of God and what it is right to investigate. . . . In this law, in fact, the will of God is explained and revealed so that each one of us may know what he needs to do. (*Metalogicon* 4, 41: PL 199, 944–45)

According to John of Salisbury, an immutable objective truth also exists, whose origin is in God, accessible to human reason and which concerns practical and social action. It is a natural law that must inspire human laws and political and religious authorities, so that they may promote the common good. This natural law is characterized by a property that John calls "equity," that is, the attribution to each person of his own rights. From this stem emerges precepts that are legitimate for all peoples, and in no way can they be abrogated. This is the central thesis of *Policraticus*, the treatise of philosophy and political theology in which John of Salisbury reflects on the conditions that render government leaders just and acceptable.

Whereas other arguments addressed in this work are linked to the historical circumstances in which it was composed, the theme of the relationship between natural law and a positive juridical order, mediated by equity, is still of great importance today. In our time, in fact, especially in some countries, we are witnessing a disturbing divergence between reason, whose task is to discover the ethical values linked to the dignity of the human person, and freedom, whose responsibility is to accept and promote them. Perhaps John of Salisbury would remind us today that the only laws in conformity with equity are those that protect the sacredness of human life and reject the licitness of abortion, euthanasia, and bold genetic experimentation, those laws that respect the dignity of marriage between a man and a woman, that are inspired by a correct secularism of the state—a secularism that always entails the safeguard of religious freedom and that pursues subsidiarity and solidarity at both the national and the international level. If this were not so, what John of Salisbury terms the "tyranny of princes," or as we would say, "the dictatorship of relativism" would end by coming to power, a relativism, as I recalled a few years ago, "which does not recognize anything as definitive and whose ultimate goal consists solely of one's own ego and desires" (Cardinal

Joseph Ratzinger, Dean of the College of Cardinals, *Homily, Mass for the Election of the Roman Pointiff,* 18 April 2005).

In my encyclical *Caritas in Veritate,* in addressing people of goodwill who strive to ensure that social and political action are never separated from the objective truth about man and his dignity, I wrote:

> Truth, and the love which it reveals, cannot be produced: they can only be received as a gift. Their ultimate source is not, and cannot be, mankind, but only God, who is himself Truth and Love. This principle is extremely important for society and for development, since neither can be a purely human product; the vocation to development on the part of individuals and peoples is not based simply on human choice, but is an intrinsic part of a plan that is prior to us and constitutes for all of us a duty to be freely accepted. (n. 52)

We must seek and welcome this plan that precedes us, this truth of being, so that justice may be born, but we may find it and welcome it only with a heart, a will, and a reason purified in the light of God.

—*16 December 2009*

PETER LOMBARD

PETER LOMBARD, A THEOLOGIAN who lived in the twelfth century, enjoyed great fame because one of his works, titled the *Sentences*, was used as a theological manual for many centuries.

So who was Peter Lombard? Although the information on his life is scarce, it is possible to reconstruct the essential lines of his biography. He was born between the eleventh and twelfth centuries, near Novara, in northern Italy, in a region that once belonged to the Lombards. For this very reason he was nicknamed "the Lombard." He belonged to a modest family, as we may deduce from the letter of introduction that Bernard of Clairvaux wrote to Gilduin, superior of the abbey of Saint-Victor in Paris, asking him to give free accommodation to Peter, who wanted to go to that city in order to study. Even in the Middle Ages not only nobles or the rich might study and acquire important roles in ecclesial and social life but also people of humble origin such as, for example, Gregory VII, the pope who stood up to Emperor Henry VI, or Maurice of Sully, the archbishop of Paris who commissioned the building of Notre Dame and who was the son of a poor peasant.

Peter Lombard began his studies in Bologna and then went to Rheims and last to Paris. From 1140, he taught at the prestigious school of Notre Dame. Esteemed and appreciated as a theologian, eight years later he was charged by Pope Eugene II to examine the doctrine of Gilbert de la Porrée that was giving rise to numerous discussions because it was held to be not wholly orthodox. Having become a priest, he was appointed bishop of Paris in 1159, a year before his death in 1160.

Like all theology teachers of his time, Peter also wrote discourses and commentaries on Sacred Scripture. His masterpiece, however, consists of the four books of the *Sentences*. This is a text which came into being for didactic purposes. According to the theological method in use in those times, it was necessary first of all to know, study, and comment on the thought of the Fathers of the Church and of the other writers deemed authoritative. Peter therefore collected a very considerable amount of documentation, which consisted mainly of the teachings of the great Latin Fathers, especially St. Augustine, and was open to the contribution of contemporary theologians. Among other things, he used an encyclopedia of Greek theology that had only recently become known to the West: *The Orthodox Faith*, composed by St. John Damascene.

The great merit of Peter Lombard is to have organized all the material that he had collected and chosen with care, in a systematic and harmonious framework. In fact, one of the features of theology is to organize the patrimony of faith in a unitive and orderly way. Thus, he distributed the "sentences," that is, the Patristic sources on various arguments, in four books. In the first book, he addresses God and the Trinitarian mystery; in the second, the work of the creation, sin, and grace; in the third, the mystery of the Incarnation and the work of redemption with an extensive exposition on the virtues. The fourth book is dedicated to the sacraments and to the last realities, those of eternal life, or *novissimi*. The overall view presented includes almost all the truths of the Catholic faith.

The concise, clear vision and clear, orderly schematic and ever consistent presentation explain the extraordinary success of Peter Lombard's *Sentences*. They enabled students to learn reliably and gave the educators and teachers who used them plenty of room for acquiring deeper knowledge. A Franciscan theologian, Alexandre of Hales, of the next generation, introduced into the *Sentences* a division that facilitated their study and consultation. Even the greatest of the thirteenth-century theologians, Albert the Great, Bonaventure of Bagnoregio, and Thomas Aquinas began their academic activity by commenting on the four books of Peter Lombard's *Sentences,* enriching them with their reflections. Lombard's text was the book in use at all schools of theology until the sixteenth century.

I emphasize how the organic presentation of faith is an indispensable requirement. In fact, the individual truths of faith illuminate each other, and in their total and unitive vision appears the harmony of God's plan of salvation and the centrality of the mystery of Christ. After the example of Peter Lombard, I invite all theologians and priests always to keep in mind the whole vision of the Christian doctrine, to counter today's risks of fragmentation and the debasement of the single truths. The *Catechism of the Catholic Church,* as well as the *Compendium* of this same catechism, offers us exactly this full picture of Christian revelation, to be accepted with faith and gratitude. However, I encourage the individual faithful and the Christian communities to make the most of these instruments to know and to deepen the content of our faith. It will thus appear to us as a marvelous symphony that speaks to us of God and of his love and asks of us firm adherence and an active response.

To get an idea of the interest that the reading of Peter Lombard's *Sentences* still inspires today, I propose two examples. Inspired by St. Augustine's commentary on the book of Genesis, Peter wonders why woman was created from man's rib and not from his head or his feet. And Peter explains: "She was formed neither as a dominator nor a slave of man but rather as his companion" (*Sentences* 3, 18, 3). Then, still on the basis of the Patristic teaching he adds: "The mystery of Christ and of the Church is represented in this act. Just as, in fact, woman was formed from Adam's rib while he slept, so the Church was born from the sacraments that began to flow from the side of Christ, asleep on the Cross, that is, from the blood and water with which we are redeemed from sin and cleansed of guilt" (*Sentences* 3, 18, 4). These are profound reflections that still apply today when the theology and spirituality of Christian marriage have considerably deepened the analogy with the spousal relationship of Christ and his Church.

In another passage in one of his principal works, Peter Lombard, treating the merits of Christ, asks himself: "Why, then does [Christ] wish to suffer and die, if his virtues were sufficient to obtain for himself all the merits?" His answer is incisive and effective: "For you, not for himself!" He then continues with another question and another answer, which seem to reproduce the discussions that went on during the lessons of medieval theology teachers: "And in what sense did he suffer and die for me? So that his passion and his death might be an example and cause for you. An example of virtue and humility, a cause of glory and freedom; an example given by God, obedient unto death; a cause of your liberation and your beatitude" (*Sentences* 3, 18, 5).

Among the most important contributions offered by Peter Lombard to the history of theology, I recall his treatise on the sacraments, of which he gave what I would call a definitive definition: "Precisely what is a sign of God's grace and a visible form of invisible grace, in such a way that it bears its image and is its cause is called a sacrament in the proper sense" (4, 1, 4). With this definition, Peter Lombard grasps the essence of the sacraments: they are a cause of grace; they are truly able to communicate divine life. Successive theologians never again departed from this vision and were also to use the distinction between the material and the formal element introduced by the "Master of the Sentences," as Peter Lombard was known. The material element is the tangible, visible reality; the formal element consists of the words spoken by the minister. For a complete and valid celebration of the sacraments, both are essential: matter, the reality with which the Lord visibly touches us, and the word that conveys the spiritual significance. In baptism, for example, the material element is the water that is poured on the head of the child, and the formal element is the formula: "I baptize you in the name of the Father, of the Son, and of the Holy Spirit." Peter Lombard, moreover, explained that the sacraments alone objectively transmit divine grace and they are seven: baptism, the eucharist, penance, the unction of the sick, orders, confession, and matrimony (cf. *Sentences* 4, 2, 1).

It is important to recognize how precious and indispensable for every Christian is the sacramental life, in which the Lord transmits this matter in the community of the Church, and touches and transforms us. As the *Catechism of the Catholic Church* says, the sacraments are "powers that come forth from the body of Christ, which is ever-living and life-giving. They are actions of the Holy Spirit" (n. 1116). I urge priests, especially ministers in charge of souls, to have an intense sacramental life themselves in the first place in order to be of help to the faithful. May the celebration of the sacraments be impressed with dignity and decorum and encourage personal recollection and community participation, the sense of God's presence and missionary zeal. The sacraments are the great treasure of the Church, and it is the task of each one of us to celebrate them with spiritual profit. In them an ever-amazing event touches our lives: Christ, through the visible signs, comes to us, purifies us, transforms us, and makes us share in his divine friendship.

—*30 December 2009*

St. Francis of Assisi

HERE I PRESENT THE FIGURE OF FRANCIS, an authentic "giant" of holiness, who continues to fascinate a great many people of all age groups and every religion.

"A sun was born into the world." With these words, in the *Divine Comedy* (*Paradiso*, Canto 11), the great Italian poet Dante Alighieri alludes to Francis's birth, which took place in Assisi either at the end of 1181 or the beginning of 1182. As part of a rich family—his father was a cloth merchant—Francis lived a carefree adolescence and youth, cultivating the chivalrous ideals of the time. At age twenty, he took part in a military campaign and was taken prisoner. He became ill and was freed. After his return to Assisi, a slow process of spiritual conversion began within him, which brought him gradually to abandon the worldly lifestyle that he had adopted thus far.

The famous episodes of Francis's meeting with the leper—to whom, dismounting from his horse, he gave the kiss of peace—and of the message from the crucifix in the small Church of St. Damian date to this period. Three times Christ on the Cross came to life and told him: "Go, Francis, and repair my church in ruins." This simple occurrence of the word of God heard in the Church of St. Damian contains a profound symbolism. At that moment, St. Francis was called to repair the small church, but the ruinous state of the building was a symbol of the dramatic and disquieting situation of the Church herself.

At that time, the Church had a superficial faith that did not shape or transform life, a scarcely zealous clergy, and a chilling of love. It was an interior destruction of the Church that also brought a decomposition of unity, with the birth of heretical movements. Yet there at the center of the Church in ruins was the Crucified Lord, and he spoke: he called for renewal; he called Francis to the manual labor of repairing the small Church of St. Damian, symbol of a much deeper call to renew Christ's own Church, with her radical faith and her loving enthusiasm for Christ.

This event, which probably happened in 1205, calls to mind another similar occurrence that took place in 1207: Pope Innocent III's dream. In it, he saw the Basilica of St. John Lateran, the mother of all churches, collapsing and one small and insignificant religious brother supporting the church on his shoulders to prevent it from falling. On the one hand, it is interesting to note that it is not the pope who was helping to prevent the church from collapsing but rather a small and insignificant brother, whom the pope recognized in Francis when he later came to visit. Innocent III was a powerful pope, who had a great theological formation and great political influence; nevertheless, he was not the one to renew the Church; the small, insignificant religious was. It was St. Francis, called by God. On the other hand, however, it is important to note that St. Francis does not renew the Church without or in opposition to the pope, but only in communion with him. The two realities go together: the successor of Peter, the bishops, the Church founded on the succession of the Apostles and the new charism that the Holy Spirit brought to life at that time for the Church's renewal. Authentic renewal grew from these together.

Let us return to the life of St. Francis. When his father Bernardone reproached him for being too generous to the poor, Francis, standing before the bishop of Assisi, in a symbolic gesture, stripped off his clothes, thus showing he renounced his paternal inheritance. Just as at the moment of creation, Francis had nothing, only the life that God gave him, into whose hands he delivered himself. He then lived as a hermit, until, in 1208, another fundamental step in his journey of conversion took place. While listening to a passage from the Gospel of Matthew— Jesus' discourse to the apostles whom he sent out on mission—Francis felt called to live in poverty and dedicate himself to preaching. Other companions joined him, and in 1209 he traveled to Rome, to propose to Pope Innocent III his plan for a new form of Christian life. He received a fatherly welcome from that great pontiff, who, enlightened by the Lord, perceived the divine origin of the movement inspired by Francis. The *Poverello* of Assisi understood that every charism, as a gift of the Holy Spirit, existed to serve the Body of Christ, which is the Church; therefore, he always acted in full communion with the ecclesial authorities. In the life of the saints, there is no contradiction between prophetic charism and the charism of governance, and if tension arises, they know to patiently await the times determined by the Holy Spirit.

Actually, several nineteenth-century and also twentieth-century historians have sought to construct a so-called historical Francis, behind the traditional depiction of the saint, just as they sought to create a so-called historical Jesus behind the Jesus of the Gospels. This historical Francis would not have been a man of the Church, but rather a man connected directly and solely to Christ, a man who wanted to bring about a renewal of the People of God, without canonical forms or hierarchy. The truth is that St. Francis really did have an extremely intimate relationship with Jesus and with the Word of God, that he wanted to pursue *sine glossa*: just as it is, in all its radicality and truth. It is also true that initially he did not intend to create a religious order with the necessary canonical forms. Rather, he simply wanted, through the Word of God and the presence of the Lord, to renew the People of God, to call them back to listening to the Word and to literal obedience to Christ. Furthermore, he knew that Christ was never "mine" but is always "ours," that "I" cannot possess Christ; that "I" cannot rebuild in opposition to the Church, her will and her teaching. Instead, it is only in communion with the Church built on the apostolic succession that obedience too to the Word of God can be renewed.

It is true that Francis had no intention of creating a new order, but solely that of renewing the People of God for the Lord who comes. He understood, however, through suffering and pain that everything must have its own order and that the law of the Church is necessary to give shape to renewal. Thus, he placed himself fully, with his heart, in communion with the Church, with the pope, and with the bishops. He always knew that the center of the Church is the eucharist, where the body of Christ and his blood are made present through the priesthood, the eucharist, and the communion of the Church. Wherever the priesthood and the eucharist and the Church come together, it is there alone that the word of God also dwells. The real historical Francis was the Francis of the Church, and precisely in this way he continues to speak to nonbelievers and believers of other confessions and religions as well.

Francis and his friars, who were becoming ever more numerous, established themselves at the Portiuncula, or the Church of Santa Maria degli Angeli, the sacred place par excellence of Franciscan spirituality. Even Clare, a young woman of Assisi from a noble family, followed the school of Francis. This became the origin of the Second Franciscan order, that of the Poor Clares, another experience destined to produce outstanding figures of sainthood in the Church.

Innocent III's successor Pope Honorius III, with his papal bull *Cum Dilecti* in 1218 supported the unique development of the first Friars Minor, who started missions in different European countries, and even in Morocco. In 1219, Francis obtained permission to visit and speak to the Muslim sultan Malik al-Klmil, to preach the gospel of Jesus there too. I highlight this episode in St. Francis's life, which is very timely. In an age when there was a conflict underway between Christianity and Islam, Francis, intentionally armed only with his faith and personal humility, traveled the path of dialogue effectively. The chronicles tell us that he was given a benevolent welcome and a cordial reception by the Muslim sultan. It provides a model that should inspire today's relations between Christians and Muslims: to promote a sincere dialogue, in reciprocal respect and mutual understanding (cf. *Nostra Aetate* 3). It appears that later, in 1220, Francis visited the Holy Land, thus sowing a seed that would bear much fruit: his spiritual sons would, in fact, make of the sites where Jesus lived a privileged space for their mission. It is with gratitude that I think today of the great merits of the Franciscan custody of the Holy Land.

On his return to Italy, Francis turned over the administration of his order to his vicar, Br. Pietro Cattani, while the pope entrusted the rapidly growing order's protection to Cardinal Ugolino, the future Pope Gregory IX. For his part, the founder, dedicated completely to his preaching, which he carried out with great success, compiled his Rule, which was then approved by the pope.

In 1224, at the hermitage in La Verna, Francis had a vision of the Crucified Lord in the form of a seraph, and from that encounter he received the stigmata from the Seraph Crucifix, thus becoming one with the Crucified Christ. It was a gift, therefore, that expressed his intimate identification with the Lord.

The death of Francis—his *transitus*—occurred on the evening of 3 October 1226, in the Portiuncula. After having blessed his spiritual children, he died, lying on the bare earthen floor. Two years later, Pope Gregory IX entered him in the roll of saints. A short time after, a great basilica in his honor was constructed in Assisi, still today an extremely popular pilgrim destination. There pilgrims can venerate the saint's tomb and take in the frescoes by Giotto, an artist who has magnificently illustrated Francis's life.

It has been said that Francis represents an *alter Christus*, that he was truly a living icon of Christ. He has also been called "the brother of Jesus." Indeed, this was his ideal: to be like Jesus, to contemplate Christ in the Gospel, to love him intensely and to imitate his virtues. In particular, he wished to ascribe interior and exterior poverty with a fundamental value, which he also taught to his spiritual sons. The first Beatitude of the Sermon on the Mount—"Blessed are the poor in spirit, for theirs is the kingdom of heaven" (Mt 5:3)—found a luminous fulfillment in the life and words of St. Francis. Truly, the saints are the best interpreters of the Bible. As they incarnate the word of God in their own lives, they make it more captivating than ever, so that it really speaks to us. The witness of Francis, who loved poverty as a means to follow Christ with dedication and total freedom, continues to be for us too an invitation to cultivate interior poverty in order to grow in our trust of God, also by adopting a sober lifestyle and a detachment from material goods.

Francis's love for Christ expressed itself in a special way in the adoration of the blessed sacrament of the eucharist. In the *Fonti Francescane* (*Writings of St. Francis*), one reads such moving expressions as: "Let everyone be struck with fear, let the whole world tremble, and let the heavens exult, when Christ, the Son of the living God, is present on the altar in the hands of a priest. O stupendous dignity! O humble sublimity, that the Lord of the universe, God and the Son of God, so humbles himself that for our salvation he hides himself under an ordinary piece of bread" (Francis of Assisi, *Scritti*, Editrici Francescane [Padova 2002], 401).

I also recall a piece of advice that Francis gave to priests: "When you wish to celebrate Mass, in a pure way, reverently make the true sacrifice of the most holy body and blood of our Lord Jesus Christ" (Francis of Assisi, *Scritti*, 399). Francis always showed great deference toward priests and asserted that they should always be treated with respect, even in cases where they might be somewhat unworthy personally. The reason he gave for this profound respect was that they receive the gift of consecrating the eucharist. Dear brothers in the priesthood, let us never forget this teaching: the holiness of the eucharist appeals to us to be pure, to live in a way that is consistent with the mystery we celebrate.

From love for Christ stems love for others and also for all God's creatures. This is yet another characteristic trait of Francis's spirituality: the sense of universal brotherhood and love for creation, which inspired the famous *Canticle of Creatures*. This too is an extremely timely message. As I recalled in my encyclical *Caritas in Veritate*, development is sustainable only when it respects creation and does not damage the environment (cf. nn. 48–52); and in the message for the World Day of Peace this year, I also underscored that even building stable peace is linked to respect for creation. Francis reminds us that the wisdom and benevolence of the Creator is expressed through creation. He understood nature as a language in which God speaks to us, in which reality becomes clear, and we can speak *of* God and *with* God.

Francis was a great saint and a joyful man. His simplicity, his humility, his faith, his love for Christ, his goodness toward every man and every woman brought him gladness in every circumstance. Indeed, there subsists an intimate and indissoluble relationship between holiness and joy. A French writer once wrote that there is only one sorrow in the world: not to be saints, that is, not to be near to God. Looking at the testimony of St. Francis, we understand that this is the secret of true happiness: to become saints, close to God!

May the Virgin Mary, so tenderly loved by Francis, obtain this gift for us. Let us entrust ourselves to her with the words of the *Poverello* of Assisi himself: "Blessed Virgin Mary, no one like you among women has ever been born in the world, daughter and handmaid of the most high King and heavenly Father, mother of our Most Blessed Lord Jesus Christ, spouse of the Holy Spirit. Pray for us to your most blessed and beloved Son, Lord and Master" (Francis of Assisi, *Scritti*, 163).

—*27 January 2010*

St. Clare of Assisi

ONE OF THE BEST-LOVED SAINTS is without a doubt St. Clare of Assisi, who lived in the thirteenth century and was a contemporary of St. Francis. Her testimony shows us how indebted the Church is to courageous women, full of faith like her, who can give a crucial impetus to the Church's renewal.

So who was Clare of Assisi? To answer this question, we possess reliable sources: not only the ancient biographies, such as that of Tommaso da Celano, but also the *Proceedings* of the cause of her canonization that the pope promoted only a few months after Clare's death and that contain the depositions of those who had lived a long time with her.

Born in 1193, Clare belonged to a wealthy, aristocratic family. She renounced her noble status and wealth to live in humility and poverty, adopting the lifestyle that Francis of Assisi recommended. Although her parents were planning a marriage for her with some important figure, as was then the custom, Clare, with a daring act inspired by her deep desire to follow Christ and her admiration for Francis, at the age of eighteen left her family home and, in the company of a friend, Bona di Guelfuccio, made her way in secret to the Friars Minor at the little Church of the Portiuncula. It was the evening of Palm Sunday in 1211. In the general commotion, a highly symbolic act took place: while his companions lit torches, Francis cut off Clare's hair and she put on a rough penitential habit. From that moment, she had become the virgin bride of Christ, humble and poor, and she consecrated herself totally to him. Like Clare and her companions, down through history innumerable women have been fascinated by love for Christ which, with the beauty of his divine person, fills their hearts. And the entire Church, through the mystical nuptial vocation of consecrated virgins, appears what she will be forever: the pure and beautiful bride of Christ.

In one of the four letters that Clare sent to St. Agnes of Prague, the daughter of the king of Bohemia, who wished to follow in Christ's footsteps, she speaks of Christ, her beloved spouse, with nuptial words that may be surprising but are nevertheless moving:

> When you have loved [him] you shall be chaste; when you have touched [him] you shall become purer; when you have accepted [him] you shall be a virgin. Whose power is stronger, whose generosity is more elevated, whose appearance more beautiful, whose love more tender, whose courtesy more gracious. In whose embrace you are already caught up; who has adorned your breast with precious stones . . . and placed on your head a golden crown as a sign [to all] of your holiness. (*First Letter to Blessed Agnes of Prague: FF, 2862*)

Especially at the beginning of Clare's religious experience, Francis of Assisi was not only a teacher to Clare whose teachings she was to follow but also a brotherly friend. The friendship between these two saints is a very beautiful and important aspect. Indeed, when two pure souls on fire with the same love for God meet, they find in their friendship with each other a powerful incentive to advance on the path of perfection. Friendship is one of the noblest and loftiest human sentiments, which divine grace purifies and transfigures. Like St. Francis and St. Clare, other saints too experienced profound friendship on the journey toward Christian perfection. Examples are St. Francis de Sales and St. Jane Frances de Chantal. As St. Francis de Sales himself wrote: "It is a blessed thing to love on earth as we hope to love in heaven, and to begin that friendship here which is to endure forever there. I am not now speaking of simple charity, a love due to all mankind, but of that spiritual friendship which binds souls together, leading them to share devotions and spiritual interests, so as to have but one mind between them" (*The Introduction to a Devout Life 3*, 19).

After spending a period of several months at other monastic communities, resisting the pressure of her relatives, who did not at first approve of her decision, Clare settled with her first companions at the Church of San Damiano, where the Friars Minor had organized a small convent for them. She lived in this monastery for more than forty years, until her death in 1253. A firsthand description has come down to us of how these women lived in those years at the beginning of the Franciscan movement. It is the admiring account of Jacques de Vitry, a Flemish bishop who came to Italy on a visit. He declared that he had encountered a large number of men and women of every social class who, having "left all things for Christ, fled the world. They called themselves Friars Minor and Sisters Minor and are held in high esteem by the lord pope and the cardinals. . . . The women live together in various homes not far from the city. They receive nothing but live on the work of their own hands. And they are deeply troubled and pained at being honored more than they would like to be by both clerics and lay people" (*Letter of October* 1216: *FF*, 2205, 2207).

Jacques de Vitry had perceptively noticed a characteristic trait of Franciscan spirituality about which Clare was deeply sensitive: the radicalism of poverty associated with total trust in divine providence. For this reason, she acted with great determination, obtaining from Pope Gregory IX or, probably, already from Pope Innocent III, the so-called *Privilegium Paupertatis* (cf. *FF*, 3279). On the basis of this privilege, Clare and her companions at San Damiano could not possess any material property. This was a truly extraordinary exception in comparison with the canon law then in force, but the ecclesiastical authorities of that time permitted it, appreciating the fruits of evangelical holiness that they recognized in the way of life of Clare and her sisters. This shows that even in the centuries of the Middle Ages, the role of women was not secondary but on the contrary considerable. In this regard, it is useful to remember that Clare was the first woman in the Church's history who composed a written rule, submitted for the pope's approval, to ensure the preservation of Francis of Assisi's charism in all the communities of women—large numbers of which were already springing up in her time—that wished to draw inspiration from the example of Francis and Clare.

In the Convent of San Damiano, Clare practiced heroically the virtues that should distinguish every Christian: humility, a spirit of piety, and penitence and charity. Although she was the superior, she wanted to serve the sick sisters herself and joyfully subjected herself to the most menial tasks. In fact, charity overcomes all resistance, and whoever loves, joyfully performs every sacrifice. Her faith in the real presence of Christ in the eucharist was so great that twice a miracle happened. Simply by showing to them the most blessed sacrament, she turned back the Saracen mercenaries, who were on the point of attacking the convent of San Damiano and pillaging the city of Assisi.

Such episodes, like other miracles whose memory lives on, prompted Pope Alexander IV to canonize her in 1255, only two years after her death, outlining her eulogy in the bull on the Canonization of St. Clare. In it we read: "How powerful was the illumination of this light and how strong the brightness of this source of light. Truly this light was kept hidden in the cloistered life; and outside them shone with gleaming rays; Clare, in fact, lay hidden, but her life was revealed to all. Clare was silent, but her fame was shouted out" (*FF*, 3284). And it is today as it was, dear friends: those who change the world for the better are holy; they transform it permanently, instilling in it the energies that only love inspired by the gospel can elicit. The saints are humanity's great benefactors!

Saint Clare's spirituality, the synthesis of the holiness she proposed, is summed up in the fourth letter she wrote to St. Agnes of Prague. Saint Clare used an image very widespread in the Middle Ages that dates back to Patristic times: the mirror. And she invited her friend in Prague to reflect herself in that mirror of the perfection of every virtue which is the Lord himself. She wrote:

> Happy, indeed, is the one permitted to share in this sacred banquet so as to be joined with all the feelings of her heart [to Christ] whose beauty all the blessed hosts of the heavens unceasingly admire, whose affection moves, whose contemplation invigorates, whose generosity fills, whose sweetness replenishes, whose remembrance pleasantly brings light, whose fragrance will revive the dead, and whose glorious vision will bless all the citizens of the heavenly Jerusalem, because the vision of him is the *splendor of everlasting glory, the radiance of everlasting*

light, and a mirror without tarnish. Look into this mirror every day,
O Queen, spouse of Jesus Christ, and continually examine your face
in it, so that in this way you may adorn yourself completely, inwardly
and outwardly. . . . In this mirror shine blessed poverty, holy humility,
and charity beyond words. (*Fourth Letter to Blessed Agnes of Prague*:
FF, 2901–03)

Grateful to God for giving us saints who speak to our hearts and
offer us an example of Christian life to imitate, I end with the same
words of blessing that St. Clare composed for her sisters and which the
Poor Clares, who play a precious role in the Church with their prayer and
with their work, still preserve today with great devotion. These are words
in which the full tenderness of her spiritual motherhood emerges: "I give
you my blessing now while living, and after my death, in as far as I may:
nay, even more than I may, I call down on you all the blessings that the
Father of mercies has bestowed and continues to bestow on his spiritual
sons and daughters both in heaven and on earth, and with which a spiritual father and mother have blessed and will bless their spiritual sons and
daughters. Amen" (*FF*, 2856).

—*15 September 2010*

St. Dominic de Guzmán

HAVING PRESENTED THE LUMINOUS FIGURE of Francis of Assisi and also Clare of Assisi, I talk now about another saint of the same period who made a fundamental contribution to the renewal of the Church of his time: St. Dominic, the Founder of the Order of Preachers, also known as Dominican Friars.

His successor at the head of the order, Blessed Jordan of Saxony, gives a complete picture of St. Dominic in the text of a famous prayer: "Your strong love burned with heavenly fire and God-like zeal. With all the fervor of an impetuous heart and with an avowal of perfect poverty, you spent your whole self in the cause of the apostolic life" and in preaching the gospel. It is precisely this fundamental trait of Dominic's witness that is emphasized: he always spoke *with* God and *of* God. Love for the Lord and for neighbor, the search for God's glory and the salvation of souls in the lives of saints, always go hand in hand.

Dominic was born at Caleruega, Spain, in about 1170. He belonged to a noble family of Old Castille and, supported by a priest uncle, was educated at a famous school in Palencia. He distinguished himself straightaway for his interest in the study of Sacred Scripture and for his love of the poor, to the point of selling books, which in his time were a very valuable asset, in order to support famine victims with the proceeds.

Ordained a priest, he was elected canon of the Cathedral Chapter in Osma, his native diocese. Although he may well have thought that this appointment might bring him a certain amount of prestige in the Church and in society, he did not view it as a personal privilege or as the beginning of a brilliant ecclesiastical career but, rather, as a service to carry out with dedication and humility. Are not a career and power temptations from which not even those who have a role of guidance and governance in the Church are exempt? I recalled this during the consecration of several bishops: "We do not seek power, prestige, or esteem for ourselves. . . . We know how in civil society and often also in the Church things suffer because many people on whom responsibility has been conferred work for themselves rather than for the community" (16 September 2009).

The bishop of Osma, a true and zealous pastor whose name was Didacus, soon spotted Dominic's spiritual qualities and wanted to avail himself of his collaboration. Together they went to northern Europe, on the diplomatic missions entrusted to them by the king of Castille. On his travels, Dominic became aware of two enormous challenges for the Church of his time: the existence of people who were not yet evangelized on the northern boundaries of the European continent, and the religious schism that undermined Christian life in the south of France, where the activity of certain heretical groups was creating a disturbance and distancing people from the truth of the faith. So it was that missionary action for those who did not know the light of the gospel and the work of the reevangelization of Christian communities became the apostolic goals that Dominic resolved to pursue.

It was the pope, to whom Bishop Didacus and Dominic went to seek advice, who asked Dominic to devote himself to preaching to the Albigensians, a heretical group that upheld a dualistic conception of reality, that is, with two equally powerful creator principles, good and evil. This group consequently despised matter as coming from the principle of evil. They even refused marriage, and went to the point of denying the Incarnation of Christ and the sacraments in which the Lord "touches" us through matter, and the resurrection of bodies. The Albigensians esteemed the poor and austere life—in this regard they were even exemplary—and criticized the riches of the clergy of that time. Dominic enthusiastically accepted this mission and carried it out with the example of his own poor and austere existence, gospel preaching, and public discussions. He devoted the rest of his life to this mission of preaching the good news. His sons were also to make St. Dominic's other dreams come true: the mission *ad gentes,* that is, to those who do not yet know Jesus and the mission to those who lived in the cities, especially the university cities, where the new intellectual trends were a challenge to the faith of the cultured.

This great saint reminds us that in the heart of the Church a missionary fire must always burn. It must be a constant incentive to make the first proclamation of the gospel and, wherever necessary, a new evangelization. Christ, in fact, is the most precious good that the men and women of every time and every place have the right to know and love! And it is comforting to see that in the Church today too there are many pastors and lay faithful alike, members of ancient religious orders and new ecclesial movements, who spend their lives joyfully for this supreme ideal, proclaiming and witnessing to the gospel!

Many other men then joined Dominic de Guzmán, attracted by the same aspiration. In this manner, after the first foundation in Toulouse, the Order of Preachers gradually came into being. Dominic, in fact, in perfect obedience to the directives of the popes of his time, Innocent III and Honorius III, used the ancient Rule of St. Augustine, adapting it to the needs of apostolic life that led him and his companions to preach as they traveled from one place to another but then returning to their own convents and places of study, to prayer, and community life. Dominic wanted to give special importance to two values he deemed indispensable for the success of the evangelizing mission: community life in poverty and study.

First, Dominic and his friar preachers presented themselves as mendicants, that is, without vast estates to be administered. This element made them more available for study and itinerant preaching and constituted a practical witness for the people. The internal government of the Dominican convents and provinces was structured on the system of chapters, which elected their own superiors, who were subsequently confirmed by the major superiors; thus, it was an organization that stimulated fraternal life and the responsibility of all the members of the community, demanding strong personal convictions. The choice of this system was born precisely from the fact that as preachers of the truth of God, the Dominicans had to be consistent with what they proclaimed. The truth studied and shared in charity with the brethren is the deepest foundation of joy. Blessed Jordan of Saxony said of St. Dominic: "All men were swept into the embrace of his charity, and, in loving all, he was beloved by all. . . . He claimed it his right to rejoice with the joyful and to weep with the sorrowful" (*Libellus de principiis Ordinis Praedicatorum autore Iordano de Saxonia*, ed. H. C. Scheeben [*Monumenta Historica Sancti Patris Nostri Dominici*, Romae, 1935]).

Second, with a courageous gesture, Dominic wanted his followers to acquire sound theological training, and he did not hesitate to send them to the universities of the time, even though a fair number of clerics viewed these cultural institutions with diffidence. The Constitutions of the Order of Preachers give great importance to study as a preparation for the apostolate. Dominic wanted his friars to devote themselves to it without reserve, with diligence and with piety—a study based on the soul of all theological knowledge, that is, on Sacred Scripture, and respectful of the questions asked by reason. The development of culture requires those who carry out the ministry of the Word at various levels to be well trained. I therefore urge all those, pastors and laypeople alike, to cultivate this "cultural dimension" of faith, so that the beauty of the Christian truth may be better understood and faith may be truly nourished, reinforced, and also defended. I ask seminarians and priests to esteem the spiritual value of study. The quality of the priestly ministry also depends on the generosity with which one applies oneself to the study of the revealed truths.

Dominic, who wished to found a religious order of theologian-preachers, reminds us that theology has a spiritual and pastoral dimension that enriches the soul and life. Priests, the consecrated religious, and also all the faithful may find profound "inner joy" in contemplating the beauty of the truth that comes from God, a truth that is ever timely and ever alive. Moreover, the motto of the Friar Preachers, *contemplata aliis trader*, helps us to discover a pastoral yearning in the contemplative study of this truth because of the need to communicate to others the fruit of one's own contemplation.

When Dominic died, in 1221 in Bologna, the city that declared him its patron, his work had already had widespread success. The Order of Preachers, with the Holy See's support, had spread to many countries in Europe for the benefit of the whole Church. Dominic was canonized in 1234, and it is he himself who, with his holiness, points out to us two indispensable means for making apostolic action effective. In the very first place is Marian devotion, which he fostered tenderly and left as a precious legacy to his spiritual sons who, in the history of the Church, have had the great merit of disseminating the prayer of the Holy Rosary, so dear to the Christian people and so rich in gospel values: a true school of faith and piety. In the second place, Dominic, who cared for several women's monasteries in France and in Rome, believed unquestioningly in the value of prayers of intercession for the success of the apostolic work. Only in heaven will we understand how much the prayer of cloistered religious effectively accompanies apostolic action! To each and every one of them I address my grateful and affectionate thoughts.

May the life of Dominic de Guzmán spur us all to be fervent in prayer, courageous in living out our faith, and deeply in love with Jesus Christ. Through his intercession, let us ask God always to enrich the Church with authentic preachers of the gospel.

—*3 February 2010*

St. Anthony of Padua

WE DISCUSSED ST. FRANCIS OF ASSISI; here I present another saint who belonged to the first generation of the Friars Minor: Anthony of Padua, or of Lisbon, as he is also called with reference to his native town. He is one of the most popular saints in the whole Catholic Church, venerated not only in Padua, where a splendid basilica has been built that contains his mortal remains, but also throughout the world. Dear to the faithful are the images and statues that portray him with the lily—a symbol of his purity—or with the Child Jesus in his arms, in memory of a miraculous apparition mentioned in several literary sources.

With his outstanding gifts of intelligence, balance, apostolic zeal, and, primarily, mystic fervor, Anthony contributed significantly to the development of Franciscan spirituality.

He was born into a noble family in Lisbon in about 1195 and was baptized with the name of Fernando. He entered the Canons, who followed the monastic Rule of St. Augustine, first at St. Vincent's monastery in Lisbon and later at that of the Holy Cross in Coimbra, a renowned cultural center in Portugal. He dedicated himself with interest and solicitude to the study of the Bible and of the Church Fathers, acquiring the theological knowledge that was to bear fruit in his teaching and preaching activities.

The event that represented a decisive turning point on his life happened in Coimbra. It was there, in 1220, that the relics were exposed of the first five Franciscan missionaries who had gone to Morocco, where they had met with martyrdom. Their story inspired in young Fernando the desire to imitate them and to advance on the path of Christian perfection. Thus, he asked to leave the Augustinian Canons to become a Friar Minor. His request was granted and, having taken the name of Anthony, he too set out for Morocco. But divine providence disposed otherwise. After an illness, he was obliged to return to Italy and, in 1221, participated in the famous "Chapter of the Mats" in Assisi, where he also met St. Francis. He then lived for a period in complete concealment in a convent at Forlì in northern Italy, where the Lord called him to another mission.

Invited, in somewhat casual circumstances, to preach on the occasion of a priestly ordination, he showed himself to be endowed with such knowledge and eloquence that his superiors assigned him to preaching. Thus, he embarked on apostolic work in Italy and France that was so intense and effective that it induced many people who had left the Church to retrace their footsteps. Anthony was also one of the first, if not the first, theology teachers of the Friars Minor. He began his teaching in Bologna with the blessing of St. Francis who, recognizing Anthony's virtues, sent him a short letter that began with these words: "I would like you to teach the brethren theology." Anthony laid the foundations of Franciscan theology which, cultivated by other outstanding thinkers, was to reach its apex with St. Bonaventure of Bagnoregio and Blessed Duns Scotus.

Having become provincial superior of the Friars Minor in northern Italy, Anthony continued his ministry of preaching, alternating it with his office of governance. When his term as provincial came to an end, he withdrew to a place near Padua where he had stayed on various other occasions. Barely a year later, he died at the city gates on 13 June 1231. Padua, which had welcomed him with affection and veneration in his lifetime, has always accorded him honor and devotion. Pope Gregory IX himself, having heard him preach, described him as the "Ark of the Testament" and, subsequent to miracles brought about through his intercession, canonized him in 1232, only a year after his death.

In the last period of his life, Anthony put in writing two cycles of sermons, titled respectively *Sunday Sermons* and *Sermons on the Saints,* destined for the Franciscan order's preachers and teachers of theological studies. In these sermons, he commented on the texts of Scripture presented by the liturgy, using the Patristic and medieval interpretation of the four senses: the literal or historical, the allegorical or christological, the tropological or moral, and the anagogical, which orients a person to eternal life. Today, it has been rediscovered that these senses are dimensions of the one meaning of Sacred Scripture and that it is right to interpret Sacred Scripture by seeking the four dimensions of its words. Saint Anthony's sermons are theological and homiletical texts that echo the live preaching in which Anthony proposes a true and proper itinerary of Christian life. The richness of spiritual teaching contained in the sermons was so great that in 1946 Venerable Pope Pius XII proclaimed Anthony a Doctor of the Church, attributing to him the title "Doctor Evangelicus," since the freshness and beauty of the gospel emerge from these writings. We can still read them today with great spiritual profit.

In these sermons, St. Anthony speaks of prayer as a loving relationship that impels one to speak gently with the Lord, creating an ineffable joy that sweetly enfolds the soul in prayer. Anthony reminds us that prayer requires an atmosphere of silence, which does not mean distance from external noise but rather is an interior experience that aims to remove the distractions caused by a soul's anxieties, thereby creating silence in the soul itself. According to this prominent Franciscan Doctor's teaching, prayer is structured in four indispensable attitudes, which in Anthony's Latin are defined as *obsecratio, oratio, postulatio, gratiarum actio.* We might translate them in the following manner. The first step in prayer is confidently opening one's heart to God; this is not merely accepting a word but opening one's heart to God's presence. Next is speaking with God affectionately, seeing him present with oneself; then comes a very natural thing presenting our needs to him; and last, praising and thanking him.

In St. Anthony's teaching on prayer, we perceive one of the specific traits of the Franciscan theology that he founded: namely, the role assigned to divine love, which enters into the sphere of the affections, of the will, and of the heart, and which is also the source from which flows a spiritual knowledge that surpasses all other knowledge. In fact, it is in loving that we come to know.

Anthony writes further: "Charity is the soul of faith, it gives it life; without love, faith dies" (*Sermones Dominicales et Festivi* 2 [Messagero, Padua 1979], 37).

It is only the prayerful soul that can progress in spiritual life: this is the privileged object of St. Anthony's preaching. He is thoroughly familiar with the shortcomings of human nature, with our tendency to lapse into sin, which is why he continuously urges us to fight the inclination to avidity, pride, and impurity instead practicing the virtues of poverty and generosity, of humility and obedience, of chastity and of purity. At the beginning of the thirteenth century, in the context of the rebirth of the city and the flourishing of trade, the number of people who were insensitive to the needs of the poor increased. This is why on various occasions Anthony invites the faithful to think of the true riches, those of the heart, which make people good and merciful and permit them to lay up treasure in heaven. "O rich people," he urged them, "befriend . . . the poor; welcome them into your homes: it will subsequently be they who receive you in the eternal tabernacles in which is the beauty of peace, the confidence of security, and the opulent tranquility of eternal satiety" (ibid., 29).

Is not this perhaps a very important teaching today too, when the financial crisis and serious economic inequalities impoverish many people and create conditions of poverty? In my encyclical *Caritas in Veritate,* I recall: "The economy needs ethics in order to function correctly—not any ethics whatsoever, but an ethics that is people-centered" (n. 45).

Anthony, in the school of Francis, always put Christ at the center of his life and thinking, of his action and of his preaching. This is another characteristic feature of Franciscan theology: Christocentrism. Franciscan theology willingly contemplates and invites others to contemplate the mysteries of the Lord's humanity, the man Jesus, and in a special way the mystery of the nativity: God who made himself a child and gave himself into our hands, a mystery that gives rise to sentiments of love and gratitude for divine goodness.

Not only the nativity, a central point of Christ's love for humanity, but also the vision of the Crucified One inspired in Anthony thoughts of gratitude to God and esteem for the dignity of the human person, so that all believers and nonbelievers might find in the Crucified One and in his image a life-enriching meaning. Saint Anthony writes: "Christ who is your life is hanging before you, so that you may look at the Cross as in a mirror. There you will be able to know how mortal were your wounds that no medicine other than the blood of the Son of God could heal. If you look closely, you will be able to realize how great your human dignity and your value are. . . . Nowhere other than looking at himself in the mirror of the Cross can man better understand how much he is worth" (*Sermones Dominicales et Festivi* 3, 213–14).

In meditating on these words, we are better able to understand the importance of the image of the Crucified One for our culture, for our humanity that is born from the Christian faith. Precisely by looking at the Crucified One, we see, as St. Anthony says, how great are the dignity and worth of the human being. At no other point can we understand how much the human person is worth, precisely because God makes us so important, considers us so important that, in his opinion, we are worthy of his suffering; thus, all human dignity appears in the mirror of the Crucified One, and our gazing upon him is ever a source of acknowledgment of human dignity.

May Anthony of Padua, so widely venerated by the faithful, intercede for the whole Church and especially for those who are dedicated to preaching; let us pray the Lord that he will help us learn a little of this art from St. Anthony. May preachers, drawing inspiration from his example, be effective in their communication by taking pains to combine solid and sound doctrine with sincere and fervent devotion. Let us pray that priests and deacons will carry out with concern this ministry of the proclamation of the Word of God, making it timely for the faithful, especially through liturgical homilies. May they effectively present the eternal beauty of Christ, just as Anthony recommended: "If you preach Jesus, he will melt hardened hearts; if you invoke him, he will soften harsh temptations; if you think of him, he will enlighten your mind; if you read of him, he will satisfy your intellect" (*Sermones Dominicales et Festivi* 3, 59).

—*10 February 2010*

St. Bonaventure

Interpreter of Francis

I talk now about St. Bonaventure of Bagnoregio. I confide to you that in broaching this subject I feel a certain nostalgia, for I am thinking back to my research as a young scholar on this author, who was particularly dear to me. My knowledge of him had quite an impact on my formation. A few months ago, with great joy, I made a pilgrimage to the place of his birth, Bagnoregio, an Italian town in Lazio that venerates his memory.

Saint Bonaventure, in all likelihood born in 1217, died in 1274. Thus, he lived in the thirteenth century, an epoch in which the Christian faith which had deeply penetrated the culture and society of Europe inspired imperishable works in the fields of literature, the visual arts, philosophy, and theology. Among the great Christian figures who contributed to the composition of this harmony between faith and culture, Bonaventure stands out, a man of action and contemplation, of profound piety and prudent government.

He was called Giovanni di Fidanza. An episode that occurred when he was still a boy deeply marked his life, as he himself recounts. He fell seriously ill, and even his father, who was a doctor, gave up all hope of saving him from death. So his mother had recourse to the intercession of St. Francis of Assisi, who had recently been canonized. And Giovanni recovered.

The figure of the *Poverello* of Assisi became even more familiar to him several years later when he was in Paris, where he had gone to pursue his studies. He had obtained a master of arts diploma, which we could compare with that of a prestigious secondary school in our time. At that point, like so many young men in the past and also today, Giovanni asked himself a crucial question: "What should I do with my life?" Fascinated by the witness of fervor and evangelical radicalism of the Friars Minor, who had arrived in Paris in 1219, Giovanni knocked at the door of the Franciscan convent in that city and asked to be admitted to the great family of St. Francis's disciples. Many years later, he explained the reasons for his decision: he recognized Christ's action in St. Francis and in the movement he had founded. Thus, he wrote in a letter addressed to another friar: "I confess before God that the reason which made me love the life of blessed Francis most is that it resembled the birth and early development of the Church. The Church began with simple fishermen and was subsequently enriched by very distinguished and wise teachers;

the religion of Blessed Francis was not established by the prudence of men but by Christ" (*Epistula de tribus quaestionibus ad magistrum innominatum*, in *Opere di San Bonaventura. Introduzione generale* [Rome 1990], 29).

So it was that in about the year 1243 Giovanni was clothed in the Franciscan habit and took the name Bonaventure. He was immediately sent to study and attended the Faculty of Theology of the University of Paris, where he took a series of very demanding courses. He obtained the various qualifications required for an academic career earning a bachelor's degree in Scripture and in the *Sentences*. Thus, Bonaventure studied profoundly Sacred Scripture, the *Sentences* of Peter Lombard—the theology manual in that time—and the most important theological authors. He was in contact with the teachers and students from across Europe who converged in Paris; and he developed his own personal thinking and a spiritual sensitivity of great value with which, in the following years, he was able to infuse his works and his sermons, thus becoming one of the most important theologians in the history of the Church. It is important to remember the title of the thesis he defended in order to qualify to teach theology, the *licentia ubique docendi,* as it was then called. His dissertation was titled *Questions on the Knowledge of Christ.* This subject reveals the central role that Christ always played in Bonaventure's life and teaching. We may certainly say that the whole of his thinking was profoundly Christocentric.

In those years in Paris, Bonaventure's adopted city, a violent dispute was raging against the Friars Minor of St. Francis Assisi and the Friars Preachers of St. Dominic de Guzmán. Their right to teach at the university was contested, and doubt was even being cast upon the authenticity of their consecrated life. Of course, the changes introduced by the mendicant orders in the way of understanding religious life, of which I have spoken in previous chapters, were so entirely new that not everyone managed to understand them. Then it should be added that, just as sometimes happens even among sincerely religious people, human weakness, such as envy and jealousy, came into play. Although Bonaventure was confronted by the opposition of the other university masters, he had already begun to teach at the Franciscans' chair of theology, and, to respond to those who were challenging the mendicant orders, he composed a text titled *Evangelical Perfection.* In this work, he shows how the Mendicant orders, especially the Friars Minor, in practicing the vows of poverty, chastity, and obedience, were following the recommendations of the gospel itself. Over and above these historical circumstances, the teaching that Bonaventure provides in this work of his and in his life remains very timely: the Church is made more luminous and beautiful by the fidelity to their vocation of those sons and daughters of hers who not only put the evangelical precepts into practice but, by the grace of God, are called to observe their counsels and thereby, with their poor, chaste, and obedient way of life, to witness to the gospel as a source of joy and perfection.

The storm blew over, at least for a while, and through the personal intervention of Pope Alexander VI in 1257, Bonaventure was officially recognized as a doctor and master of the University of Paris. However, he was obliged to relinquish this prestigious office because in that same year the general chapter of the order elected him minister general.

Bonaventure fulfilled this office for seventeen years with wisdom and dedication, visiting the provinces, writing to his brethren, and at times intervening with some severity to eliminate abuses. When Bonaventure began this service, the order of Friars Minor had experienced an extraordinary expansion: there were more than thirty thousand friars scattered throughout the West, with missionaries in North Africa, the Middle East, and even in Peking. It was necessary to consolidate this expansion and especially to give it unity of action and of spirit in full fidelity to Francis's charism. In fact, different ways of interpreting the message of the saint of Assisi arose among his followers, and they ran the real risk of an internal split. To avoid this danger, in 1260 the general chapter of the order in Narbonne accepted and ratified a text proposed by Bonaventure in which the norms regulating the daily life of the Friars Minor were collected and unified. Bonaventure, however, foresaw that, regardless of the wisdom and moderation which inspired the legislative measures, they would not suffice to guarantee communion of spirit and hearts. It was necessary to share the same ideals and the same motivations.

For this reason, Bonaventure wished to present the authentic charism of Francis, his life and his teaching. Thus, he zealously collected documents concerning the *Poverello* and listened attentively to the memories of those who had actually known Francis. This inspired a historically well-founded biography of the saint of Assisi, titled *Legenda Maior*. It was redrafted more concisely and hence titled *Legenda minor*. Unlike the Italian term, the Latin word does not mean a product of the imagination but, on the contrary, *Legenda* means an authoritative text, "to be read" officially. Indeed, the general chapter of the Friars Minor in 1263, meeting in Pisa, recognized St. Bonaventure's biography as the most faithful portrait of their founder, and so it became the saint's official biography.

What image of St. Francis emerged from the heart and pen of his follower and successor St. Bonaventure? The key point: Francis is an *alter Christus,* a man who sought Christ passionately. In the love that impelled Francis to imitate Christ, he was entirely conformed to Christ. Bonaventure pointed out this living ideal to all Francis's followers. This ideal, valid for every Christian yesterday, today, and forever, was also proposed as a program for the Church in the third millennium by my predecessor Venerable John Paul II. This program, he wrote in his letter *Nova Millennio Ineunte,* is centered "in Christ himself, who is to be known, loved, and imitated, so that in him we may live the life of the Trinity, and with him transform history until its fulfillment in the heavenly Jerusalem" (n. 29).

In 1273, St. Bonaventure experienced another great change in his life. Pope Gregory X wanted to consecrate him a bishop and to appoint him a cardinal. The pope also asked him to prepare the Second Ecumenical Council of Lyons, a most important ecclesial event, for the purpose of reestablishing communion between the Latin Church and the Greek Church. Bonaventure dedicated himself diligently to this task but was unable to see the conclusion of this ecumenical session because he died before it ended. An anonymous papal notary composed a eulogy to Bonaventure that gives us a conclusive portrait of this great saint and excellent theologian. "A good, affable, devout, and compassionate man, full of virtue, beloved of God and human beings alike. . . . God, in fact, had bestowed upon him such grace that all who saw him were pervaded by a love that their hearts could not conceal" (cf. J. G. Bougerol, *Bonaventura*, in A. Vauchez, ed. *Storia dei santi e della santità cristiana*, vol. 6, *L'epoca del rinnovamento evangelico* [Milan 1991], 91).

Let us gather the heritage of this holy Doctor of the Church, who reminds us of the meaning of our life with the following words: "On earth . . . we may contemplate the divine immensity through reasoning and admiration; in the heavenly homeland, on the other hand, through the vision, when we are likened to God and through ecstasy . . . we shall enter into the joy of God" (*La conoscenza di Cristo, q. 6, conclusione*, in *Opere di San Bonaventura. Opuscoli Teologici / 1* [Rome 1993], 187).

Guiding the Franciscan Legacy

Having presented the life and personality of St. Bonaventure of Bagnoregio, I continue by reflecting on part of his literary opus and on his doctrine.

As I have already said, among St. Bonaventure's various merits was the ability to interpret authentically and faithfully St. Francis of Assisi, whom he venerated and studied with deep love. In a special way, in St. Bonaventure's day, a trend among the Friars Minor known as the "Spirituals" held that St. Francis had ushered in a totally new phase in history and that the "eternal Gospel," of which Revelation speaks, had come to replace the New Testament. This group declared that the Church had now fulfilled her role in history. They said that she had been replaced by a charismatic community of free people guided from within by the Spirit, namely the "Spiritual Franciscans."

This group's ideas were based on the writings of a Cistercian abbot, Joachim of Fiore, who died in 1202. In his works, he affirmed a Trinitarian rhythm in history. He considered the Old Testament as the age of the Father, followed by the time of the Son, the time of the Church. The third age was to be awaited, that of the Holy Spirit. The whole of history was thus interpreted as a history of progress: from the severity of the Old Testament to the relative freedom of the time of the Son, in the Church, to the full freedom of the Sons of God in the period of the Holy Spirit. This, finally, was also to be the period of peace among humankind, of the reconciliation of peoples and of religions.

Joachim of Fiore had awakened the hope that the new age would stem from a new form of monasticism. Thus, it is understandable that a group of Franciscans might have thought it recognized St. Francis of Assisi as the initiator of the new epoch and his order as the community of the new period—the community of the age of the Holy Spirit—that left behind the hierarchical Church in order to begin the new Church of the Spirit, no longer linked to the old structures. Hence, they ran the risk of very seriously misunderstanding St. Francis's message, of his humble fidelity to the gospel and to the Church. This error entailed an erroneous vision of Christianity as a whole.

Saint Bonaventure, who became minister general of the Franciscan order in 1257, had to confront grave tension in his order precisely because of those who supported the above-mentioned trend of the Franciscan Spirituals and who followed Joachim of Fiore. To respond to this group and to restore unity to the order, Saint Bonaventure painstakingly studied the authentic writings of Joachim of Fiore, as well as those attributed to him, and, bearing in mind the need to present the figure and message of his beloved St. Francis correctly, he wanted to set down a correct view of the theology of history. St. Bonaventure actually tackled the problem in his last work, a collection of conferences for the monks of the studium in Paris. He did not complete it, and it has come down to us through the transcriptions of those who heard him. It is titled *Hexaëmeron,* in other words, an allegorical explanation of the six days of the creation. The Fathers of the Church considered the six or seven days of the creation narrative as a prophecy of the history of the world, of humanity. For them, the seven days represented seven periods of history, later also interpreted as seven millennia. With Christ, we should have entered the last, that is, the sixth period of history, which was to be followed by the great sabbath of God. Saint Bonaventure hypothesizes this historical interpretation of the account of the days of the creation, but in a very free and innovative way. To his mind, two phenomena of his time required a new interpretation of the course of history.

The first: the figure of St. Francis, the man totally united with Christ even to communion with the stigmata, almost an *alter Christus,* and, with St. Francis, the new community he created, different from the monasticism known until then. This phenomenon called for a new interpretation, as an innovation of God which appeared at that moment. *The second:* the position of Joachim of Fiore, who announced a new monasticism and a totally new period of history, going beyond the revelation of the New Testament, demanded a response. As minister general of the Franciscan order, St. Bonaventure had immediately realized that with the spiritualistic conception inspired by Joachim of Fiore, the order would become ungovernable and logically move toward anarchy. In his opinion, this had two consequences: The first, the practical need for structures and for insertion into the reality of the hierarchical Church, of the real Church, required a theological foundation. This was partly because the others, those who followed the spiritualist concept, upheld what seemed to have a theological foundation. The second, while taking into account the necessary realism made it essential not to lose the newness of the figure of St. Francis.

How did St. Bonaventure respond to the practical and theoretical needs? Here I can only provide a very basic summary of his answer, and it is in certain aspects incomplete:

1. Saint Bonaventure rejected the idea of the Trinitarian rhythm of history. God is one for all history and is not tritheistic. Hence, history is one, even if it is a journey and, according to St. Bonaventure, a journey of progress.

2. Jesus Christ is God's last word—in him, God said all, giving and expressing himself. More than himself God cannot express or give. The Holy Spirit is the Spirit of the Father and of the Son. Christ himself says of the Holy Spirit: "He will bring to your remembrance all that I have said to you" (Jn 14:26), and, "He will take what is mine and declare it to you" (Jn 16:15). Thus, there is no loftier gospel; there is no other Church to await. Therefore, the Order of St. Francis too must fit into this Church, into her faith and into her hierarchical order.

3. This does not mean that the Church is stationary, fixed in the past, or that there can be no newness within her. *Opera Christi non deficiunt, sed proficiunt:* Christ's works do not go backward, they do not fail but progress, the saint said in his letter *De Tribus Quaestionibus.* Thus, St. Bonaventure explicitly formulates the idea of progress, and this is an innovation in comparison with the Fathers of the Church and the majority of his contemporaries. For Bonaventure, Christ was no longer the end of history, as he was for the Fathers of the Church, but rather its center. History does not end with Christ but begins a new period. The following is another consequence: until that moment, the idea that the Fathers of the Church were the absolute summit of theology predominated; all successive generations could only be their disciples. Saint Bonaventure also recognized the Fathers as teachers forever, but the phenomenon of

St. Francis assured him that the riches of Christ's word are inexhaustible and that new light could also appear to the new generations. The oneness of Christ also guarantees newness and renewal in all the periods of history. The Franciscan order, of course, as he emphasized, belongs to the Church of Jesus Christ, to the apostolic Church, and cannot be built on utopian spiritualism. Yet, at the same time, the newness of this order in comparison with classical monasticism was valid, and St. Bonaventure—as I said in my previous chapter—defended this newness against the attacks of the secular clergy of Paris: the Franciscans have no fixed monastery; they may go everywhere to proclaim the gospel. It was precisely the break with stability, the characteristic of monasticism, for the sake of a new flexibility that restored to the Church her missionary dynamism.

At this point, it might be useful to say that today too there are views that see the entire history of the Church in the second millennium as a gradual decline. Some see this decline as having already begun immediately after the New Testament. In fact, *Opera Christi non deficiunt, sed proficiunt*: Christ's works do not go backward but forward. What would the Church be without the new spirituality of the Cistercians, the Franciscans, and the Dominicans, the spirituality of St. Teresa of Avila and St. John of the Cross, and so forth? This affirmation applies today too: *Opera Christi non deficiunt, sed proficiunt*, they move forward. Saint Bonaventure teaches us the need for overall, even strict discernment, sober realism, and openness to the newness that Christ gives his Church through the Holy Spirit. And while this idea of decline is repeated, another idea, this "spiritualistic utopianism," is also reiterated. Indeed, we know that after the Second Vatican Council, some were convinced that everything was new, that there was a different Church, that the preconciliar Church was finished, and that we had another, totally "other" Church—an anarchic utopianism! And thanks be to God, the wise helmsmen of the barque of St. Peter, Pope Paul VI, and Pope John Paul II, on the one hand, defended the newness of the council and, on the other, defended the oneness and continuity of the Church, which is always a Church of sinners and always a place of grace.

4. In this regard, St. Bonaventure, as minister general of the Franciscans, took a line of government which showed clearly that the new order could not, as a community, live at the same "eschatological height" as St. Francis, in whom Bonaventure saw the future world anticipated, but guided at the same time by healthy realism and by spiritual courage. Francis had to come as close as possible to the maximum realization of the Sermon on the Mount, which for St. Francis was *the* rule, but nevertheless bore in mind the limitations of the human being, who is marked by original sin.

Thus, we see that for St. Bonaventure, governing was not merely action but above all was thinking and praying. At the root of his government, we always find prayer and thought; all his decisions are the result of reflection, of thought illumined by prayer. His intimate contact with Christ always accompanied his work as minister general, and therefore he composed a series of theological and mystical writings that express the soul of his government. They also manifest his intention of guiding the order inwardly, that is, of governing not only by means of commands and structures but also by guiding and illuminating souls, orienting them to Christ.

I mention only one of these writings, which are the soul of his government and point out the way to follow, both for the individual and for the community: the *Itinerarium mentis in Deum* (*The Mind's Road to God*), which is a "manual" for mystical contemplation. This book was conceived in a deeply spiritual place: Mount La Verna, where St. Francis had received the stigmata. In the introduction, the author describes the circumstances that gave rise to this writing: "While I meditated on the possible ascent of the mind to God, among other things there occurred that miracle which happened in the same place to the blessed Francis himself, namely the vision of the winged seraph in the form of a crucifix. While meditating upon this vision, I immediately saw that it offered me the ecstatic contemplation of Fr. Francis himself as well as the way that leads to it" (cf. *The Mind's Road to God,* Prologue, 2: *Opere di San Bonaventura. Opuscoli Teologici* / 1 [Rome 1993], 499).

The six wings of the seraph thus became the symbol of the six stages that lead humans progressively from the knowledge of God, through the observation of the world and creatures, and through the exploration of the soul itself with its faculties, to the satisfying union with the Trinity through Christ, in imitation of St. Francis of Assisi. The last words of St. Bonaventure's *Itinerarium,* which respond to the question of how it is possible to reach this mystical communion with God, should be made to sink to the depths of the heart:

> If you should wish to know how these things come about [the mystical communion with God], interrogate grace, not doctrine; desire, not intellect; the cry of prayer, not the pursuit of study; the spouse, not the teacher; God, not man; darkness, not clarity; not light, but the fire that inflames all and transports one to God with fullest unction and burning affection. . . . Let us then . . . pass over into darkness; let us impose silence on cares, concupiscence, and phantasms; let us pass over *with the Crucified Christ from this world to the Father,* so that when the Father is shown to us we may say with Philip, "*It is enough for me.*" (cf. ibid., 7, 6)

Let us accept the invitation addressed to us by St. Bonaventure, the Seraphic Doctor, and learn at the school of the divine Teacher: let us listen to his word of life and truth that resonates in the depths of our soul. Let us purify our thoughts and actions so that he may dwell within us and that we may understand his divine voice, which draws us toward true happiness.

Theologian of Love

Saint Bonaventure of Bagnoregio is an eminent theologian, who deserves to be set beside another great thinker, a contemporary of his, St. Thomas Aquinas. Both scrutinized the mysteries of revelation, making the most of the resources of human reason in the fruitful dialogue between faith and reason that characterized the Christian Middle Ages. This interchange made it a time of great intellectual vigor, as well as of faith and ecclesial renewal, which is often not sufficiently emphasized.

Other similarities link the two: Both Bonaventure, a Franciscan, and Thomas, a Dominican, belonged to the mendicant orders, which, with their spiritual freshness, as I mentioned previously, renewed the whole Church in the thirteenth century and attracted many followers. They both served the Church with diligence, passion, and love, to the point that they were invited to take part in the Ecumenical Council of Lyons in 1274, the very same year in which they died. Thomas while he was on his way to Lyons, Bonaventure while the council was taking place. Even the statues of the two saints in St. Peter's Square are parallel. They stand right at the beginning of the colonnade, starting from the façade of the Vatican Basilica; one is on the left wing and the other on the right. Despite all these aspects, in these two great saints we can discern two different approaches to philosophical and theological research which show the originality and depth of the thinking of each.

A first difference concerns the concept of theology. Both doctors wondered whether theology was a practical or a theoretical and speculative science. Saint Thomas reflects on two possible contrasting answers. The first says: theology is a reflection on faith, and the purpose of faith is that the human being become good and live in accordance with God's will. Hence, the aim of theology would be to guide people on the right, good road; thus, it is basically a practical science. The other position says: theology seeks to know God. We are the work of God; God is above our action. God works right action in us; so theology essentially concerns not our own doing but knowing God, not our own actions. Saint Thomas's conclusion is: theology entails both aspects: it is theoretical, and it seeks to know God ever better; and it is practical: it seeks to orient our life to the good. But there is a primacy of knowledge: above all, we must know God and then continue to act in accordance with God (*Summa Theologiae* 1a, q. 1, art.

4). This primacy of knowledge in comparison with practice is significant to St. Thomas's fundamental orientation.

Saint Bonaventure's answer is very similar, but the stress he gives is different. Saint Bonaventure knows the same arguments for both directions, as does St. Thomas. But in answer to the question as to whether theology was a practical or a theoretical science, St. Bonaventure makes a triple distinction. He extends the alternative between the theoretical (the primacy of knowledge) and the practical (the primacy of practice), adding a third attitude, which he calls "sapiential," and affirming that wisdom embraces both aspects. And he continues: wisdom seeks contemplation (as the highest form of knowledge), and has as its intention especially *ut boni fiamus*, that we become good (cf. *Breviloquium,* Prologue, 5). He then adds: "Faith is in the intellect in such a way that it provokes affection. For example: the knowledge that Christ died 'for us' does not remain knowledge but necessarily becomes affection, love (*Proemium in I Sent.* q. 3).

Bonaventure's defense of theology is along the same lines, namely, of the rational and methodical reflection on faith. He lists several arguments against engaging in theology—perhaps also widespread among a section of the Franciscan friars and also present in our time: that reason would empty faith, that it would be an aggressive attitude to the Word of God, that we should listen to and not analyze the Word of God (cf. *Letter of Saint Francis of Assisi to Saint Anthony of Padua*). The saint responds to these arguments against theology, which demonstrate the perils that exist in theology itself saying: it is true that there is an arrogant manner of engaging in theology, a pride of reason that sets itself above the Word of God. Yet real theology, the rational work of the true and good theology, has another origin, not the pride of reason. One who loves wants to know his beloved better and better; true theology does not involve reason and its research prompted by pride, *sed propter amorem eius cui assentit*—"[but is] motivated by love of the One who gave his consent" (*Proemium in I Sent.* q. 2) and wants to be better acquainted with the beloved: this is the fundamental intention of theology. Thus, in the end, for St. Bonaventure, the primacy of love is crucial.

Consequently, St. Thomas and St. Bonaventure define the human being's final goal, one's complete happiness, in different ways. For St. Thomas, the supreme end, to which our desire is directed, is to see God. In this simple act of seeing God, all problems are solved: we are happy; nothing else is necessary. Instead, for St. Bonaventure, the ultimate destiny of the human being is to love God, to encounter him, and to be united in his and our love. For him, this is the most satisfactory definition of our happiness.

Along these lines, we could also say that the loftiest category for St. Thomas is the true, whereas for St. Bonaventure it is the good. It would be mistaken to see a contradiction in these two answers. For both of them, the true is also the good, and the good is also the true; to see God is to love, and to love is to see. Hence, it was a question of their different interpretation of a fundamentally shared vision. Both emphases have given shape to different traditions and different spiritualities and have thus shown the fruitfulness of the faith: one in the diversity of its expressions.

Let us return to St. Bonaventure. It is obvious that the specific emphasis he gave to his theology, of which I have given only one example, is explained on the basis of the Franciscan charism. The *Poverello* of Assisi, notwithstanding the intellectual debates of his time, had shown with his whole life the primacy of love. He was a living icon of Christ in love with Christ, and thus he made the figure of the Lord present in his time. He did not convince his contemporaries with his words but rather with his life. In all St. Bonaventure's works, precisely also his scientific works, his scholarly works, one sees and finds this Franciscan inspiration; in other words one notices that his thought starts with his encounter with the *Poverello* of Assisi. However, in order to understand the practical elaboration of the topic "primacy of love," we must bear in mind yet another source: the writings of the so-called Pseudo-Dionysius, a Syrian theologian of the sixth century who concealed himself behind the pseudonym of Dionysius the Areopagite. In the choice of this name, he was referring to a figure in the Acts of the Apostles (cf. 17:34). As we have seen, this theologian had created a liturgical theology and a mystical theology and had spoken extensively of the different orders of angels. His writings were translated into Latin in the ninth century. At the time of St. Bonaventure—we are in the thirteenth century—a new tradition appeared that aroused the interest of the saint and of other theologians of his century. Two things in particular attracted St. Bonaventure's attention.

1. Pseudo-Dionysius speaks of nine orders of angels, whose names he had found in Scripture and then organized in his own way, from the simple angels to the seraphim. Saint Bonaventure interprets these orders of angels as steps on the human creature's way to God. Thus, they can represent the human journey, the ascent toward communion with God. For St. Bonaventure, there is no doubt: St. Francis of Assisi belonged to the Seraphic order, to the supreme order, to the choir of seraphim; that is, he was a pure flame of love. And this is what Franciscans should have been. But St. Bonaventure knew well that this final step in the approach to God could not be inserted into a juridical order but is always a special gift of God. For this reason, the structure of the Franciscan order is more modest, more realistic, but nevertheless must help its members to come ever closer to a seraphic existence of pure love. We noted in the prior chapter this synthesis between sober realism and evangelical radicalism in the thought and action of St. Bonaventure.

2. St. Bonaventure, however, found in the writings of Peusdo-Dionysius another element, an even more important one. Whereas for St. Augustine the *intellectus*, the seeing with reason and the heart, is the ultimate category of knowledge, Pseudo-Dionysius takes a further step: in the ascent toward God, one can reach a point in which reason no longer sees. But in the night of the intellect, love still sees. It sees what is inaccessible to reason. Love goes beyond reason; it sees further; it enters more profoundly into God's mystery. Saint Bonaventure was fascinated by this vision, which converged with his own Franciscan spirituality. It is precisely in the dark night of the Cross that divine love appears in its full grandeur; where reason no longer sees, love sees. The final words of his *The Journey of the Mind into God* can seem to be a superficial interpretation, an exaggerated expression of devotion devoid of content. Instead, when read in the light of St. Bonaventure's theology of the Cross, they are a clear and realistic expression of Franciscan spirituality: "If you seek in what manner these things occur [that is, the ascent toward God] interrogate grace, not doctrine; desire, not intellect; the cry of prayer, not the pursuit of study . . . not light, but the fire that inflames all and transports one to God" (7, 6). All this is neither anti-intellectual nor antirational: it implies the process of reason but transcends it in the love of the Crucified Christ. With this transformation of the mysticism of Pseudo-Dionysius, St. Bonaventure is placed at the source of a great mystical current that has greatly raised and purified the human mind: it is a lofty peak in the history of the human spirit.

This theology of the Cross, born of the encounter of Pseudo-Dionysius's theology and Franciscan spirituality, must not make us forget that St. Bonaventure also shares with St. Francis of Assisi his love for creation, his joy at the beauty of God's creation. On this point I cite a sentence from the first chapter of the *Journey*: "He who is not brightened by such splendors of created things is blind; he who does not awake at such clamors is deaf; he who does not praise God on account of all these effects is mute; he who does not turn toward the First Principle on account of such indications is stupid" (1, 15).

The whole creation speaks loudly of God, of the good and beautiful God; of God's love. Hence, for St. Bonaventure, the whole of our life is a "journey," a pilgrimage, an ascent to God. But with our own strength alone, we are incapable of climbing to the loftiness of God. God himself must help us, must "pull" us up. Thus, prayer is necessary. Prayer, says the saint, is the mother and the origin of the upward movement—*sursum actio*, an action that lifts us up, Bonaventure says. Accordingly, I conclude with the prayer with which he begins his *Journey*: "Let us therefore say to the Lord Our God: "Lead me forth, Lord, in thy way, and let me step in thy truth; let my heart be glad, that it fears thy name"" (1, 1).

—3, 10, and 17 March 2010

St. Matilda of Hackeborn

Saint Matilda of Hackeborn, one of the great figures of the convent of Helfta, lived in the thirteenth century. Her sister, St. Gertrude the Great, tells of the special graces that God granted to St. Matilda in the sixth book of *Liber specialis gratiae* (*Book of Special Grace*), which states: "What we have written is very little in comparison with what we have omitted. We are publishing these things solely for the glory of God and the usefulness of our neighbor, for it would seem wrong to us to keep quiet about the many graces that Matilda received from God, not so much for herself, in our opinion, but for us and for those who will come after us" (Mechthild von Hackeborn *Liber specialis gratiae*, 6, 1).

This work was written by St. Gertrude and by another sister of Helfta and has a unique story. At the age of fifty, Matilda went through a grave spiritual crisis, as well as physical suffering. In this condition, she confided to two of her sisters who were friends the special graces with which God had guided her since childhood. However, she did not know that they were writing it all down. When she found out, she was deeply upset and distressed. However, the Lord reassured her, making her realize that all that had been written was for the glory of God and for the benefit of her neighbor (cf. ibid., 2, 25; 5, 20). This work, therefore, is the principal source to refer to for information on the life and spirituality of Matilda.

With her, we are introduced into the family of Baron von Hackeborn, one of the noblest, richest, and most powerful barons of Thuringia, related to the Emperor Frederick II, and we enter the convent of Helfta in the most glorious period of its history. The baron had already given one daughter to the convent, Gertrude of Hackeborn (1231/1232–1291/1292). Gertrude was gifted with an outstanding personality. She was abbess for forty years, capable of giving the spirituality of the convent a particular hallmark and of bringing it to an extraordinary flourishing as the center of mysticism and culture, a school for scientific and theological training. Gertrude offered the nuns an intellectual training of a high standard, which enabled them to cultivate a spirituality founded on Sacred Scripture, on the liturgy, on the Patristic tradition, on the Cistercian Rule and spirituality, with a particular love for St. Bernard of Clairvaux and William of Saint-Thierry. She was a real teacher, exemplary in all things, in evangelical radicalism and in apostolic zeal. Matilda, from childhood, accepted and enjoyed the spiritual and cultural atmosphere created by her sister, later giving it her own personal hallmark.

Matilda was born in 1241 or 1242 in the castle of Helfta. She was the baron's third daughter. When she was seven, she went with her mother to visit her sister Gertrude in the convent of Rodersdorf. She was so enchanted by this environment that she ardently desired to belong to it. She entered as a schoolgirl and in 1258 became a nun at the convent, which in the meantime had moved to Helfta, to the property of the Hackeborns. She was distinguished by her humility, her fervor, her friendliness, the clarity and the innocence of her life, and by the familiarity and intensity with which she lived her relationship with God, the Virgin Mary, and the saints. She was endowed with lofty natural and spiritual qualities, such as knowledge, intelligence, familiarity with the humanities, and a marvelously sweet voice: everything suited her to being a true treasure for the convent from every point of view (ibid, *Proem.*). Thus, when "God's nightingale," as she was called, was still very young, she became the principal of the convent's school, choir mistress, and novice mistress, offices that she fulfilled with talent and unflagging zeal, not only for the benefit of the nuns but for anyone who wanted to draw on her wisdom and goodness.

Illumined by the divine gift of mystic contemplation, Matilda wrote many prayers. She was a teacher of faithful doctrine and deep humility, a counselor, comforter, and guide in discernment. We read: "She distributed doctrine in an abundance never previously seen at the convent, and alas, we are rather afraid that nothing like it will ever be seen again. The sisters would cluster around her to hear the word of God, as if she were a preacher." She was the refuge and consoler of all and, by a unique gift of God, was endowed with the grace of being able to reveal freely the secrets of the heart of each one. Many people, not only in the convent but also outsiders, religious and laypeople, who came from afar, testified that this holy virgin had freed them from their afflictions and that they had never known such comfort as they found near her. "Furthermore, she composed and taught so many prayers that if they were gathered together they would make a book larger than a Psalter" (ibid., 6, 1).

In 1261 a five-year-old girl came to the convent. Her name was Gertrude: she was entrusted to the care of Matilda, herself just twenty years of age, who taught her and guided her in the spiritual life until she not only made her into an excellent disciple but also her confidant. In 1271 or 1272, Matilda of Magdeburg also entered the convent. So it was that this place took in four great women—two Gertrudes and two Matildas—the glory of German monasticism. During her long life, which she spent in the convent, Matilda was afflicted with continuous and intense bouts of suffering, to which she added the very harsh penances chosen for the conversion of sinners. In this manner, she participated in the Lord's passion until the end of her life (cf. ibid., 6, 2). Prayer and contemplation were the life-giving *humus* of her existence: her revelations, her teachings, her service to her neighbor, her journey in faith and in love have their root and their context here. In the first book of the work, *Liber specialis gratiae,* the nuns wrote down Matilda's confidences pronounced on the feasts of the Lord, the saints and, especially, of the Blessed Virgin. This saint had a striking capacity for living the various elements of the liturgy, even the simplest, and bringing it into the daily life of the convent. Some of her images, expressions, and applications are at times distant from our sensibility today, but, if we were to consider monastic life and her task as mistress and choir mistress, we should grasp her rare ability as a teacher and educator who, starting from the liturgy, helped her sisters to live intensely every moment of monastic life.

Matilda gave an emphasis in liturgical prayer to the canonical hours, to the celebrations of Holy Mass, and especially to holy communion. Here she was often rapt in ecstasy in profound intimacy with the Lord in his most ardent and sweetest heart, carrying on a marvelous conversation in which she asked for inner illumination, while interceding in a special way for her community and her sisters. At the center of Matilda's vision are the mysteries of Christ, which the Virgin Mary constantly recommends to people so that they may walk on the path of holiness: "If you want true holiness, be close to my Son; he is holiness itself that sanctifies all things" (ibid., 1, 40). The whole world, the Church, benefactors, and sinners were present in her intimacy with God. For her, heaven and earth were united.

Her visions, her teachings, the events of her life are described in words reminiscent of liturgical and biblical language. In this way, it is possible to comprehend her deep knowledge of Sacred Scripture, which was her daily bread. She had constant recourse to the Scriptures, making the most of the biblical texts read in the liturgy, and drawing from them symbols, terms, countryside, images, and famous figures. She had a special love for the Gospel:

> The words of the Gospel were marvelous nourishment for her and in her heart stirred feelings of such sweetness that, because of her enthusiasm, she was often unable to finish reading it. . . . The way in which she read those words was so fervent that it inspired devotion in everyone. Thus, when she was singing in the choir, she was completely absorbed in God, uplifted by such ardor that she sometimes expressed her feelings in gestures. . . . On other occasions, since she was rapt in ecstasy, she did not hear those who were calling or touching her and came back with difficulty to the reality of the things around her. (ibid., 6, 1)

In one of her visions, Jesus himself recommended the Gospel to her; opening the wound in his most gentle heart, he said to her: "consider the immensity of my love: if you want to know it well, nowhere will you find it more clearly expressed than in the Gospel. No one has ever heard expressed stronger or more tender sentiments than these: 'As my father has loved me, so I have loved you (Jn 15:9)'" (ibid., 1, 22).

Personal and liturgical prayer, especially the Liturgy of the Hours and Holy Mass, are at the root of St. Matilda of Hackeborn's spiritual experience. In letting herself be guided by Sacred Scripture and nourished by the bread of the eucharist, she followed a path of close union with the Lord, ever in full fidelity to the Church. This is also a strong invitation to us to intensify our friendship with the Lord, especially through daily prayer and attentive, faithful, and active participation in Holy Mass. The liturgy is a great school of spirituality.

Her disciple Gertrude gives a vivid picture of St. Matilda of Hackeborn's last moments. They were very difficult but illumined by the presence of the Blessed Trinity, of the Lord, of the Virgin Mary, and of all the saints, even of Gertrude's sister by blood. When the time came in which the Lord chose to gather her to him, she asked him to let her live longer in suffering for the salvation of souls, and Jesus was pleased with this further sign of her love.

Matilda was fifty-eight years old. The last leg of her journey was marked by eight years of serious illness. Her work and the fame of her holiness spread far and wide. When her time came, "the God of majesty . . . the one delight of the soul that loves him . . . sang to her: 'Come, you blessed of my Father' . . . and he united her with his glory (ibid., 6, 8).

May St. Matilda of Hackeborn commend us to the Sacred Heart of Jesus and to the Virgin Mary. She invites us to praise the Son with the heart of the Mother, and to praise Mary with the heart of the Son: "I greet you, O most deeply venerated Virgin, in that sweetest of dews which from the Heart of the Blessed Trinity spread within you; I greet you in the glory and joy in which you now rejoice forever, you who were chosen in preference to all the creatures of the earth and of heaven even before the world's creation! Amen" (ibid., 1, 45).

—*29 September 2010*

St. Gertrude the Great

St. Gertrude the Great brings us once again to the monastery of Helfta, where several of the Latin-German masterpieces of religious literature were written by women. Gertrude belonged to this world. She is one of the most famous mystics, the only German woman to be called "Great," because of her cultural and evangelical stature: her life and her thought had a unique impact on Christian spirituality. She was an exceptional woman, endowed with special natural talents and extraordinary gifts of grace, the most profound humility, and ardent zeal for her neighbor's salvation. She was in close communion with God both in contemplation and in her readiness to go to the help of those in need.

At Helfta, she measured herself systematically, so to speak, with her teacher, Matilda of Hackeborn, of whom I spoke in the last chapter. Gertrude came into contact with Matilda of Magdeburg, another medieval mystic, and grew up under the wing of Abbess Gertrude, motherly, gentle, and demanding. From these three sisters she drew precious experience and wisdom; she worked them into a synthesis of her own, continuing on her religious journey with boundless trust in the Lord. Gertrude expressed the riches of her spirituality not only in her monastic world but also and above all in the biblical, liturgical, Patristic, and Benedictine contexts, with a highly personal hallmark and great skill in communicating.

Gertrude was born on 6 January 1256, on the Feast of the Epiphany, but nothing is known of her parents or of the place of her birth. Gertrude wrote that the Lord himself revealed to her the meaning of this first uprooting: "I have chosen you for my abode because I am pleased that all that is lovable in you is my work. . . . For this very reason, I have distanced you from all your relatives, so that no one may love you for reasons of kinship and that I may be the sole cause of the affection you receive" (*The Revelations* 1, 16: Siena 1994, 76–77).

When she was five years old, in 1261, Gertrude entered the monastery for formation and education, a common practice in that period. Here she spent her whole life, the most important stages of which she herself points out. In her memoirs, she recalls that the Lord equipped her in advance with forbearing patience and infinite mercy, forgetting the years of her childhood, adolescence, and youth, which she spent, she wrote,

in such mental blindness that I would have been capable . . . of thinking, saying, or doing without remorse everything I liked and wherever I could, had you not armed me in advance, with an inherent horror of evil and a natural inclination for good and with the external vigilance of others. I would have behaved like a pagan . . . in spite of desiring you

since childhood, that is, since my fifth year of age, when I went to live
in the Benedictine shrine of religion to be educated among your most
devout friends. (ibid., 2, 23, 140–41.)

Gertrude was an extraordinary student. She learned everything that
can be learned of the sciences of the *trivium* and *quadrivium*, the education of that time; she was fascinated by knowledge and threw herself
into profane studies with zeal and tenacity, achieving scholastic successes
beyond every expectation. If we know nothing of her origins, she herself
tells us about her youthful passions: literature, music and song, and the
art of miniature painting captivated her. She had a strong, determined,
ready, and impulsive temperament. She often says that she was negligent;
she recognizes her shortcomings and humbly asks forgiveness for them.
She also humbly asks for advice and prayers for her conversion. Some
features of her temperament and faults were to accompany her to the end
of her life, so as to amaze certain people who wondered why the Lord
had favored her with such a special love.

From being a student, Gertrude moved on to dedicate herself totally
to God in monastic life. For twenty years, nothing exceptional occurred:
study and prayer were her main activities. Because of her gifts, she shone
out among the sisters; she was tenacious in consolidating her knowledge
of culture in various fields. Nevertheless, during Advent of 1280, she
began to feel disgusted with all this and realized the vanity of it all. On
27 January 1281, a few days before the Feast of the Purification of the
Virgin, toward the hour of Compline in the evening, the Lord with his
illumination dispelled her deep anxiety. With gentle sweetness, he calmed
the distress that anguished her, a torment that Gertrude saw even as a
gift of God, "to pull down that tower of vanity and curiosity which,
although I had both the name and habit of a nun, alas, I had continued
to build with my pride, so that at least in this manner I might find the
way for you to show me your salvation" (ibid., 2, 87). She had a vision
of a young man who, in order to guide her through the tangle of thorns
that surrounded her soul, took her by the hand. In that hand, Gertrude
recognized "the precious traces of the wounds that abrogated all the acts
of accusation of our enemies" (ibid., 2, 1, 89), and thus recognized the
One who saved us with his blood on the Cross: Jesus.

From that moment, her life of intimate communion with the Lord
was intensified, especially in the most important liturgical seasons,
Advent–Christmas, Lent–Easter, the feasts of Our Lady, even when illness prevented her from going to the choir. This was the same liturgical
humus as that of Matilda her teacher; but Gertrude describes it with simpler, more linear images, symbols, and terms that are more realistic; and
her references to the Bible, to the Fathers, and to the Benedictine world
are more direct.

Her biographer points out two directions in what we might describe as her own particular "conversion": in *study*, with the radical passage from profane, humanistic studies to the study of theology, and in *monastic observance*, with the passage from a life that she describes as negligent, to the life of intense, mystical prayer, with exceptional missionary zeal. The Lord, who had chosen her from her mother's womb and who since her childhood had made her partake of the banquet of monastic life, called her again with his grace "from external things to inner life and from earthly occupations to love for spiritual things." Gertrude understood that she was remote from him, "in the region of unlikeness," as she said with Augustine; that she had dedicated herself with excessive greed to liberal studies, to human wisdom, overlooking spiritual knowledge, depriving herself of the taste for true wisdom; she was then led to the mountain of contemplation where she cast off her former self to be reclothed in the new. "From a grammarian she became a theologian, with the unflagging and attentive reading of all the sacred books that she could lay her hands on or contrive to obtain. She filled her heart with the most useful and sweet sayings of Sacred Scripture. Thus, she was always ready with some inspired and edifying word to satisfy those who came to consult her while having at her fingertips the most suitable scriptural texts to refute any erroneous opinion and silence her opponents" (ibid., 1, 1, 25).

Gertrude transformed all this into an apostolate: she devoted herself to writing and popularizing the truth of faith with clarity and simplicity, with grace and persuasion, serving the Church faithfully and lovingly so as to be helpful to and appreciated by theologians and devout people. Little of her intense activity has come down to us, partly because of the events that led to the destruction of the monastery of Helfta. In addition to *The Herald of Divine Love* and *The Revelations*, we still have her *Spiritual Exercises*, a rare jewel of mystical spiritual literature.

In religious observance, Gertrude was "a firm pillar . . . a very powerful champion of justice and truth" (ibid., 1, 1, 26), her biographer says. By her words and example, she kindled great fervor in other people. She added to the prayers and penances of the monastic rule others with such devotion and such trusting abandonment in God that she inspired in those who met her an awareness of being in the Lord's presence. In fact, God made her understand that he had called her to be an instrument of his grace. Gertrude herself felt unworthy of this immense divine treasure, and confesses that she had not safeguarded it or made enough of it. She exclaimed: "Alas! If you had given me to remember you, unworthy as I am, by even only a straw, I would have viewed it with greater respect and reverence that I have had for all your gifts!" (ibid., 2, 5, 100). Yet, in recognizing her poverty and worthlessness, she adhered to God's will, "because," she said,

I have so little profited from your graces that I cannot resolve to believe that they were lavished upon me solely for my own use, since no one can thwart your eternal wisdom. Therefore, O giver of every good thing who has freely lavished upon me gifts so undeserved, [enable] that, in reading this, the heart of at least one of your friends may be moved at the thought that zeal for souls has induced you to leave such a priceless gem for so long in the abominable mud of my heart. (ibid., 2, 5, 100–101.)

Two favors in particular were dearer to her than any other, as Gertrude herself writes:

The stigmata of your salvation-bearing wounds, which you impressed upon me, as it were, like a valuable necklace, in my heart, and the profound and salutary wound of love with which you marked it. You flooded me with your gifts of such beatitude that even were I to live for a thousand years with no consolation neither interior nor exterior, the memory of them would suffice to comfort me, to enlighten me, to fill me with gratitude. Further, you wished to introduce me into the inestimable intimacy of your friendship by opening to me in various ways that most noble sacrarium of your divine being, which is your divine heart. . . . To this accumulation of benefits you added that of giving me as advocate the Most Holy Virgin Mary, your mother, and often recommended me to her affection, just as the most faithful of bridegrooms would recommend his beloved bride to his own mother. (ibid., 2, 23, 145)

Looking forward to never-ending communion, she ended her earthly life on 17 November 1301 or 1302, at the age of about forty-six. In the seventh exercise, that of preparation for death, St. Gertrude wrote: "O Jesus, you who are immensely dear to me, be with me always, so that my heart may stay with you and that your love may endure with me with no possibility of division; and bless my passing, so that my spirit, freed from the bonds of the flesh, may immediately find rest in you. Amen" (*Spiritual Exercises* [Milan, 2006], 148).

It seems obvious to me that these are not only things of the past, of history; rather, St. Gertrude's life lives on as a lesson of Christian life, of an upright path, and shows us that the heart of a happy life, of a true life, is friendship with the Lord Jesus. And this friendship is learned in love for Sacred Scripture, in love for the liturgy, in profound faith, in love for Mary, so as to be ever more truly acquainted with God himself and hence with true happiness, which is the goal of our life.

—*6 October 2010*

St. Elizabeth of Hungary

ANOTHER GREAT WOMAN OF THE MIDDLE AGES who inspired the greatest admiration is St. Elizabeth of Hungary, also called St. Elizabeth of Thuringia.

Elizabeth was born in 1207; historians dispute her birthplace. Her father was Andrew II, the rich and powerful king of Hungary. To reinforce political ties, he had married the German Countess Gertrude of Andechs-Meran, sister of St. Hedwig, who was wife to the Duke of Silesia. Elizabeth, together with her sister and three brothers, spent only the first four years of her childhood at the Hungarian court. She liked playing, music, and dancing; she recited her prayers faithfully and already showed special attention to the poor, whom she helped with a kind word or an affectionate gesture.

Her happy childhood was suddenly interrupted when some knights arrived from distant Thuringia to escort her to her new residence in central Germany. In fact, complying with the customs of that time, Elizabeth's father had arranged for her to become a princess of Thuringia. The Landgrave or Count of this region was one of the richest and most influential sovereigns in Europe at the beginning of the thirteenth century, and his castle was a center of magnificence and culture. Yet the festivities and apparent glory of castle life concealed the ambition of feudal princes, who were frequently warring with each other and in conflict with the royal and imperial authorities.

In this context, the Landgrave Hermann very willingly accepted the betrothal of his son Ludwig to the Hungarian princess. Elizabeth left her homeland with a rich dowry and a large entourage, including her personal ladies-in-waiting, two of whom were to remain faithful friends to the very end. It is they who left us the precious information on the childhood and life of the saint.

They reached Eisenach after a long journey and made the ascent to the Fortress of Wartburg, the strong castle towering over the city. It was here that the betrothal of Ludwig and Elizabeth was celebrated. In the ensuing years, while Ludwig learned the knightly profession, Elizabeth and her companions studied German, French, Latin, music, literature, and embroidery. Despite the fact that political reasons had determined their betrothal, a sincere love developed between the two young people, enlivened by faith and by the desire to do God's will. On his father's death, when Ludwig was eighteen years old, he began to reign over Thuringia.

Elizabeth, however, became the object of critical whispers because her behavior was incongruous with court life. Hence, their marriage celebrations were far from sumptuous, and a part of the funds destined for the banquet were donated to the poor.

With her profound sensitivity, Elizabeth saw the contradictions between the faith professed and Christian practice. She could not bear compromise. Once, on entering a church on the Feast of the Assumption, she took off her crown, laid it before the crucifix, and, covering her face, lay prostrate on the ground. When her mother-in-law reprimanded her for this gesture, Elizabeth answered: "How can I, a wretched creature, continue to wear a crown of earthly dignity when I see my King Jesus Christ crowned with thorns?"

Elizabeth behaved to her subjects in the same way that she behaved to God. Among the *Sayings of the Four Maids*, we find this testimony: "She did not eat any food before ascertaining that it came from her husband's property or legitimate possessions. While she abstained from goods procured illegally, she also did her utmost to provide compensation to those who had suffered violence" (nn. 25 and 37).

She is a true example for all who have roles of leadership: the exercise of authority, at every level, must be lived as a service to justice and charity, in the constant search for the common good.

Elizabeth diligently practiced works of mercy: she would give food and drink to those who knocked at her door, procured clothing, paid debts, cared for the sick, and buried the dead. Coming down from her castle, she often visited the homes of the poor with her ladies-in-waiting, bringing them bread, meat, flour, and other food. She distributed the food personally and attentively checked the clothing and mattresses of the poor. This behavior was reported to her husband, who not only was not displeased but answered her accusers, "So long as she does not sell the castle, I am happy with her!"

The miracle of the loaves that were changed into roses fits into this context: while Elizabeth was on her way with her apron filled with bread for the poor, she met her husband, who asked her what she was carrying. She opened her apron to show him and, instead of bread, it was full of magnificent roses. This symbol of charity often features in depictions of St. Elizabeth.

Elizabeth's marriage was profoundly happy: she helped her husband to raise his human qualities to a supernatural level, and he, in exchange, stood up for his wife's generosity to the poor and for her religious practices. Increasingly admired for his wife's great faith, Ludwig said to her, referring to her attention to the poor, "Dear Elizabeth, it is Christ whom you have cleansed, nourished, and cared for." A clear witness to how faith and love of God and neighbor strengthen family life and deepen ever more the matrimonial union.

The young couple found spiritual support in the Friars Minor, who began to spread through Thuringia in 1222. Elizabeth chose from among them Friar Rodeger (Rüdiger) as her spiritual director. When he told her about the event of the conversion of Francis of Assisi, a rich young merchant, Elizabeth was even more enthusiastic in the journey of her Christian life.

From that time, she became even more determined to follow the poor and crucified Christ, present in poor people. Even when her first son was born, followed by two other children, this saint never neglected her charitable works. She also helped the Friars Minor to build a convent at Halberstadt, of which Friar Rodeger became superior. For this reason, Elizabeth's spiritual direction was taken on by Conrad of Marburg.

The farewell to her husband was a hard trial, when, at the end of June in 1227, Ludwig IV joined the Crusade of the Emperor Frederick II. He reminded his wife that this was traditional for the sovereigns of Thuringia. Elizabeth answered him: "Far be it from me to detain you. I have given my whole self to God, and now I must also give you." However, fever decimated the troops, and Ludwig himself fell ill and died in Otranto before embarking, in September 1227. He was twenty-seven years old. When Elizabeth learned the news, she was so sorrowful that she withdrew in solitude; but then, strengthened by prayer and comforted by the hope of seeing him again in heaven, she began to attend to the affairs of the kingdom.

However, another trial was lying in wait for Elizabeth. Her brother-in-law usurped the government of Thuringia, declaring himself to be the true heir of Ludwig and accusing Elizabeth of being a pious woman incapable of ruling. The young widow, with three children, was banished from the castle of Wartburg and went in search of a place of refuge. Only two of her ladies remained close to her. They accompanied her and entrusted the three children to the care of Ludwig's friends. Wandering through the villages, Elizabeth worked wherever she was welcomed, looked after the sick, spun thread, and cooked.

During this calvary, which she bore with great faith, patience, and dedication to God, a few relatives who had stayed faithful to her and viewed her brother-in-law's rule as illegal, restored her reputation. So it was that at the beginning of 1228, Elizabeth received sufficient income to withdraw to the family's castle in Marburg, where her spiritual director, Fra Conrad, also lived. It was he who reported the following event to Pope Gregory IX:

> On Good Friday in 1228, having placed her hands on the altar in the chapel of her city, Eisenach, to which she had welcomed the Friars Minor, in the presence of several friars and relatives, Elizabeth renounced her own will and all the vanities of the world. She also wanted to resign all her possessions, but I dissuaded her out of love for the poor. Shortly afterward, she built a hospital, gathered the sick and

invalids, and served at her own table the most wretched and deprived. When I reprimanded her for these things, Elizabeth answered that she received from the poor special grace and humility. (*Epistula magistri Conradi* 14–17)

We can discern in this affirmation a certain mystical experience similar to that of St. Francis: the *Poverello* of Assisi declared in his testament, in fact, that serving lepers, which he at first found repugnant, was transformed into sweetness of the soul and of the body (*Testamentum* 1–3). Elizabeth spent her last three years in the hospital she founded, serving the sick and keeping wake over the dying. She always tried to carry out the most humble services and repugnant tasks. She became what we might call a consecrated woman in the world (*soror in saeculo*) and, with other friends clothed in gray habits, formed a religious community. It is not by chance that she is the patroness of the Third Order Regular of St. Francis and of the Franciscan Secular Order.

In November 1231, she was stricken with a high fever. When the news of her illness spread, may people flocked to see her. After about ten days, she asked for the doors to be closed so that she might be alone with God. In the night of 17 November, she fell asleep gently in the Lord. The testimonies of her holiness were so many and such that after only four years Pope Gregory IX canonized her. That same year, the beautiful church built in her honor at Marburg was consecrated.

In St. Elizabeth, we see how faith and friendship with Christ create a sense of justice, of the equality of all, of the rights of others, and how they create love, charity. And from this charity is born hope too, the certainty that we are loved by Christ and that the love of Christ awaits us, thereby rendering us capable of imitating Christ and of seeing Christ in others. Saint Elizabeth invites us to rediscover Christ, to love him, and to have faith and thereby to find true justice and love, as well as the joy that one day we shall be immersed in divine love, in the joy of eternity with God.

—*20 October 2010*

St. Albert the Great

ONE OF THE GREAT MASTERS OF MEDIEVAL THEOLOGY is St. Albert the Great. The title "Great" (*Magnus*), with which he has passed into history indicates the vastness and depth of his teaching, which he combined with holiness of life. However, his contemporaries did not hesitate to attribute to him titles of excellence even then. One of his disciples, Ulric of Strasbourg, called him the "wonder and miracle of our epoch."

Albert was born in Germany at the beginning of the thirteenth century. When he was still young, he went to Italy, to Padua, the seat of one of the most famous medieval universities. He devoted himself to the study of the so-called liberal arts: grammar, rhetoric, dialectics, arithmetic, geometry, astronomy, and music, that is, to culture in general, demonstrating that characteristic interest in the natural sciences which was soon to become the favorite field for his specialization. During his stay in Padua, Albert attended the church of the Dominicans, whom he then joined with the profession of religious vows. Hagiographic sources suggest that Albert came to this decision gradually. His intense relationship with God; the Dominican friars' example of holiness; hearing the sermons of Blessed Jordan of Saxony, St. Dominic's successor as the master general of the Order of Preachers, were the decisive factors that helped him to overcome every doubt and even to surmount his family's resistence. God often speaks to us in the years of our youth and points out to us the project of our life. As it was for Albert, so also for all of us, personal prayer, nourished by the Lord's Word, frequent reception of the sacraments, and the spiritual guidance of enlightened people are the means to discover and follow God's voice. Albert received the religious habit from Blessed Jordan of Saxony.

After his ordination to the priesthood, Albert's superiors sent him to teach at various theological study centers annexed to the convents of the Dominican fathers. His brilliant intellectual qualities enabled him to perfect his theological studies at the most famous university in that period, the University of Paris. From that time on, St. Albert began his extraordinary activity as a writer, which he was to pursue throughout his life.

Prestigious tasks were assigned to him. In 1248, he was charged with opening a theological studium at Cologne, one of the most important regional capitals of Germany, where he lived at different times and which became his adopted city. He brought with him from Paris an exceptional student, Thomas Aquinas. The sole merit of having been St. Thomas's teacher would suffice to elicit profound admiration for St. Albert. A relationship of mutual esteem and friendship developed between these two great theologians, human attitudes that were very helpful in the development of this branch of knowlege. In 1254, Albert was elected provincial of the Dominican fathers' *Provincia Teutoniae* "Teutonic Province," which included communities scattered over a vast territory in central and northern Europe. He distinguished himself for the zeal with which he exercised this ministry, visiting the communities and constantly recalling his confreres to fidelity, to the teaching and example of St. Dominic.

Albert's gifts did not escape the attention of the pope of that time, Alexander IV, who wanted Albert with him for a certain time at Anagni, where the popes went frequently, in Rome itself, and at Viterbo, in order to avail himself of Albert's theological advice. The same supreme pontiff appointed Albert bishop of Regensburg, a large and celebrated diocese but which was going through a difficult period. From 1260 to 1262, Albert exercised this ministry with unflagging dedication, succeeding in restoring peace and harmony to the city, in reorganizing parishes and convents, and in giving a new impetus to charitable activities.

In the year 1263–1264, Albert preached in Germany and in Bohemia at the request of Pope Urban IV. He later returned to Cologne and took up his role as lecturer, scholar, and writer. As a man of prayer, science, and charity, his authoritative intervention in various events of the Church and of the society of the time were acclaimed: above all, he was a man of reconciliation and peace in Cologne, where the archbishop had run seriously afoul of the city's institutions; he did his utmost during the Second Council of Lyons, in 1274, summoned by Pope Gregory X, to encourage union between the Latin and Greek Churches after the separation of the great schism with the East in 1054. He also explained the thought of Thomas Aquinas, which had been the subject of objections and even quite unjustified condemnations.

Albert died in his cell at the Convent of the Holy Cross, Cologne, in 1280, and was very soon venerated by his confreres. The Church proposed him for the veneration of the faithful with his beatification in 1622 and with his canonization in 1931, when Pope Pius XI proclaimed him Doctor of the Church. This was certainly an appropriate recognition of this great man of God and outstanding scholar, not only of the truths of the faith but of a great many other branches of knowledge. Indeed, with a glance at the titles of his very numerous works, we realize that there was something miraculous about his culture and that his encyclopedic interests led him not only to concern himself with philosophy and theology, like other contemporaries of his, but also with every other discipline then known, from physics to chemistry, from astronomy to minerology, from botany to zoology. For this reason, Pope Pius XII named him patron of enthusiasts of the natural sciences and also called him *Doctor universalis* precisely because of the vastness of his interests and knowledge.

Of course, the scientific methods that St. Albert the Great used were not those that came to be established in the following centuries. His method consisted simply in the observation, description, and classification of the phenomena he had studied, but it was in this way that he opened the door for future research.

He still has a lot to teach us. Above all, St. Albert shows that there is no opposition between faith and science, despite certain episodes of misunderstanding that have been recorded in history. A person of faith and prayer, as was St. Albert the Great, can serenely foster the study of the natural sciences and progress in knowledge of the micro- and macrocosm, discovering the laws proper to the subject, since all this contributes to fostering thirst for and love of God. The Bible speaks to us of creation as of the first language through which God, who is supreme intelligence, who is the *Logos*, reveals to us something of himself. The Book of Wisdom, for example, says that the phenomena of nature, endowed with greatness and beauty, is like the works of an artist through which, by analogy, we may know the author of creation (cf. Wis 13:5). With a classical similitude in the Middle Ages and in the Renaissance, one can compare the natural world to a book written by God that we read according to the different approaches of the sciences (cf. *Address to the Participants in the Plenary Meeting of the Pontifical Academy of Sciences,* 31 October 2008; *L'Osservatore Romano,* English edition, 5 November 2008, 6). How many scientists, in fact, in the wake of St. Albert the Great, have carried on their research inspired by wonder at and gratitude for a world which, to their eyes as scholars and believers, appeared and appears as the good work of a wise and loving creator! Scientific study is then transformed into a hymn of praise. Enrico Medi, a great astrophysicist of our time, whose cause of beatification has been introduced, wrote:

> O you mysterious galaxies . . . I see you, I calculate you, I understand you, I study you and I discover you, I penetrate you and I gather you. From you I take light and make it knowledge, I take movement and make it wisdom, I take sparkling colors and make them poetry; I take you stars in my hands and, trembling in the oneness of my being, I raise you above yourselves and offer you in prayer to the Creator that through me alone you stars can worship. (*Le Opere. Inno alla creazione*)

Saint Albert the Great reminds us that there is friendship between science and faith and that through their vocation to the study of nature, scientists can take an authentic and fascinating path of holiness.

His extraordinary open-mindedness is also revealed in a cultural feat that he carried out successfully, that is, the acceptance and appreciation of Aristotle's thought. In St. Albert's time, in fact, knowledge was spreading of numerous works by this great Greek philosopher, who lived a quarter of a millenium before Christ, especially in the sphere of ethics and metaphysics. They showed the power of reason, explained lucidly and clearly the meaning and structure of reality, its intelligibility, and the value and purpose of human actions. Saint Albert the Great opened the door to the complete acceptance in medieval philosophy and theology of Aristotle's philosophy, which was subsequently given a definitive form by St. Thomas. This reception of a pagan pre-Christian philosophy, let us say, was an authentic cultural revolution in that epoch. Yet many Christian thinkers feared Aristotle's philosophy, a non-Christian philosophy, especially because, presented by his Arab commentators, it had been interpreted in such a way, at least in certain points, as to appear completely irreconcilable with the Christian faith. Hence, a dilemma arose: are faith and reason in conflict with each other or not?

This is one of the great merits of St. Albert: with scientific rigor, he studied Aristotle's works, convinced that all that is truly rational is compatible with the faith revealed in the Sacred Scriptures. In other words, St. Albert the Great thus contributed to the formation of an autonomous philosophy, distinct from theology and united with it only by the unity of the truth. So it was that in the thirteenth century, a clear distinction came into being between these two branches of knowledge, philosophy and theology, which, in conversing with each other, cooperate harmoniously in the discovery of the authentic human vocation, thirsting for truth and happiness: and it is above all theology, which St. Albert defined as "emotional knowledge," that points out to human beings their vocation to eternal joy, a joy that flows from full adherence to the truth.

Saint Albert the Great was capable of communicating these concepts in a simple and understandable way. An authentic son of St. Dominic, he willingly preached to the People of God, who were won over by his words and by the example of his life. Let us pray to the Lord that learned theologians will never be lacking in Holy Church, wise and devout like St. Albert the Great, and that he may help each one of us to make our own the "formula of holiness" that he followed in his life: "to desire all that I desire for the glory of God, as God desires for his glory all that he desires," in other words always to be conformed to God's will, in order to desire and to do everything only and always for his glory.

—*24 March 2010*

St. Thomas Aquinas

His Life and Context

We continue our meditation on some of the great thinkers of the Middle Ages. We recently looked at the great figure of St. Bonaventure, a Franciscan, and here I discuss the one whom the Church calls the *Doctor Communis*, namely, St. Thomas Aquinas. In his encyclical *Fides et Ratio*, my venerable predecessor Pope John Paul II recalled that "the Church has been justified in consistently proposing St. Thomas as a master of thought and a model of the right way to do theology" (n. 43). It is not surprising that, after St. Augustine, among the ecclesiastical writers mentioned in the *Catechism of the Catholic Church*, St. Thomas is cited more than any other, at least sixty-one times! He was also called the *Doctor Angelicus*, perhaps because of his virtues and, in particular, the sublimity of his thought and the purity of his life.

Thomas was born between 1224 and 1225 in the castle that his wealthy noble family owned at Roccasecca near Aquino, not far from the famous abbey of Monte Cassino, where his parents sent him to receive the first elements of his education. A few years later, he moved to Naples, the capital of the kingdom of Sicily, where Frederick II had founded a prestigious university. Here the thinking of the Greek philosopher Aristotle was taught without the limitations imposed elsewhere. The young Thomas was introduced to it and immediately perceived its great value. However, it was above all in those years that he spent in Naples that his Dominican vocation was born. Thomas was, in fact, attracted by the ideal of the order recently founded by St. Dominic. However, when he was clothed in the Dominican habit, his family opposed this decision and he was obliged to leave the convent and spend some time at home.

In 1245, by which time he had come of age, he was able to continue on the path of his response to God's call. He was sent to Paris to study theology under the guidance of another saint, Albert the Great, of whom we spoke previously. A true and deep friendship developed between Albert and Thomas. They learned to esteem and love each other to the point that Albert even wanted his disciple to follow him to Cologne, where he had been sent by the superiors of the order to found a theological studium. Thomas then once again came into contact with all of Aristotle's works and his Arab commentators, which Albert described and explained.

In this period, the culture of the Latin world was profoundly stimulated by the encounter with Aristotle's works, which had long remained unknown. They were writings on the nature of knowledge, on the natural sciences, on metaphysics, on the soul, and on ethics; and they were full of information and intuitions that appeared valid and convincing. All this formed an overall vision of the world that had been developed without and before Christ, and with pure reason, and seemed to impose itself on reason as "the" vision itself; accordingly, seeing and knowing this philosophy had an incredible fascination for the young. Many accepted enthusiastically, indeed with acritical enthusiasm, this enormous baggage of ancient knowledge that seemed to be able to renew culture advantageously and to open totally new horizons. Others, however, feared that Aristotle's pagan thought might be in opposition to the Christian faith and refused to study it. Two cultures converged: the pre-Christian culture of Aristotle, with its radical rationality, and the classical Christian culture. Certain circles, moreover, were led to reject Aristotle by the presentation of this philosopher which had been made by the Arab commentators Avicenna and Averroës. Indeed, it was they who had transmitted the Aristotelian philosophy to the Latin world. For example, these commentators had taught that human beings have no personal intelligence but that there is a single universal intelligence, a spiritual substance common to all, that works in all as "one": hence, a depersonalization of humanity. Another disputable point passed on by the Arab commentators was that the world was eternal like God. This, understandably, unleashed never-ending disputes in the university and clerical worlds. Aristotelian philosophy was continuing to spread even among the populace.

Thomas Aquinas, at the school of Albert the Great, did something of fundamental importance for the history of philosophy and theology, I would say for the history of culture: he made a thorough study of Aristotle and his interpreters, obtaining for himself new Latin translations of the original Greek texts. Consequently, he no longer relied solely on the Arab commentators but was able to read the original texts for himself. He commented on most of the Aristotelian opus, distinguishing between what was valid and was dubious or to be completely rejected, showing its consonance with the events of Christian revelation and drawing abundantly and perceptively from Aristotle's thought in the explanation of the theological texts he was uniting. In short, Thomas Aquinas showed that a natural harmony exists between Christian faith and reason. And this was the great achievement of Thomas who, at that time of clashes between two cultures—when it seemed that faith would have to give in to reason—showed that they go hand in hand. Insofar as reason appeared incompatible with faith, it was not reason, and what appeared to be faith was not faith if it was in opposition to true rationality; thus, he created a new synthesis that formed the culture of the centuries to come.

Because of his excellent intellectual gifts, Thomas was summoned to Paris to be professor of theology on the Dominican chair. Here he began his literary production, which continued until his death and has something miraculous about it: he commented on Sacred Scripture because the professor of theology was above all an interpreter of Scripture; and he commented on the writings of Aristotle. He composed powerful systematic works, among which stands out his *Summa Theologiae*, as well as treatises and discourses on various subjects. He was assisted in the composition of his writings by several secretaries, including his confrere, Reginald of Piperno, who followed him faithfully and to whom he was bound by a sincere brotherly friendship marked by great confidence and trust. This is a characteristic of saints: they cultivate friendship because it is one of the noblest manifestations of the human heart and has something divine about it, just as Thomas himself explained in some of the *quaestiones* of his *Summa Theologiae*. He writes in it: "It is evident that charity is the friendship of man for God" and for "all belonging to him" (*ST* 2, q. 23, a. 1).

He did not stay long or permanently in Paris. In 1259, he took part in the general chapter of the Dominicans in Valenciennes, where he was a member of a commission that established the order's program of studies. Then from 1261 to 1265, Thomas was in Orvieto. Pope Urban IV, who held him in high esteem, commissioned him to compose liturgical texts for the feast of *Corpus Christi*, established subsequent to the eucharistic miracle of Bolsena. Thomas had an exquisitely eucharistic soul. The most beautiful hymns that the liturgy of the Church sings to celebrate the mystery of the real presence of the body and blood of the Lord in the eucharist are attributed to his faith and his theological wisdom. From 1265 until 1268, Thomas lived in Rome, where he probably directed a studium, that is, a study house of his order, and where he began writing his *Summa Theologiae* (cf. Jean-Pierre Torrell, *Tommaso d'Aquino. L'uomo e il teologo* [Casale Monf., 1994], 118–84).

In 1269, Thomas was recalled to Paris for a second cycle of lectures. His students understandably were enthusiastic about his lessons. One of his former pupils declared that a vast multitude of students took Thomas's courses, so many that the halls could barely accommodate them; and this student added, making a personal comment, that "listening to him brought him deep happiness." Thomas's interpretation of Aristotle was not accepted by all, but even his adversaries in the academic field, such as Godfrey of Fontaines, for example, admitted that the teaching of Friar Thomas was superior to others for its usefulness and value and served to correct that of all the other masters. Perhaps also in order to distance him from the lively discussions that were going on, his superiors sent him once again to Naples to be available to King Charles I, who was planning to reorganize university studies.

In addition to study and teaching, Thomas also dedicated himself to preaching to the people. And the people too came willingly to hear him. I would say that it is truly a great grace when theologians are able to speak to the faithful with simplicity and fervor. The ministry of preaching, moreover, helps theology scholars themselves to have a healthy pastoral realism and enriches their research with lively incentives.

The last months of Thomas's earthly life remain surrounded by a particular, I would say, mysterious atmosphere. In December 1273, he summoned his friend and secretary Reginald to inform him of his decision to discontinue all work because he had realized, during the celebration of Mass subsequent to a supernatural revelation, that everything he had written until then "was worthless." This is a mysterious episode that helps us to understand not only Thomas's personal humility but also the fact that, however lofty and pure it may be, all we manage to think and say about the faith is infinitely exceeded by God's greatness and beauty, which will be fully revealed to us in heaven. A few months later, more and more absorbed in thoughtful meditation, Thomas died while on his way to Lyons to take part in the Ecumenical Council convoked by Pope Gregory X. He died in the Cistercian abbey of Fossanova, after receiving the viaticum with deeply devout sentiments.

The life and teaching of St. Thomas Aquinas could be summed up in an episode passed down by his ancient biographers. While, as was his wont, the saint was praying before the crucifix in the early morning in the chapel of St. Nicholas in Naples, Domenico da Caserta, the church sacristan, overheard a conversation. Thomas was anxiously asking whether what he had written on the mysteries of the Christian faith was correct. And the Crucified One answered him: "You have spoken well of me, Thomas. What is your reward to be?" And the answer Thomas gave him was what we too, friends and disciples of Jesus, always want to tell him: "Nothing but yourself, Lord!" (ibid., 320).

Faith and Reason

I continue my presentation of St. Thomas Aquinas, a theologian of such value that the study of his thought was explicitly recommended by the Second Vatican Council in two documents, the decree *Optatam totius*, on the training of priests, and the declaration *Gravissimum Educationis*, which addresses Christian education. Indeed, already in 1880 Pope Leo XIII, who held St. Thomas in high esteem as a guide and encouraged Thomistic studies, chose to declare him patron of Catholic schools and universities.

The main reason for this appreciation is not only explained by the content of his teaching but also by the method he used, especially his new synthesis of and distinction between philosophy and theology. The Fathers of the Church were confronted by different philosophies of a Platonic type in which a complete vision of the world and of life was presented, including the subject of God and of religion. In competing with these philosophies, they themselves had worked out a complete vision of reality, starting with faith and using elements of Platonism to respond to the essential questions of men and women. They called this vision, based on biblical revelation and formulated with a Platonism corrected in the light of faith, "our philosophy." The word "philosophy" was not, therefore, an expression of a purely rational system and, as such, distinct from faith but rather indicated a comprehensive vision of reality, constructed in the light of faith but used and conceived of by reason—a vision that naturally exceeded the capacities proper to reason but as such also fulfilled it.

For St. Thomas, the encounter with the pre-Christian philosophy of Aristotle (who died in about 322 B.C.E.) opened up a new perspective. Aristotelian philosophy was obviously a philosophy worked out without the knowledge of the Old and New Testaments, an explanation of the world without revelation, through reason alone. And this consequent rationality was convincing. Thus, the old form of the Fathers' "our philosophy" no longer worked. The relationship between philosophy and theology, between faith and reason, needed to be rethought. A "philosophy" existed that was complete and convincing in itself, a rationality that preceded the faith, followed by "theology," a form of thinking with the faith and in the faith. The pressing question was this: are the worlds of rationality, philosophy conceived of without Christ, and the world of faith compatible? Or are they mutually exclusive? Elements that affirmed the incompatibility of these two worlds were not lacking, but St. Thomas was firmly convinced of their compatibility—indeed, that philosophy worked out without the knowledge of Christ was awaiting, as it were, the light of Jesus to be complete. This was the great "surprise" of St. Thomas that determined the path he took as a thinker. Showing this independence of philosophy and theology and, at the same time, their reciprocal relationality was the historic mission of the great teacher. And thus, it can be understood that in the nineteenth century, when the incompatibility of modern reason and faith was strongly declared, Pope Leo XIII pointed to St. Thomas as a guide in the dialogue between them. In his theological work, St. Thomas supposes and concretizes this relationality. Faith consolidates, integrates, and illumines the heritage of truth that human reason acquires. The trust with which St. Thomas endows these two instruments of knowledge, faith and reason, may be traced back to the conviction that both stem from the one source of all truth, the divine *Logos*, which is active in both contexts, that of creation and that of redemption.

Together with the agreement between reason and faith, we must recognize on the other hand that they avail themselves of different cognitive procedures. Reason receives a truth by virtue of its intrinsic evidence, mediated or unmediated; faith, on the contrary, accepts a truth on the basis of the authority of the Word of God that is revealed. Saint Thomas writes at the beginning of his *Summa Theologiae:*

> We must bear in mind that there are two kinds of sciences. There are some which proceed from a principle known by the natural light of the intelligence, such as arithmetic and geometry and the like. There are some which proceed from principles known by the light of a higher science: thus the science of perspective proceeds from principles established by geometry, and music from principles established by arithmetic. So it is that sacred doctrine is a science, because it proceeds from principles established by the light of a higher science, namely, the science of God and the blessed. (1a, q. 1, a. 2)

This distinction guarantees the autonomy of both the human and the theological sciences. However, it is not equivalent to separation but, rather, implies a reciprocal and advantageous collaboration. Faith, in fact, protects reason from any temptation to distrust its own abilities, stimulates it to be open to ever broader horizons, keeps alive in it the search for foundations, and, when reason itself is applied to the supernatural sphere of the relationship between God and humans, faith enriches his work. According to St. Thomas, for example, human reason can certainly reach the affirmation of the existence of one God, but only faith, which receives the divine revelation, is able to draw from the mystery of the love of the Triune God.

Moreover, it is not only faith that helps reason. Reason, too, with its own means can do something important for faith, making it a threefold service that St. Thomas sums up in the preface to his commentary on the *De Trinitate* of Boethius: "Demonstrating those truths that are preambles of the faith; giving a clearer notion, by certain similitudes, of the truths of the faith; resisting those who speak against the faith, either by showing that their statements are false or by showing that they are not necessarily true" (q. 2, a. 3). The entire history of theology is basically the exercise of this task of the mind, which shows the intelligibility of faith, its articulation and inner harmony, its reasonableness, and its ability to further human good. The correctness of theological reasoning and its real cognitive meaning are based on the value of theological language which, in St. Thomas's opinion, is principally an analogical language. The distance between God, the Creator, and the being of God's creatures is infinite; dissimilitude is ever greater than similitude (cf. *Enchiridion Symbolorum,* 806). Nevertheless, in the whole difference between creator and creatures, an analogy exists between the created being and the being of the Creator, which enables us to speak about God with human words.

Saint Thomas not only based the doctrine of analogy on exquisitely philosophical argumentation but also on the fact that with revelation God himself spoke to us and therefore authorized us to speak of him. I consider it important to recall this doctrine. In fact, it helps us get the better of certain objections of contemporary atheism, which denies that religious language is provided with an objective meaning and instead maintains that it has solely a subjective or merely emotional value. This objection derives from the fact that positivist thought is convinced that humanity does not know *being* but solely the functions of reality that can be experienced. With St. Thomas and with the great philosophical tradition, we are convinced that, in reality, man does not only know the functions, the object of the natural sciences, but also knows something of being itself—for example, he knows the person, the *you* of the other, and not only the physical and biological aspect of his being.

In the light of this teaching of St. Thomas, theology says that however limited it may be, religious language is endowed with sense because we touch being like an arrow aimed at the reality it signifies. This fundamental agreement between human reason and Christian faith is recognized in another basic principle of Aquinas's thought. Divine grace does not annihilate but presupposes and perfects human nature. The latter, in fact, even after sin, is not completely corrupt but wounded and weakened. Grace, lavished upon us by God and communicated through the mystery of the Incarnate Word, is an absolutely free gift with which nature is healed, strengthened, and assisted in pursuing the innate desire for happiness in the heart of every man and of every woman. All the faculties of the human being are purified, transformed, and uplifted by divine grace.

An important application of this relationship between nature and grace is recognized in the moral theology of St. Thomas Aquinas, which proves to be of great timeliness. At the center of his teaching in this field, he places the new law, which is the law of the Holy Spirit. With a profoundly evangelical gaze, he insists on the fact that this law is the grace of the Holy Spirit given to all who believe in Christ. The written and oral teaching of the doctrinal and moral truths transmitted by the Church is united to this grace. Saint Thomas, emphasizing the fundamental role in moral life of the action of the Holy Spirit, of grace, from which flow the theological and moral virtues, makes us understand that all Christians can attain the lofty perspectives of the Sermon on the Mount if they live an authentic relationship of faith in Christ, if they are open to the action of his Holy Spirit. However, Aquinas adds, "Although grace is more efficacious than nature, yet nature is more essential to man, and therefore more enduring" (*Summa Theologiae*, 1a–2ae, q. 94, a. 6, ad 2), which is why, in the Christian moral perspective, there is a place for reason, which is capable of discerning natural moral law. Reason can recognize this by considering what it is good to do and what it is good to avoid in order to achieve that felicity which everyone has at heart, which also implies a responsibility toward others and, therefore, the search for the common good. In other words, the human, theological, and moral virtues are rooted in human nature. Divine grace accompanies, sustains, and impels ethical commitment; but, according to St. Thomas, all human beings, believers and nonbelievers alike, are called to recognize the needs of human nature expressed in natural law and to draw inspiration from it in the formulation of positive laws, namely, those issued by the civil and political authorities to regulate human coexistence.

When natural law and the responsibility it entails are denied, this dramatically paves the way to ethical relativism at the individual level and to totalitarianism of the state at the political level. The defense of universal human rights and the affirmation of the absolute value of the person's dignity postulate a foundation. Does not natural law constitute this foundation, with the nonnegotiable values that it indicates? Venerable John Paul II wrote in his encyclical *Evangelium Vitae* words that are still very up to date: "It is therefore urgently necessary, for the future of society and the development of a sound democracy, to rediscover those essential and innate human and moral values which flow from the very truth of the human being and express and safeguard the dignity of the person: values which no individual, no majority, and no state can ever create, modify, or destroy, but must only acknowledge, respect, and promote" (n. 71).

To conclude, Thomas presents to us a broad and confident concept of human reason: *broad* because it is not limited to the spaces of the so-called empirical-scientific reason, but open to the whole being and thus also to the fundamental and inalienable questions of human life; and *confident* because human reason, especially if it accepts the inspirations of Christian faith, is a promoter of a civilization that recognizes the dignity of the person, the intangibility of the person's rights, and the cogency of his or her duties. It is not surprising that the doctrine on the dignity of the person, fundamental for the recognition of the inviolability of human rights, developed in schools of thought that accepted the legacy of St. Thomas Aquinas, who had a very lofty conception of the human creature. He defined it, with his rigorously philosophical language, as "what is most perfect to be found in all nature—that is, a subsistent individual of a rational nature" (*Summa Theologiae* 1a, q. 29, a. 3).

The depth of St. Thomas Aquinas's thought—let us never forget it—flows from his living faith and fervent piety, which he expressed in inspired prayers, such as this one in which he asks God: "Grant me, O Lord my God, a mind to know you, a heart to seek you, wisdom to find you, conduct pleasing to you, faithful perseverance in waiting for you, and a hope of finally embracing you."

A Theological Vision

Even more than seven hundred years after his death, we can learn much from St. Thomas Aquinas. My predecessor Pope Paul VI also said this in a discourse he gave at Fossanova on 14 September 1974 on the occasion of the seventh centenary of St. Thomas's death. He asked himself: "Thomas, our teacher, what lesson can you give us?" And he answered with these words: "Trust in the truth of Catholic religious thought, as defended, expounded, and offered by him to the capacities of the human mind" (*Address in Honor of St. Thomas Aquinas in the Basilica*, 14 September 1974; *L'Osservatore Romano*, English edition, 26 September 1974, 4). In Aquino moreover, on that same day, again with reference to St. Thomas, Paul VI said, "All of us who are faithful sons and daughters of the Church can and must be his disciples, at least to some extent!" (*Address in the Square at Aquino*, 14 September 1974, 5).

Let us too, therefore, learn from the teaching of St. Thomas and from his masterpiece, the *Summa Theologiae*. It was left unfinished, yet it is a monumental work: it contains 512 questions and 2,669 articles. It consists of concentrated reasoning in which the human mind is applied with clarity and depth to the mysteries of faith, alternating questions with answers in which St. Thomas deepens the teaching that comes from Sacred Scripture and from the Fathers of the Church, especially St. Augustine. In this reflection, in meeting the true questions of his time, which are also often our own questions, St. Thomas, also by employing the method and thought of the ancient philosophers, and of Aristotle in particular, thus arrives at precise, lucid, and pertinent formulations of the truths of faith in which truth is a gift of faith, shines out and becomes accessible to us for our reflection. However, this effort of the human mind—Aquinas reminds us with his own life—is always illumined by prayer, by the light that comes from on high. Only those who live with God and with his mysteries can also understand what they say to us.

In his *Summa* of theology, St. Thomas starts from the fact that God has three different ways of being and existing: First, God exists in himself; he is the beginning and end of all things, which is why all creatures proceed from him and depend on him. Second, God is present through his grace in the life and activity of the Christian, of the saints. Last, God is present in an altogether special way in the person of Christ, here truly united to the man Jesus, and active in the sacraments that derive from his work of redemption. Therefore, the structure of this monumental work (cf. Jean-Pierre Torrell, *La "Summa" di San Tommaso* [Milan, 2003], 29–75), a quest with "a theological vision" for the fullness of God (cf. *Summa Theologiae* 1a q. 1, a. 7), is divided into three parts and is illustrated by the *Doctor Communis* himself, St. Thomas, with these words: "Because the chief aim of sacred doctrine is to teach the knowledge of

God, not only as he is in himself, but also as he is the beginning of things and their last end, and especially of rational creatures, as is clear from what has already been said, therefore, we shall treat: (1) of God; (2) of the rational creature's advance toward God; (3) of Christ, who as man, is our way to God" (ibid., 1, q. 2). It is a circle: God in himself, who comes out of himself and takes us by the hand, in such a way that with Christ we return to God, we are united to God, and God will be all things to all people.

The first part of the *Summa Theologiae* thus investigates God in himself, the mystery of the Trinity and of the creative activity of God. In this part, we also find a profound reflection on the authentic reality of the human being, inasmuch as the person has emerged from the creative hands of God as the fruit of his love. On the one hand, we are dependent created beings; we do not come from ourselves; yet, on the other, we have a true autonomy so that we are not only something apparent—as certain Platonic philosophers say—but a reality desired by God as such and possessing an inherent value.

In the second part, St. Thomas considers the human being, impelled by grace, in his or her aspiration to know and love God in order to be happy in time and in eternity. First of all, the author presents the theological principles of moral action, studying how, in the free choice of the human being to do good acts, reason, will, and passions are integrated, to which is added the power given by God's grace through the virtues and the gifts of the Holy Spirit, as well as the help offered by moral law. Hence, the human being is a dynamic being who seeks himself, seeks to become himself, and, in this regard, seeks to do actions that build him up, that make him truly human; and here the moral law comes into it. Grace and reason itself, the will and the passions enter too. On this basis, St. Thomas describes the profile of the person who lives in accordance with the Spirit and thus becomes an image of God. Here Aquinas pauses to study the three theological virtues, faith, hope, and charity, followed by a critical examination of more than fifty moral virtues, organized around the four cardinal virtues of prudence, justice, temperance, and fortitude. He then ends with a reflection on the different vocations in the Church.

In the third part of the *Summa*, St. Thomas studies the mystery of Christ—the way and the truth through which we can reach God the Father. In this section, he writes almost unparalleled pages on the mystery of Jesus' Incarnation and passion, adding a broad treatise on the seven sacraments, for it is in them that the divine Word Incarnate extends the benefits of the Incarnation for our salvation, for our journey of faith toward God and eternal life. God is, as it were, materially present with the realities of creation and thus touches us in our inmost depths.

In speaking of the sacraments, St. Thomas reflects in a special way on the mystery of the eucharist, for which he had such great devotion, the early biographers claim, that he would lean his head against the Tabernacle, as if to feel the throbbing of Jesus' divine and human heart. In one of his works, commenting on Scripture, St. Thomas helps us to understand the excellence of the sacrament of the eucharist when he writes: "Since this [the eucharist] is the sacrament of our Lord's passion, it contains in itself the Jesus Christ who suffered for us. Thus, whatever is an effect of our Lord's passion is also an effect of this sacrament. For this sacrament is nothing other than the application of our Lord's passion to us" (cf. *Commentary on John*, ch. 6, lect. 6, n. 963). We clearly understand why St. Thomas and other saints celebrated Holy Mass shedding tears of compassion for the Lord who gave himself as a sacrifice for us, tears of joy and gratitude.

Let us fall in love with this sacrament! Let us participate in Holy Mass with recollection, to obtain its spiritual fruits; let us nourish ourselves with this body and blood of our Lord, to be ceaselessly fed by divine grace! Let us willingly and frequently linger in the company of the blessed sacrament in heart-to-heart conversation!

All that St. Thomas described with scientific rigor in his major theological works, such as, precisely, the *Summa Theologia*, and the *Summa contra gentiles*, was also explained in his preaching, both to his students and to the faithful. In 1273, a year before he died, he preached throughout Lent in the Church of San Domenico Maggiore in Naples. The content of those sermons was gathered and preserved: they are the *Opuscoli*, in which he explains the Apostles' Creed, interprets the prayer of the Our Father, explains the Ten Commandments, and comments on the Hail Mary. The content of the Doctor Angelicus's preaching corresponds with virtually the whole structure of the *Catechism of the Catholic Church*. Actually, in catechesis and preaching, in a time like ours of renewed commitment to evangelization, these fundamental subjects should never be lacking: what *we believe*, and here is the creed of the faith; what *we pray*, and here is the Our Father and the Hail Mary; and what *we live*, as we are taught by biblical revelation. And here is the law of the love of God and neighbor and the Ten Commandments, as an explanation of this mandate of love.

I propose some simple, essential, and convincing examples of the content of St. Thomas's teaching. In his booklet on the Apostles' Creed, he explains the value of faith. Through it, he says, the soul is united to God and produces, as it were, a shot of eternal life; life receives a reliable orientation, and we overcome temptations with ease. To those who object that faith is foolishness because it leads to belief in something that does not come within the experience of the senses, St. Thomas gives a very articulate answer and recalls that this is an inconsistent doubt, for human intelligence is limited and cannot know everything. Only if we were able to know all visible and invisible things perfectly would it be genuinely foolish to accept truths out of pure faith. Moreover, it is impossible to live, St. Thomas observes, without trusting in the experience of others, wherever one's own knowledge falls short. It is thus reasonable to believe in God, who reveals himself, and in the testimony of the Apostles: they were few, simple, and poor, grief-stricken by the crucifixion of their teacher. Yet many wise, noble, and rich people converted very soon after hearing their preaching. In fact, this is a miraculous phenomenon of history, to which it is far from easy to give a convincing answer other than that of the Apostle's encounter with the Risen Lord.

In commenting on the article of the creed on the Incarnation of the divine Word, St. Thomas makes a few reflections. He says that the Christian faith is strengthened in considering the mystery of the Incarnation; hope is strengthened at the thought that the Son of God came among us, as one of us, to communicate his own divinity to human beings; charity is revived because there is no more obvious sign of God's love for us than the sight of the creator of the universe making himself a creature, one of us. Finally, in contemplating the mystery of God's Incarnation, we feel kindled within us our desire to reach Christ in glory. Using a simple and effective comparison, St. Thomas remarks: "If the brother of a king were to be far away, he would certainly long to live beside him. Well, Christ is a brother to us; we must therefore long for his company and become of one heart with him" (*Opuscoli teologico-spirituali* [Rome, 1976], 64).

In presenting the prayer of the Our Father, St. Thomas shows that it is perfect in itself, since it has all five of the characteristics that a well-made prayer must possess: trusting, calm abandonment; a fitting content because, St. Thomas observes, "it is quite difficult to know exactly what it is appropriate and inappropriate to ask for, since choosing among our wishes puts us in difficulty" (ibid., 120); and then an appropriate order of requests; the fervor of love; and the sincerity of humility.

Like all the saints, St. Thomas had a great devotion to Our Lady. He described her with a wonderful title: *Triclinium totius Trinitatis; triclinium,* that is, a place where the Trinity finds rest since, because of the Incarnation, in no creature as in her do the three divine persons dwell and feel delight and joy at dwelling in her soul full of grace. Through her intercession, we may obtain every help.

With a prayer that is traditionally attributed to St. Thomas and that in any case reflects the elements of his profound Marian devotion, we too say: "O most blessed and sweet Virgin Mary, Mother of God . . . I entrust to your merciful heart . . . my entire life. . . . Obtain for me as well, O most sweet Lady, true charity with which from the depths of my heart I may love your most Holy Son, our Lord Jesus Christ, and, after him, love you above all other things . . . and my neighbor, in God and for God."

—*2, 16, and 23 June 2010*

MARGUERITE D'OINGT

WITH MARGUERITE D'OINGT, we are introduced to Carthusian spirituality, which draws its inspiration from the evangelical synthesis lived and proposed by St. Bruno. We do not know the date of her birth, although some place it around 1240. Marguerite came from a powerful family of the old nobility of Lyons, the Oingt. We know that her mother was also called Marguerite, that she had two brothers—Giscard and Louis—and three sisters: Catherine, Elizabeth, and Agnes. The latter followed her to the Carthusian monastery, succeeding her as prioress.

We have no information on her childhood, but from her writings it seems that she spent it peacefully in an affectionate family environment. In fact, to express God's boundless love, she valued images linked to the family, with particular reference to the figure of the father and of the mother. In one of her meditations, she prays:

> Most gentle Lord, when I think of the special graces that you have given me through your solicitude: first of all, how you took care of me since my childhood and how you removed me from the danger of this world and called me to dedicate myself to your holy service, and how you provided everything that was necessary for me: food, drink, dress, and footwear (and you did so) in such a way that I had no occasion to think of these things but of your great mercy. (Marguerite d'Oingt, *Scritti Spirituali, Meditazione 5*, 100 [Cinisello Balsamo, 1997], 74)

Again from her meditations, we know that she entered the Carthusian monastery of Poleteins in response to the Lord's call, leaving everything behind and accepting the strict Carthusian Rule in order to belong totally to the Lord, to be with him always. She wrote:

> Gentle Lord, I left my father and my mother and my siblings and all the things of this world for love of you; but this is very little, because the riches of this world are but thorns that prick; and the more one possesses, the more unfortunate one is. And because of this, it seems to me that I left nothing other than misery and poverty; but you know, gentle Lord, that if I possessed a thousand worlds and could dispose of them as I pleased, I would abandon everything for love of you; and even if you gave me everything that you possess in heaven and on earth, I would not consider myself satiated until I had you, because you are the life of my soul. I do not have and do not want to have a father and mother outside of you. (ibid., *Meditazione 2*, 32, 59)

We also have little data on her life in the Carthusian monastery. We know that in 1288 she became its fourth prioress, a post she held until her death on 11 February 1310. From her writings, however, we do not deduce particular stages in her spiritual itinerary. She conceived the entirety of life as a journey of purification up to full configuration with Christ. He is the book that is written, which is inscribed daily in her own heart and life, in particular his saving passion. In the work *Speculum*, referring to herself in the third person, Marguerite stresses that by the Lord's grace "she had engraved in her heart the holy life that Jesus Christ God led on earth, his good example and his good doctrine. She had placed the gentle Jesus Christ so well in her heart that it even seemed to her that he was present and that he had a closed book in his hand, to instruct her" (ibid., 1, 2–3, 81). "In this book she found written the life that Jesus Christ led on earth, from his birth to his ascension into heaven" (ibid., 1, 12, 83). Every day, beginning in the morning, Marguerite dedicated herself to the study of this book. And, when she had looked at it well, she began to read the book of her own conscience, which showed the falsehoods and lies of her own life (cf. ibid., 1, 6–7, 82); she wrote about herself to help others and to fix more deeply in her heart the grace of the presence of God, so as to make every day of her life marked by comparison with the words and actions of Jesus, with the Book of his life. And she did this so that Christ's life would be imprinted in her soul in a permanent and profound way, until she was able to see the Book internally, that is, until contemplating the mystery of God Trinity (cf. ibid., 2, 14–22; 3, 23–40, 84–90).

Through her writings, Marguerite gives us some traces of her spirituality, enabling us to understand some features of her personality and of her gifts of governance. She was a very learned woman; she usually wrote in Latin, the language of the erudite, but she also wrote in Provençal, and this too is a rarity: thus, her writings are the first of those known to be written in that language. She lived a life rich in mystical experiences described with simplicity, allowing one to intuit the ineffable mystery of God, stressing the limits of the mind to apprehend it and the inadequacy of human language to express it. Marguerite had a linear personality, simple, open, of gentle affectivity, great balance, and acute discernment, able to enter into the depths of the human spirit, discerning its limits, its ambiguities, but also its aspirations, the soul's élan toward God. She showed an outstanding aptitude for governance, combining her profound mystical spiritual life with service to her sisters and to the community. Significant in this connection is a passage of a letter to her father. She wrote: "My dear father, I wish to inform you that I am very busy because of the needs of our house, so that I am unable to apply my mind to good thoughts; in fact, I have so much to do that I do not know which way to turn. We did not harvest the wheat in the seventh month of the year, and our vineyards were destroyed by the storm. Moreover, our church is in such a sorry state that we are obliged to reconstruct it in part" (ibid., *Lettere* 3, 14, 127).

A Carthusian nun thus describes the figure of Marguerite: "Revealed through her work is a fascinating personality, of lively intelligence, oriented to speculation and at the same time favored by mystical graces: in a word, a holy and wise woman who is able to express with a certain humor an affectivity altogether spiritual" (*Una Monaca Certosina*; *Certosine*, in *Dizionario degli Istituti di Perfezione* [Rome, 1975], col. 777). In the dynamism of mystical life, Marguerite valued the experience of natural affections, purified by grace, as a privileged means to understand more profoundly and to second divine action with greater alacrity and ardor. The reason lies in the fact that the human person is created in the image of God and is therefore called to build with God a wonderful history of love, allowing oneself to be totally involved in God's initiative.

The God-Trinity, the God-love who reveals himself in Christ fascinated her, and Marguerite lived a relationship of profound love for the Lord and, in contrast, sees human ingratitude to the point of betrayal, even to the paradox of the Cross. She says that the Cross of Christ is similar to the bench of travail. Jesus' pain is compared with that of a mother. She wrote:

> The mother who carried me in her womb suffered greatly in giving birth to me, for a day or a night, but you, most gentle Lord, were tormented for me not only for one night or one day, but for more than thirty years! . . . How bitterly you suffered because of me throughout your life! And when the moment of delivery arrived, your work was so painful that your holy sweat became as drops of blood, which ran down your whole body to the ground. (ibid., *Meditazione* 1, 33, 59)

In evoking the accounts of Jesus' passion, Marguerite contemplated these sorrows with profound compassion. She said:

> You were placed on the hard bed of the cross, so that you could not move or turn or shake your limbs as a man usually does when suffering great pain, because you were completely stretched and pierced with the nails . . . and . . . all your muscles and veins were lacerated. . . . But all these pains . . . were still not sufficient for you, so much so that you desired that your side be pierced so cruelly by the lance that your defenseless body should be totally ploughed and torn and your precious blood spurted with such violence that it formed a long path, almost as if it were a current.

Referring to Mary, she said: "It was no wonder that the sword that lacerated your body also penetrated the heart of your glorious mother who so wanted to support you . . . because your love was loftier than any other love" (ibid., *Meditazione* 2, 36–39, 42, 60–61).

Marguerite d'Oingt invites us to meditate daily on the life of sorrow and love of Jesus and that of his mother, Mary. Here is our hope, the meaning of our existence. From contemplation of Christ's love for us are born the strength and joy to respond with the same love, placing our life at the service of God and of others. With Marguerite, we also say: "Gentle Lord, all that you did, for love of me and of the whole human race, leads me to love you, but the remembrance of your most holy passion gives unequaled vigor to my power of affection to love you. That is why it seems to me that. . . . I have found what I so much desired: not to love anything other than you or in you or for love of you" (ibid., *Meditazione* 2, 46, 62).

At first glance, this figure of a Medieval Carthusian nun, as well as her life and her thought, seems distant from us, from our life, from our way of thinking and acting. But if we look at the essential aspect of this life, we see that it also affects us and that it would also become the essential aspect of our own existence.

We have heard that Marguerite considered the Lord as a book. She fixed her gaze on the Lord; she considered him a mirror in which her own conscience also appeared. And from this mirror, light entered her soul. She let into her own being the Word, the life of Christ, and thus she was transformed; her conscience was enlightened; she found criteria and light and was cleansed. It is precisely this that we also need: to let the words, life, and light of Christ enter our conscience so that it is enlightened, understands what is true and good and what is wrong. May our conscience be enlightened and cleansed. Rubbish is not only on different streets of the world. There is also rubbish in our consciences and in our souls. Only the light of the Lord, his strength and his love, cleanses us, purifies us, showing us the right path. Therefore, let us follow holy Marguerite in this gaze fixed on Jesus. Let us read the book of his life; let us allow ourselves to be enlightened and cleansed, to learn the true life.

—*3 November 2010*

JOHN DUNS SCOTUS

ANOTHER IMPORTANT FIGURE in the history of theology is Blessed John Duns Scotus, who lived at the end of the thirteenth century. An ancient epitaph on his tombstone sums up the geographical coordinates of his biography: "Scotland bore me, England received me, France taught me, Cologne in Germany holds me." We cannot disregard this information, partly because we know very little about the life of Duns Scotus. He was probably born in 1266 in a village called, precisely, "Duns," near Edinburgh.

Attracted by the charism of St. Francis of Assisi, he entered the family of the Friars Minor and was ordained a priest in 1291. He was endowed with a brilliant mind and a tendency for speculation which earned him the traditional title of *Doctor Subtilis*, "Subtle Doctor." Duns Scotus was oriented to the study of philosophy and theology at the famous universities of Oxford and of Paris. Having successfully completed his training, he embarked on teaching theology at the Universities of Oxford and Cambridge and then of Paris, beginning by commenting, like all the bachelors of theology of his time, on the *Sentences* of Peter Lombard. Indeed, Duns Scotus's main works are the mature fruit of these lessons and take the name of the places where he taught: *Ordinatio* (called in the past *Opus Oxoniense*–Oxford), *Reportatio Cantabrigiensis* (Cambridge), *Reportata Parisiensia* (Paris). One can add to these at least the *Quodlibeta* (or *Quaestiones quodlibetales*), a quite important work consisting of twenty-one questions on various theological subjects. Duns Scotus distanced himself from Paris, after a serious dispute broke out between King Philip IV the Fair and Pope Boniface VIII, rather than sign a document hostile to the pope as the king requested of all religious, preferring voluntary exile. Thus, he left the country, together with the Franciscan friars, out of love for the See of Peter.

This event invites us to remember how often in the history of the Church believers have met with hostility and even suffered persecution for their fidelity and devotion to Christ, to the Church, and to the pope. We all look with admiration at these Christians who teach us to treasure as a precious good faith in Christ and communion with the successor of Peter, hence with the universal Church.

However, friendly relations between the king of France and the successor of Boniface VIII were soon restored, and in 1305 Duns Scotus was able to return to Paris to lecture on theology with the title of *Magister regens* ("regent master"), now we would say "Professor." Later, his superiors sent him to Cologne as professor of the Franciscan Studium of Theology, but he died on 8 November 1308, when he was only forty-three years old, leaving nevertheless a consistent opus.

Because of the fame of his holiness, his cult soon became widespread in the Franciscan order, and Venerable Pope John Paul II, wishing to confirm it, solemnly beatified him on 20 March 1993, describing him as the "minstrel of the Incarnate Word and defender of Mary's Immaculate Conception" (*Solemn Vespers*, St. Peter's Basilica; *L'Osservatore Romano*, n. 3, 24 March 1993, 1). These words sum up the important contribution that Duns Scotus made to the history of theology. First of all, he meditated on the mystery of the Incarnation. Unlike many Christian thinkers of the time, he held that the Son of God would have been made man even if humanity had not sinned. He says in his *Reportatio Parisiensis*: "To think that God would have given up such a task had Adam not sinned would be quite unreasonable! I say, therefore, that the fall was not the cause of Christ's predestination and that if no one had fallen, neither the angel nor man, in this hypothesis Christ would still have been predestined in the same way" (in *III Sent.*, d. 7, 4). This perhaps somewhat surprising thought crystallized because, in the opinion of Duns Scotus, the Incarnation of the Son of God, planned from all eternity by God the Father, at the level of love is the fulfillment of creation and enables every creature, in Christ and through Christ, to be filled with grace and to praise and glorify God in eternity. Although Duns Scotus was aware that, in fact, because of original sin, Christ redeemed us with his passion, death, and resurrection, he reaffirmed that the Incarnation is the greatest and most beautiful work of the entire history of salvation, that it is not conditioned by any contingent fact but is God's original idea of ultimately uniting with himself the whole of creation, in the person and flesh of the Son.

As a faithful disciple of St. Francis, Duns Scotus liked to contemplate and preach the mystery of the saving passion of Christ, as the expression of the loving will, of the immense love of God, who reaches out with the greatest generosity, irradiating his goodness and love (cf. *Tractatus de primo principio*, c. 4). Moreover, this love was not only revealed on Calvary but also in the most blessed eucharist, for which Duns Scotus had a very deep devotion and which he saw as the sacrament of the real presence of Jesus and as the sacrament of unity and communion that induces us to love each other and to love God, as the supreme good we have in common (cf. *Reportatio Parisiensis*, in *IV Sent.*, d. 8, q. 1, n. 3). As I wrote in my "Letter for the International Congress in Cologne Marking the Seventh Centenary of the Death of Blessed Duns Scotus," citing the thought of our author: "Just as this love, this charity, was at the origin of all things, so too our eternal happiness will be in love and charity alone: 'willing, or the loving will, is simply eternal life, blessed and perfect'" (*AAS* 101 [2009], 5).

This strongly "Christocentric" theological vision opens us to contemplation, wonder, and gratitude: Christ is the center of history and of the cosmos—it is he who gives meaning, dignity, and value to our lives! As Pope Paul VI proclaimed in Manila, I too would like to cry out to the world: Christ "reveals the invisible God, he is the firstborn of all creation, the foundation of everything created. He is the Teacher of mankind, and its Redeemer. He was born, he died, and he rose again for us. He is the center of history and of the world; he is the one who knows us and who loves us; he is the companion and the friend of our life. . . . I could never finish speaking about him" (*Homily*, Mass at Quezon Circle, Manila; 29 November 1970).

Not only Christ's role in the history of salvation but also that of Mary is the subject of the *Doctor Subtilis's* thought. In the times of Duns Scotus, the majority of theologians countered with an objection that seemed insurmountable, the doctrine which holds that Mary Most Holy was exempt from original sin from the very first moment of her conception: in fact, at first sight the universality of the redemption brought about by Christ might seem to be jeopardized by such a statement, as though Mary had had no need of Christ or his redemption. Therefore, the theologians opposed this thesis. Thus, to enable people to understand this preservation from original sin, Duns Scotus developed an argument that was later, in 1854, also to be used by Blessed Pope Pius IX when he solemnly defined the Dogma of the Immaculate Conception of Mary. And this argument is that of "preventive redemption," according to which the Immaculate Conception is the masterpiece of the redemption brought about by Christ because the very power of his love and his mediation obtained that the mother of Jesus be preserved from original sin. Therefore, Mary is totally redeemed by Christ, but already before her conception. Duns Scotus's confreres, the Franciscans, accepted and spread this doctrine enthusiastically, and other theologians, often with a solemn oath, strove to defend and perfect it.

In this regard, I highlight a fact that I consider relevant. Concerning the teaching on the Immaculate Conception, important theologians like Duns Scotus enriched what the People of God already spontaneously believed about the Blessed Virgin and expressed in acts of devotion, in the arts, and in Christian life in general with the specific contribution of their thought. Thus, faith both in the Immaculate Conception and in the bodily Assumption of the Virgin was already present in the People of God, while theology had not yet found the key to interpreting it in the totality of the doctrine of the faith. The People of God therefore precede theologians, and this is all thanks to that supernatural *sensus fidei*, namely, that capacity infused by the Holy Spirit that qualifies us to embrace the reality of the faith with humility of heart and mind. In this sense, the People of God is the "teacher that goes first" and must then be more deeply examined and intellectually accepted by theology. May theologians always be ready to listen to this source of faith and retain the humility and simplicity of children! I mentioned this a few months ago, saying: "There have been great scholars, great experts, great theologians, teachers of faith who have taught us many things. They have gone into the details of Sacred Scripture . . . but have been unable to see the mystery itself, its central nucleus. . . . The essential has remained hidden! . . . On the other hand, in our time there have also been 'little ones' who have understood this mystery. Let us think of St. Bernadette Soubirous; of St. Thérèse of Lisieux, with her new interpretation of the Bible that is 'nonscientific' but goes to the heart of Sacred Scripture" (*Homily, Mass for the Members of the International Theological Commission*, Pauline Chapel, Vatican City, 1 December 2009).

Lastly, Duns Scotus has developed a point to which modernity is very sensitive. It is the topic of freedom and its relationship with the will and with the intellect. The author underlines freedom as a fundamental quality of the will, introducing an approach that lays greater emphasis on the will. Unfortunately, in later authors, this line of thinking turned into a voluntarism, in contrast to the so-called Augustinian and Thomist intellectualism. For St. Thomas Aquinas, who follows St. Augustine, freedom cannot be considered an innate quality of the will but the fruit of the collaboration of the will and the mind. Indeed, an idea of innate and absolute freedom—as it evolved, precisely, after Duns Scotus—placed in the will that precedes the intellect, both in God and in humans, risks leading to the idea of a God who would not even be bound to truth and good. The wish to save God's absolute transcendence and diversity with such a radical and impenetrable accentuation of his will does not take into account that the God who revealed himself in Christ is the divine *Logos*, who acted and acts full of love for us. Of course, as Duns Scotus affirms, love transcends knowledge and is capable of perceiving ever better than thought, but it is always the love of the God who is *Logos* (cf. Benedict XVI, *Address at the University of Regensburg*, 12 September 2006). In the human being too, the idea of absolute freedom, placed in the will, forgetting the connection with the truth, does not know that freedom itself must be liberated from the limits imposed on it by sin. All the same, the Scotist vision does not fall into these extremes: for Duns Scotus, a free act is the result of the concourse of intellect and will, and if he speaks of a "primacy" of the will, he argues this precisely because the will always follows the intellect.

In speaking to Roman seminarians, I recalled that "since the beginning and throughout all time but especially in the modern age freedom has been the great dream of humanity" (*Discourse at the Roman Major Seminary*, 20 February 2009). Indeed, in addition to our own daily experience, modern history actually teaches us that freedom is authentic and helps with building a truly human civilization only when it is reconciled with truth. If freedom is detached from truth, it becomes, tragically, a principle of the destruction of the human person's inner harmony, a source of domination by the strongest and the violent and a cause of suffering and sorrow. Freedom, like all the faculties with which the human being is endowed, increases and is perfected, Duns Scotus says, when the human being is open to God, making the most of the disposition to listen to God's voice: when we listen to divine revelation, to the Word of God in order to accept it, a message reaches us that fills our life with light and hope, and we are truly free.

Blessed Duns Scotus teaches us that in our life the essential is to believe that God is close to us and loves us in Jesus Christ, and therefore to cultivate a deep love for him and for his Church. We on earth are witnesses of this love. May Mary Most Holy help us to receive this infinite love of God, which we will enjoy eternally to the full in heaven, when our soul is at last united to God forever in the communion of saints.

—7 July 2010

St. Bridget of Sweden

On the eve of the Great Jubilee in anticipation of the Year 2000, the Venerable John Paul II proclaimed St. Bridget of Sweden co-patroness of the whole of Europe. I now present her, her message, and the reasons why—still today—this holy woman has much to teach the Church and the world.

We are well acquainted with the events of St. Bridget's life because her spiritual fathers compiled her biography in order to further the process of her canonization immediately after her death in 1373. Bridget was born seventy years earlier, in 1303, in Finster, Sweden, a northern European nation that for three centuries had welcomed the Christian faith with the same enthusiasm as that with which the saint had received it from her parents, very devout people who belonged to noble families closely related to the reigning house.

We can distinguish two periods in this saint's life.

The first was characterized by her happily married state. Her husband was called Ulf, and he was governor of an important district of the kingdom of Sweden. The marriage lasted for twenty-eight years, until Ulf's death. Eight children were born, the second of whom, Karin (Catherine), is venerated as a saint. This is an eloquent sign of Bridget's dedication to her children's education. Moreover, King Magnus of Sweden so appreciated her pedagogical wisdom that he summoned her to court for a time, so that she could introduce his young wife, Blanche of Namur, to Swedish culture. Bridget, who was given spiritual guidance by a learned religious who initiated her into the study of the Scriptures, exercised a very positive influence on her family, which, thanks to her presence, became a true "domestic church." Together with her husband, she adopted the Rule of the Franciscan Tertiaries. She generously practiced works of charity for the poor; she also founded a hospital. At his wife's side, Ulf's character improved, and he advanced in the Christian life. On their return from a long pilgrimage to Santiago de Compostela, which they made in 1341 with other members of the family, the couple developed a project of living in continence; but a little while later, in the tranquility of a monastery to which he had retired, Ulf's earthly life ended. This first period of Bridget's life helps us to appreciate what today we could describe as an authentic "conjugal spirituality": together, Christian spouses can make a journey of holiness sustained by the grace of the sacrament of marriage. It is often the wife, as happened in the life of Bridget and Ulf, who with her religious sensitivity, delicacy, and gentleness succeeds in persuading her husband to follow a path of faith. I am thinking with gratitude of the

many women who, day after day, illuminate their families with their witness of Christian life, in our time too. May the Lord's Spirit still inspire
holiness in Christian spouses today, to show the world the beauty of
marriage lived in accordance with the gospel values: love, tenderness,
reciprocal help, fruitfulness in begetting and in raising children, openness
and solidarity to the world, and participation in the life of the Church.

The second period of Bridget's life began when she was widowed. She
did not consider another marriage, in order to deepen her union with the
Lord through prayer, penance, and charitable works. Therefore, Christian widows too may find in this saint a model to follow. In fact, upon
the death of her husband, after distributing her possessions to the poor—
although she never became a consecrated religious—Bridget settled near
the Cistercian monastery of Alvastra. Here began the divine revelations
that were to accompany her for the rest of her life. Bridget dictated them
to her confessors-secretaries, who translated them from Swedish into
Latin and gathered them in eight volumes titled *Revelationes* (*Revelations*). A supplement followed these books called, precisely, *Revelationes
extravagantes* (*Supplementary Revelations*).

Saint Bridget's *Revelations* have a very varied content and style. At
times, the revelations are presented in the form of dialogues between the
divine persons, the Virgin Mary, the saints, and even demons; they are
dialogues in which Bridget also takes part. At other times, instead, a specific vision is described; and in yet others what the Virgin Mary reveals to
her concerning the life and mysteries of the Son. The value of St. Bridget's
Revelations, sometimes the object of criticism, Venerable John Paul II
explained in his Letter *Spes Aedificandi*: "The Church, which recognized
Bridget's holiness without ever pronouncing on her individual revelations, has accepted the overall authenticity of her interior experience" (n.
5). Indeed, reading these *Revelations* challenges us on many important
topics. For example, the description of Christ's passion, with very realistic details, frequently recurs. Bridget always had a special devotion to
Christ's passion, contemplating in it God's infinite love for human beings.
She boldly places these words on the lips of the Lord who speaks to her:
"O my friends, I love my sheep so tenderly that were it possible I would
die many other times for each one of them that same death I suffered for
the redemption of all" (*Revelationes* 1, c. 59). The sorrowful motherhood
of Mary, which made her Mediatrix and Mother of Mercy, is also a subject that recurs frequently in the *Revelations*.

In receiving these charisms, Bridget was aware that she had been
given a gift of special love on the Lord's part: "My Daughter," we read
in the first book of *Revelations*, "I have chosen you for myself; love
me with all your heart . . . more than all that exists in the world" (c.
1). Bridget, moreover, knew well and was firmly convinced that every
charism is destined to build up the Church. For this very reason, many

of her revelations were addressed in the form of admonishments, even severe ones, to the believers of her time, including the religious and political authorities, that they might live a consistent Christian life; but she always reprimanded them with an attitude of respect and of full fidelity to the magisterium of the Church and, in particular, to the successor of the Apostle Peter.

In 1349, Bridget left Sweden for good and went on pilgrimage to Rome. She was not only intending to take part in the Jubilee of the Year 1350 but also wished to obtain from the pope approval for the rule of a religious order that she was intending to found, called after the Holy Savior and made up of monks and nuns under the authority of the abbess. This is an element we should not find surprising: in the Middle Ages, monastic foundations existed with both male and female branches, but with the practice of the same monastic Rule that provided for the abbess's direction. In fact, in the great Christian tradition, the woman is accorded special dignity and—always based on the example of Mary, Queen of Apostles—a place of her own in the Church, which, without coinciding with the ordained priesthood, is equally important for the spiritual growth of the community. Furthermore, the collaboration of consecrated men and women, always with respect for their specific vocation, is of great importance in the contemporary world.

In Rome, in the company of her daughter Karin, Bridget dedicated herself to a life of intense apostolate and prayer. And from Rome, she went on pilgrimage to various Italian shrines, in particular to Assisi, the homeland of St. Francis, for whom Bridget had always had great devotion. Finally, in 1371, her deepest desire was crowned: to travel to the Holy Land, to which she went accompanied by her spiritual children, a group that Bridget called "the friends of God." In those years, the popes lived at Avignon, a long way from Rome: Bridget addressed a heartfelt plea to them to return to the See of Peter, in the Eternal City. She died in 1373, before Pope Gregory XI returned to Rome definitively.

Bridget was buried temporarily in the Church of San Lorenzo in Panisperna in Rome, but in 1374 her children Birger and Karin took her body back to her homeland, to the monastery of Vadstena, the headquarters of the religious order St. Bridget had founded. The order immediately experienced a considerable expansion. In 1391, Pope Boniface IX solemnly canonized her.

Bridget's holiness, characterized by the multiplicity of her gifts and the experiences that I have wished to recall in this brief biographical and spiritual outline, makes her an eminent figure in European history. In coming from Scandinavia, St. Bridget bears witness to the way Christianity had deeply permeated the life of all the peoples of this continent. In declaring her co-patroness of Europe, Pope John Paul II hoped that St. Bridget—who lived in the fourteenth century, when Western Christianity had not yet been wounded by division—may intercede effectively with God to obtain the grace of full Christian unity so deeply longed for. Let us pray, dear brothers and sisters, for this same intention, which we have very much at heart, and that Europe may always be nourished by its Christian roots, invoking the powerful intercession of St. Bridget of Sweden, a faithful disciple of God and co-patroness of Europe.

—*27 October 2010*

ST. CATHERINE OF SIENA

WE NOW REFLECT ON A WOMAN who played an eminent role in the history of the Church: St. Catherine of Siena. The century in which she lived—the fourteenth—was a troubled period in the life of the Church and throughout the social context of Italy and Europe. Yet, even in the most difficult times, the Lord does not cease to bless his people, bringing forth saints who give a jolt to minds and hearts, provoking conversion and renewal.

Catherine is one of these and still today speaks to us and impels us to walk courageously toward holiness, to be ever more fully disciples of the Lord.

Born in Siena in 1347, into a very large family, she died in Rome in 1380. When Catherine was sixteen years old, motivated by a vision of St. Dominic, she entered the Third Order of the Dominicans, the female branch known as the Mantellate. While living at home, she confirmed her vow of virginity—made privately when she was still an adolescent—and dedicated herself to prayer, penance, and works of charity, especially for the benefit of the sick.

When the fame of her holiness spread, she became the protagonist of an intense activity of spiritual guidance for people from every walk of life: nobles and politicians, artists and ordinary people, consecrated men and women and religious, including Pope Gregory XI, who was living at Avignon in that period and whom she energetically and effectively urged to return to Rome.

Catherine traveled widely to press for the internal reform of the Church and to foster peace among the states. It was also for this reason that Venerable Pope John Paul II chose to declare her co-patroness of Europe: may the old continent never forget the Christian roots that are at the origin of its progress and continue to draw from the Gospel the fundamental values that assure justice and harmony.

Like many of the saints, Catherine knew great suffering. Some even thought that they should not trust her, to the point that in 1374, six years before her death, the general chapter of the Dominicans summoned her to Florence to interrogate her. They appointed Raymund of Capua, a learned and humble friar and a future master general of the order, as her spiritual guide. Having become her confessor and also her "spiritual son," he wrote a first complete biography of the saint. She was canonized in 1461.

The teaching of Catherine, who learned to read with difficulty and learned to write in adulthood, is contained in the *Dialogue of Divine*

Providence or *Libro della Divina Dottrina*, a masterpiece of spiritual literature, in her *Epistolario* and in the collection of her prayers. Her teaching is endowed with such excellence that, in 1970, Pope Paul VI declared her a Doctor of the Church, a title that was added to those of co-patroness of the city of Rome—at the wish of Blessed Pius IX—and of Patroness of Italy—in accordance with the decision of Venerable Pius XII.

In a vision that was ever present in Catherine's heart and mind, Our Lady presented her to Jesus, who gave her a splendid ring, saying to her: "I, your Creator and Savior, espouse you in the faith, that you will keep ever pure until you celebrate your eternal nuptials with me in heaven" (Blessed Raimondo da Capua, *S. Caterina da Siena, Legenda maior*, n. 115, Siena 1998). This ring was visible to her alone. In this extraordinary episode, we see the vital center of Catherine's religious sense, and of all authentic spirituality: Christocentrism. For her, Christ was like the spouse with whom a relationship of intimacy, communion, and faithfulness exists. He was the best beloved whom she loved above any other good. This profound union with the Lord is illustrated by another episode in the life of this outstanding mystic: the exchange of hearts. According to Raymond of Capua, who passed on the confidences Catherine received, the Lord Jesus appeared to her "holding in his holy hands a human heart, bright red and shining." He opened her side and put the heart within her, saying: "Dearest daughter, as I took your heart away from you the other day, now, you see, I am giving you mine, so that you can go on living with it forever" (ibid.). Catherine truly lived St. Paul's words, "It is no longer I who live, but Christ who lives in me" (Gal 2:20).

Like the Sienese saint, every believer feels the need to be conformed with the sentiments of the heart of Christ, to love God and one's neighbor as Christ himself loves. And we can all let our hearts be transformed and learn to love like Christ in a familiarity with him that is nourished by prayer, by meditation on the Word of God, and by the sacraments, above all by receiving holy communion frequently and with devotion. Catherine also belongs to the throng of saints devoted to the eucharist with which I concluded my Apostolic Exhortation *Sacramentum Caritatis* (cf. n. 94). The eucharist is an extraordinary gift of love that God continually renews to nourish our journey of faith, to strengthen our hope, and to inflame our charity, to make us more and more like him.

A true and authentic spiritual family was built up around Catherine's strong and genuine personality; people fascinated by the moral authority of this young woman with a most exalted lifestyle were at times also impressed by the mystical phenomena they witnessed, such as her frequent ecstasies. Many put themselves at Catherine's service and above all considered it a privilege to receive spiritual guidance from her. They called her "mother" because, as her spiritual children, they drew spiritual nourishment from her. Today, too, the Church receives great benefit from the exercise of spiritual motherhood by so many women, lay and consecrated, who nourish souls with thoughts of God, who strengthen the people's faith, and direct Christian life toward ever loftier peaks. "Son, I say to you and call you," Catherine wrote to one of her spiritual sons, Giovanni Sabbatini, a Carthusian, "inasmuch as I give birth to you in continuous prayers and desire in the presence of God, just as a mother gives birth to a son" (*Epistolario, Lettera* n. 141: *To Fr Giovanni de' Sabbatini*). She would usually address the Dominican Fr. Bartolomeo de Dominici with these words: "Most beloved and very dear brother and son in Christ sweet Jesus."

Another trait of Catherine's spirituality is linked to the gift of tears. They express an exquisite, profound sensitivity, a capacity for being moved and for tenderness. Many saints have had the gift of tears, renewing the emotion of Jesus himself, who did not hold back or hide his tears at the tomb of his friend Lazarus and at the grief of Mary and Martha or at the sight of Jerusalem during his last days on this earth. According to Catherine, the tears of saints are mingled with the blood of Christ, of which she spoke in vibrant tones and with symbolic images that were very effective: "Remember Christ crucified, God and man. . . . Make your aim the Crucified Christ; hide in the wounds of the Crucified Christ and drown in the blood of the Crucified Christ" (*Epistolario, Lettera* n. 16: *Ad uno il cui nome si tace* ["to one who remains anonymous"]). Here we can understand why, despite her awareness of the human shortcomings of priests, Catherine always felt very great reverence for them: through the sacraments and the word, they dispense the saving power of Christ's blood.

The Sienese saint always invited the sacred ministers, including the pope, whom she called "sweet Christ on earth," to be faithful to their responsibilities, motivated always and only by her profound and constant love of the Church. She said before she died: "In leaving my body, truly I have consumed and given my life in the Church and for the Holy Church, which is for me a most unique grace" (Raimondo da Capua, *S. Caterina da Siena, Legenda maior*, n. 363). Hence, we learn from St. Catherine the most sublime science: to know and love Jesus Christ and his Church. In the *Dialogue of Divine Providence*, she describes Christ with an unusual image, as a bridge flung between heaven and earth. This bridge consists of three great stairways constituted by the feet, the side, and the mouth of Jesus. Rising by these stairways, the soul passes through the three stages of every path to sanctification: detachment from sin, the practice of the virtues and of love, sweet and loving union with God.

Let us learn from St. Catherine to love Christ and the Church with courage, intensely and sincerely. Therefore, let us make our own St. Catherine's words that we read in the *Dialogue of Divine Providence* at the end of the chapter that speaks of Christ as a bridge: "Out of mercy you have washed us in his blood; out of mercy you have wished to converse with creatures. O crazed with love! It did not suffice for you to take flesh, but you also wished to die! . . . O mercy! My heart drowns in thinking of you: for no matter where I turn to think, I find only mercy" (ch. 30, 79–80).

—24 November 2010

JULIAN OF NORWICH

I STILL REMEMBER WITH GREAT JOY the apostolic journey I made in the United Kingdom in 2009. England is a land that has given birth to a great many distinguished figures who enhanced Church history with their testimony and their teaching. One of them, venerated both in the Catholic Church and in the Anglican Communion, is the mystic Julian of Norwich, on whom I wish to reflect here.

The very scant information on her life in our possession comes mainly from her *Revelations of Divine Love in Sixteen Showings*, the book in which this kindly and devout woman set down the content of her visions.

It is known that she lived from 1342 until about 1430, turbulent years both for the Church, torn by the schism that followed the pope's return to Rome from Avignon, and for the life of the people who were suffering the consequences of a long, drawn-out war between the kingdoms of England and of France. God, however, even in periods of tribulation, does not cease to inspire figures such as Julian of Norwich to recall people to peace, love, and joy.

As Julian herself recounts, in May 1373, most likely on the thirteenth of that month, she was suddenly stricken with a very serious illness that in three days seemed to be carrying her to the grave. After the priest, who hastened to her bedside, had shown her the Crucified One, not only did Julian rapidly recover her health but she received the sixteen revelations that she subsequently wrote down and commented on in her book, *Revelations of Divine Love*.

And it was the Lord himself, fifteen years after these extraordinary events, who revealed to her the meaning of those visions. "'Would you learn to see clearly your Lord's meaning in this thing? Learn it well: Love was his meaning. Who showed it to you? Love. . . . Why did he show it to you? For Love.' . . . Thus I was taught that Love was our Lord's meaning" (Julian of Norwich, *Revelations of Divine Love* 86).

Inspired by divine love, Julian made a radical decision. Like an ancient anchoress, she decided to live in a cell located near the church called after St. Julian, in the city of Norwich—in her time an important urban center not far from London. She may have taken the name of Julian precisely from that saint to whom was dedicated the church in whose vicinity she lived for so many years, until her death.

This decision to live as a "recluse," the term in her day, might surprise or even perplex us. But she was not the only one to make such a choice. In those centuries, a considerable number of women opted for this form of life, adopting rules specially drawn up for them, such as the rule compiled by St. Aelred of Rievaulx.

These anchoresses, or recluses, in their cells, devoted themselves to prayer, meditation, and study. In this way, they developed a highly refined human and religious sensitivity that earned them the veneration of the people. Men and women of every age and condition in need of advice and comfort would devoutly seek them. It was not, therefore, an individualistic choice; precisely with this closeness to the Lord, Julian developed the ability to be a counselor to a great many people and to help those who were going through difficulties in this life.

We also know that Julian too received frequent visitors, as is attested by the autobiography of another fervent Christian of her time, Margery Kempe, who went to Norwich in 1413 to receive advice on her spiritual life. This is why, in her lifetime, Julian was called "Dame Julian," as is engraved on the funeral monument that contains her remains. She had become a mother to many.

Men and women who withdraw to live in God's company acquire, by making this decision, a great sense of compassion for the suffering and weakness of others. As friends of God, they have at their disposal a wisdom that the world—from which they have distanced themselves—does not possess and they amiably share it with those who knock at their door. I therefore recall with admiration and gratitude the women and men's cloistered monasteries. Today more than ever, they are oases of peace and hope, a precious treasure for the whole Church, especially since they recall the primacy of God and the importance, for the journey of faith, of constant and intense prayer.

It was precisely in the solitude infused with God that Julian of Norwich wrote her *Revelations of Divine Love*. Two versions have come down to us, one that is shorter, probably the older, and one that is longer. This book contains a message of optimism based on the certainty of being loved by God and of being protected by his providence.

In this book, we read the following wonderful words: "And I saw full surely that ere God made us he loved us; which love was never lacking nor ever shall be. And in this love he has made all his works; and in this love he has made all things profitable to us; and in this love our life is everlasting . . . in which love we have our beginning. And all this shall we see in God, without end" (*Revelations of Divine Love*, ch. 86).

The theme of divine love recurs frequently in the visions of Julian of Norwich, who, with a certain daring, did not hesitate to compare them also to motherly love. This is one of the most characteristic messages of her mystical theology. The tenderness, concern, and gentleness of God's kindness to us are so great that they remind us, pilgrims on earth, of a mother's love for her children. In fact, the biblical prophets also sometimes used this language that calls to mind the tenderness, intensity, and totality of God's love, which is manifested in creation and in the whole history of salvation that is crowned by the Incarnation of the Son.

God, however, always excels all human love, as the prophet Isaiah says: "Can a woman forget her sucking child, that she should have no compassion on the son of her womb? Even these may forget, yet I will never forget you" (Is 49:15).

Julian of Norwich understood the central message for spiritual life: God is love, and it is only if one opens oneself to this love, totally and with total trust, and lets it become one's sole guide in life, that all things are transfigured. True peace and true joy found, one is able to radiate it.

I emphasize another point. The *Catechism of the Catholic Church* cites the words of Julian of Norwich when it explains the viewpoint of the Catholic faith on an argument that never ceases to be a provocation to all believers (cf. nn. 304–13, 314). If God is supremely good and wise, why do evil and the suffering of innocents exist? The saints themselves asked this very question. Illumined by faith, they give an answer that opens our hearts to trust and hope: in the mysterious designs of providence, God can draw a greater good even from evil, as Julian of Norwich wrote: "Here I was taught by the grace of God that I should steadfastly hold me in the Faith . . . and that . . . I should take my stand on and earnestly believe in . . . that 'all manner of thing shall be well'" (*The Revelations of Divine Love*, ch. 32).

Yes, God's promises are ever greater than our expectations. If we present to God, to his immense love, the purest and deepest desires of our heart, we shall never be disappointed. "And all will be well," "all manner of things shall be well": this is the final message that Julian of Norwich transmits to us and that I am also proposing to you today.

—1 December 2010